BACKGROUNDS OF
EUROPEAN LITERATURE

The Political, Social,
and Intellectual Development
behind the Great Books
of Western Civilization

Second Edition

D1501020

ROD W.   VINCENT F. HOPPER
Colorado Women's College   *New York University*

PRENTICE-HALL, INC.
Englewood Cliffs, New Jersey

0-13-056317-X

Library of Congress Catalog Card Number 73-18864

Printed in the United States of America

10 9 8 7 6 5 4 3 2 1

PRENTICE-HALL INTERNATIONAL, INC., London
PRENTICE-HALL OF AUSTRALIA, PTY. LTD., Sydney
PRENTICE-HALL OF CANADA, LTD., Toronto
PRENTICE-HALL OF INDIA PRIVATE LIMITED, New Delhi
PRENTICE-HALL OF JAPAN, INC., Tokyo

Preface

This book provides, in compact form, a general survey of the principal historical and cultural events that have shaped Western Europe from ancient times to the present. It traces the main currents of European civilization from their sources in Classical secular culture and Hebraic religious ideals, through their fusion with the Gothic achievements of medieval times, down to their intricate blending in the cultures of modern nations.

The text is intended for students at the college level and may be used in several ways:

1. to provide background material for a course on the origins and principal movements of Western civilization as they were reflected in European literature;
2. to supply integration, purpose, and direction for a course in which a limited number of Great Books are studied;
3. as a supplementary volume for general courses concerned with Occidental literature or with European culture patterns.

To add to the book's usefulness as a classroom supplement, lists of suggested readings for further study are offered after discussions of principal topics, and for convenient review a chronology of significant events is given at the end of each part.

In this second edition, the authors have added much new material to the last section of the book covering the period from 1500 to the present. The chapter on the Renaissance

iii

has been expanded to include brief treatments of the Counter-Reformation and of the Spanish *Siglo de Oro*. Two entirely new chapters have been added to cover the period
from the end of World War I to the present. The lists of
readings have been completely updated.

This book grew out of the authors' experience in teaching courses in European literature. They found that examination of great literary works themselves was not very
fruitful for their students unless those students had prior
knowledge of the cultures in which those works were produced. Intelligent reading of an ancient Greek tragedy, for
example, requires at least a knowledge of Periclean Athens
and of Greek dramatic form and stage conditions, and
usually some acquaintance with ancient Greek religion and
mythology. In the same way, Plato becomes much more
meaningful after a review of earlier Greek philosophy. For
a course dealing with selected Great Books that are inevitably widely separated in time as well as in subject matter,
by beginning with works from ancient Greece and Rome,
then turning to passages or books from the Old and New
Testaments, and finally observing the amalgamation of
Classicism and Hebraism in later Western literature, the
teacher can intelligently arrange a coherent program of
readings from past to present.

In their choice of material to be treated in this volume
and in making decisions concerning the extensiveness of
such treatment, the authors have been guided by the needs
of students as these needs became apparent in the classroom. While it is not intended to be an exhaustive history
of Western culture, this handbook nevertheless aspires to be
enlightening on the principal cultural influences that have
contributed to making modern man the complex creature
that he is.

The authors wish to express their appreciation to Mrs.

Tess Kushel for her assistance in the preparation of the manuscript of the first edition, and to Professor Herbert W. Edwards of New York University for his critical reading of some of the sections. Gratitude is especially owed to Professor Albert C. Baugh for his many helpful suggestions and gracious guidance in the total process of planning and completing this volume. For the second edition, thanks are again due to Professor Edwards and also to Professor Harold A. Schofield of Colorado Women's College for their reading of the new material. Our wives have proved indispensable in the preparation of the manuscript.

R. W. H.
V. F. H.

Contents

vi

PART II. HEBRAISM

PART III. THE MEDIEVAL FUSION

PART IV. THE MODERN SPIRIT

Charts, Maps, and Illustrations

chapter 1

OUR CULTURAL HERITAGE

We of the twentieth century are apt to pride ourselves a great deal on our individualism. Yet, try as we may to be ourselves, we are very much what custom, society, and the cultural traditions of the past have made us. To put it another way, we were born yesterday, but the world wasn't. All that we learn as we grow up is selected from what was discovered or invented in the past, sometimes the very remote past. Our most cherished ideas and social attitudes were formulated by those who lived before us. Even our daily habits and ways of thinking are products of centuries of cultural growth.

This culture into which we are born is an amalgam of great complexity, representing a fusion of the achievements of many previous civilizations. Three of these, the Classical, the Hebraic, and the Gothic, seem to have been particularly prominent in shaping the present Western world. Of course, many very important individual contributions (such as Arabic numerals) originated elsewhere, but the main stream of European civilization had its twin sources in ancient Classical and Hebraic times with a major tributary added by the later Gothic invasions.

1

Classicism, which originated in Greece and was continued in ancient Rome, was the principal contributor to that aspect of our life which is usually referred to as secular. Our school system, our civic institutions, our sciences, and many of our arts and crafts trace their origins to Classical inspiration. The distinctive qualities of the Classical point of view arose from the circumstance that the leaders of the ancient civilizations of Greece and Rome were continually striving for a clear-eyed understanding of the realities of life. They were insatiably curious about the nature of the world in which they found themselves, and they were so much given to speculation that they produced the greatest philosophers of all time. In fact, the intellectual atmosphere of the Classical world encouraged individual thinking to such a degree that scarcely any modern theory is not traceable to an origin there. With the simultaneous ambition to create a sane and orderly society in which human dignity would be respected and human achievement consequently encouraged, they emphasized form and symmetry in life as in their arts. Being distrustful of uncontrolled emotional impulse, they sought to create broad principles of rational and balanced conduct which would result in the cultivation of mind and body and spirit. The ennoblement of man as a rational animal was the ultimate achievement of ancient Classicism.

At approximately the same time, in a small area known as Palestine, another desire to comprehend the universe as a coherent and purposeful whole led to the devotion to one God and gave rise to the richest expressions of religious feeling known to Western man. Here was a different attitude toward life which glorified man as the child of a loving Father, who was the creator of the universe and whose favorite creation was the human race. To learn how to serve God, to understand the difference between right and wrong, to be humble before one's Maker—these were the ideals which Hebraic leaders expounded to their followers. There was a very great deal that was rational in these preachings, but the special quality of Hebraism was the glorification of the pure in heart rather than the brilliant in intellect. Our seven-day week with its day of rest was transmitted to us from Hebraism, and many of the most deeply felt artistic achievements of the Western world, together with the very language and imagery of many English and European poets, are indebted to Hebraic literature for their inspiration. Even when one examines the theories of such influential modern thinkers as Rousseau and the ensuing cults and philosophical schools devoted to right feeling rather than right thinking, one wonders how many of these "modern" ideas would have come into being without the impetus of Hebraic ideology.

Before the first century A.D. these two independent cultural attitudes began to be aware of each other. In the first century Christianity, which originated in Hebraism, began to spread throughout the Classical world and to adopt Classical traditions, including a great deal of Platonic theology. When Christianity became the official religion of the Roman Empire, the blend of the two culture patterns was essentially completed, although the many conflicts so produced distressed thoughtful individuals and occasioned many heated arguments. Such conflicts have never been fully resolved, as is witnessed by the never-ending debates between science and religion and the many troubled individual religious doubts and wonderings of our own time. But the presence in every town of some sort of a municipal building and school is a symbol of our inescapable Classical heritage just as the local church evidences the continuity of the Hebraic attitude toward life. The American twenty-five-cent piece bears the inscription "Liberty," a Classical ideal, on the same side of the coin as the Hebraic "In God We Trust."

The temporary setback to Western civilization known as the Dark Ages was occasioned by the Gothic invasions. Their most obvious immediate effect was the destruction or dimming of the composite Judaeo-Classical culture in Europe. But when the recovery known as the Middle Ages took place, the appearance of new ideas and attitudes indicates that the Goths had also contributed something of their own to the Occident. Restless energy, or love of activity, was primary among these contributions, but reinforcement of the ideal of individual liberty, a fascinated interest in the grotesque, a mystical regard for women, and the concept of personal loyalty to a chief were also influential in creating the patterns of medieval and later European life.

The reintroduction of Classical learning through the Moslem conquests in Spain is a partial explanation of the ensuing Renaissance when Classicism seemed to be dominant. The Reformation is explainable as a resurgence of Hebraic religious feeling. The Neo-Classic Age and the following period of the Enlightenment were inspired by Classical models, but the theories of the Romantic Movement and of many of the nineteenth-century German philosophers emphasize the intuitive approach to knowledge upon which Hebraism was built. Meanwhile, Gothic urgency had been very much in evidence in the physical and mental activities of Europeans from the Middle Ages on.

It is not particularly worth while to attempt to analyze every aspect of contemporary civilization with the object of indicating its reflection of one or more of these three cultural patterns. It is very illuminating, however, to recognize these three forces in their early and purer phases and to observe how the blending took place. Such interpretation will be given in the following chapters, beginning with a careful analysis of the three cultures and then proceeding more briefly with descriptions of ensuing cultural movements and trends. As a final preliminary preparation for this journey through Western civilization, it may be helpful to think of mankind in Aristotle's terms as made up of heart, mind, and will, and to observe how the heart of modern man has been influenced by Hebraic religious feelings, his mind trained by Classical methods, and, less certainly, his energy inherited from or stimulated by the example of his Gothic ancestors.

Part I

CLASSICISM

chapter 2

HELLENISM:
THE GREEK SPIRIT

I. PRE-GREEK CULTURE

Sometime about two thousand years before Christ, back among the unrecorded moments of history, a tribe of un-lettered, pastoral nomads made a routine decision which ultimately proved to be one of the most important in the history of the world. These undistinguished tribesmen, whose original home had been somewhere among the grass-lands of the lower Danube, in the course of many genera-tions had wandered south and west, always in search of new pastures for their flocks, until they had reached Thrace on the northern shore of the Aegean Sea. Here they had met a problem: should they continue westward toward the Adriatic, or should they turn southward to follow the in-viting and fertile shores of the Aegean? Though they were unaware of it at the time, their answer to this, for them, commonplace problem was to determine much of the future of Western civilization.

Since all we know of these early tribesmen consists pre-ponderantly of poetic and anthropological conjecture, we can only guess at the reasoning behind their choice of routes. But whatever their thinking might have been, their decision was a most fortunate one. By turning to the south, they and other racially similar tribes who followed their trail over the course of the next millennium unwittingly directed their steps toward the long-established civilization of the Mediterranean, which they were ultimately to stimulate and vitalize into the brightest cultural achievement in the history of man. To be sure, it was many centuries after they had first turned south until the more aggressive of these Central European tribesmen reached and merged with the great but decaying Mycenean culture at the lower end of the Hellenic peninsula. But in so doing, they laid the cornerstone of western history, for it proved to be this happy combination of Eastern refinement and love of beauty and Indo-European vigor and energy which set in motion the superb achievements of the Greeks, achievements to which mankind must forever remain in grateful indebtedness.

The union of Indo-European and Mycenean strains did not in itself account for all that is excellent in subsequent Greek culture. When the first tribesmen began to penetrate the Peloponnesus, the world was already old and had already compiled a notable record of social and technical achievement. For example, in the narrow 600-mile-long valley between the Tigris and Euphrates rivers, the successive civilizations of Sumeria, Babylon, and Assyria had developed writing, metallurgy, weaving, and other arts and crafts to a degree only slightly to be improved upon by succeeding ages. They had also reached an advanced state of knowledge in the sciences, particularly in mathematics and astronomy, and had developed architecture of great beauty and structural skill. Coincidentally, in Egypt there flourished a vigorous culture which in its comprehensiveness, its stamina, and its technical resourcefulness was one of the wonders of history. In agriculture, industry, science, and the practical and fine arts, the contributions of Egypt were astounding in their scope and were surpassed but seldom even by the Greeks themselves. And in Persia, by the sixth century B.C., when the Greeks were just beginning to emerge as an important factor in the Mediterranean world, the warlike despots of that mighty empire had already developed military service to heights that would not again be achieved until the great age of Rome. Greek life borrowed freely and copiously from all of these older cultures. It made few improvements over their best accomplishments in the material aspects of living, and it even appropriated many of the intellectual concepts of the past and incorporated them into the rich life of the Hellenic mind.

What was there about the Greeks, then, that made their heritage to mankind so unique? The answer lies indubitably in the noble Greek concept of the importance and dignity of the individual. For all their brilliant achievements, the pre-Greek civilizations were despotic and narrow. Human life was plentiful and cheap; the vast illiterate masses were virtually—or actually—slaves, subject to the harsh, rigid control of a few privileged aristocrats who were fortunate enough to be the accepted followers of an all-powerful ruler. Furthermore, even these aristocrats had no real security, for their privileges, their property, and their very lives were granted them only through the favor of their king and could be forfeited at any moment as a result of the merest prompting of the royal whim. It is quite understandable, therefore, that under such conditions of absolute rule, concepts such as that of the dignity of the individual should have escaped entirely the mind of the Babylonian, the Assyrian, the Persian, or the Egyptian. The thesis of the Sophists, that man was the measure of all things, or the Greek belief that man's greatest obligation to society and to the gods was to develop his own individual capacity for excellence would have seemed to the pre-Greek (if he could have comprehended such concepts at all) to be sacrilege, subversion, or advanced lunacy.

The result of this lack of recognition of individual worth is easily apparent. Despite the rich legacies of pre-Greek culture, the earlier eras were singularly and consistently devoid of humanistic thought. Their science was largely applied, not pure; their politics despotism; their religion and philosophy superstition of the wildest sort; and their literature all but non-existent. Their writing was for the most part hieroglyphic, not grammatical, and as such was capable of representing only the most rudimentary and standardized pictorial situations, with no capacity whatever for individual expression or for finer shades of meaning.

But above all, their state of mind was closed. To pre-Greek man, the preservation of *order* was more important than the precarious business of social or intellectual experimentation. "The strength of Egypt is to sit still," said Herodotus, but his tone was sardonic, for he knew that he was diagnosing the malady of a dying culture. The great genius of the Greeks, on the other hand, lay in their ability to conceive of the simultaneous existence of order *and* progress. To them both individual and group development seemed quite possible within a system of life that was at once rational, well-proportioned, moderate, and—above all—relatively free. It is this spirit of individual freedom within the framework of moderation and social responsibility which explains the apparent modernity of the Greeks. It also shows why, in less than two centuries, they could advance from a condition of political and intellectual vacuity to become an enlightened polity that produced the greatest single body of literature and thought known to man. This achievement becomes all the more remarkable when one considers that in the more than two thousand years between the development of graphic communication by the Sumerians (about 3500 B.C.) and the merging of Indo-

European and Mycenean culture in the Peloponnesus we have only a handful of sporadic or fragmentary examples of imaginative writing.

II. THE GREEK MIND

Embarking on the treacherous sea of generalization, we shall try to classify the most salient characteristics of Hellenism as they manifest themselves in that all-too-facile abstraction we shall call the "Greek Mind." To do so with a reasonable degree of concreteness, let us introduce ourselves into the consciousness of a hypothetical intelligent Greek student in the early stages of manhood. What qualities would he be seeking to develop in his still-forming character?

Broadly speaking, he would say in answer to our opening question, his goal was _areté_, a word the Greeks used for education in general, but which could more exactly be translated as _excellence_. Above all things, our young Greek student would wish to excel, to rise above his fellows and above his own human indolence as much as his natural capacities would permit. But upon our asking him as to the particular category of life in which he desired to excel, he would show only bewilderment. The question would appear to him to be nonsense. To develop one capacity without developing all others would seem to him the very converse of excellence. He could only blurt out: "What category? Why, in all categories, of course," an answer which he would probably deliver in the exasperated tone one adopts when explaining the obvious to a backward child.

But, we would reason with him, nobody can possibly reach an ultimate state of perfection in all things, or even in a very limited number of things. Wouldn't it be better to choose one field of activity—a specialty—and develop that at the expense of some other attainments? How could one expect to compete with his fellows if he were satisfied to become merely a jack of all trades?

His answers to these questions would be courteous but final. He would concede with regret that perfection in anything is impossible, even for the gods, but would maintain that it is the duty of every human being, as a lesser imitation of the gods, to strive to attain as great a degree of perfection as his natural gifts permit. As for the developing of a specialty (and he would have had some difficulty in understanding the word at first), do you gentlemen mean to try to develop some talent to *excess*, like the juggler or the rope dancer in the public square? Do you mean for one to imitate the parrot, who can utter a few words but who is useless for anything else? Surely you are joking; you are forgetting the forest to see only the trees. Such "specialties" are for barbarians, not for Greeks. Does a man have only one arm, one leg, one organ of sense? No, he has many features, many senses, many potential abilities. It is his duty to develop all of these in proportion, to preserve a balance and symmetry of attainment, both of body and of mind. To do otherwise would be to become a monstrosity.

As for competing with one's fellows, our young Greek would understand that well, for he has competed with them in the gymnasium and on the athletic field from childhood. But the purpose of this competition, he would insist, is not primarily to win or to eliminate his neighbor from the race. Rather it is to test one's own achievement, to show up one's own weaknesses and to spur oneself on to a further stage of development. Altogether, he would hint, your sense of *areté* is a little naive. It is true that foreigners often possess peculiarly one-sided ideas of education, but such notions are certainly not compatible with Greek standards.

Nettled but not entirely routed by his answer, we would attempt one more question. We understand that our young Greek's education has consisted largely of physical training, military science, music, dancing, rhetoric, philosophy, and mathematics. What is the practical value of all these studies? Are they really useful in adult life?

To this query our young friend's reply would again assume the tone of patient exasperation. Useful? Practical? Is there any possible point to doing anything that is not useful or practical? Is it even conceivable to employ means without an end? Don't you realize that the worst tortures conceived by the Greek mind were the *pointless* ones, like that of Sisyphus who, for his misdeeds, was forced in Hades to roll a heavy stone painfully and repeatedly uphill? Of course Greek studies have a purpose, the purpose of making a good and useful citizen. Physical training and military science preserve one's health and school him to endure the rigors of defending the state; dancing gives him the grace and good bearing necessary to the dignity of citizenship; rhetoric, philosophy, and music give him the vocal training, a sense of the polished phrase, and the grasp of ideas indispensable to making him an effective speaker in the public forum; while mathematics (together with music) instill the restraining sense of proportion and regularity which will prevent his embarking thoughtlessly upon the aforementioned hobby of "specialization."

Asked to give examples of the result of this type of education, he would point to Sophocles, a man of impressive physical proportions and beauty, who also had distinguished himself as a general, priest, political leader, tragic dramatist, and lover of life, and who, even at the age of ninety, had been able to write such a dramatic masterpiece as *Oedipus at Colonus*. Or there was Plato, an even more beautiful physical specimen, who had won many athletic prizes, had written music and dramatic poetry (which he despised, it is true), had founded the Academy, where his philosophical dialogues had served as textbooks, and who had died in his sleep at the age of eighty after having spent the night enjoying himself at a convivial wedding celebration. Of course not everybody can be a Sophocles or a Plato, but he can at least attempt, within his own limitations, to match the purposefulness, the versatility, and the proportion of their lives. After such a demonstration of the Greek sense of personal excellence, we would probably begin to grasp the significance of Edith Hamilton's remark that until we can conceive of a modern society where all-American football players are also our best poets, philosophers, and political leaders, we cannot wholly understand the spirit of Greek life.[1]

From our young Greek's answers we can easily extract the essence of Hellenism. We can perceive the desire for order, proportion, and restraint demonstrated in the sculpture of a Phidias or a Praxiteles; we can see the rational, practical humanism, the balanced sense of individual freedom and political responsibility, which resulted in the great social democracy of Periclean Athens. Further examination of Greek literature and art would only serve to intensify our awareness of the Greek passion for wholeness, for individual integrity, and for the sheer excitement of living. The great heroes of legend and history—Odysseus, Pericles, Socrates—were men of *areté* who loved life and lived it fully, with ingenuity, courage, and yet usually with moderation. The tragic failures—Oedipus, Alcibiades, Alexander— were on the other hand men whose good intentions were wrecked by a fatal lack of restraint and proportion, especially in their sense of self-esteem. It was no idle whim that prompted the inscribing of the temple of Apollo at Delphi with two unforgettable exhortations: "Know Thyself" and "Nothing in Excess." Rather, the one who selected those mottoes must have known, with that characteristically Greek propensity for getting at the essence of things, that

[1] Edith Hamilton, *The Greek Way to Western Civilization* (Mentor, 1948).

in five words he was anatomizing the mind of an entire civilization.

Much has been written about the classic sense of beauty. The Greeks themselves were always talking about it and striving to achieve *kalos* (beauty) and avoid *aischos* (ugliness) to such a degree that these words almost attained the ethical connotation of "good" and "bad." Beauty, like all abstractions, is almost impossible to define, but to the Greek, the words inscribed on the temple of Apollo came close to sufficiency in their suggestion of human aspiration conditioned by moderation, proportion, and humility.

SUGGESTED READINGS

See end of Chapter 8 for suggested readings.

chapter 3

THE GREEK
HISTORICAL BACKGROUND

I. EARLY AEGEAN CULTURE

Unwary laymen, reading about the Greeks, are often tempted to conceive of a heroic, beautiful, intellectual race which miraculously achieved the highest form of culture practically overnight, with no indebtedness to other races and nations. In reality, Hellenism was a wonder but not a miracle, the result of a fortunate combination of geographical, economic, military, and cultural circumstances too complex to be explained in a few easy generalizations. Like all other civilizations, that of the Greeks passed through several stages of development from the crudest tribal society to the amazing sophistication represented by Periclean Athens. To make the picture more complicated, the level of development varied among the city-states which constituted Hellenic society, with the lower Peloponnesus predominating during the earlier years, Miletus (in Asia Minor) then taking the ascendency until 500 B.C., Athens dominating the Golden Age from 500 to 300, and Macedonia and other areas taking transitory and undecisive precedence during the long period of decline.

Altogether, Hellenic culture represented a long, slow development marked by a considerable amount of political confusion—confusion of sufficient moment to prevent the Aegean world from ever attaining anything nearly approaching a national unity or a cultural uniformity. In reality, the Greeks were a most variegated society, a slowly developed melting-pot civilization, full of confusion and contradictions, torn with internecine warfare and misunderstanding, and yet a society which, all in all, achieved through its philosophers, poets, and historians the highest state of intellectual excellence the world has ever known.

We have seen that the Central European tribes which invaded the Aegean brought little with them in the form of culture. Rather, they found culture awaiting them as they pushed southward into the Peloponnesus and encountered the rich heritage of Mycenae. Unlike the Normans in England, they acquired their culture with their conquests and, in winning the lands of their predecessors, were themselves won by the achievements of the vanquished. But the roots of Hellenism go deeper even than Mycenae; they stretch through the Aegean into Crete and, in all probability, back into ancient Egypt.

For our purposes, we shall consider that Aegean civilization began on the island of Crete (or Minos, as it was sometimes known to the Greeks) in the so-called Minoan Period (3400-1400 B.C.). The settlers of Crete were mainly from North Africa, which lay four hundred miles by sea to the South, and their subsequent culture shows strong evidence of Egyptian influences. Archaeologists have identified three distinct epochs in Cretan life: the unimportant Early Minoan (to 2300 B.C.); the Middle Minoan (2300-1800), contemporary with the age of Hammurabi in Babylon; and the late Minoan (1800-1400), contemporaneous with the great temple period of Egypt. This last epoch left behind it an extensive treasure of painting, sculpture, and metalwork, some writings in linear script,[1] and the palace of Cnossus sensationally unearthed by Sir Arthur Evans in 1900.

The government of the island throughout its history seems to have been one of extreme despotism, and the type of civilization predominantly urban, if we can believe the *Iliad*'s reference to the "ninety cities of Crete." The most important of these cities, Cnossus, was burned to the ground in 1400 B.C., probably as a result of a combination of civil war and foreign invasion. The downfall of Cnossus marked the end of Minoan civilization, a catastrophe brought about as much through the exhaustion of the island's slender natural resources as through military conquest.

Besides the large number of art objects excavated by archaeologists, Crete has left us an important body of mythology, much of which was adopted by the Greeks. The hero tales of Minos and Daedalus and the legends of Theseus, Ariadne, and the Minotaur are all of Cretan origin and later figured largely in Greek literature. But after 1400 B.C. Crete, though several times a military objective, ceased to be of any considerable importance and contributed nothing further to the world's cultural progress.

Aegean civilization next flowered around two cities: Mycenae in southern Greece and Ilium (the much-fabled Troy) near the Dardanelles in Asia Minor. Despite the wide geographical separation of these two cities, their civilization

---

[1] Some of the writings, which Evans classified as Linear B, have been deciphered by Michael Ventris (1922-1956) and have been shown to be written in a form of Greek used about 1400 B.C., 500 years earlier than that of any previously known texts in the language. Since Evans's first discoveries, fragments of about 5,000 additional tablets have been unearthed.

Still other writings, known as Linear A, have yet to be deciphered, although scholars are making some progress toward a solution of this problem. See John Chadwick, *The Decipherment of Linear B* (Cambridge, 1958) and Leonard B. Palmer, *Myceneans and Minoans: Aegean Prehistory in the Light of the Linear B Tablets* (1962).

seems to have been almost a common one. The Myceneans appear to have been of the same mixed stock as the Minoans, but the inhabitants of Ilium, like the Greeks who ultimately conquered them, were apparently a combination of Mediterranean and Balkan ethnic strains. So similar were the patterns of life in Mycenae and Troy, however, that it is possible to consider them both under the general heading of Mycenean civilization.

Mycenean life, while far from devoid of artistic achievement, was also highly commercial. Both Mycenae and Ilium dominated important trade routes, and the latter seems to have been a particularly prosperous mercantile center, with most of its inhabitants engaged in a mixture of legitimate shipping and open piracy. The city's strategic situation near the Dardanelles enabled it to levy tolls on all foreign ships passing through that always important shipping artery, and it was probably the abuse of this monopoly that became the primary cause of the Trojan War. At Mycenae, excavations show that city also to have been as much a fortress as it was a trading center, and its military and economic strength, together with its high standard of living, gives good reason for its attractiveness to the wandering Greek tribes from the north.

Most of what we know about Mycenean civilization is derived from the dramatic findings of the German archaeologist Heinrich Schliemann. Convinced that the Homeric epics were at least partly based upon actual happenings, Schliemann in 1868 organized the first of a series of archaeological expeditions to Mycenean territories. Braving the ridicule of his colleagues and of the learned world in general, Schliemann boldly set out to find the site of the fabled city of Troy. His first attempts were failures, but in 1871 he met with a success beyond his most optimistic dreams. For Schliemann not only found the site of Troy but he also discovered that at least *nine* "cities" had existed between 3000 B.C. and A.D. 500 in that very spot. None of these "cities" had been unusually large; some had been mere hamlets, others modest-sized towns. The Homeric Troy is generally identified as the Sixth City,[2] a medium-sized settlement whose destruction by fire about 1184 B.C. gives historical support to Homer's story of the Greek victory over the Trojans.

Following his spectacular discoveries near the Dardanelles, Schliemann transferred his activities to the Peloponnesus, and in 1875 unearthed the ruins of the city of Mycenae. Ten years later he discovered the site of the nearby town of Tiryns. The importance of these last discoveries cannot be overestimated, for in bringing to light the skeletons of these ancient settlements, Schliemann also uncovered much hitherto unknown material concerning Mycenean history and everyday civilization. Perhaps his most exciting discovery was that of a tomb-like structure containing six occupied graves and many ornaments of beaten gold and other metals. One of these graves contained the corpse of what had obviously been a very high dignitary, probably a king, whom Schliemann controversially declared to be Agamemnon himself. The German archaeologist also uncovered the groundwork of a large building, probably a royal palace, and excavated several smaller beehive-like structures of marble. The function of these last is undetermined, although Schliemann has some evidence for his claim that one of them served at one time as the "treasury of Atreus."

Schliemann's discoveries established many hitherto unknown facts about Mycenean culture. It is clear that this culture had reached a high point in artistic achievement and that it also, about 1400 B.C., had been the most powerful military force in the Aegean, with successful conquests of Crete and Troy and even profitable raids on Egyptian

2 More recent discoveries indicate that it may have been the seventh city to be built on this site.

coastal towns to its credit. It was also established that the first infiltrations of Greek tribes into the Mycenean world were gradual and peaceful, permitting a slow fusion of the two racial strains until the European element somehow or another intruded itself into the royal line. According to Greek tradition, the house of Atreus and his son Agamemnon, which ruled Mycenae just before and during the Trojan war, was Greek rather than Semitic in origin, and Schliemann's discoveries tend to substantiate the legend.

II. THE INDO-EUROPEAN INVASIONS

It is now time to backtrack a bit from the days of Mycenean glory to trace the movements of those European bands whose decision to migrate into the Aegean was noted in the very opening of this section of the book, and whose fusion with Mycenean culture shaped the subsequent history of the Aegean world. The first group of European tribesmen to reach the southern tip of the Hellenic peninsula were the Arcadians, a small and apparently peaceful band who, according to legend, lived an idyllic pastoral life which seems to have had little influence on Mycenean society. Much more decisive was the effect of the next wave of Greeks, the Achaeans. These people, much superior to the Arcadians in number and in energy, poured steadily into the Peloponnesus and, without evoking general warfare, eventually became the rulers of Mycenae. The Achaeans were unquestionably the catalytic agents in forming early Greek civilization; it was they who had the vitality, the practicality, and at the same time the nobility and dignity that characterize the Greeks of Homeric legend. Homer constantly refers to the Greeks as the Achaeans, leaving little doubt that it was this tribe which was the true founder of Hellenism.

The Achaeans were followed into the Peloponnesus by the Dorians, a tribe of fierce warriors which successfully

sacked Mycenae about 1100 B.C.[3] The Dorians seem to have
had little of the regenerative tendencies of the Achaeans;
their civilization was far more primitive, militaristic, and
destructive and has left little or nothing in the way of
cultural monuments. Nevertheless, the Dorians for nearly
one thousand years remained the undisputed rulers of the
Peloponnesus, and their capital city of Sparta became as
important as Athens itself in shaping subsequent Greek
history.

Many other European tribes came into the Aegean, but
none seems to have reached the Peloponnesus in any numbers. The Aeolians, a large but relatively unimportant
group, settled in the north and in Asia Minor about 1150
B.C. Far more important were the Ionians, a small band
which about 1030 B.C. reached the area of Attica, where
they were probably merged with a group of Achaean ref-
ugees from the Dorian conquest. Together these people settled in and around the city of Athens, a fishing and shipping town which for the next few centuries played no great
part in Greek history, but which later achieved strength and
prosperity by its economic and colonial expansion throughout the Aegean islands and over onto the opposite shore of
Asia Minor.

By approximately 1000 B.C. the period of migration was
over, and the next two centuries were marked largely by
the slow growth of states, the most important of which were
Thessaly, Boeotia, Aetolia, Megara, Corinth, Argos, Sparta,
and Attica. Although of common racial stock, these states
were generally mutually antagonistic politically, but at
the same time they attained a reasonably homogeneous cultural development which they themselves recognized as
"Hellenic." This culture, they felt, set them apart from the
rest of the peoples of the world, whom they spoke of as

---

[3] The fire marks of this destructive victory are still visible on the
walls of the royal palace excavated by Schliemann.

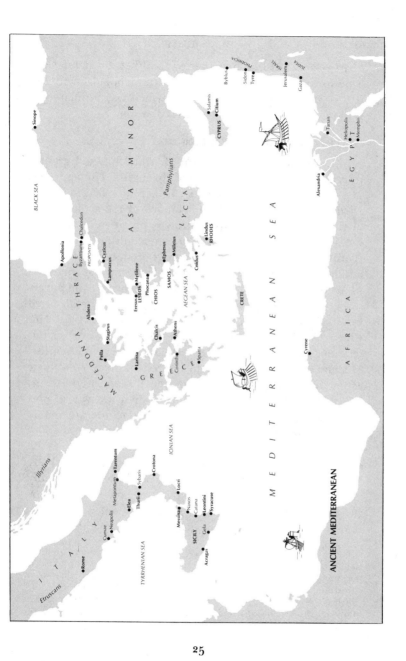

ANCIENT MEDITERRANEAN

"barbarians."[4] It is to be regretted that they did not develop a political unity to match their cultural homogeneity, for it was this lack of political fusion which was ultimately to lead to the downfall of Hellenic civilization.

III. THE HOMERIC AGE (1200-900 B.C.)

Most of the foregoing pattern of tribal flux and gradual integration took place before and during the Homeric Age, so called because it represents the period reflected in the *Iliad* and the *Odyssey*. Little is known of the actual events of this seminal era in Greek history, but it is certain that it was a time of great turbulence and military activity. It is only natural that such times should produce great leaders, fabulous adventurers, and deeds of spectacular heroism. Many of these deeds and not a few of the heroes and adventurers have been immortalized, in exaggerated or idealized form no doubt, in the wealth of legends and epic tales with which Greek literature abounds. The well-known characters in these tales—Jason, Agamemnon, Odysseus, Achilles, Menelaus, Hector, Aeneas, and the rest—probably had their actual historical counterparts in the leaders of the time, many of whom fought in an actual Trojan war whose aims were, as we have seen, somewhat less romantic and noble than those recorded by Homer.

In this formative period of Greek history, it is to be expected that a man's worth would be measured largely by his capacity for heroism and physical endurance. It is only natural, therefore, that the Homeric poems, which mirror the events of this time, should reflect the violence and the highly personal standards of distinction held by the people

---

4 The word *barbarian* did not have the same contemptuous connotation with the Greeks that it bears today. It carried the approximate meaning of "outsider" to the Greeks, who though feeling their own culture to be superior to that of the barbarian, readily recognized the worth of certain foreign elements and welcomed them into their midst. Many of the technicians and educators in Athens were actually of "barbarian" descent.

of that age. But even more valuable is the Homeric capacity for vivid portrayal of the domestic civilization of the early Greeks. In the absence of more scientific historical sources, therefore, we must turn largely to Homer and, to a lesser degree, to his contemporary, Hesiod, for our knowledge of how people lived and died in the formative days of the Hellenic era.

Apart from military activity, life in the Homeric period was rural and pastoral, with the small village being the most important economic unit. Agriculture, stock-breeding, and simple handcrafts were the principal activities, with a very reasonable spread of wealth between rich and poor. Great luxuries were unknown, and even the leaders of the community lived in rough houses and enjoyed a standard of living little different from that of the ordinary laborer. Because of this equitable spread of the necessities of life, it was possible for every man to live adequately. Slavery and forced labor were rare and men enjoyed a social equality generally found only in far more primitive societies. Odysseus, for example, fought side by side with his swineherd, and the suitors in Odysseus' palace saw no social objection to having a goatherd among their number at the banquet table.

Dress, food, and social intercourse were simple and restrained; the period seems to have been generally quite free from the moral and physical excesses which marred much of later classical life. By the end of the period, however, the inevitable phenomenon of economic dislocation became apparent. The old paternalistic and equalitarian clan rule gradually gave way to monarchy, and with monarchy came class antagonisms with a resultant centralization of wealth and power in the few and a reduction to peonage of the many.

IV. THE AGE OF KINGS (900-700 B.C.)

The two centuries following the time of Homer and

Hesiod are spoken of as the Age of Kings and could with equal appropriateness be called the dark age of Greek history. In this period the humanism and personal freedom which so strongly characterize the Greek spirit and Greek creative arts were apparently largely extinguished by the blight of arbitrary despotic government. We know but little of the life and events of the Age of Kings, possibly because of this despotic rule, which seems to have discouraged creative or historically valuable writing.

The leading monarchies of this period were those of Argos, Sparta, Athens, and Thebes. In these cities the royal administration, though strict, was apparently efficient and just. But even in these monarchies the power of the ruler was gradually undermined by that of the leading nobles, who eventually reduced the king to a mere figurehead or eliminated him altogether. By 700 the monarchies had generally disappeared and had been replaced by baronial rivalries so severe as to reduce political life to a shambles and eventually to destroy the nobility itself as a social class. Strong men, not necessarily noble, began to force their way into political circles and sometimes to assume personal and quite extra-legal one-man rule. With these upstart rulers, the Age of Kings ended and the day of the tyrants began.

V. THE AGE OF THE TYRANTS (700-500 B.C.)

In modern speech a tyrant is one who rules oppressively and unjustly, but to the Greeks the word signified a person without royal ancestry who seizes control of a government and rules *de facto* if not *de jure*. In principle, the Greeks did not admire this type of usurper any more than we do today, but the fact remains that many of their tyrants, particularly those in Athens, were able men who earned popular support despite their irregular accession. In fact, the tyrant was virtually forced to be a good ruler, for the Greeks considered it an obligation to dethrone and even murder an oppressor.

Throughout history irregular rulers of all types have arisen out of unstable social conditions, and in Athens, the city-state upon which we shall concentrate during the remainder of this historical survey, we find no exception to the rule. Under the kings, Athens had found herself in constant confusion; there had been no codification of the laws and no economic planning. On the other hand, there had been tremendous dislocation of wealth and privilege. More and more farmers and small businessmen were forced into slavery because they could not compete with the spiralling financial power of the rich. Large landholders, viewing the rapidly rising merchant princes with suspicion, further accelerated the economic chaos by deliberately selling their crops to foreign consumers rather than to their own cities, hoping thereby to cause urban unrest which would unsettle their commercial rivals. Furthermore, in her relations with other cities, Athens was constantly bickering and fighting, and although the usual Greek inter-city warfare was often a desultory, spare-time affair, fought without a great deal of bloodshed during the slack agricultural season, the cumulative effect of this sporadic squabbling was disastrous to the Athenian economy. These unsettled conditions encouraged the overthrow of the kings and nobles in favor of the seemingly "strong men," the tyrants, who gave the impression of being able to straighten out the difficulties once they were in power. But at the same time, the very conditions which sponsored tyranny also made it necessary for the tyrant to be effective in his rule lest he be summarily replaced by another who promised to do the job better.

As a result of this compulsion to establish order, the age of the tyrants was highly constructive and, in a sense, acted as the seeding time of the great democratic institutions of Periclean Athens. Throughout the period there took place a gradual evolution of codified law. Aristocratic landholdings were slowly broken up and redistributed to farm workers, and colonization was encouraged in order to bolster

Athenian commerce. Public works were undertaken on an ever-increasing scale, and there was even official support given to education and the fine arts.

Perversely enough, one of the most instrumental factors in the development of democratic institutions was the adoption during the seventh century of oriental military tactics. The Greek method of warfare was based upon the phalanx, or solid line of foot soldiers armed with shield and spear, whose closely massed formation presented a formidable barrier to enemy attack. Much more powerful than the Homeric system of individual combat between carefully trained aristocrats, the phalanx with its relatively simple technique of pushing and spearing required little training and made it possible to assemble an army made up of common people in a few weeks' time, as compared to the many years of schooling required for preparing a warrior for individual combat of the Homeric type.

The Greeks greatly improved upon Eastern military tactics in one important respect: they used an army, not of nameless slaves whipped into battle by monolithic officers, but rather of free men who fought for a country and for institutions they loved and respected and which allowed them to live as human beings in an atmosphere of relative liberty and personal opportunity. Again and again in Greek military history we find the Hellenic armies triumphing over superior numbers by sheer force of patriotic spirit; it was this great love of the Hellenic warrior for his *polis* (city-state) that was the real "secret weapon" of the Greeks.

Among the many Athenian leaders during the Age of Tyrants, four names in particular stand out: Draco, Solon, Pisistratus, and Cleisthenes. Under Draco, in 621 B.C., an attempt was made to correct the chaos of Athenian law. Before 621, legal quarrels or actions against the public good had been decided largely by custom or whim, and a gigantic task presented itself to anyone who tried to reduce this amorphous mass of unwritten legal tradition to a recorded body of law. The results of Draco's efforts in this direction, known as the Draconian Code, were a step in the right direction, but his code left much to be desired, particularly in regard to the control of irresponsible agricultural and business practices and to the dangerous custom of permitting enslavement for debt. The great mass of people were as badly off as before, with no hope for the betterment of their condition under a legal system which encouraged the accumulation of wealth by the few at the expense of the many.

Under Solon, in 594 B.C., many of the abuses of the Draconian Code were corrected. Solon wiped out all land mortgages, abolished enslavement for debt, and provided trial by citizen jury. The rich grumbled at these reforms, asserting that the aristocratic arbiter was a traitor to his class. But at the same time they realized that further economic dislocation might ruin them completely, and reluctantly they acquiesced to the new measures. Solon also divided the population into four groups according to annual income and assigned privileges and obligations to each group. Under this system, the wealthy paid higher taxes than the poor, but were eligible to higher offices. This early form of income tax resulted in a state that was frankly a plutocracy, but considering the many evils the law corrected, it represented great progress. The principal fault of Solon's work was that, in his zeal for codification, he made so many laws and assigned so many penalties that complete enforcement was impossible and respect for law consequently declined.

One of the most colorful figures in Athenian history was Pisistratus, who played a leading role in politics for over half a century and who was undisputed leader of Athens from 546 to 527 B.C. Part mountebank and part enlightened statesman, Pisistratus captured the fancy of the Athenians as much by his sense of the dramatic as by his generally constructive measures. It is said that he once engineered a political coup by riding through the streets of Athens in the company of an impressively statuesque woman whom he boldly represented to the gullible as being the goddess Athene herself come personally to favor his cause. Another time he curried sympathy by tearing his garments to rags and covering them with blood before presenting himself in public with the story that a foul attempt had been made on his life. But despite this rabble-rousing foolery, Pisistratus ruled with justice and did much to improve Athenian living conditions with an enlightened program of public works. He also earned the gratitude of the world by instituting the Greek drama as a state-supported institution and by reawakening interest in the Homeric poems through publicly subsidized Homeric recitals. It was also under this tyrant, and probably directly because of his influence, that the Homeric poems were edited and set down in their present form. Altogether, it must be said that the ascendancy of Pisistratus, though often marred by low political scoundrelism, was both culturally and socially one of the most constructive periods in Athenian history.

With Cleisthenes, who ruled at the turn of the sixth century, legislative reforms were instituted which brought Athenian government to the threshold of its greatest period of democratic rule. Cleisthenes ended the confusing practice of voting by clans and instead divided the populace into *demes,* or districts. He instituted the *Boule,* or council, made up of representatives from each district, and thus made it possible for all geographical and economic divisions of the populace to receive a proper voice in the government. He also instituted political ostracism, a practice of discouraging the rise of tyrants through the temporary exile of any citizen whose activities were deemed in an annual referendum to be contrary to the public good. A description of the machinery of Athenian government, as perfected by Cleisthenes, will be given later. Suffice it to say for the present that this wise, statesmanlike, and politically dedicated man made it possible through his leadership for Athens to pass from the generally profitable but politically dangerous practice of rule by tyrants and demagogues into the bold, unique, utterly unprecedented democratic system which proved to be the greatest single achievement of the ancient world.

VI. THE PERSIAN WARS (497-479 B.C.)

The seven centuries which elapsed between the Trojan war and the time of Cleisthenes had been occupied mostly in the slow evolution of domestic institutions within the Greek city-states. Now, at the opening of the glorious fifth century, the Hellenic world found itself faced with its first great international challenge in the form of the powerful and aggressive Persian Empire. During the reign of Cyrus the Great (550-529), Persia had reached the peak of her domestic development and had also overthrown her chief rival, Babylonia, to become the leading power in Asia Minor. Still bursting with military energy after the death of Cyrus, Persia, under Cyrus' brilliant but half-insane son Cambyses, had gone on to conquer and annex Egypt and to dream of eventually holding sway over the entire eastern Mediterranean. One of the obstacles to the achievement of this dream was the Hellenic world, which controlled important commercial and military sites and which had no intention of knuckling down to the brash aggressiveness of her powerful eastern neighbor. After Cambyses had committed suicide in 522, his successor, Darius, turned his attention to eliminating all obstacles to complete Persian domination of the area, with particular concentration on the problem of entirely eliminating Greek opposition.

Darius was a great general and an even greater administrator, and the skill with which he organized his extensive domain fell little short of genius. He divided his empire into twenty provinces or satrapies, each under the direction of a satrap carefully chosen for his unquestioning accep-

tance of the royal will. These satraps were carefully supervised by agents and secret police of the emperor, who
reported directly to Darius in the event of any sign of dis-
loyalty or personal ambition on the part of the provincial
governors. To make sure that such news travelled fast, Darius constructed great highways from the capital to the most
remote parts of his domain, and over these roads couriers
passed tirelessly back and forth bearing news of all significant happenings within the land. In addition to his advanced system of communications, Darius developed a
police system which watched over the actions of public and
private citizens alike with such sinister efficiency as to discourage any thought of unpatriotic action or maladminis-
tration. And climaxing Persian power was its immense slave
army, the fiercest and most ruthlessly disciplined body of
the ancient world. Altogether the Persians, led by their
ambitious emperor, constituted a seemingly insuperable
threat to the future existence of Greek civilization.

By 516 Darius had conquered all the lands to the east
and south of his capital, had annexed the Greek territory of
Ionia in Asia Minor, and had cast the die of further conquest to the west by crossing the Bosphorus into Europe.
By 500 the Persian army stood on the very borders of Hellenic Greece, poised for what looked to be an easy conquest
of the peninsula. But Darius, accustomed to think of government only as a rule of force, had not understood the
extent to which the Greeks would resist any threat to
curtail their precious heritage of freedom. Not being ready
at the time to meet the Persian hordes face to face, the
Greeks had encouraged their Ionian brothers to revolt
against Persian rule and had furnished material assistance
to the cause of Ionian freedom. The revolt failed, but it
took the Persians six years of hard and costly fighting to
subdue it and gave the Hellenic Greeks some time to prepare themselves for the blow that was soon to fall on them
also.

After the defeat of the Ionians, Athens became the next target of Persian wrath. In 490 a vast Persian armada of 140 ships and 100,000 fighting men[5] sailed boldly into the Aegean with the purpose of totally destroying the Greek city which had been so instrumental in fomenting and prolonging the Ionian revolt. Despite their long preparations, the Athenians were caught by surprise and were no match in numbers or armament for the Persian hordes. They hastily sent to Sparta for aid, but religious observances delayed the Spartan armies and when the Persians debarked before the plain of Marathon they found themselves confronted by only 10,000 poorly organized, lightly armed Athenians. But stronger than their weapons was the Athenian willingness to die for the free institutions they enjoyed and it was this determination, so far beyond the understanding of the slave-driving Persian generals, together with the clever use of pincer tactics by the Athenians, that eventually carried the day for the Greeks. Through weakening their line at strategic points to allow the Persians to rush into the gap and then by closing the breach to surround and annihilate the baffled enemy, the lightly equipped Athenians were able to decimate the slow, heavily armed Persians until by the end of the day Darius' huge expeditionary force had been entirely routed with an immense toll of casualties.

Finding themselves in full possession of the field of Marathon, the Athenians were then horrified to see the Persian galleys turning toward the undefended city of Athens itself. Despite the fatigue of a day's fighting, the Athenian army in forced march managed to negotiate the more than twenty miles between Marathon and the capital in time to anticipate the attacking Persian fleet and discourage an attempted enemy landing. Following this dou-

[5] Estimates of the size of armies by classical historians vary greatly. In this case, the estimated number of Persians has varied from 30,000 to 200,000. No one really know the true figures.

ble humiliation at the hands of the supposedly weak Athenians, the Persians abandoned their expedition. Athens, on the other hand, by virtue of its achievement became the leading power among the Greek states and the unifying force in organizing further defense against Persian aggression.

After Marathon, the Persians had gone home to lick their wounds and plan revenge. However, Darius died in 486 and it took some time for his son Xerxes to make up his mind to continue the Greek campaign. Finally in 480 Xerxes led an army of about 180,000 men down through Thrace and Macedonia and into the Hellenic peninsula, sweeping everything before him as he advanced, until he reached the pass of Thermopylae, a narrow opening between the mountains and the sea. This time it was the Spartans who were to be the heroes of the day. Here a contingent of not more than three hundred Spartans, together with some Thebans, Phocians, and Thespians, under the Spartan king, Leonidas, was standing with instructions to delay the Persian advance until the Athenian navy could arrive with reinforcements. Xerxes vainly hurled wave after wave of his troops against the few defending Greeks, but in the narrow pass the force of numbers counted for little, and as at Marathon the lightly armed Greeks were able to outmaneuver their slow-moving opponents. Finally, through the treachery of a Greek deserter, the Persians learned of a path whereby they could surround Leonidas and his group of three hundred Spartans. In the ensuing battle, Leonidas stood his ground with true Spartan courage until he and virtually all of his troop were annihilated and the Persians finally controlled the pass.

Though technically defeated at Thermopylae, the heroic defense of Leonidas did much to stiffen Greek morale. Enormous numbers of Persians had been killed in the attempt to take Thermopylae, and even Xerxes was awed by the courage of the Greeks. In desperation he is said to have exclaimed: "In what way can we conquer these men?" to be answered only by the ominous and foreboding silence of his generals.

The battle of Thermopylae also gave the Greeks the time they needed to organize their naval attack, and it was on the sea, at Salamis, that the Persian expedition was first decisively defeated. Here the Greeks won their battle through the greater flexibility of their forces and, though greatly outnumbered, were able to destroy the flower of the Persian navy. The next year (479) at Plataea a Greek army composed principally of Spartans and Athenians utterly routed the Persian forces, while the same day the few remaining ships of the Persian navy were burned at Mycale. The war was over, the great Persian Empire had suffered a defeat from which it never recovered, and Greece, temporarily unified in the face of a common enemy, was at the threshold of its Golden Age.

VII. ATHENS IN THE GOLDEN AGE (479-431 B.C.)

According to the poet Shelley, "the period which intervened between the birth of Pericles (c. 500) and the death of Aristotle (322) is undoubtedly, whether considered in itself or with reference to the effect which it has produced upon the subsequent destinies of civilized man, the most memorable in history." As a literary man, Shelley naturally extended the limits of his Golden Age to include the time of Plato and Aristotle and, from the literary standpoint, no one will dispute him. But for the greatest single period of political and social achievement, one would have to narrow Shelley's designation to include only the interval of Athenian history between the end of the Persian Wars (479) and the beginning of the disastrous Peloponnesian conflict in 431. During this all too brief half-century, Athens gained her greatest prosperity. This prosperity was achieved largely because of her tremendous political and military prestige as a result of her efforts during the Persian

Wars and also because of her highly developed commercial and financial economy. Domestically, she had miraculously achieved a type of life that was balanced and stable, with ample opportunity for persons of all classes and with relatively little abuse of power and privilege. In short, Athens during this period was able to maintain a balance of those mercurial elements of authority, freedom, intellectual culture, and individual opportunity never again matched in the history of the world.

Regrettably, this domestic equilibrium was not paralleled with a similar stability in the field of foreign relations. In diplomatic affairs, Athens made error after error, and none of these blunders was more costly than that of her conduct in regard to the Delian League. The Delian League had been formed at the conclusion of the Persian Wars. Its purpose was both defensive and offensive; it sought to protect the Aegean from any resumption of Persian aggression and at the same time it lent military aid to the Ionian Greeks in their ultimately successful war for independence from their Persian conquerors. Most of the influential cities of the central Aegean area joined with Athens in the League, but Sparta and her satellites of the Peloponnesus were ominously absent. Later this jealous rift between the two largest powers who had fought side by side against the Persians was to have tragic results, but for the present it was confined to a rather stimulating commercial competition and to obscure diplomatic maneuvering.

The advantages of a confederation of Greek city-states were obvious to all, but though quite conscious of their ethnic unity, the Greeks all through their history refused to achieve the political amalgamation they so urgently needed. The Delian League was no exception to this tendency. Once the threat of further Persian aggression had disappeared, lesser members of the confederation began to grumble at paying the annual membership tax and objected with increasing strenuousness to Athenian domination of

League affairs. Even before the conclusion of mopping-up activities against Persia, several League members, including Naxos and Thatos, had revolted and had had to be brought back into line by forcible measures. More and more, Athens was required to maintain unity by coercion. Finally she ceased to convene the Delian parliament and in 454 took the decisive step of removing the Delian treasury from the island of Delos to Athens itself. It is true that the threat of Egyptian raids against the Aegean islands made such a removal desirable, but at the same time there was no mistaking the real motive behind Athenian policy. Athens had become a major power and the Delian confederation had been transformed into an Athenian Empire.

VIII. PERICLES (c. 500-429 B.C.)

The leading figure in this Athenian metamorphosis was Pericles, whose name has been immortalized by being applied to the period representing the very peak of Greek civilization. For over thirty years, as *strategos autokrator,* or military chief of staff, he led the Athenians in peace and war, brought to its highest flowering the long, slow growth of Athenian democracy, and left behind him a sense of nobility unapproached by any other figure in the ancient world.

Though Pericles was a progressive leader in every sense of the term, he was no upstart radical. He came from one of the most blue-blooded of Athenian families, and from earliest infancy enjoyed the advantages of wealth and cultured refinement. Everything in his background should have led him to join the conservative, oligarchic party, but as Pericles matured politically he saw clearly that the trend of the times was toward enlarging the privileges of the ordinary citizen. Accordingly, throughout his career he devoted himself to the extension of democracy to the less privileged classes and to the broadening of the base of Athenian government to include matters of culture and social welfare as well as the traditional legislative, military, and police functions.

One of his earliest acts was to institute a system of pay for military and jury service; another was to grant to all citizens a small annual subsidy to cover admission charges to theatres and official sports contests. By so doing he hoped to foster creative writing, to instill a greater appreciation of the arts, and to encourage education. The wealthy conservatives sputtered about the moral disintegration that would result from these government handouts, but it would be difficult to prove that any harm was done. Pericles also incurred much criticism in some quarters when he embarked upon a large-scale program of construction. He built eight miles of fortifications known as the "Long Walls" to protect the city from a land-based attack, he constructed ships and storage warehouses for war emergencies, and balanced this military program with the construction of beautiful temples and public buildings throughout Attica. Consequent to this latter project, he was able to employ large numbers of artists, architects, and workers of all classes so that, in the words of Plutarch, "the undisciplined mechanic multitude . . . should not go without their share of public funds, and yet should not have these given them for sitting still and doing nothing."

"The Olympian," as he was called by sarcastic enemies, was not too occupied with the affairs of state to be devoid of lighter romantic moments. Though many years married, he formed an alliance with Aspasia, a highly intelligent and educated courtesan from Megara who had rejected the empty and sheltered life led by respectable Athenian women in favor of an existence which, while socially dubious, brought with it the physical and intellectual freedom she desired. Aspasia in her mature years ran a school of rhetoric and philosophy which, although nominally intended for the daughters of the wealthy, was also attended by such famous men as Socrates, Euripides, Alcibiades, Anaxagoras, Pheidias, and, of course, Pericles himself. Eventually Pericles and his wife were amicably divorced and Aspasia became, in effect, the first lady of the land. Ironically enough, Pericles could not marry her because of a short-sighted law he himself had instituted forbidding legal marriage between Athenians and foreigners. Despite the sneering jibes of Pericles' political enemies, Aspasia was a devoted and distinguished companion, worthy of her protector's greatness, and an active contributor to many of his most constructive civic deeds.

Yet inspired as was the thirty-year leadership of Pericles, it was not all to the good. Much of the extensive public works program was financed by exacting tribute from satellite states, which made for increasingly bad feeling between Athens and her weaker Delian allies. Even more rash was his expropriation of the treasury of the Delian League and the spending of funds intended for all member states in the League for purely Athenian improvements. This frankly imperialistic attitude was intensified by Pericles' successors and caused a hatred of Athens which did much to result in her eventual downfall in the Peloponnesian Wars.

Also, Periclean government was weak in its failure to devise a civil service for the routine jobs of administration. Because the Greeks were extremely apprehensive of creating a bureaucracy, these jobs were left to amateurs whose actions were often conditioned by political or purely emotional considerations.

But the greatest evil of all lay in the very excellence of Pericles' rule. For a generation the Athenians became so used to relying upon the strong man at the controls that they became politically shiftless and negative, and when Pericles finally died in the Plague of 429 there was no statesman of developed stature to take his place. Athenian government rapidly degenerated into a cynical, opportunistic demagoguery, with men of no moral or civic qualifications scrambling for power and avid for personal gain. The integrity, strength, and philosophical enlightenment of Pericles were gone, and the glory of Athens was tragically soon to follow in their wake.

IX. THE PELOPONNESIAN WARS (459-404 B.C.)

Periclean rule, despite its general excellence, could not have prevented the inevitable death struggle between Athens and Sparta. Long before the death of Pericles, the die of internecine warfare had been cast in the formation of the Delian League, which constituted a serious military and commercial threat to Sparta and her allies in the Peloponnesian Confederation. In the first years of the League, Athens had followed a program of Spartan appeasement, but with the coming to power of Pericles, appeasement was abandoned in favor of a "get tough" policy toward the Peloponnesian cities. For nearly thirty years (459-431) a state of cold war existed between the Delian League and the Peloponnesian Confederation with Athens doing everything possible to steal the Confederation's markets in Italy and to undermine Spartan power over her allies. Occasionally the cold war developed warmer phases in the form of naval blockades and desultory battles against Spartan satellites, but for the most part the first phase of the Peloponnesian conflict was one of diplomatic and economic strategy.

In 445 a Thirty-Year Peace was signed which stipulated that Sparta should maintain her land supremacy while allowing Athens a free hand on the sea, but the effect of this treaty was merely to preserve the status quo. It was only a question of time before the situation between the rival cities became intolerable, and in 431 that long-delayed moment arrived. From 431 to 404 Greece was plunged into a ruthless, frustrating, inconclusive war which proved eventually to be suicidal for Hellenic civilization.

Before outlining the course of the Peloponnesian War, it would be profitable to give a brief description of the nature of Spartan society. Though only one hundred miles apart as the crow flies, Athens and Sparta were as distant as the poles in social and political organization. Athens was a citizen democracy, Sparta a peculiar form of monarchy with two kings (who were mere figureheads) and a board of five Ephors, who ruled with absolute sway.[6] Both cities used slaves to perform the necessary labors of life, but while Athens treated her slaves with decency and humanity, Sparta governed hers with iron discipline and harsh cruelty. This discipline was felt to be necessary because the Spartan populace contained 200,000 slaves as against only 8,000 masters, and the fear of uprising on the part of the ill-used, numerically superior helots continually haunted the thoughts of the master class.

In the training of the citizen body the Athenians, as we have seen, sought to develop the well-balanced man. The Spartans, on the other hand, strove to encourage only the qualities of the professional soldier. Intellectual training was slight and consisted largely in extensive learning by rote, which probably accounts for the almost complete absence of Spartan creative arts. Physical culture, on the other hand, was pursued to the fullest possible extent, with great stress placed upon the development of courage, endurance, discipline, and ability to endure privations of all sorts. The young boys were taken from their families at an early age and brought up in a communal society, where they lived in barracks and conformed to military regulation in their every action. Even the women were trained in soldierly qualities and, to the horror of the sex-conscious Athenians, were required regularly to attend the gymnasia for exercise and participation in competitive sports.

The result of this kind of training was to achieve a society of superb soldiers whose military exploits both awed and terrified the Hellenic world. Such a regimen could produce a Leonidas, who with his valiant Three Hundred

[6] There was also a council of twenty-eight elders elected by, but not from, the people. The real power lay with the Ephors, however.

fought to the death at Thermopylae, and it could produce a Pausanias, who led his troop to victory over the force of an overwhelming Persian attack at Plataea. But it could not produce a nation of free men, it could not produce an idea, it could not produce a society capable of progress and development. In his great *History of the Peloponnesian Wars,* Thucydides points to this rigidity as the great weakness of Spartan society.

They were conservative and slow to act even in emergencies. Cautious even when caution was unnecessary, they never dared put out their full strength . . . . Where others thought of adding to their possession, the Spartans were haunted by the fear of losing what they had.

And yet it was this nation of militaristic robots who defeated the free Athenians in the senseless carnage of the Peloponnesian Wars. But the Athens which fell in 404 was an Athens going fat and soft in imperialism and demagoguery, an Athens which represented a sorry state of decline from the early days of Pericles. The moral to be drawn would seem to be not that "might makes right" but rather that "eternal vigilance is the price of democracy."

The events of the Peloponnesian War need be traced only in barest outline. The actual fighting started when Athens intervened in the revolt of Corcyra against her mother state of Corinth. Since Corinth in turn was an ally of Sparta, this action by Athens was deemed to have broken the Thirty-Year Peace and a general conflagration between Attica and the Peloponnesus was not long in following. The fighting had hardly begun when the Athenians were critically weakened by a plague which decimated the city's population and carried off Pericles himself. The great leader's post as *strategos autokrator* was taken by Cleon, a brave soldier but a gross and ignorant demagogue who failed to inspire or even elicit the respect of the populace.

The war dragged on through year after year of costly and indecisive fighting until both sides were so exhausted that in 421 they signed the Peace of Nicias and returned disconsolately to their wasted homelands.

The Peace of Nicias was hardly more than a desperate two-party agreement between Athens and Sparta. Both major powers neglected their allies and divided disputed powers and territories among themselves, thus engendering great anger among other states who had participated in the ten years of fighting. It was only a question of time before this understandable disgruntlement would develop into a resumption of armed conflict. To keep her allies in line, Athens had to resort to the most extreme coercive measures, including the total extermination of the island town of Melos.

At the same time, demagogues at home kept the war fever alive as a means of holding their own power. The most notorious of these warmongers was Alcibiades, nephew of Pericles, pupil of Socrates, and one of the most brilliantly gifted men in history. Because of his great charm and his indisputable talents, Alcibiades was able to wheedle the Athenians into supporting his plan for a campaign against the islands of Sicily, with the object of encircling Sparta and cutting her off from the western Mediterranean. In 415 the ill-advised expedition was launched, with Athens in a foolhardy mood staking her very existence upon its successful outcome.

The story of the Sicilian campaign is one of the darkest in history. The Sicilians, bitterly defending their homeland, inflicted defeat after defeat upon their tormentors and finally forced a large part of the Athenian army into a desperate retreat, virtually without food and water. Many died of thirst or starvation on the way; others were killed in great numbers in guerilla warfare. Finally, in a last stand on the Assinarus river, the last vestiges of the Athenian army were destroyed or captured, many being killed as they forgot personal defense in their frenzy to slake their thirst in the bloody waters. Those who were not killed were taken into slavery, where most of them died of neglect laboring in the stone quarries of Syracuse. As Thucydides puts it:

> The immensity of this event was without parallel in the . . . war and, in my opinion, in all that we know of Greek history. It was also of unparalleled glory to the victors and humiliation to the vanquished . . . army, fleet, everything perished in total ruin, and of many only few returned home.

As though the Sicilian defeat were not terrible enough in itself, the campaign, as might have been expected, touched off the even worse situation of Spartan resumption of the war against Athens. Advised by Alcibiades, who had deserted to the enemy, the Spartans in 413 entered Attica itself and the Athenians found themselves in a state of siege. They gathered what allies they could and for nearly ten years fought with dogged weariness against superior numbers, conniving intrigue at home, and depletion of their physical and natural resources. In 405 they were routed in a naval engagement in the Hellespont and shortly afterward, with their fleet destroyed, their food supply almost gone, and their allies in revolt, they were forced to witness the humiliating spectacle of the unopposed Spartan navy entering the harbor of Athens to occupy the city and destroy its fortifications. With this destruction was also shattered all Athenian hope of ever regaining her past political and cultural glory.

X. THE DECLINE OF GREECE (404-146 B.C.)

The end of the Peloponnesian Wars marked not only the defeat of Athens; it also was the beginning of the rapid disintegration of Hellenic civilization. To be sure, the best work of Plato and Aristotle was still in the future, but it takes more than the teachings of philosophers to make a great society. Politically, Athens had begun to decline with the death of Pericles, and after her defeat in the war, Hellenic leadership fell to powers far less enlightened and socially developed than she. After the Spartan triumph, the mantle of leadership naturally fell to the victor in the war, but Sparta's conservative and static way of life hardly fitted her for the role. It was not long before her position was being strongly disputed by other cities, with Thebes and Syracuse being especially strong rivals. For the next sixty-five years all manner of destructive jockeying for power further hastened the decline of the Hellenic world. From 350 to 338, following the brief ascendencies of Sparta, Thebes, and Syracuse, Athens regained some measure of her former leadership for another short period, but the great days were over.

Meanwhile, as the Greek cities were unsystematically destroying themselves, a foreign power was rising to the north in Macedonia, and by 346 B.C. some Athenian leaders, including the orator Demosthenes, realized that the real menace to Hellenic freedom was embodied in the Macedonian king Philip. After much time-wasting debate, Athens declared war on her latest rival, but was easily defeated in 338 B.C., whereupon Greece rapidly came under the domination of Philip. After Philip was assassinated two years later, his brilliant but erratic son Alexander the Great succeeded to the throne and ruled for fourteen violent and bloody years, during which time he conquered nearly all of the Mediterranean world and much of Asia Minor. Although Alexander's gigantic empire disintegrated rapidly after his premature death at thirty-two, Macedonian supremacy continued another half-century, though with diminishing strength.

Consequent with the dispersion of power within, there rose the menace of foreign invasion from without. By 275 B.C. the Gauls were nibbling at the borders of the Hellenistic world, and though the Gallic incursions were short-lived and indecisive, their effect upon the morale of the defenders was seriously destructive. Far more alarming than the Gauls was the growing menace of a rising Rome. The story of the century and a quarter after 275 B.C. is a sad one of accelerating Hellenistic weakness and decline in the face of the young and powerful aggressor to the West. From 214 B.C. onward, the disciplined Roman armies were able to defeat the Macedonians almost at will and to annex more and more former Greek-Macedonian territory, until in 146 B.C. the entire Aegean area, now reduced to military and cultural unimportance, was incorported unceremoniously into the vast machinery of Rome.

SUGGESTED READINGS

See end of Chapter 8 for suggested readings.

chapter 4

GREEK RELIGION

I. ORIGINS

Like Greek civilization in general, Greek religion derived largely from Cretan and Mycenean sources and was transmuted gradually to meet the needs of the more rational and less mystical European invaders. Of the original type of worship of these invaders, we have not the slightest notion. But that they were deeply responsive to spiritual ideas is indicated by the major role played by religion throughout the history of Greek life. It is also evident that they must have had some previous sacred ceremonials and beliefs, for otherwise they would merely have adopted Mycenean forms *in toto,* without effecting the significant changes they made in the predominantly Oriental outlook of their predecessors.

Cretan and Mycenean religion was apparently based upon the nature myth of conception, growth, death, and rebirth, as represented by the seasons and by the concrete generative phenomena of plant and animal life. Their gods and goddesses represented various aspects of this life, with the principal divinities being directly related to the idea of fertility, both in relation to crops and to human life. Be-

49

cause women more clearly symbolize the concept of propagation, the most important Cretan-Mycenean deities were female, with Cybele, the earth goddess, being the most significant of all.

At first glance, Greek religion seems to have been a far cry from the primitive nature worship of Crete and Mycenae. Whereas the earlier beliefs stressed the female functions of gestation and birth, the Greeks celebrated the male principle of fertilization and raised the male qualities of strength, aggressiveness, and courage over the more passive and ministrative feminine propensities. Furthermore, as time went on, the Greek religious outlook became far less concerned with natural phenomena than with the more sophisticated ethical problems of man's relationship with his fellows; even in Homeric times the gods were seen as being more interested in problems of war, government, and human virtue than in such rudimentary affairs as the passage of the seasons or the productivity of field and family.

But this seeming divergency between Greek and Mycenean religion is more apparent than real. Scholars, particularly in the nineteenth century, have carefully pointed out the parallels between Greek and Eastern mythology and have even shown that, of all the deities on Mount Olympus, hardly one existed who cannot be traced back directly to the nature worship of Crete and Mycenae. The very names of most of the Olympians are seldom of Greek origin and, despite the switch in sexual emphasis from female to male principles, the fertility motif emerges as being as fundamental to primitive Greek as it was to Oriental worship.

It will not be necessary for us to document the conclusions scholars have reached on the common nature of Greek and earlier Mediterranean sacred beliefs. The only point to be stressed from the preceding paragraphs is that religion, like all other aspects of civilization, is a dynamic institution. Though often seemingly conservative and resistant to change, it nevertheless is continually altering to meet the needs of succeeding ages, each with its own peculiar problems. Greek religion was no exception to this process. It passed through many stages, from the early nature worship hypothecated by the scholars, through an age of myth and fable, to the heroic Olympian period of Homer, which in turn shaded gradually into the more abstract, ethical, and sophisticated approach indicated by the Greek drama. Throughout these various metamorphoses, individual religious concepts were sometimes rational, sometimes mystical, but by the fifth century sacred beliefs had managed to achieve a reasonable synthesis of reason and emotion, of ethics and mysticism.

Because of the constant evolution of Hellenic religion from early times through the Age of Pericles, it would be well to be wary of flat statements concerning its nature and thought content. One should remember that Greek literature covers a period of nearly a thousand years and that the ideas reflected over this period underwent many alterations as Greek civilization met the challenge of the passing centuries. At the same time, one should bear in mind that although the details and interpretations changed from time to time, the stream of Greek religious beliefs was broad, deep, and powerful, and did more than any other single force to direct the conduct of Greek life.

II. THE GREEK VIEW OF THE CREATION [1]

As in the Hebraic conception of the beginnings of things, the universe was believed by the Greeks to have originated in darkness and chaos. Probably because of the Hellenic love of form, light, and order, the pre-world was imagined

[1] Alternate names of the principal gods are given in parentheses in the following account. Some of the gods had more than one Greek name. Many of them were later identified with Roman deities and consequently acquired Latin names.

as a place of negatives, of the absence of the qualities which the Greeks admired. Out of Chaos, therefore, came Nox (Night), which was conceived of as a kind of abstract entity, and Erebus, the place of death.

But from Nox and Erebus, by an unexplained miracle, Eros (Love) was born, presaging the formation of a world of order and beauty. Eros generated Aether (Light) and Hemera (Day) as his first children, followed by Gaea (Mother Earth) and Ouranos (Father Heaven). The fact that these earliest entities were conceived of simultaneously as natural phenomena and as gods is a basic clue to an understanding of the common Greek habit of personifying inanimate objects and abstract ideas. The multitude of gods resulted from this fanciful delight in visualizing concrete personalities as representative of the intangible and super-human things of life.

The children of Ouranos and Gaea were the gigantic Titans, several of whom became favorite subjects among Greek and Roman writers. War broke out among the gods when one of the Titans, Cronus (Saturn or Father Time) rebelled against his father. Victorious in this first heavenly revolution, he took over the rule of the universe together with his sister-wife Rhea (Ops) and lorded it over his fellows Atlas, Prometheus, Epimetheus, and Oceanus.

Fearful of a similar revolution by his own offspring, Cronus swallowed them as they were born, until Rhea secretly hid his sixth child, Zeus (Jove, Jupiter), and allowed him and his succeeding younger brothers Hades (Pluto, Dis) and Poseidon (Neptune) to grow to manhood. When Zeus came of age he fulfilled his father's fears by leading a revolt against the Titans which succeeded in dethroning Cronus. Known thereafter as "father of gods and men," he divided the universe with his brothers. To Hades he gave command of the underworld, which became the habitation of the dead and was known as Hades after the name of the god.

He assigned the ocean to Poseidon and kept earth and heaven for himself. The abode of the gods was believed to be on high Mount Olympus where snow or rain never fell and where the gods feasted on nectar, laughed, quarrelled, became angry, loved, and made merry like any other group of intimate friends.

Having conquered Cronus, Zeus put the other Titans to work at various tasks. Atlas was forced to support the world on his shoulders. To Epimetheus was assigned the task of creating animals and men. True to his name, which means "afterthought," he endowed the animal kingdom, which he created first, with so many good qualities like swiftness, strength, fur, and wings that he had nothing left to give man to make him even equal to the beasts. Consequently he appealed to his brother Prometheus. Prometheus, whose name means "forethought," had already taken the precaution of stealing fire from Zeus which he had kept secreted in a hollow reed. This he gave to man, and with it man created his weapons for self-protection and his crafts and arts for self-improvement. In Aeschylus' *Prometheus Bound* this gift of fire is made symbolic of all the qualities which make man superior to the animals.

Because of his defiance of Zeus, Prometheus was punished by being chained to a rock where, in his lonely eminence, he taunted Zeus with the secret foreknowledge of his own eventual liberation and the downfall of Zeus himself. In an attempt to force him to reveal this secret, Zeus sent an eagle to gnaw daily at his liver which grew back every night so that it might be reconsumed the next day. No one shared the secret of Prometheus until Io, a fellow-sufferer from the power of Zeus, aroused his sympathy. A mortal woman, she had been desired by Zeus, who threw a cloud over the earth so that his wife Hera (Juno) would not discover his love-making. But the cloud itself aroused Hera's suspicions. She came upon the lovers suddenly, and Zeus attempted to save the situation by transforming Io into a cow. Hera begged the cow as a gift. Zeus saw no valid way of refusing her without making her more suspicious, so he cravenly granted her request. Hera then placed the cow under the supervision of Argus, the hundred-eyed watchman of the gods. Zeus tried to rescue Io by sending Hermes to tell stories and play to Argus in an attempt to lull all of his eyes to sleep at once. When the last eye finally closed, Hermes killed Argus. The practical-minded Hera used the eyes to embroider the tail of her favorite bird, the peacock, on whose plumage they may still be seen. She also continued to persecute her husband's paramour by sending a brize or gad-fly to keep the cow-shaped Io in motion and to pursue her on her flight through the entire Mediterranean world.

When the forlorn Io paused in her wanderings before the rock to which the rebellious Titan was chained, Prometheus comforted her by predicting that Zeus would ultimately change her back to a woman and that a descendant of hers, Heracles (Hercules), would shoot the eagle and set him free. He also predicted that Zeus would have a child by the sea-nymph Thetis who would overthrow his father. This prediction did not actually come to pass because Heracles, after freeing Prometheus, sufficiently tempered the pride of both Zeus and Prometheus to effect a reconciliation between them, at which point Prometheus revealed his secret. Zeus, having learned wisdom from Prometheus, did not carry through his projected love affair with Thetis and consequently retained his throne. The Greek habit of giving their gods human attributes is again revealed in this conception that the gods, like men, can learn by experience and grow in wisdom with the passing of time.

Meanwhile, the creation of humanity had started earthly troubles as well as heavenly conflicts. The first woman was created on Mount Olympus by the gods themselves. Each of the Olympian divinities gave some of his own particular power in this creation, with Aphrodite sharing her beauty, Hera her domestic virtues, Athene her wisdom, and so forth. For this reason, the first woman was named Pandora, or "gift of all." She was then sent to earth to serve as a punishment for man because he had been the receiver of stolen goods (the fire of Zeus) and had become so clever and gifted. The gods had given Pandora a box which she was forbidden to open. Unable to control her feminine curiosity, she opened the lid and released all the evils which have ever since plagued humanity. In panic, Pandora slammed the cover down and succeeded in preserving the last remaining thing in the casket, which was Hope. A more logical variant of this legend narrates that Hope was one of the many gifts Prometheus gave to man.

III. THE OLYMPIAN GODS

Meanwhile Zeus, in his role of father of the gods, continued to divert himself with many love affairs with both goddesses and mortal women. His wife Hera was eternally jealous, and the immortal lord of the universe often found himself in the role of a henpecked husband, engaging in numerous escapades and priding himself on eluding the vigilance of his wife.

Students of Greek literature often find the marital infidelities and bickerings of the gods singularly inappropriate to beings of divine stature and greatness, but to the Greeks the situation presented no problem whatsoever. As in many early religions, the chief of the gods served as both nature spirit and hero. Zeus was not only a symbol of power and strength but was also the prototype of the male principle. It is only natural, therefore, that he should have been seen as the father of many children, although the Greeks, being monogamists, could not adopt the Oriental custom of giving their chief god many wives to accommodate his progenitive tendencies.

But while they rejected polygamy, the Greeks saw nothing particularly shocking in extra-marital activity, especially in a god who was empowered to have and do what he pleased. In this respect, the Greeks were aristocratic in their reactions. They believed in social rank and in the privileges and responsibilities that go with rank. If the gods have to bear the great burden of directing the affairs of men, it is no more than fair that they assume special privileges in return for their efforts. Whatever these immortals chose to do was right because their doing so made it right.

At the same time, the Greeks realized that many of these arbitrary actions were privileges reserved for the gods and were not to be imitated or demanded by mere mortals. For man to covet these privileges for himself would be to commit *hubris,* the worst of all crimes, in which a common mortal arrogantly attempts to place himself on a level with the divine. The Greeks were singularly free from the element of terror, and fear of the gods was a concept quite foreign to their thoughts, but in this one respect they saw their divinities in terms of wrath and retribution. The gods were jealous of their powers and would not for a moment tolerate man's assuming the prerogatives of the gods himself. Such *hubris* brought with it inevitable and often horrible punishment, and though few sinners in Greek legend are portrayed as undergoing eternal torture, those few have invariably been guilty of supreme arrogance toward the gods.

With all their power and privilege, however, the Olympians were not omnipotent. Although they existed on a far higher level than men and were stronger, wiser, nobler, and more beautiful than they, they were not by any means the be-all and the end-all. They too were ruled by higher forces in that they were subject to the predeterminations of *Moira,* or fate. Often they knew this fate in advance, but at the same time they were powerless to do anything about it.

Zeus, for example, could not prevent the slaying of his favorite mortal son Sarpedon during the siege of Troy, although he was aware in advance that the boy would die. He also was unable to carry out a desired union with the sea-nymph Thetis when he learned that it was fated that the son of Thetis would be stronger than his father.

Another limitation on the powers of the gods was the often-overlooked fact that, unlike many divinities, they were not essentially creators. They did not build the universe. They could create and destroy lesser forms of life, but they had no power to fashion matter itself, nor could they combat in any conceivable degree what had been destined from the beginning. It is well to bear in mind that the Olympians themselves had evolved over eons of time and only after several previous dynasties had existed. Thus they must never be equated with the Judeo-Christian concept of God the Creator.

The Olympian gods were therefore relative rather than absolute divinities. The Greeks saw them as limited and faulty, but still far above humanity and worthy of imitation in everything save the assumption of privilege. To have conceived of them as perfect would have been difficult for the Greeks, who would have looked upon perfection as being so remote from possibility as to be impractical in human affairs. They preferred to see their deities as noble and dignified, as existing on a level of glory ever beyond the reach of man, and yet not so far beyond earthly qualities that man could not see reflected in himself, however poorly, some of the characteristics of a god.

IV. THE DESCENT OF MAN

But while viewing himself thus in the mirror of divinity, the Greek was still conscious of his relative unworthiness. He did not place so much emphasis as the Christians on the factor of man's depravity, it is true, but he nevertheless tended to take a rather dim view of the present state of society in contrast to the great days of the legendary past.

According to Hesiod, man has passed through several ages, each one inferior to the one which preceded it. In the Golden Age, he lived without toil in a world of eternal spring, where nature provided food in abundance and where the weather was so mild as to make shelter unnecessary. Since there was abundance for all, war and strife were non-existent and private property unknown. The next age was that of silver, which introduced the four seasons and thereby made it necessary for men to work in order to provide food and shelter against the privations of winter. Thus the concept of property began to develop and with it the seeds of individual jealousies and conflicts. The third age was that of bronze, in which the element of strife came into being. This strife, however, was at first merely competitive action entirely unmarked by the wickedness that characterizes the modern struggle for existence. The Bronze Age was followed by one of demigods, in which many of the great heroes of myth and story roamed the earth performing deeds still extolled by the poets. But this brilliant period soon departed, to be succeeded by the present Age of Iron, in which man has become vicious, predatory, and corrupted by the desire for money and power. Thus the Greeks, in their own way, concurred with the Hebraic doctrine of the fall of man.[2]

[2] There is also a flood legend among the Greeks, which tells of Zeus destroying humanity by flood after becoming disgusted by its corruptness. However one couple, Deucalion and Pyrrha, were warned in advance of the catastrophe and built an ark which rode the storm safely. When the waters receded, the ark grounded on Mount Parnassus. Deucalion and Pyrrha then proceeded to repopulate the earth by throwing stones over their shoulders; wherever the stones landed, men sprang up full-grown. There is some doubt, however, that this rather unorthodox method of propagation succeeded in producing human beings any more virtuous than they had been before the flood.

V. THE CULT OF APOLLO

So far we have been discussing what may be termed the Homeric, or classical, aspects of Greek religion. We must now turn to a consideration of the sacred beliefs and practices of the sixth century and following, in order to have a better understanding of the moral and ethical problems presented by the life and art of the Golden Age.

It is to be expected that with the growing complexity of Greek civilization through the post-Homeric centuries, religious concepts should assume less of the heroic-mythological flavor of earlier times and should put increased stress upon the moral or allegorical interpretation of the gods and their deeds. From the writings of the fifth century, it is evident that the educated Greeks no longer thought of divinities of Mount Olympus as actual beings in the Homeric sense, but rather as personifications of ideals and as metaphorical standard-setters of human behavior. For instance, the young Zeus of *Prometheus Bound* represents the power principle of rule, whereas his antagonist, Prometheus, stands for knowledge or cunning. Both characters are extreme in their attitudes and learn only after suffering and struggle to moderate their respective attitudes. The play teaches, among other things, that wisdom in government consists largely of a combination of the Zeus-principle and the Prometheus-principle, that authority and knowledge are sterile by themselves and can be useful only when used together and when both are tempered by kindness and sympathy. Dozens of other examples could be given of the allegorical, rather than literal, use of Olympian concepts in Greek literature of the Golden Age. Altogether, it may be said that before the opening of the fifth century, Greek religion had emerged from its folk stage and had entered the period of reason and sophistication.

One of the most important of the gods in this second

stage of religious development was Apollo, who represented the concept of rational orderliness. As such, he was regarded as the giver of law, both moral and political, and to worship him most effectively one would closely observe the strictures of decency and of the state. The compulsion to this observance came more from within than from without, more from fear of loss of self-respect than from fear of legal punishment. The walls of the temple of Apollo at Delphi bristled with maxims which testified to the need for cultivation of rational self-restraint: "Curb thy spirit," "Observe the limit," "Hate *hubris*," "Keep a reverent tongue," "Fear authority," "Bow before the divine," "Glory not in strength," and, most important of all, "Know thyself," and "Nothing in excess." [3]

Perhaps the best interpretation of Apollonian principles is to be found in the Greek drama. Although the drama grew out of the legend of Apollo's opposite number, Dionysus, the message of most of the individual plays is predominantly Apollonian in tone. In most of these works, the audience is warned by the example of legendary figures to shun the arrogance that leads to *hubris*, to reverence the gods and bow to fate, and above all, to exercise *sophrosyné* (moderation) in all things. Violations of these principles leads to personal misery and destruction and might even bring on *até*, a curse which settles on a family or community, for generations if necessary, until the situation is righted and the wrath of the god appeased. Since this moral message is present in nearly every surviving Greek tragedy, one might almost consider the drama as being the Bible of Apollo just as the Homeric poems were the Bible of "classical" Olympian religion.

[3] In addition to displaying these homilies, the temple of Delphi also housed the oracle, or priestess, of Apollo, who dispensed more particular, though often ambiguous, advice on all matters from personal problems to major political policy.

Besides being the source of moral principles, Apollo also was looked upon as being the interpreter (and in some city-states also the giver) of political law. Public violations of all kinds were regarded as direct offenses against the god, whose presence was invoked in all trials of civic offenders. In meting out punishment, the concept of restitution was followed. The offender was made to appease the wrath of Apollo by restoring to the injured party that which had been taken from him or its equivalent, plus a fine to compensate for the disturbance to the victim's peace of mind. In cases of assault or murder, primitive Greek justice required punishment in kind on the basis of an eye for an eye. Without this compensation, the soul of the injured party would not be able to attain peace after death but would be barred from the realm of souls and would come back to plague the offenders and their posterity. In later and more sophisticated concepts of justice, this direct eye-for-eye principle was modified to take into consideration the circumstances of the case. Punishments were meted out according to the degree as well as to the intent of the crime, and proper consideration was given to the motives behind the action. If the identity of the lawbreaker were unknown, justice was done by publicly cursing him and relying on this curse to plague him and his family until he confessed his crime and made proper restitution.

From these general examples, we can see that Apollo acted as the balance wheel of Greek civilization, the preserver of the equilibrium of individual and state alike. His will was understood through the use of reason; he was worshipped through reasonable restraint and moderation, and in cases of violation of his laws, appeased through a measured, rational type of punishment. In the arts his spirit is manifested in the cool, balanced symmetry of the temple, the dignified calm of the statue, the restrained gesture of farewell on mortuary sculpture, or the lesson of *sophrosyné* underlying the dramatic tragedy. More than any other god, his spirit dominated the life and thought of the Greeks, and it is the influence of this spirit that results in the balanced, logical, orderly approach to life that we regard as representing the essence of Classicism.

VI. THE CULT OF DIONYSUS

Although the spirit of Apollo seems to predominate in Greek life and art, one would not be wise to assume that Hellenism was entirely devoid of the elements of mysticism, emotion, and ecstasy that constitute an important part of all human experience. To have ruled out these elements would have been to violate the very balance that Greek civilization sought to maintain, and the Greeks, despite their seeming restraint, were no people to have denied themselves any satisfying aspect of life. Cults devoted to the worship of the senses and emotions, though often frowned upon for their excesses, existed at all times during Greek history and ultimately became sufficiently respectable (if considerably more restrained) to be accepted as an official form of religious observance in nearly all Greek cities. The most important of these cults was that of Dionysus, the god of the vine, whose rites ultimately gave rise to the development of the drama.

Dionysus was only a half-god (he had a mortal mother) and is not mentioned as a divinity by Homer. He was the son of Zeus and Semele, daughter of King Cadmus of Thebes, and his birth was irregular in the extreme. Zeus was so madly in love with Semele that he promised on his oath to refuse her nothing. Hera, the jealous wife of the All-Father, prompted Semele in a dream to desire to see her lover in all his celestial splendor, and accordingly the eager girl made that request. Zeus tried to dissuade her, but she insisted, and the god, on the terms of his oath, had to comply. He appeared before Semele as a bolt of lightning which struck her dead, and thus Hera had her revenge. At the time of her death, Semele had been pregnant with Zeus' child, and Zeus saved the foetus by snatching it from the ashes of its unfortunate mother and hiding it in his own thigh until it was ready for birth.

Semele's sister Ino desired to adopt the newborn Dionysus as her own, but the enraged Hera punished her for this impious wish by driving her and her husband mad and causing them to destroy their own offspring. Then, to save the infant from the further wrath of Hera, Zeus sent him in the care of Hermes to the valley of Nysa, where he was brought up by the Hyades, a group of nymphs whom Zeus later rewarded by making them into stars.

On reaching maturity, the troubles of Dionysus were resumed. Nobody in his own country would accept him as a divinity, and he was forced to wander over the face of the earth, teaching men the culture of the vine and acquiring a band of disciples, known as maenads or sileni (the Romans called them bacchantes from Bacchus, the Roman name of Dionysus). These followers were devoted to growth and fertility, but they were also wild, intemperate, and even bloodthirsty at times. Perhaps some of our modern prejudice against drunkenness and unrestrained living was implanted in ancient times by the destructive excesses of these too zealous votaries of the joy of life. Certainly the arrival of Dionysus and his wild-eyed band was regarded by his contemporaries with feelings of somewhat less than welcome. He was bitterly opposed by Lycurgus, king of Thrace, and driven from the country into the sea. In his native Thebes, he was imprisoned by his cousin King Pentheus, and was forced to destroy his tormentor by making all the Theban women so drunk that, in a frenzy, they turned upon their ruler and tore him to bits. On another occasion, Dionysus was captured by pirates and saved himself from torture only by putting on a medicine-show display of magic to impress the rudimentary minds of his captors. He caused the pirate ship to stand still in a billowing wind, made wine drip from the sails and green vines to blossom from the mast. Then, as a grand finale, he turned himself into a roaring lion and so terrified his oppressors that they jumped overboard to their death. Eventually, he was accepted by the gods as one of their own and, after a lifetime of earthly suffering, went to Olympus to take his rightful place among the immortals.[4]

Not until the sixth century was Dionysus fully appreciated by the Greeks. Only then did the contradictory aspects of his nature become clear. Wine, fertility, the joy of life, were seen as great assets to man, but they were also understood as cruel destructive forces if abused. Properly used, they could give man the vitality, ecstasy, and hope that are necessary in coping with the difficulties of existence; they could give him a sense of creativeness and growth that makes of life a positive, rather than a negative and despairing experience. It was in this sense of affirmation that the Greeks in the sixth century b.c. developed the great Dionysiac festivals that gave birth to the Drama.

Of these the Greater Dionysia, in March, was the most important. It was a three- to five-day affair devoted to street parades, dramatic production of comedy and tragedy, and ceremonial rites to supplicate the god and assure the fertility of the coming year's crops. Another festival, the Lenaea or Lesser Dionysia, was held in December to celebrate the

---

[4] Another version of Dionysus, apparently Cretan in origin but revived by the Orphic cult in Greek times, equates him with the Cretan god Zagreus, who was born to Zeus and Persephone after Zeus had visited the underworld in the form of a serpent. Persecuted by the jealous Hera, Dionysus was forced to assume many disguises, but he finally met his end when he was torn to pieces by the Titans while he was in the form of a bull. This accounts for the barbaric Cretan rite in the worship of Dionysus-Zagreus of falling upon and consuming a live bull, from which re-enactment of the death of Dionysus the worshippers symbolically partook of the flesh of the god himself.

arrival of Dionysus for his annual three-months' visit.[5] Since this visit coincided exactly with the period when Apollo was traditionally absent for his annual journey to the land of the Hyperboreans, it was possible eventually to merge the worship of the two divinities and to dedicate the temples of Apollo during the winter months as temporary sanctuaries of Dionysus. By the fifth century this merger of the Apollonian and Dionysian elements was complete, and Greek religion officially assumed the qualities of reason and emotion, of restraint and ecstasy, that are the necessary ingredients of true spiritual fulfillment.

VII. THE MYSTERIES

No outline of Greek religion would be complete without at least brief mention of the Orphic and the Eleusinian mysteries. The former cult, which is connected most prominently with the Pythagorean order of mystics in southern Italy (see p. 138), is derived from the legend of Orpheus, the young musician who played and sang so sweetly that he could charm the animals and even move stones with his melodies. But when he lost his wife Euridice, Orpheus was so downcast that even the gods were moved and allowed him to descend into Hades to bring Euridice back to earth. The condition was made, however, that he would not look upon his wife's face until she emerged from the underworld. Unfortunately, at the very portals of earth, Orpheus could not resist the desire to gaze upon Euridice, and as a result of this violation of the gods' will she was again taken from him and returned to Hades. In his sorrow, Orpheus thereupon took up his lyre and sang so poignantly of his loss that the gods relented and once more restored the beloved Euridice to life.

[5] It is interesting to note how these two festivals coincide both in time and function with the Christian celebration of Christmas and Easter.

So runs the legend, and a pretty one it is, made doubly beautiful by the familiar music of Gluck's opera. But to the Orphic cult the principal elements of the tale were not the romantic ones so much as the presentation of Orpheus as one who had visited Hades and returned. The story was interpreted not only as a nature myth in which the death and rebirth of Euridice represented the crop cycle but also as the basis of a belief in immortality, in which the individual is seen as living many lives in succeeding incarnations. The immortal factor in human existence was the soul, which after death returned to the underworld, where it was purified during a stay of one thousand years, after which it returned to earth in another body. The Orphics conceived of life as a wheel which rotated so that part of its course would be in light and part in darkness. The soul was seen as being attached to the spokes of the wheel, emerging for a time into the light (life) and plunging once more into the shadows of death. However, the soul longs to escape from this constant motion and to free itself from the wheel to attain rest, a state arrived at only when the soul reaches complete purity. Thus, the Orphics maintained, the individual should live as virtuously as possible so that through succeeding incarnations his soul might become increasingly pure and might eventually escape from the wheel into eternal peace.

Onto this body of belief, the Orphics grafted an extensive and complicated body of dogma and authority based upon the supposed writings of Orpheus himself. A priestly class was instituted to interpret those works and to encourage and maintain the strict observance of the rites of the order. The underworld was interpreted as being not merely the realm of the dead but also a place of rewards and punishments, with the wicked souls being sent for purgation to the fiery pit of Tartarus and less culpable spirits being assigned to categories of Hades where they might dwell in relative bliss or misery, according to their deserts, while awaiting their next incarnation. The greatest spirits were sent to the Elysian Fields, or Realm of the Blessed, which, though seen probably as a temporary resting place, nevertheless represented the highest form of bliss short of the spaceless, timeless nothingness attained by the completely purified soul.

Although the Orphics were of relatively minor importance during Greek times, their cult was fairly prominent during the fifth and fourth centuries B.C. and extremely so much later, during the days of the Roman Empire. The most notable example of Orphism in literature is found in the story of Aeneas' descent into the underworld in Book VI of Virgil's *Aeneid,* but an even more remarkable indication of the influence of the cult is found in the direct parallels between the tenets of Orphism and several of the most fundamental points of Christian theology.

More important than Orphism in Greek civilization, but considerably less clearly defined, was the cult of the Eleusinian mysteries.[6] Votaries of this order, which in the fifth century became the official religion of Athens, were sworn in under pain of death to keep secret the rites of the mysteries, and so well has the secret been preserved that we know nothing of what went on during these religious observances. That the procedure must have been extremely impressive there is no doubt; many have testified in writing to the awesomeness of the ritual. According to the poet Pindar, "Blessed is he who goes beneath the earth having seen these things; he knows the end of life and he knows its god-given beginnings." From this statement and many similar hints it is evident that the Eleusinian mysteries, like those of Orpheus, were based upon the seasonal myth and probably were also concerned with the immortality of the

[6] So called because the rites were held at Eleusis, a small town about twelve miles from Athens.

soul. The legend upon which they were built, however, was not that of Orpheus but rather the equally familiar one of Persephone, daughter of the grain-goddess Demeter. After having been stolen from her mother by Hades, god of the underworld, Persephone was allowed by the gods to return to earth during the spring and summer growing season on condition that she would spend the remaining six months with her husband in the realms of the dead.

Unlike the Orphics, however, the votaries of Eleusis had no body of written authority, no known dogma, and no known professional priestly class. The rites were performed at stated times during the year by trained amateurs whose regular vocation had nothing to do with religion. Nevertheless, the mysteries made a deep impression upon Athenian thought, and reflections of the mysticism of Eleusis are found in Greek literature from Aeschylus to Plato and beyond.

It remains merely to say a word concerning the average Greek's attitude toward religious worship. It seems evident from the beginning that Greek society was strongly devout and that the individual Greek was constantly concerned with the problem of achieving moral excellence and spiritual growth. Nevertheless, the Greeks had little formal religion as it is known today. They observed sacred festivals, sacrificed animals to their gods, and believed in oracles and omens. They even had an amateur priesthood, as we have seen. But with all these elements of ritualistic worship, they would still have been baffled at the concept of a formal established church with an elaborate ecclesiastical hierarchy exercising spiritual and even temporal authority. Equally puzzling would have been the doctrine of man's intrinsic wickedness or that of spending one's days in suffering and self-denial in preparation for the rewards and punishments of the life to come. To most Greeks death represented an unwelcome but not painful removal from the earth to some vague but not unpleasant state in Hades. They were not terrified at its approach, because it meant to them only a temporary separation from their friends and families and a change to an existence that was only inactive and dull at its worst. The idea of rewards and punishments in the future life did not bother most of them. Such things were reserved for only the very noble and the very wicked; the average man was not likely to experience either.

Still more puzzling would have been the Christian idea of the struggle between the flesh and the spirit and of the degraded nature of the former. Although Platonic philosophy leans somewhat toward this distinction, the Greeks in general were not obsessed by feelings of self-contempt. Man was faulty, to be sure, but not naturally wicked. To be naturally wicked would be a paradox, a contradiction in terms, for how could a thing be wicked if it is natural? The promptings of the flesh are part of the business of living and are necessary to man's existence. Life is to be enjoyed, and worldly and sensual pursuits are parts of its immense attractiveness.

This is not to say that the Greeks were libertines or degenerates. In fact, by our own standards, their morals, particularly in Athens, were relatively high, even though their attitude toward life might strike us as being dubious. We have seen that their Apollonian beliefs did not countenance excess. Their whole concept of respectability was based upon moderation (*sophrosyné*), and nothing was more contemptible than the man who failed to exercise restraint at all times. The drunkard, the glutton, the sexual libertine, the arrogant snob: all were hateful in Greek eyes because they were unbeautiful and stupid, because they violated the two principles which stood uppermost in Athenian ethical teachings: *Know thyself,* and *Nothing in excess.*

Altogether then, Hellenic religion was predominantly ethical rather than mystical and dogmatic. Greek youths studied ethics from earliest childhood; Greek literature and thought is packed with an ever-present ethical consciousness. They loved life, sought happiness on earth, and refused to worry about the future, but that love of life, that happiness, and that peace of mind were based upon stern principles of justice and decency. As is natural in human beings, they did not always live up to their principles, but neither did they render themselves socially useless by brooding over their imagined natural wickedness. All in all, their "pagan" ideas seem no worse than man's notions in any age and their behavior only extreme enough to mark them as a race full of vitality, with a healthy and refreshing zest for life.

Principal Divinities of Greek Mythology

THE TITANS

The descendants of **Ouranos** (Father Heaven) and **Gaea** (Mother Earth). The first generation consisted of six sons: **Oceanus, Koros, Krios, Hyperion, Iapetus,** and **Cronus** (Kronus, Saturn) and six daughters: **Theia, Rhéa, Themis, Mnemosyne** (Memory), **Phoebe,** and **Tethys.** The marriage of Iapetus with his sister Themis produced **Prometheus** and **Epimetheus,** while a collateral union with the sea-nymph **Clymene** produced **Atlas.** Cronus married Rhea and became the leader of the Titans and father of **Zeus, Poseidon,** and **Hades.** These three brothers later turned against their father, overthrew him, and founded the Olympian dynasty.

THE OLYMPIANS: The "Twelve"

Of the many major and minor gods in the Olympian dynasty, the most important are the **Twelve,** a group chosen by the Greeks themselves as the key figures in the Olympian group and the basis for most of their religious observances. Greek law is also to some extent derived from the concept of the Twelve, and the Greek in both court proceedings and in ordinary conversation took his oath "by the Twelve." The divinities constituting this group were:

Zeus (Jupiter, Jove)—Leader of the Olympians, god of lightning, and representative of the power principle.

Hera (Juno)—Wife of Zeus and goddess of marriage and domestic stability.

Poseidon (Neptune)—God of the sea. Often called "the earth-shaker," possibly because the Greeks attributed earthquakes to marine origin.

Hades (Pluto, Dis)—God of the underworld and presider over the realm of the dead. Also connected with the nature myth by his marriage to **Persephone** (Proserpine) who spent half her time on earth (the growing season) and half in the underworld (the winter period). Hades does not represent death itself, that function being relegated to a lesser divinity called **Thanatos.**

Pallas Athene (Minerva)—Goddess of wisdom, but also associated with many other concepts from warfare to arts and crafts. Her birth was remarkable, since she sprang full-armed from the forehead of Zeus. She was the patron goddess of Athens and to them represented the art of civilized living.

Phoebus Apollo—Son of Zeus and **Leto,** daughter of the Titans Krios and Phoebe. Sun-god, archer, musician, god of truth, light, and healing. Represented the principle of intellectual beauty. At the temple dedicated to him at Delphi, the oracle divulged in cryptic language the will of the gods.

Artemis (Cynthia, Diana)—Twin sister of Apollo, virgin goddess of the moon and of the hunt.

Aphrodite (Venus)—Daughter of Zeus and **Dione** in one version; in another supposed to have risen from the waves. Goddess of love and physical beauty.

Hephaestus (Vulcan)—Lame blacksmith god who forged the thunderbolts of Zeus. The much-deceived husband of Aphrodite.

Hermes (Mercury)—Son of Zeus and **Maia,** daughter of Atlas. Messenger and general handyman of Zeus; god of commerce, traders, travellers, and thieves.

Ares (Mars)—Son of Zeus and Hera, god of war.

Hestia (Vesta)—Virgin sister of Zeus, goddess of the hearth and home. Served in Rome by the sacred sisterhood of the Vestal Virgins. Later replaced among the Twelve by *Dionysus.*

Dionysus (Bacchus)—God of wine, son of Zeus and the mortal woman Semele. Like Demeter, connected with the principle of

DYNASTIES OF THE MAJOR GODS

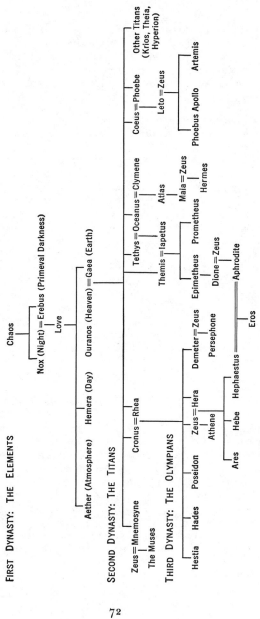

FIRST DYNASTY: THE ELEMENTS

Chaos

Nox (Night) = Erebus (Primeval Darkness)

Love

Aether (Atmosphere)   Hemera (Day)   Ouranos (Heaven) = Gaea (Earth)

SECOND DYNASTY: THE TITANS

Cronus = Rhea

Zeus = Mnemosyne
The Muses

Tethys = Oceanus = Clymene

Themis = Iapetus   Atlas   Maia = Zeus
                                      Hermes

Epimetheus   Prometheus

Dione = Zeus

Eros   Aphrodite

Coeus = Phoebe   Other Titans (Krios, Theia, Hyperion)

Leto = Zeus

Phoebus Apollo   Artemis

THIRD DYNASTY: THE OLYMPIANS

Demeter = Zeus
Persephone

Zeus = Hera
Athene

Hebe   Hephaestus

Ares

Hestia   Hades   Poseidon

fertility and, like Persephone, represented the nature myth by dying in the autumn and being reborn in the spring. The Eleusinian mysteries were dedicated to all three fertility deities and the festivals of Dionysus were periods of wild, bacchantic rejoicing. Since plays were usually performed at these festivals, Dionysus also became god of the theatre. Represented the ecstatic principle as opposed to the intellectual principle signified by Phoebus Apollo.

LESSER OLYMPIANS

Demeter (Ceres)—Sister of Zeus and goddess of agriculture. Mother of Persephone and symbol of fertility.

Eros (Cupid)—Eternal child of Hephaestus and Aphrodite, spirit of love whose mischievous darts have caused many of the world's troubles.

Pan—Son of Hermes, woodland god with goat-like horns and hoofs; player of pipes and supervisor of rustic gaieties.

Nemesis—Avenging goddess, the principle of retribution.

Hebe—Goddess of youth and cupbearer to the gods.

Iris—Goddess of the rainbow and sometimes, like Hermes, messenger of the gods.

Hymen—God of the marriage festival.

The Three Graces—Aglaia (Splendor), **Euphrosyne** (Mirth), and **Thalia** (Good Cheer). Daughters of Zeus and **Eurynome,** a sea-nymph and daughter of Oceanus. Represented the principle of the happy life, and always considered as a single unit.

The Nine Muses—daughters of Zeus and Mnemosyne (Memory). Spirits of learning and the arts, as follows: **Clio** (history), **Urania** (astronomy), **Melpomene** (tragedy), **Thalia** (comedy), **Terpsichore** (dance), **Calliope** (epic poetry), **Erato** (love poetry), **Polyhymnia** (sacred poetry), and **Euterpe** (lyric poetry).

The Erinyes (Furies)—**Tisiphone, Megaera,** and **Alecto.** Represented the pangs of conscience and relentlessly hounded wrongdoers.

The Three Fates allotted to each man his destiny. **Clotho** spun the thread of life, **Lachesis** wove it into a pattern which determined the kind of life which would be led, and **Atropos** cut it, terminating existence.

SUGGESTED READINGS

See end of Chapter 8 for suggested readings.

chapter 5

GREEK MYTHS AND LEGENDS

I. THE ORIGIN OF THE TROJAN WAR

The most famous legend in the world is that of the Trojan War. No other conflict has created more heroes or produced more fabulous deeds; no other theme has been more nobly sung by poets throughout the ages. In its inspiration of the *Iliad* and the *Odyssey* it gave us more than great literature, for in these earliest of recorded works we can find the very wellsprings of Western culture.

Troy was founded by Dardanus, who gave his name to the Dardanelles and was the son of Zeus and the ocean-nymph Electra. It was after Dardanus' grandson Tros that the city was named, though the classical writers often refer to the place as Ilium, after Tros' eldest son Ilos. The citadel attacked by the Greeks was built by Ilos, after an oracle had advised him to follow a brindled cow he had won as a prize in a wrestling contest and to build his capital wherever she first stopped to rest. Ilos obeyed instructions, built the city, and named it after his father. The place was blessed by Zeus, who delegated the goddess Athene to watch over its welfare.

Under Ilos, Troy pursued a peaceful pastoral existence,

but under the rule of Ilos' son Laomedon the city, possibly as a result of increased prosperity and a greater concern with the outside world, turned to thoughts of national defense. With the invaluable help of the gods Poseidon and Apollo, Laomedon built the walls of Troy, but on the completion of his project refused to pay his divine helpers the wages he had promised. Muttering threats, the two gods departed and Athene in sympathy withdrew her protection from the city. Thus was Troy, through its chicanery, abandoned by the divine powers.

Laomedon was succeeded on the throne by his son Priam, whose wife Hecuba bore him five children: Hector, Paris, Cassandra, Polyxena, and Polydorus. Just before the birth of Paris, Hecuba was told by an oracle that her second son would bring fire and destruction to Troy, so that Hecuba, subordinating maternal love to her country's welfare, consented to have the child exposed to die. As is customary in mythology, however, the infant Paris was rescued by a shepherd and brought up to tend flocks in total ignorance of his royal origin.

Meanwhile the gods, who had sworn destruction to Troy, were moving toward their purpose with all the smooth indirection traditionally characteristic of high diplomatic circles. The process began at an important state wedding: that of King Peleus and the sea-nymph Thetis, who were destined to become the parents of the Greek hero Achilles. All the notables of Mount Olympus were present except Eris, goddess of Discord, who for obvious reasons had been left off the invitation list. Seeking revenge, Eris threw into the banquet hall a golden apple inscribed *To the Fairest*. In the resulting feminine uproar attending the awarding of this prize, the field of contenders was finally narrowed down to three: Hera, Athene, and Aphrodite. Zeus, knowing women too well to risk his life in judging their beauty, shrewdly appointed as mediator the innocent Paris who had been tending his flocks on nearby Mount Ida. In order to assist their judge to make a decision, each contending goddess promised him a reward for his favorable answer. Hera offered to make him ruler of the richest realm on earth, Athene promised him wisdom and manliness, but Aphrodite, with her shrewd knowledge of the impulses of young men, offered him the most beautiful woman in the world as his wife. Of course, Paris found Aphrodite's bribe irresistible and the Goddess of Love won the day.

For a long time Paris waited for Aphrodite to redeem her promise and then, resigning himself to the untrustworthiness of the mighty, married the wood-nymph Oenone and settled down to a blissful domestic existence. At last he wandered to Troy, where he was recognized as the long-lost son of King Priam and restored to his rightful position in society. He continued to live with Oenone, however, until one day a royal whim sent him unconsciously on the way to achieving Aphrodite's bribe and with it his long-predicted destiny as destroyer of Troy.

It seems that King Priam's sister Hesione had been abducted many years before by Heracles, who had given her to the Greek Telamon to wed. Now Priam, somewhat belatedly, expressed a desire to rescue his sister, and Paris was delegated to carry out this difficult task. Paris' brother Deiphobus warned the Trojan Council that the mission would bring the Greeks in hordes against Troy, but Paris, feeling that Aphrodite would protect him, convinced the city Fathers that his efforts would succeed. He was thereupon equipped with a huge fleet and a powerful army and sent on his way. Arriving without untoward incident in Sparta, he found King Menelaus away and his queen, the beauteous Helen, bored in his absence and ready to welcome any foreign prince by way of diversion. The transcendent loveliness of Helen inflamed Paris as it had all men who looked on her, and she in turn was not indifferent to the handsome Trojan warrior. Soon Paris had forgotten all about his wife Oenone, to say nothing of his intended rescue of Hesione. With a few followers he made his way to the royal palace, stormed it successfully and carried off Helen as his prize. The Spartan queen, mindful of protocol, made some show of resistance, but her heart was not in the effort and soon she was sailing to Troy with Paris, apparently quite contented with her lot.

On the journey back, the sea-god Nereus cursed Paris for his deed and predicted a bloody war leading to the fall of Troy, and it was not long before the Greeks began to make this prophecy good. Menelaus, the wronged husband, reminded the several Greek leaders of a vow they had taken years before to protect the honor of Helen, and soon all Hellas was responding to the call to arms. Only the wily Odysseus temporarily withheld his support. Believing it a wasted effort to plunge an entire land into conflict over a weak-willed woman, he feigned madness in order to escape having to keep his word. When emissaries of Menelaus arrived to enlist his aid, he acted like a lunatic, yoked an ox and an ass to a plow and with this ill-matched pair plowed and harrowed his fields and scattered salt instead of seed into the furrows. The emissaries were not convinced by this buffoonery, however, and terminated Odysseus' play-acting by placing his young son Telemachus in the line of Odysseus' harrow. When the father lifted the harrow to avoid the body of his son, he betrayed his sanity and was forced to join the army.

The future hero Achilles also almost avoided military service. When he was still a small child, his mother Thetis, fearing that her son might eventually lose his life in a war, had dressed him as a girl. By the time of the abduction of Helen, however, the youth's changing voice and sprouting beard made it impossible for him to continue the masquerade. The authorities soon penetrated his disguise and demanded his services, whereupon Achilles promised to enlist and to contribute fifty ships to the campaign.

Thus the Greeks organized for their most glorious exploit, and with the energetic Agamemnon as commander-in-chief, the armies gathered at the Boeotian port of Aulis and prepared to embark in a thousand ships to storm Troy and avenge the honor of Greek womanhood.

But Fate had still another obstacle to place in the way of the Greeks. Agamemnon, during a hunting expedition, had impiously killed a sacred deer of the goddess Artemis, and in revenge the goddess stilled the winds and forced the Greek ships to lie idly in the harbor of Aulis for weeks on end. Desperate, Agamemnon turned to Calchas the seer for advice, and Calchas prophesied that only the sacrifice of Agamemnon's beloved daughter Iphigenia would appease Artemis' anger and restore the propitious wind. The horrified Agamemnon shrank from taking this step, but his sense of duty and the pleas of the other Greek heroes finally spurred him to action. Summoning his daughter on the pretext that she was to marry the hero Achilles, he led her to the sacrificial altar, where Calchas was waiting with the knife to strike the fatal blow. Too late Iphigenia realized what was expected of her and begged her father to spare her life. But Agamemnon was adamant, and the dutiful girl prepared herself for the sacrificial stroke. Then a miracle happened. Just as Calchas plunged the knife into Iphegenia's throat the girl disappeared and in her place on the altar there lay a deer with blood flowing from its neck. At the last instant Artemis had provided a substitute victim, though Iphegenia herself had disappeared. At the same moment the wind sprang up and the Greeks, shouting with joy at the double deliverance, rushed to their ships and weighed anchor for Troy.

The most famous account of the Trojan war is, of course, the *Iliad,* but it is to be remembered that that magnificent poem covers only one brief episode in the ten-year struggle. Between the time of the departure from Aulis and the opening of Homer's epic nine years elapsed, years rich with adventure for the campaigning Greeks. First, the hero Philoctetes was bitten by an adder during a shore excursion and had to be left behind to die. Then the Greek armada landed by mistake at Mysia, on the coast of Asia Minor, and fought a bloody battle with their allies, the Mysians, thinking them to be Trojans. Before the error was discovered, King Telephus was struck by the spear of Achilles, whose weapon inflicted wounds that defied cure. Upon learning that they were fighting allies, the Greeks tried in every way to right the wrong they had committed. They sent for learned physicians to assuage the pain of Telephus' wound and waited for weeks until the unfortunate king was made more comfortable. Eventually, Telephus was cured when the oracle directed that his wounds be filled with filings from the spear that had inflicted it.

These unfortunate events consumed the better part of three months, and it was early spring by the time the thousand ships finally reached Troy. A vast camp was laid out, and the Trojans quaked in terror at the strength of the enemy forces. Fighting began almost immediately, but for nine years the war dragged on with little advantage gained by either side. Then the Greeks captured and killed the boy Polydorus, son of King Priam of Troy. This outrage fanned the hatred and zeal of the Trojans and the war developed to a climactic intensity. It is at this point, in the tenth year of the war, that the *Iliad* begins.

II. THE HOUSE OF ATREUS

Of all the accursed families in literature, the House of Atreus ranks as the most unfortunate. Through generation after generation marked by murder, deception, adultery, blasphemy, cannibalism, and insanity, the descendants of Tantalus nevertheless preserved a power and dignity that amounted almost to grandeur and caused what would have been mere perversion in ordinary mortals to attain the stature of true tragedy. With the exception of Tantalus, the founder of the line, most members of the tribe seem to have been more unfortunate than downright vicious. Usually their intentions were of the best, and certainly there is no impugning their courage and resourcefulness as leaders, but in almost every instance they fell into wickedness in spite of themselves. At any rate, no family has been more celebrated in classical literature; the names of Tantalus, Niobe, Pelops, Agamemnon, Menelaus, Clytemnestra, Iphegenia, Electra, and Orestes are familiar to readers of all ages, and their deeds and misadventures form the very core of classical fiction.

Like most ancient Greek families, the House of Atreus traces its ancestry back to Zeus himself. Among the many mortal children of the god, Tantalus was the most favored, for he was allowed to eat nectar and ambrosia with the immortals, and the dignitaries of Olympus would even condescend occasionally to banquet in Tantalus' home. Apparently Tantalus' head was turned by all this glory, for he became arrogant and eventually tried by a horrible trick to humble the very gods who had raised him above his fellow men. At one of the banquets he gave to the Olympians, Tantalus served them with a stew containing the flesh of his own son Pelops. By making his guests unwitting cannibals, he hoped to prove that they were not all-knowing or infallible. Naturally, his insane egotism backfired in his own face. The gods immediately recognized the nature of the loathsome dish and punished the perverted sinner by placing him in a pool in Hades and causing him to be tormented eternally by hunger and thirst. Whenever he stooped to drink the water, it would recede from his lips; whenever he reached for the abundant fruit of the trees overhead, the branches would bend beyond his grasp. Thus he remained for eternity in awful torment for that arrogance the Greeks considered the worst of all human sins.

After punishing Tantalus, the gods restored Pelops to life, but the curse of violence continued to dog the family. Pelops wooed the princess Hippodamia, but was forced in suing for her hand to compete in a chariot race with the lady's father, King Oenomaus. If Pelops won, he was to receive Hippodamia as bride; if he lost, his head was forfeit. To make sure of winning the race, Pelops bribed the king's charioteer Myrtilus to remove the lynch pins from the king's chariot and replace them with wax. Consequently, Oenomaus' car fell apart during the contest, its loyal occupant was killed, and Pelops won his lady. In best gangster fashion, the victor got rid of his accomplice Myrtilus by throwing him into the sea, an act which angered the gods and added to the subsequent misfortunes of the family.

Tantalus' daughter, Niobe, seemed for a time to have escaped the wrath of the gods, for she was happily married to Amphion, a mortal son of Zeus who was such an excellent musician that he could move stones with his playing. With Amphion, Niobe lived in comfort and security and rejoiced in her seven brave sons and her seven lovely daughters. But maternal pride soon turned her to unreason and, like her father Tantalus, Niobe began to suffer from delusions of grandeur. Scornfully she commanded that the women of Thebes leave off their worship of the goddess Leto, who had given birth to only two children, Apollo and Artemis, and transfer it to her, who had produced fourteen perfect offspring. She added to this heresy the taunt that Leto had been only a helpless nobody, whereas she, Niobe, was a great and powerful queen. She had said too much. The mighty gods of Olympus never pardoned such egotism and were ruthless in their punishment of the blasphemous. Even as Niobe uttered her boasts, she saw her fourteen sons and daughters struck dead. As a result of this divine vengeance, Niobe turned to stone, and only her tears, which flowed over the stone day and night, remained to remind the passerby of her once-human state.

In Pelops' sons, Atreus and Thyestes, the family curse manifested itself in its fullest intensity. Thyestes seduced his brother's wife, Aerope, and Atreus in revenge murdered Thyestes' two sons and served them to their own father in a stew. When Thyestes learned that he had eaten his own flesh and blood, he fled in horror, and the gods punished the perverted Atreus by visiting his country with famine and drought. Anxious to deliver his land from the wrath of the gods, Atreus consulted the oracle and was told that prosperity could not return until Thyestes was brought back. The banished brother was forthwith recalled, along with his son Aegisthus, who had been born after Thyestes in exile had added to the bubbling cauldron of family horror by seducing his own daughter.

The reconciliation between the two brothers was of very brief duration, and before long the family had resumed its normal bloody existence. Atreus threw Thyestes into prison, and Aegisthus, after a particularly treacherous intrigue, ended the brotherly feud by running a sword through his uncle. With Atreus out of the way, Thyestes assumed the throne, but before long he too fell, slain by Atreus' avenging son Agamemnon. For some reason, Aegisthus was spared; Agamemnon was eventually to have cause to regret this oversight.

The story of Agamemnon's departure for Troy after sacrificing his daughter Iphigenia has already been told. He left behind him his wife, Clytemnestra, two daughters, Chrysosthemis and Electra, and a boy, Orestes. Clytemnestra was frantic at her husband's heartless murder of Iphigenia, and in her rage the still-vengeful Aegisthus saw his chance to eliminate Agamemnon. Throughout Agamemnon's absence, Aegisthus lived with Clytemnestra as her lover, never missing an opportunity to fan her hatred with references to the sacrifice of Iphigenia or to Agamemnon's hardly celibate life at the battle-front. When Troy fell, the guilty lovers made elaborate preparations for the return of the detested husband, who soon landed to find his capital in festive array. Amidst the cheers of his people, he made his way to the palace, where he was greeted with a brazen speech of welcome by his faithless wife. Invitations were extended to all the city notables to attend a banquet in honor of the hero-king. Then Agamemnon, weary from his long journey, entered the palace and called for a warm bath. Once unarmed and in the bath, he was an easy victim.

Rushing on him with a net and daggers, Clytemnestra and Aegisthus easily overpowered the unsuspecting king and stabbed him to death.

The two conspirators made no attempt to conceal their crime. They proclaimed the deed to the people and demanded their support. Protest was impossible; Clytemnestra had a legal point in her favor, since she was presumably avenging the murder of her daughter. Besides, Aegisthus was in complete control of the army and any uprising would have been quickly quelled. So, for many years, the unsavory pair continued their rule over the unhappy country.

But the sanguinary history of the House of Atreus had still another generation to go. Directly after the murder of Agamemnon, his daughter Electra correctly surmised that her little brother Orestes would be the next victim to be despatched. Accordingly, she had him smuggled out of the country to Phocis, where he was brought up by King Strophius as brother-companion to the young prince Pylades. Electra remained at home hated and mistreated by Clytemnestra and Aegisthus, who as the years wore on became more and more apprehensive of Orestes' vengeful return. Then one day a stranger arrived and told the guilty mother of Orestes' death in a chariot race. The queen was overjoyed; the last danger had been removed. But her joy was her undoing. The stranger was Orestes himself, come by order of an oracle of Apollo to avenge the murder of Agamemnon. In his mother's unholy joy he found the final impetus for his revenge; Clytemnestra, then Aegisthus, fell victims to his sword.

The saga of the unfortunate house of Atreus might well have ended with the removal of the miserable pair, but Greek sense of the strict application of divine law made it necessary to carry the matter still further. Orestes, though he had obeyed the command of Apolio in killing his mother and her lover, was nevertheless a matricide and subject to divine punishment for his violent deed. Hardly had he committed his double revenge than the Eumenides, or Furies, descended upon him and reduced him to a frenzied madness. This madness, which in modern terms would be called a tortured conscience, caused Orestes to leave his home and seek solace in unceasing flight throughout the Hellenic world. Escape was impossible; the Furies pursued him wherever he turned. Finally, in desperation, he made his way to Delphi and prostrated himself before the oracle of Apollo, begging for mercy, and the god, touched by the appeal, promised the tortured young man a chance for deliverance. He was to go to Athens; Apollo would arrange for him a fair trial before the Athenians, who were noted for their high sense of justice. Furthermore, the presiding justice would be the goddess Athene herself.

The god was as good as his word, and on the appointed day the citizens of Athens heard the accusations of the Furies and the eloquent defense of Apollo. When the time for decision arrived, the Athenian citizenry was found to be equally divided, but Athene herself cast the deciding ballot in favor of Orestes. Thus, for the first time in ancient mythology, an ethical issue was decided upon its own merits rather than upon the inexorable dictates of divine law. The enlightenment of this mythical Athenian court substituted a concept of plastic justice for the older rule of unyielding punishment, and thereby laid the cornerstone of our present tradition of individual freedom.

After the acquittal of Orestes, the fortunes of the House of Atreus took a long-delayed turn for the better, and the last incident in the saga is a happy one. Orestes, still suffering from the effects of his long persecution by the Furies, was instructed by Apollo to go to Tauris, where he would regain his health and happiness by stealing the image of the goddess Artemis from the temple. Accompanied by his faithful friend Pylades, Orestes set forth on his mission, which was not without considerable danger, for the Taurians had the unfortunate habit of sacrificing to Artemis all strangers who came to their land. Orestes and Pylades were well aware of the risk they were running. What they did not know, however, was that Orestes' sister Iphigenia, supposedly sacrificed to Artemis years before, had really been saved by the goddess and placed on Tauris, where she had been forced by King Thaos to perform the unpleasant task of consecrating captured foreigners as divine sacrifices. Despite her grim duties, Iphigenia was a sweet and gentle maiden, and was held in high esteem by the Taurians.

Orestes and Pylades arrived at the island and were promptly captured by a herdsman and brought to Iphigenia. The priestess questioned the captives and, upon learning that they came from Argos, asked them about the history of Agamemnon and his family. They told her that Orestes and his sisters Electra and Chrysosthemis were still alive. Iphigenia, overjoyed that some members of her family were living, offered to free one of the captives so that he might carry a message for her back to Argos. Both Pylades and Orestes offered to die so that the other might live, but Iphigenia ended the debate by choosing the former as messenger. She then gave Pylades a letter addressed to Orestes, telling him that his sister Iphigenia was alive and well and eager to be rescued from her unpleasant position at Tauris. Pylades immediately handed the message to Orestes, and in this somewhat complicated manner the recognition and reunion of the long-separated brother and sister was effected.

From then on, the course of the three was clear. Under the pretext of purifying the strangers for the sacrifice, Iphigenia conducted them to the seashore, not forgetting to bring along the image of Artemis. Once arrived at the shore, it was a simple matter to make a dash for Orestes' ship and escape with both Iphigenia and the statue. Upon arriving in his native land, the now completely cured Orestes ascended his father's throne. Shortly afterward he married Hermione, daughter of Menelaus and Helen, and with her inherited the kingdom of Sparta as well. Electra married Pylades, while Iphigenia placed the image of Artemis in a temple at Athens and continued her priesthood there. Orestes ruled wisely and uneventfully until his ninetieth year, when he died after being bitten in the heel by a poisonous serpent. Thus ended the line of Tantalus, and the violent career of the House of Atreus became a closed chapter in ancient legend.

THE HOUSE OF ATREUS

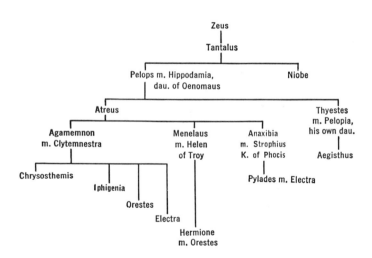

III. THE HOUSE OF CADMUS, FOUNDER OF THEBES

The King of Sidon had several sons and a daughter, Europa. One day Europa was abducted by Zeus, who assumed the form of a bull and carried his not unwilling victim on his back to the island of Crete, where she became the mother of Minos and Rhadamanthys. Meanwhile the King of Sidon, not realizing that his daughter had become the concubine of Zeus himself, sent his sons to search for her and forbade them to return to Sidon until the missing girl was located.

One of these sons, Cadmus, went to Delphi to consult the oracle of Apollo concerning his sister's whereabouts. The oracle advised him to forget about Europa and ordered him to found a city of his own instead. He was told to follow a certain heifer and to choose her first resting place as the site for his city, which was to be called Thebes. Cadmus followed the oracle's command, but before he could build his town, he was forced to kill a bloodthirsty dragon. The goddess Athene then ordered him to sow the dragon's teeth, which sprouted immediately into fully-armed warriors. These warriors turned upon one another in mortal combat, and despite Cadmus' attempts to stop the carnage, only five survived. With these five, Cadmus undertook the building of Thebes. Cadmus ruled Thebes wisely, married happily, and had five daughters and a son. Yet for all his ability and genuine good-will, Cadmus was fated to father an unhappy breed, and for many generations misfortune plagued his posterity. Of all his line, none was more unfortunate than Oedipus, whose hideous fate has been told by Sophocles in what is probably the greatest of all Greek dramas.

Oedipus was the son of King Laius of Thebes and the great-great-grandson of Cadmus. Laius had married his distant cousin Jocasta, who for a long time after her marriage had been barren. Finally the Delphic oracle had promised the unhappy pair a son, but warned that this son would murder his father. When the child was born, Laius ordered that his feet be bound and that he be exposed to die in the mountains of Cithaeron, but the shepherd who had been commissioned to perform this deed took pity on the infant and instead of leaving him to die delivered him to another shepherd, who named him Oedipus, or Swollen-Foot, because of the effect of the thongs which had bound his ankles. He then carried his charge to his master, King Polybus of Corinth. The king, who had no children of his own, was charmed by the little Oedipus and adopted him as his own. The boy grew to young manhood never suspecting his unusual origin, until one time at a banquet a drunken guest irresponsibly hinted that he was not the true son of Polybus. Burning with curiosity and receiving nothing but evasive replies from his foster-parents, Oedipus hastened to consult the oracle as to his true parentage. The oracle, instead of answering his question, gave him a far more terrible piece of news; namely, that he would murder his father and marry his mother. Horrified, Oedipus resolved never to return to Corinth lest the dismal prophecy of the oracle be fulfilled. Instead, he made his way to Boeotia.

On the way, he came to a narrow mountain pass, where he encountered a party, including an old man in a chariot, coming in the opposite direction. Since the road was too narrow for the chariot and young Oedipus to pass, an argument ensued as to which was to give way, and in the fracas which followed, the old man in the car hit Oedipus over the head with a staff. This act so aroused the youth that he killed his assailant, together with another of his party. The others escaped, and Oedipus went on his way, thinking little of what seemed only a commonplace scuffle in which he had had to defend himself against a superior force of attackers. Little did he know that the old man he had killed was King Laius, his true father. Thus, the first part of the oracle's prophecy was almost immediately fulfilled.

A short time later, Oedipus came to Thebes, where he found the citizens bemoaning a double misfortune. Their king, Laius, had been slain and, to make matters worse, a terrible monster called the Sphinx, half woman and half lion, was plaguing the town. It was the Sphinx's perverse custom to perch on a cliff before Thebes and ask passersby a question which none could answer: "What is it that goes upon four legs in the morning, two at noon, and three at night?" Upon their failure to solve the riddle, the Sphinx would descend upon her victims and tear them to bits. So serious were the inroads upon the population made by this monster that Creon, brother of Queen Jocasta and acting ruler of the city, promised the kingdom and the hand of his sister to anyone who could meet the Sphinx's challenge. To Oedipus, the query seemed of only rudimentary difficulty. When questioned by the evil one, he answered: "The answer is Man. As an infant, in the morning of his life, he goes on four legs. In full maturity, he walks upright, but in old age he requires the support of a staff." The Sphinx was so furious at receiving the correct answer that she threw herself from the precipice and was killed. The happily delivered city rewarded Oedipus by making him its ruler and giving him the hand of Queen Jocasta.

Oedipus and Jocasta ruled wisely for several years, and their union resulted in four children: two sons, Eteocles and Polynices, and two daughters, Antigone and Ismene. It was not until the children were approaching maturity that the workings of Fate began to operate openly against the royal family of Thebes. A terrible drought and subsequent plague struck the city, and once more Oedipus found it necessary to consult the oracle. This dispenser of equivocal knowledge replied that Thebes would continue to suffer until the murderer of former King Laius was brought to justice. Oedipus, in full innocence of his complicity in the killing of his predecessor, honestly set about apprehending the murderer. To aid him, he sent for the aged seer Tiresias, whose prophetic powers rivalled those of the oracle himself. The blind old man, on learning the reason for his summons, begged to be excused from his

duties and allowed to go home in peace. Oedipus persisted
in questioning him, however, until poor Tiresias had to tell
the king the stark truth: that Oedipus himself was the
murderer of Laius. Naturally, Oedipus' reaction was one of
angry disbelief, and he denounced the seer as a liar and a
quack. In this he was joined by Queen Jocasta, who scoffed
at the pretended infallibility of oracles and seers. For
hadn't the oracle predicted that her son by her first husband would slay his father? And hadn't Laius been killed
in a highway brawl in a manner quite contrary to the
oracle's prediction? Upon hearing this, Oedipus blanched
with terror. Was Laius killed on the highway? What were
the circumstances? What did he look like? Jocasta's answers
to the frenzied questioning of her husband made the matter
all too clear. The miserable Oedipus realized with horror
that Tiresias was right: the murderer of Laius was himself.
But still, there might providentially be some error. To
make sure, Oedipus sent for the sole survivor of the disaster
in the mountain pass.

While the arrival of this suddenly important figure was
being awaited, a messenger from Corinth made his appearance with the news that King Polybus had died. The message gave Oedipus a momentary feeling of hope. The oracle
had seemingly erred in this case; had it not been predicted
that he would murder his father, and had not Polybus died
peacefully of old age? But this ray of hope was only a
desperate illusion. The messenger assured Oedipus that he
should never have feared that he would murder Polybus,
because Polybus was not his father. The King had adopted
Oedipus when he was found in the mountains; the messenger himself had received the babe from a shepherd and
had taken him to the Corinthian court. At that moment the
last link in the chain of evidence against Oedipus arrived
in the person of the eagerly awaited survivor of the mountain quarrel. By a coincidence possible only in mythology,

this old man was not only a witness to the murder of Laius, but also the very shepherd who had delivered the infant Oedipus to the Corinthian messenger. The whole picture was now complete in all its awful details. Oedipus, for all his nobility of intention, had brought misfortune upon Thebes by murdering the king. Worse still, the original prophecy of the oracle had been fulfilled: the miserable king had murdered in Laius his own father and had subsequently married and had children by Jocasta, his mother. On hearing all this, Oedipus rushed into the palace to seek Jocasta, but the news had preceded him. He found her dead by her own hand in expiation of her unwitting crime. Hysterical with guilt, Oedipus tore the clasps from his kingly robe and with them put out his eyes.

Then casting aside the vestments of his office forever, he publicly announced his sins to the people of Thebes, turned over his throne to his brother-in-law Creon, and prepared to pass from the city to spend the rest of his days as a blind, conscience-tortured wanderer.

For a short while, however, Oedipus' nomadic course was postponed. Creon took pity on his suffering relative and allowed him the hospitality of the royal palace, but before long the former king's presence became a political embarrassment, and Creon sent him on his way. He was accompanied on his wanderings by his faithful daughter, Antigone, while his second daughter, Ismene, stayed behind to take care of her father's affairs in Thebes. After a long period of wandering, Oedipus and Antigone came to Colonus, near Athens, where they took refuge in the sacred wood of the Eumenides. Here the travellers were welcomed by Theseus, the noble ruler of the Athenians, and Oedipus was urged to spend the rest of his day under Athenian hospitality.

Soon after his arrival at Colonus, Oedipus was joined by his daughter Ismene, who brought fearful news of a fraternal quarrel in Thebes. Oedipus' sons Eteocles and Polynices had quarrelled over the succession to the throne; Creon had been forced to resign his regency, and Polynices, the elder brother, had set himself up as king with the understanding that his brother Eteocles would alternate with him annually as ruler. Eteocles was not content with half a loaf, however, and incited the people of Thebes to revolt and banish Polynices, who had subsequently fled to Argos and married the daughter of King Adrastus. Now, with the help of Adrastus and other powerful allies, Polynices was preparing to march against Thebes to claim his rights as ruler. Oedipus' help was needed in the crisis, Ismene told her father, and even now Creon was on the way to Athens to persuade the old man to return and to kidnap him by force if necessary. Oedipus was furious at this request; he who had been heartlessly turned out as a beggar was now asked to forgive all and help those who had tormented him. When Creon arrived, Oedipus repulsed him scornfully, and when Creon seemed about to use force, King Theseus advised the Theban leader to depart at once or suffer the attack of the powerful Athenian army. Creon discreetly left.

Shortly after Creon's departure, Polynices appeared and asked his father's blessing in the attack on Thebes, but the enraged father was not to be placated. Both his sons had treated him with unfilial contempt, now both of them could have his curse and his dire prophecy that both would welter in each other's blood.

After this painful scene, Oedipus felt that his time had come. A dreadful storm broke over the sacred wood, and Oedipus declared that it was an omen that he should enter the grove of the Eumenides alone. His faithful daughters and King Theseus accompanied him to the edge of the grove and the old man, after a touching good-by, entered alone amid the crash of thunder and rain. He immediately passed from sight; the storm miraculously ceased, and the sufferings of Oedipus were at long last ended.

Not so the problems of Thebes. This tormented city was soon plunged into the fury of a fratricidal war, with Polynices and his six allied chieftains attacking the town at each of its seven gates. Antigone and Ismene, who had returned to their native home after the death of Oedipus, awaited in terror the fulfillment of their father's curse. The battle was long and bloody, but indecisive. At last a truce was called and it was decided to settle the issue in single combat between Eteocles and Polynices. In the contest that ensued the curse of Oedipus was realized: both brothers were mortally wounded. The Theban forces then fell upon their attackers and routed them decisively. Thebes was delivered, but at terrible cost in life and strength.

Once more Creon took over the rule of the city and supervised the burying of the Theban dead. Embittered by the loss of his son Menoeceus, who was the first to die in the war, the new king gave orders that the bodies of all enemies were to remain unburied. Here he encountered the stubborn opposition of Antigone, who demanded that her brother Polynices receive the all-important last rites. Creon answered that the penalty for burying an enemy of Thebes would be death. Despite this harsh edict and despite the fearful persuasion of her timid sister Ismene, Antigone defied her uncle and conducted the forbidden rites over the body of her fallen brother. For her deed she was ruthlessly sentenced to death, but before the edict could be enforced, the distracted girl hanged herself in her cell. The death of his antagonist brought Creon no peace. His second son, Haemon, who had been engaged to Antigone, rushed to her prison and killed himself at her side. When Creon's wife, Euridice, heard of the death of her son, she too stabbed herself, and Creon, for his arrogant inflexibility, was left a humbled and broken man.

Still more humiliation was to fall upon Thebes before the story comes to an end. News of Creon's edict travelled to Athens, and the Athenians, horrified at Creon's abrogation of the Divine Law of burial, insisted on pain of attack that the enemies of Thebes be properly interred. Weakened by grief and war and in no position to dispute the Athenian might, Creon was forced to rescind his order, and the fallen were given their proper rites. Ten years later, the Epigoni, sons of the Seven Leaders against Thebes, organized to avenge the defeat of their fathers. They marched against the battle-scarred city and, finding that the entire populace had fled in terror, entered and levelled the long-suffering place to the ground.

THE HOUSE OF CADMUS

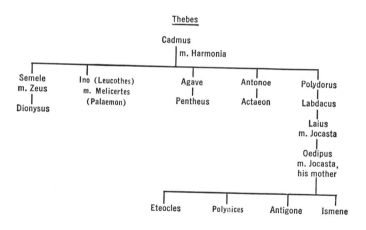

IV. JASON AND THE GOLDEN FLEECE

The far-famed voyage of the Argonauts was supposed to have taken place a generation before the Trojan War. The background of the story concerns a Greek king Athamas, who abandoned his wife Nephele to marry Ino. His first wife had reason to fear that the woman who had supplanted her in her husband's affections would also attempt to destroy their son Phrixus so that her own child might inherit the kingdom. By an elaborate ruse she arranged to have Phrixus sacrificed to the gods to avert a famine which she herself had brought about. But as the boy was being placed on the altar, a miraculous ram with golden fleece appeared from the heavens, seized both Phrixus and his sister Helle, and carried them away toward Asia. As they were crossing the Dardanelles, Helle fell into the water, wherefore the Greeks named that strait the sea of Helle or Hellespont. Phrixus was carried to Colchis on the Black Sea where he later married a princess, sacrificed the magical ram to Zeus, and presented the golden fleece to his father-in-law, King Aeetes.

The story now turns to King Aeson, an uncle of Phrixus, who had abdicated his throne in favor of his brother Pelias on condition that the rule of Pelias would continue only until Aeson's son Jason came of age. But when Jason grew up and came to claim the crown, Pelias was loath to give it up and offered to surrender the kingdom only if Jason would first prove his right to the throne by recapturing the golden fleece, which was felt to be the rightful property of the family.

Jason sent out a call for volunteers to accompany him on the expedition and commissioned the building of a great ship, which was named the Argo. The bravest heroes of the ancient world, including Hercules and Peleus, the father of Achilles, made up the band of adventurers who responded to Jason's call and who were called Argonauts after the ship on which they sailed. The voyage to Colchis was long and difficult. But after a multitude of dangerous experiences and hairbreadth escapes, Jason and most of his companions finally landed on the shores of Colchis.

After being well received by the king, Jason offered the

services of his company for the performance of any task the king should care to assign in exchange for the golden fleece. The king's astonishing response was the proposal that Jason should yoke two fire-breathing bulls to a plow, plow a field, and then sow the teeth of a dragon. He explained that the dragon's teeth would produce a crop of armed men who would spring up the instant the seed was sown and attack the sower. Jason might well have despaired of accomplishing the feat had he not already become acquainted with Medea, the king's daughter, who was a sorceress equipped with all sorts of magical potions, spells, and devices. Fortunately for Jason, Medea had been overwhelmed by a fierce passion for him upon their first meeting. Aware of her infatuation, Jason turned to her for assistance and accepted the proffer of her magic lore to enable him to perform the impossible. At the same time, Jason was so lured by her physical as well as her magical charms that he declared his love, swore eternal faithfulness to her, and begged her to return with him to Greece after the fleece had been won. Medea was naturally distraught by her betrayal of her father, but the intensity of her love for Jason offered her no alternative to casting her lot thenceforth with his.

When the time for the contest arrived, Jason covered himself and his sword with an ointment of invincibility which Medea had given him. He then successfully yoked the fiery bulls, plowed the field, and sowed the dragon's teeth. As the armed men sprang up and rushed at him, he hurled a stone into their midst as Medea had instructed him, whereat the warriors turned their weapons upon each other and completely destroyed themselves. The king had no intention of fulfilling his part of the bargain and began to plan new designs against Jason. When Medea became aware of her father's treachery, she stole secretly to Jason to tell him that he must seize the golden fleece and escape that very night. Aided again by Medea's magic, Jason killed the dragon which guarded the fleece and set out to sea together with Medea and the Argonauts.

They were hotly pursued and escaped destruction again only because of the fanatical devotion of Medea. She had taken the precaution of bringing along her younger brother Apsyrtus. Now, when the pursuers were on the verge of overtaking the Argo, she cut her brother into pieces and dropped them, one by one, over the stern of the ship. The Colchians paused to collect the pieces, delaying their pursuit and making it possible for the Argonauts to escape.

After many more trials, which they survived mainly because of Medea's craft, the Argonauts ultimately reached Greece, where they disbanded. Jason took Medea back to claim his kingdom only to discover that during his absence King Pelias had contrived the death of his father Aeson and that his mother had subsequently died of grief. Determined to avenge the death of his parents, Jason again turned to Medea, who convinced the daughters of Pelias that they might restore their father's youth by a device which she demonstrated on an old ram. She cut the ram into pieces, dropped them into a pot of boiling water, and uttered a charm, whereupon a young lamb jumped out of the pot. Carried away by the demonstration, the daughters enthusiastically administered a sleeping potion to their father, cut him up, and dropped the pieces into boiling water. But when it was time for Medea to pronounce the magical charm, she was not to be found. Because of this foul murder, public opinion in Iolchus turned against Jason and his sorceress bride, with the result that they had to flee the country.

Thus Jason never did attain the throne of Iolchus, for which he had undertaken all the adventures with the Argonauts. Instead he took refuge in Corinth, where Medea bore him three sons. For a while all was well with Jason and

Medea, but before long the frustration of never having attained the throne he deserved spurred Jason to ambitious conniving. Thrusting aside the woman who had done everything for him, he became engaged to the daughter of the king of Corinth and, to protect his intended bride from the vengeful magic of the distraught and rejected Medea, he ordered his former consort out of Corinth. Furious at this cold-hearted ingratitude, Medea got rid of her rival by sending her a poisoned robe and crown which burst into a devouring flame as soon as she had put them on. She then proceeded to kill her sons in the very sight of the horrified Jason, after which she fled the scene in a winged chariot conjured up by her magic arts. For a while she found refuge with King Aegeus in Athens, but her evil reputation dogged her steps and caused the Athenian populace to demand her exile. Forced again on her wanderings, she finally drifted into Asia Minor, where she spent her last days uneventfully in the area which was subsequently named Media in her unhappy memory.

Jason's end was no less tragic. In one version he rushed on his sword in an agony of remorse upon viewing the bodies of his murdered sons. In another and more poignant one, he lived on to a ripe and uneventful old age, wrapped in memories of hopes and dreams that had never been fulfilled, until one day, while he was musing idly alongside the hulk of his decaying Argo, a beam from the rotting ship broke off and fell on his head, ending his life.

V. THESEUS

Theseus, son of Aegeus, the king of Athens who had rescued Medea from Corinth, was one of the noblest and most revered of Greek heroes. He was brought up by his mother in southern Greece, where Aegeus had placed a pair of shoes and a sword beneath a rock. He left instructions that when the child grew strong enough to remove the boulder and claim the sword and shoes he should be sent to his father in Athens.

The child grew to be exceptionally strong, lifted the rock without difficulty, and set out to find his father. On the journey to Athens he made it a point to earn the approbation of the people by ridding the country of all evil-doers whom he encountered on the road. He was received joyfully by his father and proudly exhibited to the Athenians as the heir to the throne, an eminence which he took pains to deserve by a long succession of noble deeds.

His most famous exploit resulted from a former Athenian defeat at the hands of Minos, king of Crete. At that time, Minos had spared the city from complete destruction only on condition that every year thereafter Athens would send seven youths and seven maidens to Crete to provide food for a fearsome monster. This monster, called the Minotaur, was the half-bull, half-human offspring of Minos' wife, Pasiphae, which she had borne as the result of her unnatural passion for a bull. Annually the fourteen victims were chosen by lot until Theseus offered himself for the sacrifice with the idea of destroying the Minotaur. He set sail with the others, leaving his father heavy-hearted but with a promise that if he succeeded in his mission he would change the traditional black sail of the vessel to a white one so that news of his safe return would be known as soon as possible.

Theseus was supremely fortunate in arousing the love of Minos' daughter Ariadne. The major problem for the mighty Theseus was not the slaying of the Minotaur; he counted on his tremendous strength to accomplish that with ease. The achievement was complicated by the fact that the Minotaur was kept in a labryinth so ingeniously constructed by the master architect Daedalus that, once, inside, no one could find his way back out of the maze. It was Ariadne who supplied Theseus with the means of escape by giving him a ball of twine. He fastened the end to the door as he entered the labyrinth, unravelled the ball as he roamed about, and finally encountered the monster. He killed the Minotaur with his bare hands, picked up the twine, and followed it back to the door. Then, accompanied by Ariadne and his sacrificial companions, Theseus departed secretly for Athens.

On the return voyage, Ariadne suffered from seasickness and was put ashore on the island of Naxos to recuperate. A storm swept the ship suddenly to sea with Theseus on board. By the time Theseus succeeded in guiding the ship back to the island, Ariadne was dead. Theseus was so overcome by grief that he forgot to change the ill-omened black sails of his ship. When King Aegeus, who had been keeping constant watch for his son's return, saw the black sail, his despair caused him to hurl himself to death over the edge of the cliff into the sea, which was named the Aegean in memory of him.

The Athenians thereafter commemorated the event by sending the same ship annually to Delos, the shrine of Apollo, in fulfillment of a vow which they had made when they had entreated Apollo to vouchsafe a successful return voyage for Theseus. The city was pledged to keep itself pure while the mission was being performed, and no death sentences might be executed until the ship returned. This was the law that delayed the execution of Socrates after his conviction.

Theseus proved to be a remarkable successor to the throne. Keeping for himself only the office of Military Commander, he turned the government over to the people and established Athenian democracy. He sheltered the blinded Oedipus who was an outcast from Thebes after the discovery of his fate-imposed crimes. He warred successfully against Thebes when Creon refused burial to the bodies of those who had fought in an unsuccessful revolution in that city. Instead of permitting Thebes to be looted after his victory, he ordered only the burial of the dead, and then returned with his army to Athens.

Numerous similarly fine and heroic actions are recorded of him. He was unfortunate only in love. He lost Ariadne on his return from Crete. His second inamorata was Hippolyta, the Amazon queen whom he carried off after a war with the famous warrior-women. She bore him a son, Hippolytus, but was the cause of an invasion of Athens by the Amazons who came to rescue her. In his later life he married Phaedra, the sister of Ariadne. She kept the pattern of his luckless loves consistent by falling in love with Hippolytus and instigating thereby a series of calamities which are described in Racine's play, *Phaedra*. Theseus was ultimately treacherously killed by King Lycomedes whom he believed to be his friend. In all the stories told of him, greatness of heart is emphasized as his salient trait.

SUGGESTED READINGS

See end of Chapter 8 for suggested readings.

chapter 6

ATHENIAN DEMOCRACY IN THE GOLDEN AGE (500-322 B.C.)

I. SOCIAL DIVISIONS

In the fifth century B.C., Athenian democracy reached its highest peak and achieved the most enlightened form of government the world had yet seen. Although it was far from being a fully representative system, much less a pure democracy, it was nevertheless a remarkably equitable organization with relatively little bureaucracy and a high degree of integrity and public responsibility. At this time the city-state of Attica, with its principal city of Athens, covered an area of approximately one thousand square miles (slightly larger than that of Greater New York plus Westchester County) and had a population of about 315,000, probably half of whom lived in the capital. These 315,000 were divided into well-defined classes as follows:

A. *Citizens* (43,000). All males over twenty-one born of free Athenian parents were classed as citizens and concerned themselves primarily with the responsibilities of government. Each citizen was equal before the law and had the privilege of direct participation in law-making and state administration. In return for these privileges, the citizen body bore the expenses of the state and undertook its defense. Four classes of citizens were recognized according to wealth, and each class paid taxes in line with the extent of its property. Theoretically, the citizen was a man of leisure and independent means, though there were many gentlemen farmers and even some business men in the citizen body.

B. *Non-Citizens*. The non-citizen, or non-voting, body was constituted of about 28,500 foreign-born freemen known as *metoikoi* or metics, 115,000 slaves, and 130,000 others, including citizen women and free workers too recently risen from slavery to achieve citizenship. The metics were by no means unwanted, and their presence in Athens was even encouraged, but they took no part in the functions of the state.

The slaves were seldom Greeks after the reforms of Solon abolished enslavement for debt; for the fifth-century Athenians had a prejudice against enslaving their own kind. Rather they were military prisoners, criminals, infants rescued from exposure, or foreigners without means who voluntarily entered a state of servitude. Slaves performed most of the necessary work of the state, including manual labor, clerical duties, and many of the minor commercial functions. They also performed many of the minor official duties of the government, including those of the police force, since the Greek citizen hated bureaucracy and shrank from performing any duties which would require him to exert coercive powers over other Greeks. Strangely enough, the idea of being subject to the orders of foreign or slave policemen did not disturb him in the least, perhaps because the average Athenian, despite his highly developed sense of freedom, knew when to limit his personal whims in the interest of the public good.

Slaves had no legal rights and were bought and sold like merchandise in the open streets for prices ranging from

$50 to $1000 in modern currency. Nevertheless, the lot of the average slave in Attica was not generally oppressive. He wore no special badge of distinction, and was not expected to be cringing and servile in his manner. He was often well-educated and acted as tutor in the home of a rich citizen, where he was treated as one of the family. He could not be killed by his master, and if his condition of servitude was too brutal, he had the right to flee to a temple and ask for succor. In such cases it was customary to require that he be sold to another master. Many slaves were eventually freed by their owners or were allowed to purchase their release, so that many of the workers in Attica and not a few of the teachers and philosophers were former slaves or the sons of slaves. Slaves were permitted to marry, for despite the fact that less than half the population of Attica was free, the citizen body had no fear of being attacked and possibly overthrown by rebellious servants. It is a tribute to the humanity with which the slaves were treated that Athens was never worried by the spectre of bloody class warfare.

It might astonish one that so enlightened a people as the fifth-century Athenians should permit slavery at all, but it must be remembered that enforced servitude had existed as a matter of course in all civilizations up to that time and was taken for granted by everyone. It is to the everlasting credit of Athens that the first questionings as to the ethics of bondage emanated from her thinkers; both the Cynics and the Stoics denounced slavery, and the dramatist Euripides attacked it in his plays. Enforced servitude was never abolished in Classical times, and yet it was not until the Renaissance that the common man, whether slave or theoretically free, enjoyed the prerogatives and relatively humane treatment accorded even the lowest bondsman in the time of Pericles.

II. STATE ORGANIZATION

The Athenian government consisted of two legislative bodies and one body each for judicial, executive, military, and general supervisory functions. The legislature was made up of the *Ekklesia,* or Assembly, and the *Boule,* or Council. The *Ekklesia* was made up of all 43,000 citizens, each with equal voting rights. The attendance of all citizens was theoretically required at all legislative sessions, but this rule proved impossible to enforce. To make sure of as large a body as possible, police officers armed with whips dipped in vermilion paint patrolled the market and other loafing places on assembly days, striking every citizen in sight with their paint-smeared weapons. Persons found with vermilion stains on their clothing would be subject to a small fine and also to the ridicule of their fellows. But despite all efforts to induce attendance, actually not more than two or three thousand appeared for the ordinary weekly legislative session. And because of difficult travel conditions, most of these conscientious legislators were inhabitants of Athens itself, with the result that the agrarian suburbs usually found themelves politically at the mercy of the metropolitan commercial interests.

Meetings of the *Ekklesia* were held on a hillside known as the Pnyx. They were opened shortly after dawn with a brief ritual of prayer and sacrifice, after which regular business was in order. Speakers would call for recognition and would present their views to an often highly critical and demonstrative audience. Halting, inaudible, inept, unconvincing speakers were received with a barrage of heckling, groans, catcalls, and other verbal ridicule sufficient to strike terror into the most hardened political operator. Because of this condition, we can easily understand why the young Greek student was subjected so strenuously to the study of rhetoric, declamation, and logical expression.

Good speakers, on the other hand, were highly applauded, and there was little need for the vermilion whips in the market place on days when a popular orator was scheduled to address the assembly.

The *Ekklesia* initiated bills and resolutions and eventually rejected or passed them into law, but because the body was unwieldy, most of the actual legislative work was done in the *Boule,* or Council of Five Hundred. Cleisthenes in 507 B.C., as part of his reform program, had divided the citizen body into ten tribes or *demes* according to territorial divisions. He also had established the Council of Five Hundred, which was chosen by lot from the *Ekklesia.* At first the Council members were taken from the body at large; later a more representative system of selecting fifty councillors from each *deme* was instituted. Each council member served for one year only, so that it was possible for every citizen to serve on this important body once in his lifetime. It was the function of the *Boule* to examine all bills introduced in the *Ekklesia* and to report them favorably or unfavorably to that larger body. Thus, the Council corresponded in many ways to our own legislative committees in the House and Senate, but without the curse of our "chairmanship by seniority," since all Council members served for one year only.

In addition to its advisory function, the *Boule* also exercised important executive duties. It controlled state finances, public works and buildings, religious observances, and other civic programs. It also assumed the responsibility for steering legislation in the *Ekklesia.* For this purpose it was divided into ten *prytanies,* each of which served for one month and during that time assumed chairmanship over both Assembly and Council. Each legislative day a new chairman would be chosen for both legislative bodies, so that theoretically every Athenian citizen for one day in his life could serve as the highest functionary in the state.

Although this system was highly democratic and although it made bribery of legislators almost impossible, it was necessarily too unstable to permit of strong leadership from any one man or group of men. Before long, it was the military branch of the government which held the real power. This body consisted of ten *strategoi* elected by popular vote for one year but eligible for re-election. One of this number was chosen *strategos autokrator,* or Chief of Staff, and it was he who actually became key man in the state. The great Pericles was *strategos autokrator* (with a few short breaks) for more than a generation (463-431 B.C.) and under him Athenian "democracy" actually became a democratic monarchy.

Other governmental functions were carried out by the nine *archons,* or secondary executives, who directed the actual workings of financial affairs, public works, and so forth. There was also a large judiciary, consisting of six thousand citizens chosen by lot for a one-year term. These jurors were divided into various district courts on all judicial levels and served there as both judges and jury. The number of jurors assigned to any one trial depended upon the importance of the issue at stake; a minor litigation could be handled by a few dozen jurors, but critical issues sometimes called for several hundred to eliminate the dangers of bribery. Juries of 100 were the general rule, but in the trial of Socrates the services of 501 were enlisted.

As with members of the *Ekklesia,* the jurors reacted openly to the presentation of the case on trial. Since professional lawyers were non-existent, the plaintiff and the defendant were required to argue their differences in person. Woe to any litigant whose command of language or logic failed to meet the standards of the jury! To help the tongue-tied, professional speech writers would often prepare a case in advance. The litigant would then memorize the prepared speech and recite (not read) it to the jury. Extemporaneous skill in argumentation was not a strict necessity, since the modern system of cross-examination was generally not employed, the trial of Socrates notwithstanding. Each contestant was permitted a period of rebuttal, however, and sometimes he would put direct questions to his opponent for clarification of a disputed point. After the rebuttals were over, the jurymen would vote for the plaintiff or defendant by dropping a mussel shell or some other small object into one of two jars, each representing one party to the trial. Decision was usually reached by simple majority vote, but in serious cases a two-thirds margin might be required. Penalties assigned were usually in the form of fines, disenfranchisement, exile, or death. The last was seldom invoked and when it was called for was carried out mercifully through administration of the hemlock, a drug which painlessly put the victim into a slumber from which he never wakened. Imprisonment as a punishment was seldom used, partly because of the costly requirement of prison facilities and partly because confinement of any kind was regarded by the Greeks as being unnecessarily cruel.

Another legislative body was the *Areopagus,* a semi-honorary group composed of men who had served with distinction in one of the archonships. Under Draco and Solon, the *Areopagus* had acted solely as a court in cases of murder, assault, arson, and poisoning, but in the time of Pericles it had become a supervisory body which examined the conduct of the magistrates and educators and assumed a loose censorship of public morals. In times of emergency it could be called upon to exercise dictatorial powers, since its members were the most experienced men in the state and, being members of the *Areopagus* for life, were not subject to political opportunism.

Altogether, the Athenian system of government was an enlightened and extremely advanced organization for its time. One reason for its effectiveness lay in its slow process of development; it was the result of evolution and reform rather than violent revolution. Also it functioned within a small state clearly divided into classes, each with its privileges and responsibilities. To the Greeks, a classless society would have been an absurdity, since men are unequal in ability and many are obviously not qualified for the important business of public life. It is better, they felt, to assign a man to a definite group, outline his duties as a member of that group, and make it possible for him to rise beyond his class if his talents so warrant.

Unfortunately, the Athenian system, for all its reasonableness, carried within itself the seeds of its own destruction. The unwieldy legislative system led to more and more reliance upon one strong man—the *strategos autokrator*. So long as Athens had a Pericles to lead her, all was well, but when lesser men stepped into the leader's post the city came upon evil days. Also, Athenian foreign policy during and after the Persian Wars became more imperialistic, and the essentially local type of Athenian government was unequal to the task of directing a world power. Then too, the Athenian class system, with its flexibility which theoretically permitted even the posterity of slaves to become citizens, gradually rigidified and became ridden with jealousy, prejudice, and a suicidal desire on the part of the privileged to preserve the *status quo* in class distinctions. Before many generations had passed, Athens was to learn that the lifeblood of a democratic form of government is the constant and gradual extension of that democracy; when the democratic privilege is stultified or retracted, demagoguery and decline set in. But by the time this principle was clearly demonstrated to the Athenians, the city was already irretrievably on the road to decay.

III. MILITARY ORGANIZATION

Next in importance to his political obligations was the Athenian citizen's duty to serve in the military forces of the state. From early childhood onward, the Athenian was made aware of his responsibility to aid in the defense of his city, and much of his education, including the heavy proportion of physical training, was frankly directed toward fitting him for at least a part time military career. At eighteen, having completed his formal studies, the young Athenian was enrolled for a two-year course of military service in the *Epheboi,* or youth army, and some part of this tour of duty was spent in garrison assignment away from home. At twenty the military training period was considered over, and the citizen was thereafter liable for active service until the age of sixty. Since Athens relied largely on a conscript army, relatively few young men went in for a professional military career, but all citizens were supposed to keep themselves in proper condition to respond immediately to a call to arms. This physical requirement was taken very seriously by the Athenians, and the gymnasia were crowded every afternoon by men of all ages taking their regular exercise.

Each man was required to furnish his own arms, the basic items of armament being helmet, greaves, cuirass, shield, and short spear. Wealthier citizens could provide themselves with suits of light armor and other refinements. Assignment to companies was governed largely by the type of armor a citizen possessed, making personal wealth an important factor in the Athenian military structure. However, beyond the privilege of being placed in a company of one's economic peers, the rich man had few advantages in the Athenian army and, being well armed and generally better trained and in better condition, he could be certain that he would be called upon to bear the brunt of the fighting.

The fighting itself was hardly of the push-button variety. Rather it followed the hand-to-hand phalanx tactics previously described (see p. 30) and resembled something between a football scrimmage and a Saturday night free-for-all. Strategy consisted largely in the choice of an appropriate battlefield and the proper distribution of the corps before the fighting began; once the battle was joined anything could happen, with the issue being decided largely by strength and endurance rather than logistics and disciplined maneuver. Virtually the entire army was composed of infantry. Cavalry was not practical in the narrow Greek valleys, and battle machines, such as the catapault and battering ram, were so primitive as to be of little value except in infrequent instances of besiegement.

Despite the generally uninhibited nature of a Greek battle, certain niceties were supposed to be observed. Prisoners were not to be killed, and fellow Greeks were seldom enslaved. Battles were not fought on religious holidays or during harvest times, and to fall on one's enemy while he was sleeping, eating, or otherwise unprepared for combat, while often done, was considered rather bad form.

Since Athens was a sea power, many young men chose the navy as their division of military activity, although service therein was much less interesting than in the land forces. Because no expensive armament was needed, naval service was often chosen by the poorer class, and sometimes even slaves were enlisted on promise of freedom as a reward for their services. The Athenian ships of war were light galleys, each rowed by about sixty trained oarsmen working in teams of three seated side by side. Considerable practice and physical co-ordination were needed for the teams to function in perfect rhythm and to avoid fouling one another's oars, particularly since Athenian naval tactics relied more upon speed and flexibility of movement than strength and weight. The most effective stratagem employed by the navy was that of ramming the enemy from the side or rear. It was this tactical maneuver that so thoroughly destroyed the slow-moving Persian navy at the battle of Salamis, and once it had been proved efficient it rendered the old method of boarding for hand-to-hand combat obsolete. So long as warships continued to rely on the oar for propulsion, the ram remained the principal action of naval offense.

IV. ECONOMY

Though not richly gifted in natural resources, Athens during the Golden Age maintained a reasonably balanced economy of agriculture, crafts, and shipping. She raised grain of all kinds, olives, and grapes, and had extensive herds of sheep and goats. The grain crop was insufficient for her needs, however, and she was partly dependent upon receiving foodstuffs from abroad. On the other hand, her crafts, particularly those of ironwork and pottery, were very profitable, although they were hardly operated on a mass production basis.

But the principal source of Athenian wealth was her shipping trade, which extended over the entire Mediterranean and was the governing factor in making Athens into both the leading sea power and the most important financial center in the Hellenic world. Banking was highly developed in Athens, and her coins were a standard medium of exchange throughout the Mediterranean area. Athenian banks were able to lend money wisely, with interest rates of from 12 to 30 per cent being a routine matter. The ever-increasing volume of banking and shipping led inevitably to imperialism, both of a political and of an economic nature, and Athenian financial pressure was as much dreaded as her military strength by weaker states throughout the Aegean.

The unit of Athenian coinage was the drachma. Silver coins were minted in denominations of one, two, four, and ten drachmas, as well as in fractional pieces known as obols, worth one sixth of a drachma. One hundred drachmas were known as a mina and sixty minae constituted a talent, although no coins for these higher values were issued. The value of Athenian currency in terms of present prices is hard to determine because of the vast differences in living standards between the modern world and Periclean Athens. Laborers received three obols, or half a drachma, a day, and this might be considered a basic or subsistence wage. Skilled workers received a drachma a day and master craftsmen about two and a half drachmas. When during his trial Socrates proposed that he be fined thirty minae, he was able to name this stiff penalty only because of the promised support of his wealthy friends; he admitted that he himself could afford only one mina. Elsewhere in Greek literature a person with a fortune of fifty talents was spoken of as being a very rich man.[1]

As we have seen, the great majority of the Athenian population were workers and artisans, while the citizen body contained many persons of the leisure class. The number of citizens earning their living through the professions was rather small, since there were no lawyers, no full-time priests, no professional politicians, and very few professional military men. Teachers were usually slaves or foreigners, as were entertainers, soothsayers, and astrologers. Only medical men had true professional status in Athens, despite the many stock jokes made about the lethal effect of their ministrations. As a matter of fact, the jokes were undeserved, for Greek medicine had gone far in its knowledge of anatomy and herbology and its skill in diagnostics.

But whatever the occupation or the income of the individual Athenian, he had little to complain of in regard to taxation. Since government routine was carried on largely by slaves, low-salaried clerks, and virtually uncompensated citizens, expenses were low. What revenues were needed were derived mostly from tolls, from customs duties and,

[1] Some textbooks estimate the drachma as being worth approximately twenty-five cents in American money, but if this standard is accepted it would be necessary to multiply the purchasing power of the Greek coins by at least twenty to equate their value with current prices.

with the growth of the Athenian empire after the Persian Wars, from exorbitant levies on satellite states. Direct taxes were seldom imposed upon the individual citizen, though in time of war an income levy was sometimes resorted to. One reason for the rapidity of Athens' decline lay in her ruthless milking of dependent states within her orbit. At the first opportunity, these exploited states combined with enemies of Athens to help overthrow their hated persecutor.

V. EVERYDAY LIFE

In their everyday life, the Greeks admirably illustrate the anthropological theory that man's pattern of existence is to a great degree determined by the simple factor of climate. In lands where harsh extremes of weather prevail, men must construct sturdy houses against violent storms, must heat those houses against the blasts of winter, must own several types of clothing to suit the seasons, must work hard in mild weather to store up food for the frost periods when the fields are unproductive, and must devise useful and often complicated activities other than agriculture to keep the economy going on a year-round basis. It has been estimated that in northern temperate countries, such as the United States, more than half of a man's energy and income go into the simple providing of shelter, while another large slice of his salary is expended for foods whose prices are kept relatively high by the added expense of storing or processing for off-season use.

The Greeks, on the other hand, were troubled by no such problems of weather. Living in a country where the summers were hot and dry, the winters brief and very mild, and the growing season very nearly a year-round proposition, the Greek citizen did not have to worry about storm-tight housing, central heating, various weights and styles of clothing, or temporary shortages of perishable staples. Throughout most of the year his fields produced the grains and vegetables, his orchards the fruit, and his barns the dairy and meat products necessary for a simple but balanced diet. Since his social life was spent mostly in the open, his house could be designed for the basic necessities of sleeping and eating alone, and his pleasurable activities could consist mostly of walking, competitive sports, and conversation, without any of the expensive (and often compulsive) partying and recreational gadgetry of peoples whose lives are spent largely indoors. Altogether then, a good part of the much-praised simplicity of Greek life derived not so much from some mysterious trait of racial austerity as from the plain fact that in the salubrious and predictable Greek climate, a complicated standard of living was not necessary.

Nothing is more characteristic of the frugality of Greek life than the typical Athenian manner of dress. The men wore a simple oblong white cloth reaching to the knees, pinned at the shoulders and fastened around the waist by a sash. For cooler weather, a similar cloth was added and worn cloaklike over the shoulders. Shoes and sandals were regularly used, but hats were a rarity. Exercise was performed naked, and heavy labor very nearly so. The modern passion for variety in dress would have struck the Greek as idle and absurd; he would have much preferred to develop his individuality through sports or intellectual attainments.

Women's dress, on the other hand, was more varied and colorful. Though dyes were expensive and had to be imported, colored fabrics were used by the wives of the more prosperous citizens. While the basis of female clothing, like that of the male, was still the draped oblong cloth, individuality could be secured through arrangements of color and pattern. Hairdressing was an elaborate feminine art, and cosmetics were also judiciously employed. Indulgence in these time-consuming pursuits of self-adornment was one of the few pleasures of Greek womanhood and was tolerated by the men partly because it made their wives attractive and partly because more intellectual pursuits were considered impractical and undesirable among respectable women.

Greek houses of the Periclean period would strike modern tastes as carrying the desire for simplicity a bit too far. Dwellings were usually constructed of sun-dried clay bricks which sometimes washed away in heavy rainstorms. There were no outside windows and generally only one door. If there was any outside decoration at all, it might consist of a portico over the door, but for the most part the Greeks could see no sense in adorning their homes as though they were temples or public buildings. Ventilation and light were secured from a large inner courtyard, which also served as the main living and dining room of the house. The rooms which opened off this courtyard on every side were used for sleeping and storage, with one side being reserved exclusively for women. Dirt floors were the rule, although the wealthier families might have had tile in the courtyard. Doors consisted largely of curtains, and furniture was of the most rudimentary sort. Chairs were particularly scarce, because the Greeks regarded sitting as a wasteful barbarian custom and preferred to spend most of their waking hours on their feet. Needless to say, plumbing was non-existent, and slops were disposed of in the street. Personal cleanliness, on the other hand, was scrupulously cultivated, and no day would have been considered well spent without a visit to the public bath. Soap was unknown, but olive oil rubbed over the body and then scraped off with a flat instrument known as a strigil proved a satisfactory substitute.

Meals were frugal, but were important functions in Greek social life. Like many ancient peoples, the Greeks believed that eating in a semi-recumbent posture aided both digestion and conversation. Guests were almost always present at dinner, and to keep matters convivial a good deal of drinking was done. The usual beverage was sweet wine heavily diluted with water, and the effect of this drink was usually stimulating rather than intoxicating. More strenuous drinking bouts often took place, however, with a master of ceremonies to decide on the degree of dilution of the wine and to order the toasts. Entertainment at these bouts usually consisted of conversation and song. Occasionally professional dancers, acrobats, or musicians would be employed. Women, of course, did not attend, nor were they ever allowed in the presence of guests.

In general, the woman's position in the Greek household was that of domestic supervisor. Wives were supposed to minister to their husbands and to bring up their children. Seldom were they admitted to the more serious or intellectual aspects of their husbands' existence, nor were they allowed to hold property of their own. Throughout their lives, Greek women were under the supervision of some male: father, brother, husband, or son. Marriages were made by contract, and if anyone derived romantic satisfaction from these arbitrarily fashioned nuptials, it was considered a rare and wonderful situation. On the other hand, the Greek male was not forced to be without his romantic moments, for the institution of courtesans and mistresses was an accepted and quite respectable part of Greek life. The Athenians were noted for their high sense of morality, but that morality did not go so far as to forbid male extramarital activity. This activity, however, was supposed to be confined to the courtesan class; a wife caught in adultery would be divorced at once and disgraced forever, and a man with known propensities for philandering with his neighbors' wives would lose the respect of both society and of his fellows. It must be said that such standards managed to keep Athenian domestic life on a remarkably even keel. The average Athenian seemed to have been a good family man, to have loved his wife and children, and to have been very moderate in the indulgence of his extra-marital privileges. It seems also that visits to courtesans were not always made for sensual indulgence, because many of these women were well educated and charming as well as beautiful, and the gatherings at their homes were often more those of a respectable, highly cultivated eighteenth-century salon than those of the nineteenth-century brothel. One of these women, Aspasia, became the common-law wife of Pericles and a great power in the intellectual and political life of the city; Socrates himself paid tribute to her brilliance of mind. And yet Aspasia and her class were the exceptions, the tolerated outer fringe of a society which was, outside of the home, almost entirely male dominated. Within the narrow confines of domestic duties, Athenian wives had some small influence; in external affairs—in society and before the law—their status was so degraded as to make even the slaves seem privileged by comparison.

SUGGESTED READINGS

See end of Chapter 8 for suggested readings.

chapter 7

THE DEVELOPMENT
OF THE GREEK DRAMA

I. THE DIONYSIAC FESTIVALS

The theatre, from its very inception, has been closely allied with religion. It had its origin in ancient Greek festivals of worship and flourished throughout the Classical period as much as a religious rite as a form of entertainment. Then, after a lapse of several centuries during the early Christian era, it revived—again as part of divine worship—in the tropes, miracles, and mystery plays of the medieval period. Time and again this relationship proved embarrassing to the Church, and time and again clerical wrath has been brought down upon its unpredictable cousin, yet pulpit and stage have remained inextricably intertwined in function and appeal, until in contemporary times Maxwell Anderson has been able to compare the theatre with a cathedral and to state with plausibility that the stage has supplanted the church as a force for the spiritual betterment of man.

It is interesting that the drama, so often scorned by hell-fire preachers as a child of sin, should have had its origin in a divine peccadillo and should have grown out of the worship of an illegitimate god—the Greek Dionysus, god of fertility and wine (see p. 62).

Choral song festivals in honor of the various gods were a very early development of Greek civilization. These festivals were of rural origin, but eventually they spread to the cities and achieved their greatest development in urban surroundings. Authorities disagree as to the exact extent to which this primitive song-worship affected the growth of the drama, but it is indisputable that Greek tragedy was a direct offshoot of one form of choral festival: that devoted to the fertility myth. It is supremely important to note that the Greek theatre was not a year-round affair: its performances were confined solely to the Dionysiac festivals. Of the five annual ceremonies celebrating the god of fertility and wine, three are directly concerned with the drama. The Rustic or Lesser Dionysia, held in December in rural districts, the Lenaean or Wine-Press Festival in January, and the Greater Dionysia in March were marked by dramatic presentations which from the sixth century onward showed a rapid development in depth and complexity. The first plays were hardly more than dithyrambic odes sung in unison by a trained chorus dressed as satyrs and smeared with wine. The performance would take place on a street-corner or in a public square, for theatres were unknown until the fifth century, and the subject matter of the ode would be the trials and earthly sufferings of Dionysus. From the fact that the performers were dressed as goats (*tragodoi*) or possibly because a goat *(tragos)* was sacrificed during the recitation, the word *tragodia,* or goat-song, was applied to this and to later developments in the serious drama. (The word *drama* itself, by the way, means simply *an action* and is derived from Greek like so many other theatrical terms.)

The drama took a great step forward in the middle of the sixth century, when a poet named Thespis (compare the modern *thespian,* an actor) separated the principal actor from the chorus and had him bear the brunt of the narrative and pantomime. By thus sharpening the focus of the action, Thespis created the conception of the individual performer and, by adding a second element to the enactment of the story, injected the life-blood of opposition or struggle without which no true drama can exist. It is no wonder, then, that posterity has bestowed upon him the title of Father of the Drama. In the fifth century, Aeschylus added a second actor, and a generation later Sophocles added a third, thus greatly augmenting the flexibility of dramatic presentation. It is to be remembered, however, that although the Greek drama never contained more than three principal actors, no playwright confined himself to writing only three solo parts. One actor would usually play the part of the central figure; the others "doubled," i.e., assumed many lesser parts throughout the play. Thespis wrote many plays, but none of them has survived. Similarly, the work of other sixth-century dramatists, such as Choerilus, Pratinas, and Phrynichus, has disappeared or exists in only minute fragments.

The great flowering of the drama took place in the fifth century, with such towering figures as Aeschylus, Sophocles, Euripides, and the comedian Aristophanes producing works which still rank among the greatest creations in all literature. By this time, dramatic writing had reached its full development in classical form, and it was not until two thousand years later, with Shakespeare, that we find comparable writing for the stage. Gone were the crude, half-improvised, street-corner performances of the satyr-chorus; the theatre was now a complex, subtle, and religiously significant art-form with an especially designed theatre to house its functions and a highly professional personnel of actors, producers, playwrights, directors, and chorus members. It is to the nature of this very sophisticated fifth-century art that we now turn our attention.

II. NATURE OF THE GREEK DRAMA

It is to be emphasized that to the Greeks the drama was not mere entertainment, but a serious form of divine worship. Hence the plays were composed on a grand scale to impress the audience with the spiritual significance of the occasion. In a sense, each play was a sermon, stressing those moral concepts of restraint and humility which far more than worship of the Olympian gods, formed the true Greek religion. The most frequent ethical concept found in the classical tragedy is that of *hubris,* or the fall that follows overweening pride and arrogance.

Greek tragedy is still highly effective when presented by skilled actors, but the conventions which governed its writing and performance were radically different from those of today. Perhaps the most difficult of these conventions for the modern student to understand is that the plays were almost invariably composed on plots completely familiar to every member of the audience. The stories of Prometheus, Agamemnon, Antigone, Medea, and Oedipus were as well known to the most illiterate Greek as those of Moses, Christ, Columbus, or Washington are to us, and thus the Athenian playwright was judged not on elements of novelty or surprise but on dramatic skill, character delineation, and poetic excellence in handling thrice-familiar material. Perhaps the closest present-day parallel to this convention is the opera, where intelligent listeners familiarize themselves with the libretto beforehand in order more fully to understand and appreciate the far more important elements of musical structure, development, and performance.

The plays usually preserved the so-called "classical unities" of Time, Place, and Action; that is, they presented one dramatic episode, without sub-plots or interpolations for "comic relief," in a single setting, with action that could conceivably take place in twenty-four hours. Actual physical action on the stage was limited; the Greeks were far more interested in hearing fine poetry beautifully read than in elaborate stage-business. Besides, the high shoes (buskins) worn by tragic actors to give them grandeur of stature would tend to make rapid action awkward, if not downright ridiculous. It is for this last reason, and not because of squeamishness, that bloodshed in the Greek tragedies always took place offstage; the Greeks preferred imagining good lusty mayhem to having to view a mincing, slow, near-comic counterfeit.

Not only was the poet required to obey the unities and to fashion his tragedies from the folk-lore, mythology, and historical events of his time, but he was also required by custom to follow a fairly rigid form of dramatic construction, as follows:

1. *Prologue,* or opening speech by the principal actor. Generally this prologue was an integral part of the play and fulfilled the function of setting the scene and situation within the framework of the drama itself. In some of the plays of Euripides, a detached prologue of a purely expository, undramatic nature is found, but this device is not common until Roman times.

2. The *parodos,* or entrance of the chorus. The chorus consisted of twelve, later fifteen, members who chanted and performed a slow dance appropriate to the serious nature of the play. The delivery of the choral passages was stylized, but not rigid, and the lines themselves were composed in a fairly regular pattern with much attention to the phonic and rhythmic effect of the words employed. The most frequent type of choral construction consisted of the *strophe,* chanted by one half of the chorus, the *antistrophe* or answer by the second half, and the *epode,* or combined finale.

3. The principal body of the play follows the *parodos* and consists of dramatic *episodes* by the principal actors interspersed by choral odes (*stasima*). These episodes, gen-

erally five in number, correspond roughly to the acts of the modern drama, though they are considerably shorter. The relationship between the episodes and the choral odes varies greatly; in the earlier plays of Aeschylus the chorus comments directly upon the action and is often involved in the drama itself, whereas in the later period of Euripides the choral passages seem hardly more than atmospheric poetic entr'actes. Sometimes, in place of the *stasimon,* the dramatist will include a *commus,* or alternating passages of dialogue between the principal actor and the chorus.

4. Finally, after the sequence of episodes and choral interludes is concluded, comes the *exodus,* or departure of the chorus, much in the nature of a finale in the old Italian opera. In fact, the Greek tragedy, being a combination of acting, singing, and dancing, has much more in common with opera than with modern drama.

Greek tragedies were generally presented in tetralogies, or series of four plays, the first three of which were serious and the fourth, or satyr-play, a lighter afterpiece. Contrary to common belief, these plays were not necessarily sequential or even related in subject matter. As a matter of fact, only Aeschylus seems to have been reasonably consistent in composing his tetralogies in serial fashion. No complete tetralogy has survived, but in Aeschylus' *Agamemnon, Choephori,* and *Eumenides* we still have the three principal sections of one of the world's greatest dramatic creations; the unimportant satyr-play has been lost. Sophocles' *Oedipus, Oedipus at Colonus,* and *Antigone* follow a plot sequence, but we know that they were all composed at different times in the poet's career and thus are not parts of the same tetralogy.

One of the pleasantest customs of the Greek drama was the prize competition in which dramatic poets vied for awards of little monetary value but of great social prestige. These competitions were held during the six-day Greater

Dionysia in March. The first day of the festival would be confined to processions and general rejoicing in the manner of a Mardi Gras, but following this useful blowing off of emotional steam would come five days of poetic competition: one for dithyrambic odes, one for comedies, and three for tragedies. On each of the last three days three tetralogies by different poets would be presented. Balloting was done by ten judges, of whose votes five were chosen at random and counted and the rest destroyed without examination. Theoretically, the judges were inviolate and unprejudiced, but actually audience response played a large part in the prize award. Athenian audiences took their drama very seriously and were extremely uninhibited in manifesting their approval and disapproval of actors, playwrights, and judges. Generally the last-named considered their health and continued existence and voted with the consensus of the audience. That the judgment of the Athenian citizenry was as discerning as it was emotional is evident in the fact that they bestowed 28 first or second prizes on Aeschylus, 30 on Sophocles, and 6 on Euripides. Few other tragedians were recognized, and no complete work of any save the glorious Three survives.

III. GREEK COMEDY

Like tragedy, Greek comedy traces its origin to the early Dionysiac festivals. As we have already seen, these religious observances usually began with pageantry and uninhibited revelry, and it is from this ecstatic and licentious aspect of Dionysiac worship that Comedy developed. This origin would account for the almost unbelievable coarseness and obscenity of Greek comedy; it also explains its slapstick and quasi-improvisatory form of humor.

Comedy as a literary form developed later than tragedy, and it is natural that it should have adopted many of the formal conventions of its elder sister, such as the three-actor system, the chorus, and the general literary structure. Within this formal outline, several differences from tragedy are noted. For instance, the chorus is much larger, numbering from eighteen to twenty-four, and dresses and acts fantastically rather than with the ponderous dignity found in the older form. Also, the action in comedy is violent and constant, the actors dispensing with the high-soled buskins to make this flexibility of movement possible. In plot, the comedy generally develops around a dispute between two principal characters; in the first part of the play the dispute is set forth, in the second it is worked out and settled with a maximum of beatings, slapstick brawling, and general obscenity. Between these two main divisions of the play is the *parabasis,* or "coming forward" of the chorus. This long and often ridiculous choral passage serves as an entr'acte and often covers a change in scene and time.

It may be difficult for the modern student to understand how so free-speaking an art-form as Greek comedy could possibly have any religious connections, but it must be remembered that the Greek view of life fostered enjoyment of existence in all its aspects, provided a decent restraint were maintained. A major aspect of Dionysus himself was ecstasy and joy of life, and the comedies written as part of the festival in his honor not only express that joy but also serve as a sort of vicarious purgative of the so-called "baser emotions" of the audience.

Nor must it be thought that Greek comedy, for all its freedom of action, was composed of mere empty, noisy clowning. All of the plays of Aristophanes contained along with their foolery a great deal of extremely serious political or moral thought and used laughter as a weapon to destroy what the author considered to be social or intellectual abuses. The successors of Aristophanes were equally serious, if not so effective, in handling the problems of contemporary society. Under the spell of laughter, the Greek comedians struck at the most sacred aspects of life; it is a tribute to Greek freedom of speech and sense of humor that such caustic political critics as Aristophanes were never molested by the civil authorities. The Greeks were too healthy and resilient of mind to tolerate either a Gestapo or a Watch and Ward Society.

It is customary to divide the Attic comedy into three principal divisions according to its successive stages of growth. The Old Comedy, which flourished in the fifth century, consisted largely of political satire. In this school the leading writer was Aristophanes and from him we have the only complete Greek comedies preserved to the present time. The Middle Comedy, which developed a century later, apparently presented realistic, everyday problems such as those of marriage, moral or ethical choices, among others, much in the nature of most of our present-day comedies. Of this school, the leading writers were Antiphanes and Alexis, but none of their plays has survived. The last stage was reached in the third century with the New Comedy, an exaggerated satire of human foibles. The best exponents of this drama were Philemon and Menander, and from the few incomplete plays of the latter we can conclude that Greek comedy gradually outgrew its coarser and more slapstick aspects but in doing so lost much of its humor and fresh vitality.

IV. PRESENTATION OF GREEK DRAMA

We have seen that in early times the choral performances which anticipated the drama were given in public squares or on street corners without benefit of stage, seating arrangement, or any of the amenities of the modern theatre. It was not long, however, before more space was needed to accommodate the audience, and the presentations were moved from the city streets into the open fields. Here there was still no theatre structure as such, but one of the first "props" appeared in the *skene,* or tent, in which the actors dressed and before which, in a circle called the *orkestra,* they acted out their play. Because this *skene* interfered with vision, it was customary for the audience to gather in a semi-circle opposite the tent instead of in a circle surrounding the actors, as had been the previous custom. To improve the sight lines, it also became the custom to seat the spectators on the side of a hill from which they could look down upon the performance in comfort. From these developments, the next logical step was the building of a permanent theatre which preserved all the basic conventions of the *skene, orkestra,* and hillside semi-circular seating area. Presumably this permanent structure came about in the fifth century, though no trace of it remains. The famous Dionysiac theatre in Athens, still in a remarkably fine state of preservation, dates from the fourth century, though it may well have been a reconstruction of a less solid fifth century edifice. It is a safe assumption that the Dionysiac theatre is typical of the construction of other Greek theatres of the period.

In order to visualize the nature of the Dionysiac theatre, one need only think of a semi-circular football stadium holding 27,000 spectators flanking a playing field reduced to a 78-foot circle (see diagram). Opposite the spectators and behind the circle was a pillared structure, open at the back, with dressing rooms on either side. This was a practical development of the *skene* and served as a background for the action. The major part of the drama was played in the *orkestra* circle, around a small monument representing the altar of Dionysus. There was no raised stage in the Greek theatre; it was not until Roman times that this theatrical convention was instituted, though the Greeks had a sort of platform on wheels called the *ekkyklema* which was occasionally rolled out to represent an interior scene and served somewhat the same function as the inner stage of the

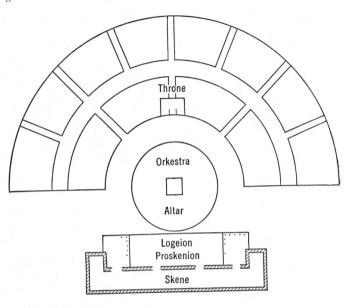

Elizabethan theatre. Apparently the *skene* offered some sort
of opportunity for scenery in the form of revolving, three-
sided prisms, and there were also trapdoors and machinery
for lowering actors from the upper part of the background
structure. Problems of acoustics and actor makeup were
partly solved by the use of the *persona,* a mask worn by the
actor and supposedly invented by Thespis. This mask not
only exaggerated the features sufficiently for them to be
distinguished a great distance from the *orkestra,* but it also
enlarged the voice by means of a small megaphone built
into the mouth. Presumably the actors doubling in secondary roles would indicate their change of character by
assuming a different mask. Incidentally these actors (called
hypokrites), along with the choristers, were subsidized and
trained by the state and were held in such esteem as to be

exempted from taxation and military service. No women appeared on the Greek stage; women's parts were apparently played by mature men and not by boys with unchanged voices as in Shakespeare's time.

The audience usually entered the theatre at daybreak and came prepared to stay until sundown. At first no admission charge was made, but later a very small fee was required. At least three tetralogies would be presented each day, and the audience worked off latent energy during the long day's proceedings by applauding or censuring the actors and throwing things—flowers or rocks as the occasion demanded—into the *orkestra*. Considering the religious nature of the gathering, the behavior of the Greek audience seems to us hardly reverent, but on the other hand, the Greeks would never have understood our church-going attitude of quiescent indulgence. Yet whatever their behavior, there was no question of the Athenian audience's encouragement of the theatre; between 480 and 380 they witnessed the premieres of more than two thousand plays—this with an annual theatrical season that lasted six days at most!

SUGGESTED READINGS

See end of Chapter 8 for suggested readings.

GREEK PHILOSOPHY
BEFORE SOCRATES

The word philosophy means literally "love of wisdom," and the philosopher, or "lover of wisdom," is generally seen as one who pursues truth in order (1) to understand the *nature* of man and his universe, (2) to determine man's *relation* to his universe, and (3) to discover the means whereby to live both wisely and well. The principal divisions of philosophy are:

(1) *Metaphysics,* or a study of man's relation to things beyond his experience, or to give it a more common interpretation, man's relation to God.

(2) *Physics,* or a study of the physical nature of the universe. Physics has now developed to a point where it is considered more of an "exact" science than a philosophy.

(3) *Ethics,* or man's relation to worldly experience and to his fellow men.

(4) *Politics,* or man's relation to the state.

I. THE MATERIALISTS

A. *The Milesian School*

Philosophical speculation of one sort or another is probably as old as man himself, but philosophy as a systematized type of intellectual endeavor is a relatively late development in history. The first "school" of Western philosophy evolved in the sixth century B.C. in the prosperous and highly civilized city of Miletus in Ionian Greece. The Milesians were the first of a long line of "hylozoic" or materialist philosophers. Their principal concern was with the nature of matter and, in attempting to determine the basic stuff of the universe, their speculations ranged from the absurd to the startlingly modern. Unfortunately, practically none of their work exists in its original form, and what we know of these earliest philosophers is gained largely from commentaries by later writers. Too often, also, we know only *what* these men believed without knowing the line of reasoning by which they reached their conclusions.

Milesian Philosophers

Thales (c. 640-546 B.C.) is considered to have been the founder of the Milesian school and the father of Western philosophy, although no work of his remains and it is not even known whether or not he wrote down any of his thoughts. From Aristotle we know that Thales believed that water was the basic universal stuff, that the earth floats upon water, and that all things are full of gods and thus have a soul, or living principle.

More interesting and imaginative than Thales was his pupil **Anaximander** (c. 611-547 B.C.), who rejected the water theory of his master and postulated that the basic universal material was an intangible element he called the *apeiron,* or "boundless," a common denominator from which all tangible materials are extracted and into which they ultimately return. Even the celestial bodies as we see them are not constant, but are merely off-shoots of larger galaxies. This concept of the plurality of worlds is amazingly modern and quite contrary to the usual philosophical thought of the ancient world. Anaximander, furthermore, foreshadowed evolutionary ideas in declaring that all life arose from water, altering its form and developing species in adapting itself to changes in environment. He also believed the earth to be a cylindrical, rotating object suspended in the vortex of the *apeiron*.

The third important Milesian philosopher, **Anaximenes** (fl. 6th century), was a pupil of Anaximander and a teacher of philosophy in the last half of the sixth century. He differed from both his predecessors in declaring *aether*, atmosphere (air and vapor), to be the world stuff, and based his conclusion presumably on the constitution of breath. Not only are all things dependent upon this element for life, but also it is mutable and can assume the form of gas, liquid, or solid under different conditions, thus being the potential basis for all matter. He held that the world was flat and that the heavenly bodies were produced by moisture rising from its surface and assuming solidity in the superheated, rarefied atmosphere aloft.

At the end of the sixth century, Ionia fell to the Persians and much of her culture was destroyed by the invaders. After Anaximenes, Miletus produced no philosophy, and for further developments in materialistic thought we must turn to other parts of the Hellenic area.

B. *"Dynamic" Philosophy: Heraclitus*

The hylozoic thinkers who followed the Milesians were largely concerned with the problem of change in the nature of matter rather than in the constitution of matter itself. The Milesians had glibly postulated the possibility of all sorts of material transformation of a basic world stuff, but later philosophers began to wonder whether or not things could really change their apparent substance and still remain the same basic element as before. Does the water which causes the seed to grow remain water in the mature plant? Is the gas that condenses into moisture still a gas or has it become something else?

To these questions **Heraclitus** (fl. 500 B.C.), an aristocratic Ephesian, answered simply that, despite appearances, "all things are one," that a common substance formed the base of even the most apparent opposites of existence. So far he was in agreement with the Milesians, but from this point he departed sharply from his predecessors. "All things are in flux," he declared. Things never are; rather, they are always *becoming* and never reach a point of rest or equilibrium. This "becoming" principle causes all things to be restless, transitory, constantly changing in form or substance. In his most famous analogy, Heraclitus pointed out that one cannot step into the same river twice, for its waters are always changing, and man himself is undergoing constant transformation and is never exactly the same person he was an instant before. Therefore, nothing really *is, was,* or *will be* unless man, by some unlikely miracle, can apply a stopwatch principle to the universe; rather all is merely a history of past forms and an indefinite future potentiality in the universal process of *becoming*.

To satisfy this view of the universe, Heraclitus decided that the common denominator of all this change must be not water, *aether,* or the *apeiron,* but rather fire, which produces both heat and light through the process of change. He further felt that this change was no chance happening, but followed a regular logical order at least theoretically understandable and predictable through the application of reason. He therefore had no use for mystical or ceremonial religion and regarded the writings of Homer and Hesiod as mere trash contrary to the rational processes of man.

C. *"Static" Philosophy: The Eleatics*

Contrary to Heraclitus, the Eleatic philosophers (so called because they flourished around Elea in southern Italy) believed change to be impossible.

Parmenides (fl. 550 B.C.), the leader of the school, argued that a thing cannot be itself and something else at the same time; either it is the one or the other, with no middle ground of "becoming." The real world, he felt, must be one homogeneous and illimitable substance, without mutation, variety, or change. If our senses tell us to the contrary, then our senses are wrong and do not reflect true reality. This distinction between the real and the perceived, with its emphasis upon the existence of truth beyond human perception, is interesting because of its foreshadowing of Platonic idealism, in which Plato makes the same distinction between the true and the apparent in the realm of ideas as does Parmenides in the field of materialism.

Later Eleatics were **Zeno of Elea** (fl. 475 B.C.), famous for his dialectical paradoxes, and **Melissus of Samos** (fl. 5th century), who added nothing essential to the argument of Parmenides, but who defended his doctrines eloquently against the compromising efforts of the Pluralists.[1]

D. *The Pluralists*

Between the exactly opposite poles of Heraclitan and Eleatic thought stood the Pluralists, who flourished in the middle of the fifth century and whose views were particularly interesting in their introduction of the atomic theory of matter.

The first of these philosophers was **Empedocles** (c. 500-430 B.C.), a Sicilian who separated all matter into the four elements of Earth, Air, Fire, and Water. These elements are

[1] Zeno of Elea must not be confused with Zeno (336-264 B.C.), the founder of the Stoic school of philosophy.

in themselves homogeneous and indestructible, but are capable of being combined in a multitude of more or less temporary forms. Thus substance and form, as we perceive them, are merely transitory blendings of the basic elements, which themselves are immutable. In this way Empedocles accounted for the factor of change without rejecting the Eleatic doctrine of a fundamentally solid and homogeneous universe. As to the agent which causes these elements to combine in an infinity of forms, Empedocles was less materialistic. He postulated that the universe was constantly being swept by the antagonistic forces of Love and Strife and that the alternation of these forces in varying degrees of intensity caused the mingling of the four basic elements.

The next development in Pluralistic thinking came with **Anaxagoras** (c. 500-428 B.C.), a native of Smyrna who spent most of his mature life in Athens as a close friend of Pericles. Anaxagoras rejected Empedocles' theory of the four elements as being too arbitrary and instead argued that all matter was made up of "seeds," each one of which contained the essence of all others but in each one of which some quality predominated over the rest. Thus, all matter is basically the same but assumes widely differing qualities through the combination of seeds, which themselves are far from homogeneous. These seeds, of course, are too small to be perceived by the senses, and thus Anaxagoras partly agreed with the Eleatics in assuming that the senses are limited and incapable of arriving at the basic material truth. At the same time, he went far in preparing the way for the atomic theory of matter developed a generation later by **Leucippus** (fl. 5th century) and **Democritus** (c. 460-362 B.C.).

Leucippus and Democritus were teacher and pupil whose views coincided so exactly that it is impossible to separate their thoughts. Together these philosophers, of whose lives we know practically nothing, attained a fame second only to that of Aristotle in the ancient world and made the greatest contribution of all the pluralistic efforts to reconcile the opposition of Heraclitan and Eleatic thought. Like the Eleatics, Leucippus and Democritus believed that the basic universal stuff was uncreated, immutable, and indestructible and that, reduced to its lowest terms, all material in the universe must become one homogeneous substance. However, they further agreed with the Pluralistic predecessors in holding that within the framework of this Eleatic universe, combinations of matter were constantly occurring through the fluctuation of imperceptibly small particles. These particles Leucippus and Democritus called atoms and postulated that, unlike the "seeds" of Anaxagoras, atoms were indivisible units of basic matter.

They further departed from their forerunners in stating that the universe is not "full," but that empty space exists in which these atoms fluctuate in constant motion. This incessant motion, moreover, is not purposeless or chaotic but rather follows a regular, if inscrutable, design. "Naught happens for nothing," Democritus said, "but everything from a ground and of necessity." In thus postulating motion and design as basic phenomena of the universe, Leucippus and Democritus established two important hypotheses of modern science. On the other hand, their conception of the atom as solid and indivisible is, of course, false and further from modern thought than is the qualitatively varying "seed" theory of Anaxagoras.

II. THE MYSTICS: PYTHAGORAS

While the Materialists from Thales to Democritus were attempting to understand the universe through an analysis of the matter composing it, other philosophers were approaching the same problem through mystical nonmaterial means. The most important of these was **Pythagoras** (c. 582-507 B.C.), a native of Samos and pupil of Anaximander who migrated to southern Italy about 530 and founded a monastic society based upon the Orphic mysteries. The Pythagorean order proliferated throughout Italy and later in Greece, whence many of its members had fled in the middle of the fifth century after serious political disturbances in Italy had made their stay there untenable. Many Greeks joined the society, and Pythagorean thought became a very influential factor in the intellectual temper of fifth-century Athens.

The Pythagoreans believed in reincarnation and sought to purify the soul to attain a nobler rebirth in the life to come (see p. 65). This purification, they believed, could be sought not only through good deeds but also through a study of the universe and a comprehension of its order and beauty. For this reason, they turned to mathematics as the key to the "music of the spheres." All things, they felt, could be explained through numbers, which are merely the symbols of the spatial and even moral qualities of the universe. They apparently arrived at this belief through observing the many numerical evidences in nature: seven stars in the large and small dipper and Pleiades, seven openings in the human head, seven mouths of the river Nile, and so forth. Infinite elaborations on the cosmic meanings of such number symbolism were worked out by the followers of Pythagoreanism, and though the system was not particularly influential on Greek thought, it became highly significant later during the Middle Ages. More important at the time were the Pythagorean contributions in pure mathematics, astronomy, and music, as well as in the mystical doctrine of reincarnation which was so important a factor in evolving Plato's ideas on the immortality of the soul.

III. PRAGMATISM: THE SOPHISTS

In sharp contrast to the mysticism of the Pythagoreans was the down-to-earth rationalism of the Sophists. With the rise of Athenian political importance in the fifth century came an attendant rise in practicality at the expense of experimentation and speculation. With greatness thrust upon her, Athens found herself the leader of the Greek world, with all the responsibilities and dangers attendant upon that position of supremacy. The magnitude of this task of leadership was frightening to many an Athenian, whose life heretofore had been rather simple, provincial, and even isolationist. To prepare himself for his new task as a responsible citizen in a rapidly expanding world, he undertook considerable special education, including instruction in the arts of practical politics.

Accordingly, there developed in Athens a group of men, many of them foreigners, who made their living by teaching the practical arts of rhetoric, including public speaking, exposition, and argumentation. These teachers, who were half-derisively called "Sophists" ("wise-guys" is the nearest translation of the term) were sometimes distinguished and conscientious men, but far more often were merely catchpenny opportunists who catered willingly to their pupils' most vulgar desires for personal advancement and showy notoriety. In teaching debate, for example, they were less careful of seeking truth than they were of seeking victory; in matters of metaphysics they were rather prone to distrust or pass over any speculation which transcended the world of the senses; their position in relation to the universe is shown in the remark of one of their number, **Protagoras** (c. 481-411 B.C.) that "man is the measure of all things." In questions of ethics they tended to favor the view that good was what one could legally get away with, and that in any case virtue was a relative matter. Before long sophistry and

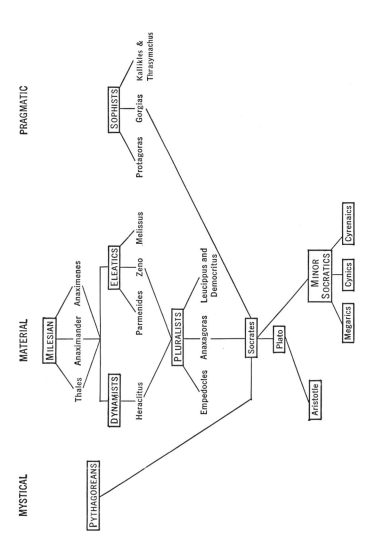

MYSTICAL MATERIAL PRAGMATIC

scoundrelism became almost synonymous terms in the minds of even those Athenians who employed Sophist teachers to aid their own personal advancement, and the utterly false association of Socrates with the Sophists in the minds of the Athenians probably contributed to the public opinion against him which brought about his execution.[2]

In all fairness, however, it must be admitted that many Sophists, such as Protagoras, were honest, conscientious men in no way to be blamed for the intellectual scoundrelism which attached itself to what was originally intended to be merely necessary instruction in the practical art of making friends and influencing people. Furthermore, the Sophists placed a salutary emphasis upon the development of the powers of reason and stimulated their pupils to develop intellectual flexibility through subjecting them to the "question and answer" type of discourse. In this form of instruction, the pupils were expected to state and develop a rational, convincing argument in the face of a barrage of leading and often shattering questions from their more experienced instructor. This method of teaching was also used by Socrates, although he rejected the Sophist interest in the worldly and the "practical"; the Socratic method was developed throughout the ensuing centuries into a highly important basic technique in the educational process.

[2] This association was brought about largely through Aristophanes' popular comedy *The Clouds,* which hilariously but quite viciously attacked Socrates as a Sophist and a quack.

SUGGESTED READINGS

(Because of the broad chronological scope of this volume, the authors have been forced to omit mention of purely literary works or studies of individual authors from the list of suggested readings. To have included even the most important volumes in these categories would have been to increase the size of the book beyond all practical proportions. Place of publication, when not mentioned, is New York.)

GENERAL

M. Arnold, "Hebraism and Hellenism" in *Culture and Anarchy* (1902); K. B. Avery, *The New Century Classical Handbook* (1962); P. Devambez et al., *The Praeger Encyclopedia of Ancient Greek Civilization* (1967); G. L. Dickenson, *The Greek Way of Life* (1931); W. Durant, *The Life of Greece* (1939); W. W. Jaeger, *Paideia: The Ideals of Greek Culture* (3 v, 1939-1945); H. D. F. Kitto, *The Greeks* (Harmondsworth, 1951); R. W. Livingston, *The Greek Genius and Its Meaning to Us* (Oxford, 1912); R. W. Livingston (ed.), *The Legacy of Greece* (Oxford, 1924); W. W. Tarn, *Hellenistic Civilization* (1961); A. J. Toynbee, *Greek Civilization and Character* (London, 1924); L. Van Hook, *Greek Life and Thought* (1930); N. P. Vlachos, *Hellas and Hellenism* (Boston, 1936); L. Whibley (ed.), *A Companion to Greek Studies* (Cambridge, 1931).

HISTORY

S. Barr, *The Will of Zeus* (1961); G. W. Botsford and C. A. Robinson, Jr., *Hellenic History* (1939); J. B. Bury, *A History of Greece* (1931); John Chadwick, *The Decipherment of Linear B* (Cambridge, 1958); M. I. Finley, *The Greek Historian* (London, 1959); C. A. Fyffe, *History of Greece* (London, 1938); Leonard B. Palmer, *Myceneans and Minoans: Aegean Prehistory in the Light of the Linear B Tablets* (1962); C. A. Robinson, *Zito Hellas* (London, 1946); M. Rostovzeff, *A History of the Ancient World* (2 v, Oxford, 1928-1930); C. G. Starr, *The Origins of Greek Civilization 1100-650 B.C.* (1961).

LITERATURE

M. Bieber, *History of the Greek and Roman Theatre* (Princeton, 1961); C. M. Bowra, *Ancient Greek Literature* (London, 1933);

L. Feder, *Crowell's Handbook of Classical Literature* (1961); H. N. Fowler, *A History of Ancient Greek Literature* (1923); M. Hadas, *A History of Greek Literature* (1950); A. E. Haigh, *The Attic Theatre* (Oxford, 1907); E. Hamilton, *The Great Age of Greek Literature* (1942); P. Harsh, *A Handbook of Classical Drama* (Palo Alto, 1944); Sir Philip Harvey, *The Oxford Companion to Classical Literature* (Oxford, 1937); G. Murray, *A History of Ancient Greek Literature* (1932); G. Murray, *The Rise of the Greek Epic* (1934); G. Norwood, *Greek Comedy* (Boston, 1932); G. Norwood, *Greek Tragedy* (Boston, 1932); G. Norwood, *The Writers of Greece* (London, 1935); H. J. Rose, *A Handbook of Greek Literature* (London, 1934); J. A. Symonds, *Studies of the Greek Poets* (London, 1920); W. C. Wright, *A Short History of Greek Literature* (1907).

MYTHOLOGY AND RELIGION

T. Bulfinch, *Mythology* (Modern Library reprint, n. d.); F. M. Cornford, *From Religion to Philosophy* (1912); F. M. Cornford, *Greek Religious Thought from Homer to the Age of Alexander* (London, 1923); F. Cumont, *Astrology and Religion among the Greeks and Romans* (1960); Sir James Frazer, *The Golden Bough* (1922); W. C. Guthrie, *The Greeks and Their Gods* (Boston, 1951); E. Hamilton, *Mythology* (1942); J. E. Harrison, *Epilegomena to the Study of Greek Religion* (Cambridge, 1921); J. E. Harrison, *Prolegomena to the Study of Greek Religion* (Cambridge, 1922); J. E. Harrison, *The Religion of Ancient Greece* (London, 1905); J. E. Harrison, *Themis: A Study of the Social Origins of Greek Religion* (Cambridge, 1912); W. W. Hyde, *Greek Religion and Its Survivals* (Boston, 1923); C. H. Moore, *The Religious Thought of the Greeks* (Cambridge, Mass., 1925); G. Murray, *Five Stages of Greek Religion* (1955); G. Murray, *Four Stages of Greek Religion* (1912); M. P. Nilsson, *Greek Folk Religion* (1961); M. P. Nilsson, *Greek Popular Religion* (1940); M. P. Nilsson, *A History of Greek Religion* (Oxford, 1949); H. J. Rose, *Ancient Greek Religion* (London, 1948); G. Schwab. *Gods and Heroes* (1946).

PHILOSOPHY

C. Bakewell, *Source Book in Ancient Philosophy* (1909); F. M. Cornford, *From Religion to Philosophy* (1957); B. A. G. Fuller, *History of Greek Philosophy* (3 v, 1922-1931); W. K. C. Guthrie,

Greek Philosophers (1960); T. A. Sinclair, *History of Greek Political Thought* (London, 1961); E. Zeller, *Outlines of the History of Greek Philosophy* (1931).

POLITICAL, ECONOMIC, SOCIAL LIFE

G. M. Calhoun, *The Business Life of Ancient Athens* (Chicago, 1926); V. G. Childe, *The Dawn of European Civilization* (6th ed., 1958); V. Ehrenberg, *The Greek State* (1960); R. Flacelière, *Love in Ancient Greece* (1962); J. B. Gittler, *Social Thought among the Early Greeks* (Athens, Ga., 1941); B. E. Hammond, *The Political Institutions of the Ancient Greeks* (London, 1895); Sir John P. Mahaffy, *Social Life in Greece from Homer to Menander* (London, 1925); H. Michell, *The Economics of Ancient Greece* (1940); New York Metropolitan Museum of Art, *The Daily Life of the Greeks and the Romans* (1933); M. C. Quenell, *Everyday Things in Archaic Greece* (London, 1931); C. E. Robinson, *Everyday Life in Ancient Greece* (Oxford, 1933); M. Rostovzeff, *The Social and Economic History of the Hellenistic World* (Oxford, 1941); G. D. Thompson, *Studies in Ancient Greek Society* (London, 1949); M. O. Wason, *Class Struggles in Ancient Greece* (London, 1947); M. O. Wason, *The Greek Political Experience: Studies in Honor of W. K. Prentice* (Princeton, 1941).

chapter 9

THE ROMAN SPIRIT

I. THE ROMAN TRINITY: DUTY, DISCIPLINE, ACHIEVEMENT

While Greece was undergoing its slow, tragic decline, another nation to the west was awkwardly but impressively lifting itself by its bootstraps. In Italy the Romans, having brought the entire peninsula under their firm domination, were restlessly seeking to extend their sway over the entire Mediterranean by means of an unremitting program of foreign conquest and enlightened colonialism. So successful was this program that within the span of a few centuries all of Europe south of the Rhine and the Danube, England, North Africa, and all those Asiatic territories touching on the Black Sea and the Mediterranean were to be incorporated into the magnificent Roman Empire, the greatest political wonder in the history of the world. Needless to say, Greece was an early victim to the new conquerors. Like the prey of a hungry python, she was swallowed whole—slowly, quietly, but with cold, inevitable efficiency. That she proved to be a nourishing meal, however, is evidenced by the eagerness with which the Romans tried to adopt Greek modes of living and to imitate Greek arts.

It is customary for professors to combine the Greek and Roman civilizations into a common culture known as Classicism. In a sense, this is a misleading practice, a mixing of oil and water. For while the Romans did try valiantly to imitate Greek ways, their pose fitted them as gracelessly as the hired finery of a provincial bridegroom. At worst, their pretensions to Attic intellectual refinement were only an ostentatious way of asserting their cultural equality with the Greeks; at best, they were sincere and inspired imitations. The contributions of Rome to the growth of the Western world were many and wonderful, to be sure, but they were *Roman,* not Greek. The Romans had their own individuality; they breathed their own atmosphere and diffused their own spirit. It is true that that spirit was not so exalted as that of the Greeks, that it suggests prose rather than the poetry of their Hellenic predecessors. But if prose it were, it was a good, solid prose, rich in its way, impressive, and worthy of attention in its own right.

Before beginning to analyze certain predominant aspects of the Roman spirit, it would be well once more to warn the reader that such a procedure will, at best, produce only the broadest generalizations. There were many Romes, historically, culturally, socially, geographically. Any attempt to choose a few universally applicable adjectives to describe a culture that covered most of the civilized world and that went through all of the social stages from stone-hut barbarism to decadent luxury would require more temerity than skill. The best one can do in a limited space is to single out a few leading qualities that manifested themselves in the arts, in politics, and in the social and economic existence of the more cultivated Romans during their best years, those of the late Republic and early Empire.

The surest approach to an understanding of Rome is the moral one. It might seem paradoxical at first that a nation of conquerors, notorious in the popular mind for its luxury and its vices, could be assayed most effectively through the medium of morality, but even a cursory examination of Roman life will confirm the fact that Rome was essentially a *dedicated* nation, devoted unswervingly to higher laws of conduct and striving conscientiously for the greater glory of the race. Even in the days of the Empire, when the achieving of great power and wealth unquestionably weakened the capacity of her leaders for energetic action, Rome never lost that sense of dedication, that mystical devotion to the State and to its divinely appointed destiny. Following the moral approach, then, we discover that the inner life of Rome may be categorized into three abstractions: Duty, Discipline, and Achievement. From the legendary founding of the city to the final destructive triumph of the Goths, this trinity never ceased to exercise its functions as the conscience of Rome and the element of idealism in its conduct of life.

A. *Duty.*

From their earliest beginnings, the Romans had conceived of man as a subordinate being, subject to higher forces and bound by those forces to an absolute compliance with moral laws. As we shall see in a later chapter, they believed in a multitude of deities—greater and lesser spirits which were assigned to every phase of daily living. Any one of these deities could make life unpleasant for the transgressor; all of them had to be propitiated regularly according to established ceremonies. Under such conditions, it was unlikely that any Roman could forget for long that he was only a man, a lesser creature in a universe filled with higher spirits and governed by rigid moral laws. But despite his subordinate position, he never looked upon himself self-pityingly as a victim of circumstance. Rather he proudly felt himself to be an instrument of the gods, the means through which they asserted their powers to minister to the comfort and welfare of man in general and of the Roman race in particular. Thus he willingly assumed his obligations, realizing that through divine guidance he was doing his part in actively carrying out the desires of the higher powers for the improvement of humanity. Never did this subservience to the higher will seem to be a humiliation, a burden, or a punishment. No man, he felt, could be a law unto himself, but with the help of the gods, he could rule the world. And through his deep-seated, long-developed sense of duty, the Roman developed qualities of mind, body, and spirit which, for a time at least, made his nation in fact the ruler of the world.

B. *Discipline.*

As a logical consequence of this sense of duty, Roman life is characterized by a spirit of discipline remarkable for its efficiency, for its reasonableness, and for the loyalty it inspired in its people. Rome was no Sparta; although sometimes cruel to slaves and captives of war, it was seldom oppressive or harsh to its citizens or to the general population of conquered countries. It permitted wide freedom of thought and expression even in political matters, was tolerant of all forms of worship that were not seditious or openly immoral, and was extremely generous in granting the precious gift of citizenship to persons in territories incorporated within the Roman State. It respected the family as a unit and permitted most of the upbringing and education of children to be carried on within the home. Beyond the custom of universal military service, there was no attempt made to transform the individual into a Spartan-like robot, an unthinking military machine existing entirely for the service of the State. And finally, there was no objection made to each individual's advancing himself economically, politically, and sometimes even socially, as far as his abilities would permit.

The Roman government could afford to be liberal in granting these privileges because it knew that it could count upon the centuries-old tradition of devotion to duty to supply most of the compensating discipline. It was well known that most Romans began to learn self-control in the cradle, that they were accustomed to accept authority from infancy, and that they had absorbed the lessons of patriotism and the glory of Rome with the very air they breathed. The government accepted implicitly the Roman tradition of respect for authority and expected nothing less than complete obedience from its people. Woe unto the individual who expected to share the benefits of Roman citizenship without accepting its responsibilities!

Altogether, the position of the Roman State was that of the stern parent. It was fair, tolerant, even enlightened in its relations with its children, but it was also unyielding in its demands for respect and total obedience. It did not terrorize, but it did punish transgressors with stern and relentless justice. It exacted much in the way of service, but it granted much in return. That its exactions were not considered excessive is seen reflected in the genuine patriotism of its subjects and in the open admiration of other nations. Throughout the Classical world, Roman citizenship was universally considered to be the greatest single privilege attainable by any man.

It was not from the State alone, however, that the Roman derived his sense of authority. As we have already seen, he was supremely conscious of his obligations to his many gods. In addition, he was trained in childhood to accept the strict rule of his father and to bow to that rule so long as his parent lived. He was taught from the cradle to put the interests of the family ahead of his own interests and to obtain the approval of the family council before taking any definitive step. His education, his career, his marriage, the naming of his children, even the selection of a vocation for his sons—all were matters for family deliberation. He accepted these restrictions willingly because he knew no different system. Nor would maturity have brought any desire to rebel against custom, for his reason would then have convinced him of his mistake. He would have seen the family as the microcosm of the State and would have bowed within his own home to that desire for order and efficiency that he had come to expect of society in general.

Beyond the authority of the gods, the State, and the family, the Roman also readily accepted the strictures of public opinion. By nature he was a conformist, anxious not to appear too different from other members of his class, fearful of being considered a maverick in the well-ordered herd. He lived, dressed, and thought in pretty much the same manner as his fellows and sought the security of group approval no less eagerly, although with considerably more dignity, than did George F. Babbitt of Floral Heights, Zenith. But while he might have resembled Sinclair Lewis's famous caricature in his social standardization, he differed radically from him in having a well-defined scale of moral values which he tried to cultivate as assiduously as a Benjamin Franklin or a Jonathan Edwards. His catalog of virtues included piety, responsibility, firmness of purpose, industry, manliness, frugality, and courtesy toward others. The ideal Roman sought also to acquire social graces and to offset excessive seriousness by cultivating a sense of humor, but at the same time he avoided the trifling, unstable, or cynical attitudes sometimes fostered by overrefinement. In his pursuit of these qualities, he was often dull and stodgy, but seldom flaccid or indifferent. The Roman character rarely sparkled, but at its best had a vitality and purposefulness that commanded attention and respect. It is this quality of *gravitas*, or moral earnestness, that formed the cornerstone of Roman society. When it was lost, as in the luxurious days of the Empire, the life of the

State went with it, and the gates of Rome were opened to the coming of the Goths.

C. *Achievement.*

Needless to say, the Romans did not live in a mystical vacuum in which they mildly accepted discipline while contemplating their duty to society. Like the Greeks, the Romans could see little sense in establishing means without an end; a devotion to ideals was understandable only so long as that devotion led to some definite conclusion. With the Greeks, however, an intellectual conclusion, in many cases, would have sufficed, but the Romans, being less given to abstract speculation than their predecessors, preferred their results to be of a more tangible nature. To the Greeks, a principle was a finished product; to the Romans it was only a tool to be employed in creating a practical good. Thus the Roman had little use for the dreamer, the idealist, or the intellectual gymnast. To such persons, his reaction would probably be: "Come down out of the clouds. Let's get down to brass tacks." It would probably be an exaggeration to state that the Roman spirit was anti-intellectual, but it would not be excessive to characterize it as being essentially pragmatic.

As a result, his creative instincts found fulfillment in the realm of the useful. He was a superb architect; his buildings, bridges, aqueducts, and public stadia were both functional and beautiful to behold. His cities and parks were magnificently planned, and he travelled on roads that were well paved, graded, and landscaped. His homes were equipped with comforts which, though meagre against those of today, were the wonder and envy of the ancient world.

The Roman was also an organizer par excellence. His institutions were run with great efficiency—his army, his government bureaus, his courts of law. With a minimum of speculation and fuss, he created a society that *worked,* that was a work of art in its way, that testified to the great ability of the Roman mind to adapt principles toward useful ends. Most of these principles, it is true, had been discovered elsewhere—in Egypt, Greece, Carthage, or more remotely in Asia—but none of them had been developed fully before Roman times. Edith Hamilton is on firm ground when she states that "in Rome, the true artist was the engineer." [1]

Unfortunately, this practicality contained within itself an inherent weakness in that it fostered a materialistic approach to life that eventually caused the breakdown of traditional Roman morality. In a sense, the very success of Roman ideals proved to be the reason for their ultimate failure. Conquest brought wealth, and Roman engineering brought comforts. Fabulous fortunes were made, and the gap between rich and poor became so great as to demoralize and ultimately unbalance even so well-disciplined a society as that of Rome. By the time of the Empire, purely monetary standards had to a large extent superseded moral principles in the scale of values. The poet Horace constantly jibed at the cupidity of the wealthy and asserted that Pecunia (Queen Money), not Augustus, was the true ruler of Rome. And Augustus himself, concerned by the materialism of his people, constantly strove to re-establish "the old morality" in their hearts and in their manner of living. But warnings and exhortations were of no more than moderate effectiveness. Practical-minded Rome was still not practical enough to attain the *sophrosyné* which guided the Greeks, and not even the Roman discipline and sense of duty could withstand forever the temptations provided by continued material success. When Rome eventually fell, its fall was as surely due to its own decadent materialism as it was to the sacking of its cities by the Goths.

[1] Edith Hamilton, *The Roman Way* (1932).

II. THE INTELLECTUAL INFLUENCE

Not least among the many reasons for Roman greatness was the ability of Rome to learn from others. Though proud of their own heritage, the Romans were far from smug concerning their institutions and customs. They were ever on the lookout for ideas and practices which would be useful to their own manner of living, and when they conquered a country, they picked its brains as systematically as they evaluated and annexed its physical wealth. Never noted for their originality, they imported most of their ideas and theories and then applied to these borrowed materials their own peculiar gift for practical development. This eclectic process of borrowing the best from other cultures is nowhere more noticeable in Roman civilization than in matters pertaining to the intellect. In education, in philosophy, in the arts, they originated little or nothing, and yet these learned activities flourished in Rome. In fact, had it not been for Roman enthusiasm for the culture of other nations, much of that culture would have been lost to the modern world, for a great deal of what we know today about the intellectual achievements of pre-Latin civilizations derives solely from Roman copies, adaptations, or translations of their works.

The richest source of artistic and intellectual material was, of course, Hellenism. It has often been remarked that, while Roman armies conquered Greece, it was Greek learning that finally conquered Rome. While this remark is more pat than accurate, it is nevertheless true that Romans fastened eagerly upon Greek culture, imported Greek teachers and poets, sent their youths to Athens to complete their education, and used Greek poetry, philosophy, drama, religion, painting, and sculpture as models for their own intellectual and spiritual life. Long before they incorporated the entire Hellenic territory into the Roman Republic (146 B.C.), they had begun to learn from the Greeks. It was from the Greek colony at Cumae in southern Italy that, back in the eighth century B.C., they first became acquainted with the alphabet, and their connection with Hellenism never ceased from that time on. Though their awareness of the greatest works of the Periclean age was postponed until the middle of the third century B.C., when receding tides of taste and the sea-change from Greek to Latin had somewhat vulgarized those sublime productions, they nevertheless took the ancient texts as their models and accepted their forms, their techniques, and their standards for artistic imitation. Never for a moment did it occur to them that the introspective, sophisticated refinements of Greek creative art were hardly appropriate materials from which to fashion the true expression of the forthright, practical, rough-and-ready Roman spirit. They knew that their imported culture was good, and cared no more whether it was appropriate than did those nineteenth-century American industrialists who imported ancient Gothic castles for their estates in Illinois and California.

Altogether, then, the greatness of Rome did not lie in her intellect. As careful custodian and transmitter of the works of the ancients, she deserves the gratitude of posterity, but her own contributions to the arts, while often excellent (and in the cases of Horace and Virgil even great), were at best imitative and a little self-conscious. The highest heritage of Rome is found rather in its heart than in its head: in its patriotism, its pride in the Roman race, its belief in its own destiny. From these qualities developed the discipline, the love of order and justice, the sense of civic responsibility, and the practical resourcefulness that made Rome the political and social mentor of the Western world.

SUGGESTED READINGS

See end of Chapter 11 for suggested readings.

chapter 10

ROMAN HISTORY

I. RACIAL BACKGROUNDS

Civilization came later to Italy than to Greece and developed much more slowly in the central Mediterranean than it had in the Aegean area. The reason for this lay more in the simple phenomenon of time-lag than in any intrinsic superiority of the Hellenic peninsula for colonization or economic development. Like Greece, Italy enjoys a warm climate suitable for year-round cultivation of crops in the south; it also possesses a range of weather conditions over its 800-mile length that permits a healthy agricultural diversification. Furthermore, Italy has the advantage of being considerably larger than Greece and of having a somewhat larger proportion of arable land. But since the waves of migration into the Mediterranean came from the east, it is only natural that the development of the Italian peninsula should have been delayed until the territories closer to the sources of migration had been well settled.

The first inhabitants of Italy came from North Africa about 3000 B.C. and were a very primitive people who left few monuments of their civilization beyond some crude stone weapons and tools which indicated that they had been largely a farming race with some knowledge of pottery and weaving. A thousand years later, traders from Crete and other parts of the eastern Mediterranean reached the peninsula. Much later, probably after 1000 B.C., Greek adventurers began to penetrate Italian territory, and eventually some of them founded colonies in the southern portion of the area.

Meanwhile in the north, after 1800 B.C., Indo-European tribes of an origin probably similar to that of the early Hellenic invaders began to arrive and gradually to work their way down into the Adriatic. The most important of these were the Italians, composed of three tribes: the Umbrians, the Samnites, and the Latins. The last settled into the central lowlands and were the immediate forerunners of the early Romans.

The most powerful early ethnic element in Italy, however, was the Etruscan. The Etruscans, or Tuscans, who gave their name to the areas they settled, arrived from the east about 800 B.C. They subjected most of central Italy and within two centuries developed a civilization of considerable stability and military power. They conquered Rome, the principal city of the Latins, in the sixth century and ruled over it for a hundred years or more. Eventually they were driven out by the Latins, but not before they had done much to organize the territory and to develop some of the basic institutions of subsequent Roman government.

Contact with other cultures, and particularly those of the more civilized East, did much to enable the early Romans to emerge from barbarism. The presence in Italy of mutual rivalries among tribes of varying ethnic origins probably eliminated the weaker peoples and prevented even the strongest from falling into a state of contented security and ultimate stagnation. Latin civilization, like that of Greece, is largely the result of the combination of vigorous Indo-European strains with the more advanced cultures, especially those of the Etruscans, the Phoenicians, and the Greeks. Ethnologically speaking, many—if not all—roads lead to Rome.

II. THE EARLY ROMAN REPUBLIC (509-146 B.C.)

Livy's monumental history, *From the Founding of the City,* gives 735 B.C. as the date of the founding of Rome, but in reality some sort of settlement had existed on the seven hills since about 1000 B.C. The strategic location of the city at a good spot for crossing the Tiber made it of considerable economic importance and from the beginning encouraged its development as a military power. From 655 to 509 B.C., however, Rome was in subjection to the Etruscans and was ruled by a single Etruscan dynasty, the Tarquins. But in 509, thanks to an alliance among the various Latin cities, the Etruscans were defeated and driven from Rome. A Roman republic based upon the regular election of two consuls was set up, and from its inception this republic dominated the affairs of virtually the entire peninsula. Neighboring Latin cities were early incorporated into the Roman sphere, and in a little more than a century the Etruscans and the Samnites were also defeated once and for all. In 390 B.C. a dangerous invasion of Celtic peoples, the Gauls, was repulsed decisively, and by 265 the Greek colonies in southern Italy had been annexed and the entire peninsula was effectively incorporated under Roman rule.

Across the Mediterranean, the wealthy city of Carthage, which had been established by the Phoenicians as a trading post, offered the chief obstacle to Rome's ultimate control of the Mediterranean world. The first Carthaginian or Punic War (264-241 B.C.) forced Carthage to cede the island of Sicily to Rome. The second Punic War, which ended in 201 B.C., was waged against Carthaginian possessions in Spain and concluded with the addition of Spain as a

Roman province. Between the second and third Punic Wars, a long series of campaigns in the East included the conquest of Macedonian Greece. Some respect for Greek learning and character kept the Romans from treating Greece like the other conquered provinces. The government was left largely in the hands of Greeks, and a minimum of tribute was exacted. Finally, a third Punic War (149-146 B.C.) destroyed Carthage and added the province of Africa, making Rome a world empire.

III. GOVERNMENT OF THE EARLY REPUBLIC

The original government of the early Romans was probably an oligarchy which soon gave way to a limited monarchy in which the king was advised by a council or senate of the Patricians (the Fathers), who were the heads of the wealthiest and oldest families. Religion was a function of the state, with the king as its head and the Patricians as priests. The strong cohesiveness of the Roman family appears also to have had its origins in these early days when the father was supreme dictator over his wife, children, and slaves. The distinctive Roman character, made up of a combination of courage, loyalty, patriotism, and enjoyment of cruelty combined with stoic endurance, became the basis of a state where the military predominated over a population of farmers and, later, artisans and tradesmen.

After the founding of the Republic in 509 B.C., Rome continued to be governed actually by a relatively small group of aristocrats who controlled the election of the consuls. As the city grew and expanded, the force of the army, which was composed of citizens and originally dominated by the Patricians, began to make itself felt in politics. The subsequent admission into the army of the lower classes brought about a gradual extension of the franchise but did little to weaken the power of the upper class. Over the centuries, various changes occurred in the evolution of

government until, by the fourth century B.C., it had crys-
talized into a relatively fixed and well-defined form.

The military and aristocratic flavor of republican Rome
resulted from the division of the citizens into classes according to property and into Centuries or army regiments. The
Patrician Class was limited to the old ruling aristocracy.
Slightly lower were the Conscript Fathers, or Conscribed
Patricians, who were admitted to the aristocratic ranks from
time to time by virtue of newly acquired wealth or power.
These were generally the outstanding business men who had
profited by the expansion of the state. At the bottom were
the masses of farmers, small-business men, artisans, and so
forth, who were known as Plebs or Plebeians. In spite of the
fact that the Plebs far outnumbered the members of the
upper classes, they had actually little power in the Popular
Assembly which elected the consuls and other magistrates.
Here, voting was done by Centuries; every Roman citizen
was automatically a member of the army and the voting
proceeded by army units to which the individuals were
assigned. Since the Patricians controlled ninety-eight Centuries and all the rest only ninety-five, the lower classes had
no chance to make themselves felt unless the Patricians
disagreed. To make up for this political inequity the Plebs
were allowed to elect ten Tribunes, who sat in the Senate
and who possessed veto power. The Tribunes, like all the
other office holders in Rome, served without salary. This
factor, in combination with the veneration generally felt
for the Fathers, resulted in the usual practice of electing
Patricians even to the office of Tribune.

Annually elected were the two Consuls at the head of the
government. They possessed veto power over each other,
could not succeed themselves, held power for one year only,
and were generally put up for election only after having
served as lesser magistrates, such as:

Praetors, who commanded the army and acted as judges;

Quaestors, who managed finance;

Aediles, who were commissioners of streets and buildings.

Irregularly elected for an eighteen-month term were other special office holders such as the Censors, who took the census, assigned citizens to Centuries, and later became supervisors of morals.

The Senate, which advised the Consuls, was made up of ex-consuls and ex-censors who were appointed to it for life after their terms of office had expired. Although the Senate met only when called by the Consuls, and then only in an advisory capacity, it became the real policy-maker of Rome because it acted as a solid continuous body, as opposed to the brief terms of the Consuls, and because it was made up of the dominant Patrician families.

The administration of the various provinces was entrusted to military governors who exacted tribute from the natives, part of which was used for local expenses and the remainder sent to Rome. Meanwhile, the character of Rome was changing as a result of the long succession of military campaigns. The population was reduced by death in battle, the power of the Senate was increased, and a big-business group came into being by financing military operations and collecting tribute. The business leaders joined the ranks of the Patricians as Conscript Fathers and came to form the first eighteen Centuries of the Patricians. Meanwhile, the influx of tribute had impoverished the Plebs whose products competed with the free imports from the provinces. Simultaneously, this easy wealth demoralized the Patrician ranks by leaving a few men in control of vast properties which they administered with the lack of concern that superabundance is apt to encourage.

IV. THE CENTURY OF REVOLUTION (146-44 B.C.)

The long-continued series of conquests had the effect of completely unbalancing the economy of Rome. Plunder from the provinces flowed into the hands of the wealthy Patricians but left the masses impoverished because of their inability to compete with slave labor at home or with the ravished imports from abroad. Under increasing threats of revolution, occasional use of the dole was made as a temporary expedient to quiet unrest. By the first century B.C., a series of earnest reforms undertaken by the Gracchi (133-118 B.C.) had been nullified by the Patricians. Similar reforms undertaken by the popular leader Marius, who was Consul six times between 118 and 100 B.C., had been only temporary in effect because of Marius' own inadequacy as a statesman. Meanwhile, the corruption in the government had become a public scandal through the revelation that the province of Numidia had been allowed to fall into the hands of the native dictator, Jugurtha, by his bribery of Roman officials.

In 90 B.C., a full-fledged social war broke out in the uprising of most of central and southern Italy against Rome. It was put down only after nine years of fighting and only by the appearance of a brilliant general, Sulla, and by the promulgation of a law which granted Roman citizenship to all communities which remained loyal to Rome. The means of this victory proved to be expensive to the Patricians. The extension of the franchise served to strengthen the popular party, and Sulla, returning to Rome at the head of his legions, used his military power to enforce his election as Consul. From this office he was able to establish a dictatorship and thus to inculcate the leadership principle in Rome, under which democratic and lawful devices were thereafter replaced by personal prestige. His army had been loyal to its general rather than to the Republic, his "election" was a meaningless formality, and his way of handling opposition was the establishment of proscription lists by which personal enemies were summarily executed as enemies of the state. The property of those proscribed was confiscated, and their children were barred from holding office.

The resulting hatreds and feuds weakened the governmental traditions of the Republic and set the stage for a long-continued struggle for power on the part of a series of ambitious men and factions whose rivalries were to culminate in the destruction of the republican form of government.

In 70 B.C., as a reward for putting down a revolt in Spain, one of Sulla's best officers, Pompey, was elected Consul, together with the wealthy Crassus, who had similarly distinguished himself by breaking up a powerful lower-class uprising led by the slave Spartacus. Simultaneously, the name of Julius Caesar began to become prominent as a leader of the popular party. In 67 B.C., Pompey left Rome to command an expedition against the pirates who had been ruining Roman trade in the Mediterranean. During his absence Caesar formed a coalition with Crassus, who supplied the necessary funds. In 65 B.C. they put up for the Consulship a ruined aristocrat named Catiline. He was defeated, but in 63 B.C. he ran again on a *Novae Tabulae* (New Records or New Deal) platform. His opponent was Cicero, a new man who was essentially a member of the middle class, but whose eloquence, astuteness, and popularity with the growing business group had made him a candidate for the Patrician party.

Cicero won the election of 63 B.C., and Catiline attempted what may have been a conspiracy or merely a protest demonstration. Whichever it was, Cicero lost no time in denouncing him to the Senate as a traitor. Catiline fled and was put to death with many of his followers by Roman troops as a conclusion to what Cicero was later overfond of referring to as "the day I saved Rome." Pompey, meanwhile, had been conducting a victorious campaign in the East. Upon his return, he reacted coldly to Cicero's proffered friendship. Probably resenting Cicero's self-imposed eminence as the savior of Rome, he joined Caesar and Crassus to form the first triumvirate. In 59 B.C. the triumvirate procured the Consulship for Caesar and Bibulus, a Patrician who was such a nonentity that the regime was often referred to as the Consulship of Julius and Caesar. Cicero was exiled for having executed without trial the leaders of the Catilinian conspiracy.

Control of Rome remained in the hands of the triumvirate until the death of Crassus in 53 B.C. Caesar was still conducting the campaigns described in his *Commentaries on the Gallic Wars,* having had himself appointed governor of Gaul at the conclusion of his term as Consul. Cicero had been recalled from exile in 57 B.C. to serve as spokesman for the triumvirate. Pompey and Crassus had been Consuls in 55 B.C.; now that Crassus was dead, renewed signs of revolution led Pompey to arrange his election as sole Consul in 52 B.C. A growing breach between the now powerful Pompey and the absent Caesar began to develop. Despite Cicero's strenuous attempts to effect a reconciliation, Caesar cast the die for civil war by crossing the Rubicon and entering Rome at the head of his armies in 49 B.C.

No match for Caesar's victorious legions, Pompey's army was destroyed and Pompey himself was killed while seeking refuge in Egypt. Shortly thereafter, Caesar arrived in Egypt to engage in a civil war on behalf of Cleopatra, a conflict in which the Alexandrian library was partly burned. After winning the war for Cleopatra, he remained with her for nine months, had a son by her named Caesarion, married her to her younger brother, and returned to Rome in 47 B.C. with the entire family group. He was voted Dictator of Rome for ten years and subsequently for life, the Senate being relegated to the role of advisory council. A superb administrator, he instituted vast social reforms, created the first newspaper by having "Daily Events" posted

on the walls of the forum, and instituted the basic arrangement of our present calendar (the Julian calendar of 365
days with an extra day for leap year).

His achievements were nevertheless nullified by his failure to establish a form of government that might outlive
him, and his assassination, planned by the aristocracy and
led by Brutus in 44 B.C., was the prelude to fifteen more
years of chaos and war. At this point, Cicero joined forces
with the assassins. Mark Antony, a Tribune, summoned
Caesar's veterans to Rome. The Senate opposed Antony by
choosing Octavian, grandnephew of Caesar named as his son
and heir in Caesar's will. Cicero joined forces with Octavian and, in fourteen speeches named the *Philippics,*
attempted to inflame the population against Antony. The
combination undermined Antony's aspirations, but Octavian, discovering that the Senate was using him as a tool,
formed a second triumvirate with Antony and Lepidus,
who had been one of Caesar's generals. In the subsequent
reign of terror, Cicero was killed, and an attempted counter-revolution organized by Brutus and Cassius was defeated. Antony celebrated his new power by a course of
sensual pleasure-seeking. Excursioning to Alexandria, he
sought out Cleopatra, became her lover, and confirmed her
and Caesarion as rulers of Egypt and Cyprus. Resenting his
high-handedness, Octavian declared war on Cleopatra.
Antony, as Cleopatra's general, was defeated in 31 B.C. and
is reported to have stabbed himself and died in Cleopatra's
arms. Cleopatra committed suicide, and Caesarion was
killed by Octavian, who was now left undisputed master of
Rome.

V. THE ROMAN EMPIRE

1. *The Golden Age* (30 B.C.-A.D. 14)

The transition from nominal republican government to
rule by emperors was accomplished by a man of extraor-

dinary vision and administrative abilities. Taking the title of Princips (Principal or Chief), Octavian restored the functions of the Senate, Assembly, and Magistrates, but retained the roles of head of the government, commander-in-chief of the standing army, and administrator of the provinces through governors appointed by him and responsible to him alone. He also created a military body known as the Praetorian Guard, picked troops sworn to loyalty to the emperor's person. The resulting novelty of peace and stability caused the grateful Senate to confer on him the name of Augustus, a term of reverence reserved heretofore for the gods. So began the tradition of the divinity of Roman emperors and the consequent weakening of the old state religion. Priests and consuls still existed, but their power remained thenceforth subordinate to the control of the emperor.

The sanity and intelligence of Octavian made the Augustan or Golden Age a period of civilized achievement. Instead of undertaking new conquests, he concerned himself with consolidation of past gains and the solidification of Roman power and prestige. Ruling for the sake of Rome, he was concerned with the physical improvement of the city and with the welfare of the citizens. The best architects, artists, scholars, and literary men were attracted to Rome, where their efforts were suitably rewarded by honor and monetary stipends which were granted by Augustus himself or by wealthy patrons who had allied themselves with his program. From the Lycaeum at Athens and from Alexandria, Greek culture and genius were brought to Rome to help in the creation of an ideal state. Roman talent was similarly encouraged and subsidized, particularly when it took the direction of glorifying patriotism and virtue. Virgil's *Aeneid* and Livy's *History* were designed not only to magnify Rome but also to restore the ancient Roman virtues and to entice a corrupted, over-sophisticated population back to sane and sober moral living.

2. *The Silver Age* (14-117)

The death of Augustus in A.D. 14 left the government so well established that the succeeding century saw the continuation of a thriving empire whose splendour was somewhat diminished only because the successors of Augustus possessed neither his abilities nor his idealism. For lack of a direct heir, the succession fell upon Tiberius, son of Augustus' first wife by another man. From 14 to 37, Tiberius exercised a strict, bitter, cruel, but undeniably able, rule. His murder placed on the throne the mad Caligula whose incredible sensual excesses and insistence on his own divinity led to his assassination in 41. He was followed by the scholarly but rather ineffectual Claudius who, in turn, was dispatched in 54 with a dish of poisoned mushrooms served by his wife, Agrippina, mother of Nero. The madness of Nero is legendary. He diverted himself with sensual and extravagant pleasures, personally competed in athletic contests, acted in the theater, displayed his musical talents, and, after a great fire, amused himself with the artistic rebuilding of Rome. A rising animosity in the army forced his suicide in 68.

Each of these emperors had held his position only through the sanction and support of the army. The administration of government continued to be competent in the main, in spite of the personal ineptitudes of the emperors, because the real work was carried on by subordinates, whose patriotism kept the welfare of Rome to the fore.

The death of Nero occasioned a year of conflict in the rivalry of four imperial candidates, but peace was resumed by the accession of the Flavians. Vespasian, Titus, and Domitian, in turn, were enlightened despots. They were succeeded in 96 by the Antonines, Nerva and Trajan, the first of a line of "philosopher kings" whose absolutism was directed toward the goal of maintaining the best, socially and culturally, for their subjects. Although the direct encouragement of scholarship provided by Augustus was, in the main, lacking, the stability of the government, the continuance of the general tradition of the Golden Age, and the opportunity for comparative freedom of expression gave scope for the diversified talents of such major writers as the philosophers Seneca and Epictetus, the epigrammatist Martial, the Greek biographer Plutarch, the embittered moralists Tacitus (in history) and Juvenal (in satire), and the dilettante Pliny.

3. *The Decline of Rome* (117-476)

After the death of Trajan in 117, signs of decay became increasingly pronounced. Less responsibility for government was assumed by the aristocratic class, who were devoting themselves mainly to personal pleasures, and old institutions like the Senate were allowed to lapse. The bureaucracy which took their places became increasingly inefficient, and emperors who fancied themselves more and more in the roles of oriental despots were in the main unable to make headway against barbarian inroads at the borders of the empire and against social and economic unbalance within. Trajan's successor, Hadrian (117-138), wearied himself with responsibilities that kept him traveling incessantly throughout the Empire but simultaneously concentrated the responsibility for government in the personality of the emperor rather than in the city of Rome. Similarly, Marcus Aurelius (161-180) undertook personally campaigns against the invaders and vast social reforms at home, but his successors lacked his integrity as well as his brains. Consequently, while a Hellenistic revival was taking place in Egypt, philosophy, science, art, and literature deserted Rome, whose leaders at best were soldier-emperors preoccupied in the main with saving the empire from dissolution and often forced to contest the imperial power itself with rival generals put up as favorites of different legions.

Under Diocletian, the enormous strain of one-man government of all Rome culminated, in 284, in a breaking up of the empire into two parts, with joint emperors ruling the East and the West respectively. In 313, Constantine reunited the empire under his sole authority, but his subsequent actions clearly foreshadowed what the future was to be. Recognizing the growing power of Christianity, which had expanded tremendously during the third century, he proclaimed it the state religion, thus officially terminating what was left of the old Roman traditions. The retreat from Rome was further signalized by his moving the capital to Byzantium on the Bosphorus, to be renamed Constantinople after him. The abandonment of Rome itself to barbarian inroads was a gradual process. In 364, the Empire was again divided. In 410, the Visigoths took and sacked Rome. In 455, the city fell to the Vandals. In 476, Romulus Augustulus, titular emperor of the West, abdicated in favor of Odoacer, who became "King of Italy," and notified Constantinople that the Western Empire was ended. Legally, "Rome" continued in Constantinople until 1453 when it was overthrown by the Turks.

SUGGESTED READINGS

See end of Chapter 11 for suggested readings.

ROMAN CULTURE

I. ECONOMY AND EVERYDAY LIFE

The life of Rome from the early days of the Republic was dominated by three powerful forces: the military, the administrative, and the agricultural. Of the three, the last was the oldest and most basic. Of necessity, Rome had from the beginning developed as an agrarian nation. Being almost totally deficient in the mineral resources necessary for establishing and maintaining an industrial economy, and being gifted by nature with rich—if not broad—fields and a wonderful growing climate, she naturally turned to agriculture as her principal means of livelihood. Her simplest citizens traditionally cultivated their own small plots of ground; her wealthiest aristocrats were gentlemen farmers. It was not until Imperial times that Rome developed anything like a substantial commercial or manufacturing economy, and even then these activities were of considerably less importance than agriculture in Roman life. It is significant that until the last days of the Republic urban Rome, though the most important city in the world, never attained a population of more than half a million.

But despite the substantial wealth of her agriculture,

Rome was far from being a self-sufficient nation, and the need for goods from abroad had from her earliest history encouraged a career of military conquest. This activity was carried out almost entirely by a civilian army, making military service the most important obligation of every Roman citizen. No matter what his domestic means of livelihood, every able-bodied male in the Republic was a soldier assigned to a permanent military troop (the Century). He was trained from childhood to accept military discipline; he was expected throughout most of his life to keep himself in good physical condition and to hold his personal affairs in such order as to permit him to answer immediately any call to his country's service.

The constant success of Roman military campaigns eventually brought about a third aspect of Roman existence: the official. The vast territories which came under Roman domination had not only to be policed, but also to be administered. Thus a large class of civil servants was created to perform the routine duties of governing the ever-expanding state. In time the country developed a highly complex bureaucracy, and the staff of office took its place beside the plow and the sword as a major factor in Latin civilization.

In a life devoted mainly to military duty, to the imposing of legal authority, and to the struggle with nature and the soil, it is natural that the Romans should have developed a strong sense of discipline and an equally strong reverence for authority, even to the point of investing family relationships with the rigid compulsiveness of the camp. The Roman family was in effect part of a small army, or clan, which traced its origin back to a common ancestor. Within this family the *paterfamilias* acted as absolute ruler. No other member had any legal rights; he alone could transact business, own property, or decide upon the marriage of his children. He even could require his sons and daughters to serve him indefinitely, until whatever time he saw fit to give them their freedom. Thus, powers of restriction over his household were virtually unlimited, though seldom abused and usually tempered somewhat by custom and public opinion. Under this patriarchal system the family developed into almost a religious concept, a symbol of higher authority, of a unity that transcended the sum of its individual parts. To have defied the will of the *paterfamilias* would have constituted more than insurrection; it would have been a form of blasphemy.

The clan relationship in Rome was emphasized by the established system of nomenclature. Each male child was given three names. His *nomen,* or middle and basic name, was the designation of the clan. His *cognomen,* or last name, was that of his particular family. Only his first name, or *praenomen,* was individually his own, and there were only fifteen first names to choose from. Other designations were sometimes added as descriptive or honorary titles to distinguish one person from another. Women were ordinarily known by the feminine version of the clan name. For example, Caesar's name was Gaius (*praenomen*) Julius (*nomen*) Caesar (*cognomen*). His daughter's name was simply Julia; women were not given *praenomina* and no especial effort was made to distinguish them as individuals; their designation by clan names was like the branding of cattle.

As a matter of fact, within these patriarchal family units, women had no rights beyond those they might gain by force of personality. They were easily divorced and were always under the legal control of some male, whether father, husband, brother, or even son. If all male relatives predeceased a woman, a guardian was appointed for her. In practice, women were not really so subservient as the legalities implied. As today, they frequently dominated the household and ordinarily seem to have been respected and admired by husbands and children. They were not kept in oriental seclusion, as were Greek women, and there seems to have been no prejudice against their obtaining some rudiments of education or taking part in group social activities. Nor were they expected to burden themselves with excessive household drudgery, for as Roman conquest brought captives from conquered territories, it became the custom to have most of the work done by slaves.

As in Greece, the labor performed by slaves covered a wide range of activity from the most menial or oppressive duties to the considerably more elevated responsibilities of land supervision, accounting, teaching, and book-copying. This custom freed the males of the family for the duties of war and government and in times of peace gave them a large amount of leisure for pleasure or for productive intellectual activity. Unfortunately the average Roman took to culture somewhat unreadily and was usually more interested in trivial activities. He filled his leisure time with social engagements, conversation in the streets and public baths, and attendance at or participation in games and religious ceremonies. At their worst, Roman pleasures were cruel and sensual, ranging from sumptuous banquets and drinking bouts to gladiatorial combats and such spectacles as the feeding of criminals and war captives to wild animals in the arena; at best they were characterized by a genuine interest in physical fitness which lasted until well into middle age or by a pleasant domesticity manifested in evenings at home spent in conversation, musical performance, or reading aloud. As Roman life came under Greek influence and became more cultivated, all Patrician children were schooled in the reading and writing of Latin and were highly trained in oratory. Recitations by the children of the family were a frequent form of home entertainment, and sometimes a group of friends would be invited to listen to a Patrician's own composition or oration. It is regrettable to relate that this somewhat tardy interest in culture was made possible only by the institution of slavery, and it is even more deplorable that the Roman masters were seldom as considerate as their much-admired Greek predecessors in their treatment of the servants who made their leisured pleasures possible.

Much has been written of the magnificence of Roman living habits, especially during the Golden Age, but the sober fact is that except for a few very wealthy persons, most Romans enjoyed few opportunities for ostentation or display. Roman houses were seldom, by modern standards, very comfortable. Built of stone around an inner court, they were generally poorly lighted, ventilated, and heated, and had little to offer by way of upholstered furniture or other refinements. In some cases, especially among the wealthy, they boasted running water and "modern" toilet facilities, but even these advances would not have removed the average Roman home from the primitive category as compared with our present-day gadget-infested households. At the same time, their large contingents of domestic slaves partly compensated for the lack of mechanical conveniences.

In public works, however, the Romans proved extremely skillful. In later times their cities were laid out scientifically, with wide, excellently paved streets crossing one another at right angles. Towns were generally divided into four square or rectangular sections, with definite functions—government, commerce, residence, and so forth—assigned to each. Public buildings, although imitative in architecture, were particularly impressive and each town had its public baths and municipal water system. The Roman aqueducts were magnificent examples of practical engineering, and some of them carried water hundreds of miles. Many have remained in use to the present day. Roman bridges also displayed a high degree of engineering skill. Altogether, the Roman city was marked by many modern features and in its concepts of orderliness, spaciousness, and architectural magnificence it has exerted a powerful influence upon modern essays in municipal planning.

II. ROMAN DRAMA

In the Roman drama, we have the key to the development of the modern stage. Although derived from the Greeks, like most Roman cultural institutions, the Roman drama nevertheless introduced a wealth of technical and literary conventions which became standard when the drama was revived in the Middle Ages. Many of these conventions, such as those governing the physical nature of the stage, have persisted with little alteration to the present day; others, such as the typing of characters and plots, have been deepened and broadened without destroying their essentially Roman bases; few have been lost altogether. British dramatists of the sixteenth and seventeenth centuries —Shakespeare, Jonson, Webster, Kyd, Marlowe—took the Roman, not the Greek, drama as their model and built their own creations on those left by Plautus, Terence, and Seneca. Molière too drew heavily upon his Classical predecessors for material, and some of his plays were hardly more than adaptations from the Latin.

But despite its profound effect upon later dramatic writing, the Roman theatre was neither highly original nor of surpassing literary merit. Strongly imitative of the Greeks, the Roman playwrights had but little of their forerunners' tragic sweep or poetic grandeur. Roman tragedy, as represented in the works of Seneca, is hollow and pompous alongside the sublimities of Aeschylus, Sophocles, and Euripides, and the comedies of Plautus and Terence, though amusing and theatrically effective, show no great advance in wit or resourcefulness over those of Aristophanes and Menander. The Greek playwrights were poets and philosophers; in the Roman plays the poetry was only clever or sententious and the philosophy, if it existed at all, only a jejune morality or a dry patriotism. In short, speaking in literary terms, the true place of Rome in the annals of dramatic history is that of an indispensable link between fifth-century Greece and the great ages of Shakespeare and Molière. Without that link, and without the genuinely original Roman contributions in stagecraft and theatre construction, the modern drama might still find itself in a chaotic and unpredictable struggle to be born.

Although the Roman literary drama differed from the Greek in that it was not concerned with religion, the first recorded stirrings of Roman folk plays occurred in Etruria in connection with the celebration of sacred rites. As in Greece, the earliest performances occurred in the form of processions, dances, and recitations during marriage, harvest, or other festivals. At first these activities were communal; later the more skilled participants were singled out to perform, while the main group was transformed into a willing and probably demonstrative audience. The first historically certain theatrical production in Rome took place during a plague in 364 B.C., when a group of Etruscan actors put on a series of dances and recitations intended to propitiate the gods and restore the health of the city. These recitations, known as Fescennine verses [1] apparently became popular with the Roman people, as were the dances performed by the visiting Etruscan *histriones*.[2]

It was only a matter of time before the Romans too developed their own professional singers and dancers and

[1] The derivation of the word *Fescennine* is still a matter of controversy. Some believe it to be derived from *Fescinnium,* the name of a town in Etruria; others feel that it is taken from *fascinum,* a phallic symbol. Since the Roman folk-drama probably originated in Etruria and since phallic symbolism is always an important element in primitive celebrations and was prominent in early Greek folk dramas, both arguments are plausible. The reader may take his choice.

[2] The name *histriones* (from which we derive our adjective *histrionic*) was applied to the Etruscan actors by the Romans as a Latin equivalent of *ister,* the Etruscan word for dancer.

the entertainments achieved more complex patterns of plot and dramatic conflict. The most important forms of entertainment put on by these actors were the *fabula Atellana* and the mime. The former was a short comic play, resembling a vaudeville turn, in which the characters were typed and easily recognizable. Among these were Macco (the clown), Bucco (the braggart), Pappus (the old fool), and Dossenus (the tricky hunchback). The plots of these plays were quite stereotyped, like those of modern burlesque shows, and were probably more distinguished for obscenity than for true wit. The mimes were coarse plays, also portraying stock situations from low life and likewise given to stock obscenities. A further development of the mime was the *pantomime,* in which one virtuoso actor played all the parts, indicating changes of character by gesture and possibly also by the use of masks.

Literary drama traditionally came into being in 240 B.C., when Livius Andronicus translated and produced a Greek tragedy and a Greek comedy at the festival of the *Ludi Romani.* These plays were in every way so far superior to anything the Romans had previously known in the theatre that adaptations of Greek plays henceforth became the principal fare on the Roman stage. Comedies were taken from Menander, Philemon and other lesser Greeks, rather than from Aristophanes, but for tragedy the great trio— Aeschylus, Sophocles, and Euripides—were the most popular. For a century after the happy innovation of Livius Andronicus the Roman theatre was in its heyday, with such tragedians as Gnaeus Naevius (c. 270-201 B.C.), Quintus Ennius (239-169 B.C.), Lucius Accius (170-c. 86 B.C.) presenting their own versions of the great Greek mythological tragedies. In comedy, the most important names were Titus Maccius Plautus (c. 254-c. 184 B.C.), Cecilius Statius (c. 219-c. 166 B.C.), and Publius Terentius Afer, known as Terence (c. 195-159 B.C.). After this golden age, the only great playwright in the Roman drama was the tragedian Seneca (4 B.C.-A.D. 65). Unfortunately, of the vast production of these writers and their colleagues, only about three dozen plays of Plautus, Terence, and Seneca have come down to us in complete form. This is a double pity, because the innumerable vanished works were probably not only of literary merit in themselves but would be also valuable as clues to the many lost Greek plays upon which they were based.

About the time of the Civil War, the Roman literary drama went into a rapid decline. It was succeeded in popularity by the mime, which became increasingly coarse and immoral. About this time women appeared for the first time on the Roman stage, taking roles of about the same subtle delicacy as those in a cheap night-club extravaganza. Before the opening of the Christian era, even these dubious entertainments had yielded in popularity to the chariot races, the gladiatorial games, and all the other bloody and depraved spectacles of the arena. Though never entirely dead, stage entertainment remained virtually non-existent from the death of Seneca until nearly nine hundred years later, when it emerged from its moribund state and, again through the combined efforts of religion and folk customs, began its slow, painful evolution into the modern drama.

Equally important with the plays themselves were the contributions made by the Romans in staging and acting conventions. Since Roman impresarios availed themselves of every possible excuse to produce their plays (during the golden century of the Roman drama more than half the calendar was marked by "feast days" appropriate for dramatic performances), the theatrical season in Italy was neither so short nor so solemnly traditional as that of Greece. Thus there was more opportunity in Rome for the development of new techniques of staging and for experimentation in the physical aspects of the theatre. One of the first Greek conventions to go was that of the acting circle, in which the actors played level with or beneath the seated audience. In Rome, the play was performed on an elevated platform, before which the audience sat or stood through continuous performances which included all types of entertainment and often lasted through the better part of a day.[3] The stage was understood by the spectators to represent a street, and playwrights respected this convention by keeping the action of the play outdoors except for whatever stage business could be clearly transacted through doors or open windows. At the rear of the stage were two crude "fronts" representing houses, and often there was an opening between these houses portraying a street running at right angles to the front stage. Actors could make entrances and exits from the houses or from any of the three street entrances; the audience understood without explanation that the right entrance led to the country, the center one to the city proper, and the left to the harbor or foreign lands. Painted backdrops were probably employed occasionally in place of the wooden fronts, and props were held to a minimum. The whole atmosphere of early Roman theatre structure was one of transitory jerry-building, and it is doubtful if any of these structures lasted longer than the festival period for which they were erected. It was not until 145 B.C. that a permanent theatre was built, and it was another ninety years before the general Pompey erected a stone playhouse having any claims to architectural beauty.[4] But even these permanent theatres, ruins of some of which

[3] The experts disagree as to whether the Roman theatre had seats or not. In Cato's time there was a law prohibiting the erection of seats for public entertainments, but it is impossible to determine how strictly this stoical ordinance was enforced.

[4] Pompey cleverly evaded the law against seats by erecting a huge amphitheatre and dedicating it as a temple of Venus. To make it legal, a small shrine containing an image of the goddess was placed at the very top of the edifice. The vast seat rows were then officially regarded as steps leading to the shrine and the stage was explained as being a ceremonial altar.

still exist, were no more than open-air structures; it was not until the seventeenth century A.D. that theatres were roofed over, and the drama attained the dignity of an indoor institution.

The costumes of the actors were taken from Greek models, with freemen wearing the *pallium,* or scarf, over the traditional Greek tunic. Old men wore white scarves, young men affected red or purple, while slaves had the tunic only. Male actors playing female parts wore long, flowing robes. Wigs of different colors were employed, although red hair was conventionally given to the slave characters. Masks were apparently not employed until very late, probably after the death of Terence. In later times it is believed that the Roman toga replaced the Greek costumes, and with the coming of Rome's age of magnificence every effort was expended to make stage performances as colorful, varied, and splendid to the eye as possible.

Some of the later Roman theatres probably had curtains, but in general the stage was open at all times. Intervals in the action were marked by vocal or instrumental music or by dancing, but there were no formal divisions into acts. The Greek chorus, as an integral part of the play, did not exist in the Roman drama, though incidental songs by the principal characters were not entirely unknown. The social position of Roman actors also differed sharply from that of the Greeks. Despite the popularity of their performances, stage people were considered undesirable and forfeited their citizenship upon entering their profession. Occasionally a great actor like Quintus Roscius could claim the friendship of the political and social lights of his time, but for the most part thespians were beyond the pale. This explains how the Roman populace, steeped in brutality and sensuality as it was, could still be shocked when the emperor Nero performed in public in the company of actors. Professionally, however, star actors had their enthusiastic followers, and those who didn't were not above maintaining a paid *claque* to guarantee applause for their performances.

Another peculiar prejudice kept the Roman dramatists from portraying pure young womanhood on the stage. Parts were written only for old women and courtesans; young girls of social acceptability were included solely by reference to their offstage actions, although often a supposed courtesan was made eligible for marriage to the young hero when she was recognized as being the long-lost daughter of a wealthy family.

Roman audiences were probably as difficult as any in the history of the theatre. Admission to early theatrical performances was free, and even in later times the prices charged were extremely low, so that even the poorest and coarsest element could attend. Frequent reference is made in the text of Roman plays to the crude, boorish, noisy behavior of this motley group. Great efforts had to be made to quiet the throng so that the play could begin, and frequent barbed references to garlic-breathed hecklers and mothers who refuse to leave their squalling babies at home indicate that the lot of the actor was not an enviable one. Audiences would not hesitate to throw refuse, wreck the theatre, and even do physical violence to the actors if the play did not please them, but on the other hand they were ready to respond tearfully to sentimental scenes and boisterously to even the crudest type of humor. If their displeasure was brutal, their approval was a heaven-storming ovation sweet to the ears of applause-hungry actors. But in their violence, Roman audiences were the eventual ruin of the art of serious entertainment. Unready for anything other than the obvious and the vulgar, they shouted down any attempts on the part of the playwright to raise popular standards of taste or refinement. Demanding more and more novelty, they soon dragged the drama down to their own debased levels, destroyed its wit, its cleverness, and whatever true poetry it may have produced. After they had done this, they deserted the theatre entirely for the obscenities of the arena, leaving to scholars and historians of the future the task of rescuing the Roman drama from oblivion and restoring it to its rightful high importance in the development of Western histrionic art.

III. ROMAN RELIGION

One of the best clues to the difference between Greek and Roman character is found in the widely divergent Hellenic and Latin concepts of religion. Greek religion from the simplest myth to the most complicated rites of the mysteries was marked by imagination, grace, flexibility, and charm. Furthermore, it had a solid—but not dogmatic—theological content that permeated the entire body of the Greek creative arts. Except for some lyric poetry, hardly a work exists that does not in some way reflect sacred beliefs; without the strong ethico-philosophical stimulus exerted by religion, Greek intellectual life would have indeed been a feeble, unprofitable thing.

Roman religion, on the other hand, was less intimate and far more formal than that of the Greeks. In early times its gods were not anthropomorphic, but spirits, and thus lent themselves poorly to the development of legend and myth. Its rites were simple to the point of being automatic, and because of this ritualistic sterility, it held only a minimum of theological and intellectual content. Most of these rites concerned themselves with propitiation, and because of the lack of humanity of the gods thus supplicated, such ceremonies carried little moral impact and hardly amounted to more than an outright buying of divine favor. It is not surprising, therefore, to find that until the time when the Romans began to cultivate Greek ways and to import Greek concepts into their own intellectual life, religion played only a small role in the Roman arts. This was especially true in literature, where the Roman author most often dwelt not upon the gods but upon his real spiritual inspiration, the State.

Since the Romans were an agrarian people, it is natural that their earliest religion should have centered upon the life of the fields and the individual home. Accustomed to believing that the human being is in all matters subject to higher authority, they could not conceive of even the most commonplace functions of existence without ascribing them to the workings of a divine spirit. Accordingly, they had gods for everything. The home was watched over by a battery of domestic divinities: a *genius*, or guardian of the house; the *manes*, or spirits of the ancestors; the *penates*, who protected the household wealth. Each domestic hearth was in the keeping of Vesta, and every door was guarded by the two-faced Janus. The fields were protected by hosts of *lares*, spirits who were assigned to all phases of agriculture: Pomona to the orchards, Faunus to the animals, Ceres for the crops, among others. There was even a *lar*, Sterculus, assigned to the manure heap! Beyond the hearth and fields, the Romans also conceived of spirits for emotions and abstract human qualities such as Anger, Fear, Virtue, Honesty, and so forth. It was the duty of the *paterfamilias* to act as the family priest and to conduct the rites to propitiate these multitudinous genii. With so many gods to appease, it is not surprising that the procedure amounted to little more than superstitious, unthinking ritual. Daily prayers, the burning of incense, and the drinking of libations made up most of these ceremonies, but often the mere naming of as many spirits as possible was regarded as a passable substitute for worship in busy times.

As Rome became urbanized and sophisticated, steps were taken to curb the proliferation of agrarian *lares* and *penates* and to formalize them into a state religion appropriate for urban as well as for rural minds. The official religion of the state centered about a sacred triad of gods: Jupiter, Juno, and Minerva. Jupiter was the ruling god. Juno, his wife, was the goddess of wisdom, crafts, and the arts. Lesser gods like Mars, Hercules, and Mercury were added to by the introduction from other countries of innumerable deities whose special celebrations crowded the calendar with over one hundred holy days. The official religious life of Rome was presided over by colleges of priests, made up mainly of Patricians. Each college had its special functions. The Pontiffs kept the records and were generally in charge of all religious matters. The Flamines supervised the burning of offerings. The function of the Augurs was to foretell the future by noting the flights of birds, examining the entrails of sacrificial animals, or utilizing other occult means of divination. There were also the sacred dancers, the Salii, and the holy brotherhood of the Luperci, priests of the wolf, who drove off evil spirits and assured fertility to women. The sacred fire of the city was kept burning by the devout service of the Vestal Virgins.

Like the rural spirit-worship (which it never succeeded in fully supplanting) the state religion was essentially formal and non-theological, although it was more imaginative and allowed for the institution of elaborate and colorful festivals in honor of its divinities. Furthermore with the adopting of Greek culture, it lent itself easily to a merging with Greek Olympianism. Jupiter, for example, became associated with Zeus, Juno with Hera, Minerva with Athene,[5] and Greek mythology quickly became incorporated into Roman religious and cultural patterns. It is to be noted, however, that while this state religion was *official,* it was not *compulsory.* The Romans were refreshingly tolerant of all forms of religion and usually felt that so long as a person committed

---

[5] See page 73 for further cross-identification of Greek and Roman gods.

no overt actions likely to endanger public safety or morality, he could believe whatever he pleased. As a result of this tolerance, the effect of the official state religion on the average citizen was simply to add one more set of divinities to the already crowded gallery of *lares* and *penates*.

But however chaotic and intellectually impoverished the Roman religion may have been, it had one very clear, positive result in that it provided that stability of character so typical of Roman life. It was a religion of absolutes; it left little room for doubt or insecurity. A man knew right from wrong, he knew how to conduct himself properly, and, if he made a mistake, he knew the rituals by which to assuage the wrath of the offended divinities. Such a religion may not have developed the intellect, but at least it afforded that spiritual security a man needs while coping with the practical problems of a busy life. Unfortunately, however, it was not the type of religion which could stand prosperity. As Rome grew wealthier and more luxurious by conquest, the moral sense of the individual citizen became dulled through easy living and monetary greed. Even the dry rituals of propitiation began to be neglected, and with their decline disappeared the principal spiritual prop of a society too long accustomed to look to authority for guidance. By the time of Augustus (30 B.C.-A.D. 14) there was frequent complaint about the loss of the "old ways," and the emperor himself tried valiantly but with only partial success to awaken the Romans to a renewed moral vigor. In order to do this, he proclaimed himself a god and directed that emperor-worship be made the new state religion.

Much has been written concerning the decadence of Roman emperor-worship, but actually the institution was of little religious importance. No Roman emperor, no matter how disordered his wits, truly believed himself to be a god, and probably no individual Roman citizen subscribed to the pretense either. The cult of the emperor was no more nor less than the veneration of the leader, a *Führer-prinzip* that has characterized most military dictatorships from Julius Caesar to Hitler and Mussolini. Roman society was always notable for its hero-worship, and always expended more spiritual and emotional energy in praising a conqueror or a great leader than it did in observing the formalities of religion. Emperor-worship was simply a means of more efficiently exerting the authoritarian principle, a *de facto* recognition that, in the last analysis, the true religion of Rome was the State.

SUGGESTED READINGS

(Place of publication, when not mentioned, is New York.)

GENERAL

C. Bailey, *The Legacy of Rome* (Oxford, 1923); V. Chapot, *The Roman World* (London, 1928); W. Durant, *Caesar and Christ* (1944); R. M. Geer, *Classical Civilization: Rome* (1940); W. C. Greene, *The Achievement of Rome* (Cambridge, Mass., 1933); E. Hamilton, *The Roman Way* (1932); F. G. Moore, *The Roman's World* (1936); G. W. White and E. C. Kennedy, *Roman History, Life, and Literature* (London, 1942).

HISTORY

G. P. Baker, *Twelve Centuries of Rome* (1934); S. Barr, *The Mask of Jove* (Philadelphia, 1966); A. E. R. Boak, *A History of Rome to 565 A.D.* (1943); J. B. Bury, *History of the Roman Empire* (n.d.); T. Frank, *Roman Imperialism* (1914); E. Gibbon, *Decline and Fall of the Roman Empire* (J. B. Bury, ed., London, 1900); M. Hadas, *A History of Rome* (1956); F. M. Heicheltherne, *A History of the Roman People* (1962); T. R. E. Holmes, *The Roman Republic and the Founder of the Empire* (1967); T. Mommsen, *History of Rome* (London, 1901); C. E. Robinson, *A History of Rome* (1935); H. H. Scullard, *A History of the Roman World from 753 to 146 B.C.* (London, 1961).

LITERATURE

M. S. Dimsdale, *A History of Latin Literature* (1915); J. W. Duff, *A Literary History of Rome* (2 v, London, 1928, 1932); J. W.

Duff, *The Writers of Rome* (London, 1937); T. Frank, *Life and Literature in the Roman Republic* (Berkeley, 1930); G. Howe and G. A. Harrer, *Roman Literature in Translation* (1924); J. W. Mackail, *Latin Literature* (1895); H. J. Rose, *A Handbook of Latin Literature* (London, 1956).

PHILOSOPHY AND RELIGION

F. Altheim, *A History of Roman Religion* (1938); C. Bailey, *Phases in the Religion of Ancient Rome* (Berkeley, 1932); A. W. Benn, *A History of Ancient Philosophy* (1912); J. B. Carter, *The Religious Life of Ancient Rome* (1911); W. W. Fowler, *The Religious Experience of the Roman People* (London, 1911); T. R. Glover, *The Conflict of Religions in the Early Roman Empire* (London, 1932); J. B. Mayor, *A Sketch of Ancient Philosophy from Thales to Cicero* (Cambridge, 1889); H. J. Rose, *Religion in Greece and Rome* (1959); E. Westermarck, *Origin and Development of the Moral Ideas* (2 v, London, 1917).

ECONOMIC, POLITICAL, SOCIAL LIFE

F. Abbott, *The Common People of Ancient Rome* (1911); F. Abbott, *A History and Description of Roman Political Institutions* (Boston, 1933); F. Abbott, *Roman Politics* (Boston, 1933); J. Carcopino, *Daily Life in Ancient Rome* (New Haven, 1940); J. A. Crook, *Law and Life of Rome* (Ithaca, 1967); S. Dill, *Roman Society from Nero to Marcus Aurelius* (London, 1905); D. R. Dudley, *The Civilization of Rome* (1962); W. W. Fowler, *Social Life at Rome in the Age of Cicero* (1929); T. Frank (ed.), *An Economic Survey of Rome* (5 v, Baltimore, 1933-1940); L. Friedlander, *Roman Life and Manners under the Early Empire* (London, 1908-1913); A. H. J. Greenridge, *Roman Public Life* (London, 1911); L. Homo, *Roman Political Institutions* (1930); H. W. Johnston, *The Private Life of the Romans* (Chicago, 1932); P. Louis, *Ancient Rome at Work* (1927); W. B. McDaniel, *Roman Private Life and Its Survivals* (Boston, 1924); U. E. Paoli, *Rome: Its People, Life, and Customs* (1963); M. Rostovtzeff, *History of the Ancient World* (2 v, Oxford, 1928); M. Rostovtzeff, *Social and Economic History of the Roman Empire* (2nd ed., Oxford, 1957); H. T. Rowell, *Rome in the Augustan Age* (1962); J. Toutain, *Economic Life of the Ancient World* (1930); H. A. Treble and K. M. King, *Everyday Life in Rome in the Time of Caesar and Cicero* (Oxford, 1931).

Chronology for Part I

THE GREEK PERIOD

(All dates before 700 are approximate.)

I. THE PRE-HOMERIC AGE (3400-1200 B.C.)

Beginning of Minoan civilization in Crete (3400); first known settlement of Troy (2870); legendary founding of Athens by the hero Cecrops and the goddess Athene (1582); beginning of Mycenean civilization (1500); Golden Age of Crete (1400-1200); Achaeans migrate from Central Europe and dominate Hellenic area (1300-1100).

II. THE HOMERIC PERIOD (1200-900 B.C.) AND THE AGE OF THE KINGS (900-700 B.C.)

A. *Historical Events*

Dorian invasion of Greece (1104); Aeolian migration (1100); Ionian migration (850); first Olympic Games (776); nobles begin to rise to power (750).

B. *Legendary and Literary Events*

Quest of the Golden Fleece (1225); war of the Seven Against Thebes (1213); Agamemnon becomes king of Mycenae (1200); Siege of Troy (1192-1183); "Homer" wrote of siege of Troy (900-840); poet Hesiod flourished (750).

III. THE AGE OF THE TYRANTS (700-500 B.C.)

A. *Historical Events*

Archonships established at Athens (683); Draconian reforms in Athens (620); Solon revises Draconian Code (594); dictatorship of Pisistratus at Athens (561-560; 546-527); Cyrus of Persia conquers Babylon (538); death of Cyrus (529); Cyrus's son Cambyses conquers Egypt (525); Darius becomes leader of Persia and continues Persian conquests (521); Cleisthenes increases Athenian democratic freedom (507).

B. Literary Events

Sappho flourished at Lesbos (600); Aesop flourished (560); Thespis "invents" the Greek Drama (534).

IV. THE GOLDEN AGE (500-322 B.C.)

A. Historical Events: The Fifth Century

Birth of Pericles (c. 500); Persian War: Ionia rebels against her Persian conquerors (499); Darius conquers Macedonia (497); battle of Marathon ends first Persian invasion of Greece (490); Xerxes resumes invasion of Greece; battles of Thermopylae and Salamis shake Persian morale (480); battles of Mycale and Plataea end Persian War (479); foundation of Delian League (477); Pericles leading figure in Athenian politics (463-431); beginning of Peloponnesian War (459); Athens seizes the Delian treasury (454); end of first phase of Peloponnesian War (446); second phase of war begins (431); plague of Athens (430-429); death of Pericles, Cleon becomes leader in Athens (429); Cleon killed in battle, Peace of Nicias ends second phase of war (421); Alcibiades leads suicidal expedition in Sicily (415-413); Spartans decisively victorious at Aegospotami (405); end of Peloponnesian Wars, Rule of Thirty Tyrants in Athens (404); Xenophon's leadership of the Ten Thousand (401).

B. Historical Events: The Fourth Century

Agesilaus king of Sparta (399-360); trial and death of Socrates (399); resurgence of the Athenian Empire (378-354); Philip becomes regent of Macedonia (359); Athens wars with Macedonia and is defeated (357-346); Alexander born (356); Philip assassinated (336); Alexander destroys Thebes and attacks Persia (335); Alexander subdues Egypt and founds Alexandria (332); Alexander in India (327-325); death of Alexander (323).

ROME

I. EARLY YEARS OF THE REPUBLIC (509-100 B.C.)

Founding of the Republic (509); alliance between Romans and Latins (493); Rome sacked by the Gauls (390); Rome rebuilt and expanding in power (387); complete subjugation of Italy and First Punic War (264-241); Second Punic War

(218-201); Spain becomes a Roman province (201); Greece placed under Roman "protection" (194); expansion into eastern Mediterranean (189); extensive poverty among Plebs becomes a national problem (157); Third Punic War (149-146); Macedonia and Asia made Roman provinces, Carthage destroyed, Rome in control of Mediterranean world (146); social reforms of Tiberius Gracchus (133); Gaius Gracchus continues reforms (123); Patricians successfully oppose reforms (118); social conflict renewed under popular Marius, consul six times, Caesar born (100).

II. THE CENTURY OF REVOLUTION (100-30 B.C.)

Social revolt of southern Italy put down by Sulla (90); Sulla's dictatorship (81); slave uprising (73); Pompey and Crassus consuls (70); Catiline defeated for consulship (65); Cicero consul and Catilinian conspiracy (63); the first triumvirate (60); consulship of Caesar and Bibulus, Cicero exiled (59); Caesar governor of Gaul (58); Cicero recalled from exile (57); Pompey and Crassus consuls (55); Pompey sole consul (52); Caesar crosses Rubicon (49); Caesar dictator of Rome (47); Caesar assassinated (44); Cicero put to death by second triumvirate (43); Antony defeated and killed (31); Octavian master of Rome (30).

III. THE AUGUSTAN OR GOLDEN AGE (30 B.C.-A.D. 14)

Augustus (Octavian) dictator of Rome (30 B.C.); government reorganized as Principate and official beginning of the Empire (27 B.C.); consolidation of Roman power, extensive program for social, economic, and cultural improvements, encouragement of artistic and literary talent for the glorification of Rome, general emulation of the Golden Age of Athens. Period ends with death of Augustus (A.D. 14).

IV. THE SILVER AGE (14-117)

A. *Emperors:* Tiberius (14), Caligula (37), Claudius (41), Nero (54), Titus (79), Domitian (81), Nerva (96), Trajan (98).

B. *Tone of Period:* Maintenance of status quo; little initiative, inspiration, originality, or progressiveness; gradual lowering of general morale and decline of traditional Roman patriotism.

V. THE DECLINE OF ROME (117-476)

    A. *Emperors:* Hadrian (117), Antoninus Pius (138), Marcus Aurelius (161), Commodus (180), Diocletian (East) and Maximian (West) (284), Constantine (313), followed by a long succession of less able rulers.

    B. *Historical Events:* The Empire divided (284) and reunited under Constantine (313); Constantinople founded (328) and dedicated to Christianity (330); the Empire again divided (364); Visigoths sack Rome (410); Vandals sack Rome (455); Romulus Augustulus, the last Western Emperor, abdicates in favor of Odoacer, King of Italy (476).

Part II

HEBRAISM

chapter 12

THE CHOSEN PEOPLE

I. HEBRAISM *vs.* CLASSICISM

While Classical civilization was making such distinctive advances towards ferreting out the secrets of an unintelligible world, the Hebrews, a very small group of people, remote and all but isolated from Mediterranean culture, were also seeking to know the nature of things. But whereas the Classic mode, as we have seen, was essentially objective, outward-going, reaching toward formalization of universal principles, the Hebraic tendency was sharply divergent: intuitive and mystic, searching for communion with the spirit rather than the outward manifestations of the universe. St. Paul was pointing out this contrast when he wrote, "The Jews demand signs and the Greeks seek wisdom." [1]

To continue Paul's oversimplification in order to emphasize the lasting impact of each civilization on the Western world, one could say that the Classical most respected Athene (wisdom) and Hephaestus (skill) while the Hebraic obeyed and worshipped the Creator of the Universe who gave his commandments to his chosen people at Mt. Sinai. The Classic world demanded and often found specific an-

[1] I Cor. 1:22.

swers to its many questions. The Hebraic world, though it also often asked questions, did not have a deep need for exhaustive explanation because the final answer it felt always and unquestionably to be in the hands of God. In this sense of inner communication with the Creator and Ruler of the Universe, together with a marvellous concept of the Creator's concern for a selected group of his Israelite children, we find the core of Hebraic emotionalism: the mystic tribal unity of a people descended from a single line (children of Abraham and of Israel [Jacob]) and chosen people of the one and only Heavenly Father.

The nature of Hebraic culture, revolving about this single concept of God's favor, is therefore inevitably quite different from that of Classical civilization. Where the Classic mind was occupied with an outward investigation into the nature of the universe and of human behavior, the Hebraic heart listened within itself to hear the voice of God. Growth in the Classic world meant clarifying, organizing, and adding to a storehouse of principles; in the Hebraic world it meant a deeper, purer, finer vision of the Creator and of his relationship to man. Instead of broad Classical principles of socially useful behavior, the Hebraic mind multiplied ritualistic laws which it believed would be pleasing to God. Athletic contests with their emphasis on skill were of less interest to the Hebrews than singing and dancing, the speech of the heart. While the Greeks and Romans sought the perfection of the civil state, the Hebrews placed full faith in their leaders, sent by God or anointed by God's priests. Knowing that the rule of Heaven was not democratic, the ancient Jews bowed before the Lord's Anointed as God's representative on earth, thus originating a theory of the divine right of kings which was to reappear many times in Western history. Interestingly enough, both cultures developed a respect for the individual, regardless of his social position. But whereas the

Classical world delighted especially to honor the man of skill, the Hebraic community listened with respect to the man who spoke with the voice of God.

The literary achievements of the two cultures are necessarily in contrast. The term *Classical* is synonymous with formalized, sophisticated art. Hebraic writings, on the other hand, are spontaneous, simple, natural. Their glory lies in their humanity, their appeals to the heart, and their moments of mystic rapture and unearthly magnificence. Possibly because emotionalism and pessimism are related or, more likely, because of the prolonged Hebraic record of manifold sufferings, the dominant tone of Hebraic writing is in sharp contrast to the usual optimism of Classical compositions; a noteworthy indication of Hebrew pessimism is the odd circumstance that the Hebrew day begins in the evening and the Hebrew year begins in the fall. Believing (unlike the Greeks and Romans) that they knew the basic secret of the universe, the Hebrews were much more interested in details of everyday life and in stories of their ancestors than in elaborate analysis of any sort. For formal, perfect, coherent, incisive speech, fanciful but disciplined imagination, deeply felt but tightly restrained utterances, one turns to Classical literature. For ecstasy, lyricism, inspired mysticism, massive grandeur, lavish and often extravagant imagery, sensuous warmth, or scenes of simple and touching domesticity, Hebraic literature is unsurpassed in the entire field of creative writing.

Both cultures were highly idealistic, each in its own way, and both had certain attitudes in common. Both Hebraic and Classical civilizations were highly self-conscious, family conscious, and certain of their superiority to all others. The ancient Hebrews, as a "chosen race," as children of a single progenitor, as removed from all foreigners or Gentiles by the rite of circumcision, were undoubtedly more exclusive than either the Greeks or the Romans. But it must not be overlooked that the Classical world was itself not free from these same exclusivist attitudes, though they were perhaps less frequently and less vehemently expressed. Similarly, mysticism was far from being a Hebraic monopoly; it flourished also in Greece and Rome, particularly in the cults of Eleusis and Orpheus. Monotheism existed in the Classical world and polytheism was not unknown to the Hebrews.

But in the most characteristic achievements of each culture, the distinction between Hebraism and Classicism is nevertheless clear. As end products of the two civilizations one might specify as peculiarly Classical the wonderfully rational but cold-blooded society of Plato's ideal state or the actual civic organization of Augustine Rome. In contrast, for a high point of Hebraic culture one might cite the two principles, love of God and love of neighbor, which Jesus selected from Hebrew scripture and specified as the two greatest commandments. Because of such ultimate achievements it is possible to say that Classicism was essentially the product of the mind; Hebraism, of the heart.

II. HISTORY OF THE ANCIENT JEWS

"Hebrew" (wanderers) they were called by the Canaanites, and the total history of the Jews is largely a story of wanderings. After an indeterminate period of nomadic existence, they became molded into a small but highly individualized nation largely as a result of persecution by others. Their early history is singularly vague. Their own records, however colorful and exact on individual details, are barren of dates until late in the story. They were too small a group to be noted in the records of surrounding nations, and even cross references of occurrences in their own history to events in other parts of the world are extremely difficult to make because the ancient Jewish historians simply ignored anything that happened in the Gentile world. Even the Egyptian monarchs with whom the

Hebrews were so intimately connected are not named as individuals but are designated simply as "pharaoh" (the ruler). As a result, all dates for early Hebrew history are approximate and are still the subject of dispute among historians.

The ancestors of the Jews, of Semitic stock like the Assyrians, Babylonians, and Phoenicians, were Bedouins living around the fringes of the Arabian desert. Probably moving in small family units or tribes, carrying crude skin tents and meager possessions with them from place to place in search of pasture land, subsisting principally on sheep, goats, milk, and cheese, they lived a very simple nomadic existence. From earliest times, they were in contact with Babylonian civilization and may have derived some of their stories (such as that of the flood) from similar Babylonian legends encountered during this earliest period in their history.

Somewhere between 2000 and 1700 B.C. pioneers like Abraham began to drift toward the more fertile regions bordering the Mediterranean. Some of them settled in Canaan, possibly acquiring the designation "Hebrew" as early as this; others were drawn to the richer civilization of Egypt. There is no reason to doubt the Biblical statement that famines in Canaan prompted increasing migrations into Egypt where government granaries helped tide the population over the "lean years." The many recorded movements back and forth between Canaan and Egypt were made possible because Egypt during this period was under the rule of a foreign dynasty known as the Hyksos or Shepherd Kings, who were friendly toward the Jews. At any rate, regardless of how or when they came to Egypt, it is clear that a large community of these Semitic peoples found prosperity in Goshen (the northeastern section of Egypt) between 1700 and 1500 B.C.

When a new national Egyptian dynasty overturned the

alien rulers, the Semitic community was apparently enslaved and put to work at hard and unrewarding labor on
national projects, possibly as a kind of revenge for the
favors shown them by previous pharaohs. If they were not
already self-conscious as a special group of people, this long
period of enslavement was more than adequate to draw
them together into a rather definite kind of social unit.

Around 1290 there emerges the first certainly historical
Hebrew leader, Moses. The fact that his name is Egyptian
by no means substantiates the surmise of some historians
that he was the illegitimate child of a king's daughter. If,
as the picturesque Jewish story narrates, he was really found
in the ark of bulrushes by a princess and brought up by
her, he would inevitably have been given an Egyptian
name. The general outline of the remainder of the story
has the ring of complete authenticity. According to the
account in Exodus, Moses was forced to flee from Egypt
after killing an Egyptian for striking a Hebrew. In view of
his later religious leadership it is very interesting to follow
the story of his flight to Midian where he married a daughter of Jethro, a priest, lived with his father-in-law for a
period of years, and later relied on Jethro's advice when
they were together in the wilderness.

After an unspecified time in Midian, Moses returned to
Egypt and obtained the consent of the pharaoh to lead the
Hebrews out of Egypt. After the memorable crossing of one
of the estuaries of the Gulf of Suez, the western arm of
water at the top of the Red Sea, they apparently attempted
a return to Canaan. Probably because of the enmity of the
intervening tribes, they were forced into a southerly detour
around the edge of the Sinai peninsula at the top of the
Red Sea. The vivid record in Exodus and Numbers of
starvation and threats of rebellion against their leader adds
to the stature of Moses, who guided them to the then active
volcano of Mt. Sinai at the south of the peninsula, where

amidst smoke, thunderings, and fire, he made a population of slaves into an independent nation, created a national religion by enjoining upon them the worship of Yahweh above all other gods, gave them a religious and ethical code in the Ten Commandments, and organized them into definite social and military units. Again the time involved is not entirely clear, but a clue in Exodus indicates forty years as the total period between the departure from Egypt and the arrival in Canaan,[2] sufficient time for a new generation to grow up and be trained as warriors. It is reasonable to assume that the journey to Mt. Sinai occupied only a short part of this time and that the remaining period was devoted principally to a long period of rest and organization somewhere to the northeast of the sacred mountain.

When Moses was apparently satisfied that his people were ready to invade Canaan, an organized northward march began. Again the extraordinarily realistic Hebraic record is filled with accounts of disaffection, backslidings, and desertions. Amidst all this Moses, one of the greatest leaders of all time, died and was succeeded by Joshua, a military man, who led the conquest of indeterminate portions of Canaan.

The record of the two hundred years immediately following the invasion (1225-1025 B.C.) is fragmentary and rather difficult to understand. Canaan at the time was ruled by a line of weak Egyptian monarchs unable to protect its inhabitants from frequent raids and invasions of neighboring tribes. The Hebrews, meanwhile, seem to have lost the impetus and unity which made their own invasion successful. Poorly organized in loose tribal units, separated from each other by Canaanites and other local peoples, evicted from their territories by encroachments of Midianites, Amelakites, Philistines, and others, they seem to have been in grave danger of disintegration. Many turned to the

[2] Ex. 16:35.

worship of local gods (Baalim, Ashtaroth, and others). Israel survived partly because of a core of the valiantly faithful, partly because of the continued strength of the southern tribe of Judah, and partly because of the appearance of a number of leaders, called Judges, who rallied from time to time a confused and disconsolate populace. One of the most remarkable elements in Jewish history is the continual ability of these people to produce inspired leaders during their most seemingly hopeless periods.

Toward the end of this dark period, the remarkable priest Samuel became the religious and temporal leader and apparently reunited and revivified the nation. At this point the most fearsome of Israel's enemies were the Philistines (a name meaning "people of the sea" and the origin of the name Palestine). Of Minoan or Greek origin, these invaders came from the Mediterranean and conducted successful warfare against the Hebrew settlements. When Samuel in his old age appointed his two sons to rule in his stead, he was opposed by the elders who demanded a king in imitation of other countries and particularly because of the necessity of strong military leadership in the face of Philistine aggression. Reluctantly Samuel acceded to their request and anointed Saul as the king. Saul was a spectacular military leader, but he was given to strange fits of despondency and temper which may have been the result of his having been placed in a position beyond his abilities.

After Saul's death in battle, Samuel chose as his successor David, a popular military leader who had ministered to Saul in his seizures and of whom the king had become insanely jealous. Under David, God's promise to Abraham to make of his seed a great nation seemed finally to be fulfilled. This many-sided monarch (poet, musician, warrior, general, administrator, religious leader) expanded Israel to occupy the greatest area in its total history and forced neighboring nations like Syria to pay tribute. His most brilliant achievement was the selection of Jerusalem as the capital of the newly united and powerful kingdom. Situated around Mount Zion, the city boasted scenic beauty and a high degree of military impregnability, and, in addition, it had the advantage of a fairly central location in Palestine. Because it was a newly captured city which had never been in the possession of any of the twelve tribes, it presented an aspect of neutrality and avoided the jealousy and resentment which would have resulted from the choice of a site in a more politically determined area. David also divided the kingdom into twelve sections, reminiscent of the original twelve tribes, and brought the Ark of the Covenant into Jerusalem, thus making the city the spiritual as well as the political center of the nation.

The reigns of David and his successor Solomon (970-930 B.C.) mark the apogee of Hebraic power and glory. The Philistines were held to a small region bordering the Mediterranean, surrounding kingdoms were forced to become subservient or at least friendly, the Hebrew Kingdom profited by amicable arrangements with traders who passed through its territories, and Solomon (with his palace, temple, wives, and concubines) set a standard of royal splendor which rivalled that of neighboring oriental potentates.

Beneath all this glory, however, there was much internal friction and discord. In spite of David's finely conceived attempts to remind the Jews of their cultural unity, there remained considerable recalcitrance among the northern tribes. Even at the height of David's career, his son Absalom had momentarily succeeded in an open rebellion, which broke out again just before David's death when Adonijah, David's second son, took over the government with the backing of the northern divisions. The prophet Nathan and David's wife Bathsheba, reinforced by some of the leading men of Jerusalem, persuaded David to name Solomon as his successor. After David's death, Solomon solidified his reign by a blood purge of his leading enemies and by the appointment of a High Priest of his own choosing. Although proverbially noted for wisdom, he continued to make enemies among his people by defection from Hebrew religious standards and by lavish personal expenditures. Solomon's glory was built by paying low wages and extorting ruinous taxes, and was supplemented by his business ventures in building a fleet of trading ships, conducting large-scale dealings in horses, and operating mines, ventures which also necessitated grossly underpaid or, more likely, slave labor. Overt signs of Solomon's precarious position were his "gift" of twenty cities to the Phoenicians and the sporadic rebellions of tributary peoples culminating in the loss of Syria.

After Solomon's death the active discontent of the northern tribes broke out into civil war upon the accession to the throne of his son Rehoboam who threatened even worse tyranny. The ten northern tribes seceded under the kingship of Jeroboam, a previous enemy of Solomon who had taken refuge in Egypt. He established the capital of the new northern kingdom at Samaria (which later became a term of reference for the whole region whose inhabitants became known as Samaritans) and apparently encouraged defection from the worship of Yahweh as a way of weakening the prestige of Jerusalem whose temple had been ordained as the central place of worship. Thenceforth the ten northern tribes were designated as the Kingdom of Israel, and the two southern tribes of the Kingdom of Judah (from which we get the term *Jew*) were all that was left to support the prestige of Jerusalem.

There followed some two hundred years of quarrellings, jealousies, and sporadic warfare between the two parts of the divided kingdom. To make matters worse, persistent raids from Egypt at the south and Syria at the north weakened both kingdoms. Syria revenged its previous servitude by exacting tribute of the northern kingdom and even forced Judah to offer lavish gifts as the price of continued independence.

In 733 B.C. Assyria (not to be confused with Syria) conquered in turn Syria and Israel, enslaved many of the inhabitants, and took over the control of both Israel and Judah. In punishment of a conspiracy of Hoshea, King of Israel, to enlist Egyptian aid against the Assyrians, a direct attack by Assyria in 721 B.C. led to the destruction of Samaria and the end of the northern kingdom. The conqueror carried away into captivity many of the leading men and replaced them with other groups drawn from different sections of the Assyrian empire. Those who remained lost their identity as Jews and became part of the mixed Samarian population. "Samaritan" was thereafter a term of contempt in Judah, but at the same time, the disappearance of these ten divisions of Israel was romanticized by the Jews into a nostalgic mourning for "the ten lost tribes."

The southern kingdom of Judah (now pathetically described as "the remnant") maintained its integrity by paying tribute to Assyria. Deeply aware of their ignominious decline from former glory and goaded by prophets who ascribed Israelite defeats to Yahweh's wrath at their moral and spiritual laxity, the Judeans gradually strengthened and deepened their religious convictions. The inspired religious teachings of Isaiah at the beginning of this period and the subsequent exhortations of Jeremiah bore fruit in what is known as the Deuteronomic Reform under King Josiah at the end of the seventh century B.C. Josiah's destruction of pagan shrines, his execution of priests of other gods, and his total crusade for a return to the purity of Yahweh worship is ascribed to the discovery of a book (believed to be all or part of Deuteronomy) "that Hilkiah the priest found in the house of the Lord" [3] in 621 B.C. Josiah also took advantage of the decline of Assyrian power by recovering Judah's independence in that same momentous year. But the interval of freedom was brief, lasting only

[3] II Kings 23:24.

until 608 B.C. when Josiah was killed in a battle with the Egyptians. His successor, after a three months' reign, capitulated completely to Egypt.

While Assyria and Egypt were contending for Palestine and while Judah was attempting to survive by casting its lot alternately with one or the other, a third power, Babylonia, was rising to a position of prominence in the Near East. In 605 B.C. the Babylonian Nebuchadnezzar defeated armies of both Assyria and Egypt, and Judah became a Babylonian province. When the puppet king Jehoiakim (encouraged by Egypt) refused to pay the annual tribute to Babylonia, Nebuchadnezzar marched into Jerusalem (597 B.C.) and deported to captivity in Babylonia many leading citizens. A subsequent rebellion under Zedekiah brought about the destruction of Jerusalem in 586 B.C. and the carrying away of a great many of the remaining Jews. Others fled into Egypt.

During the fifty years of what is known as the Babylonian captivity, remarkable religious leaders like Jeremiah held the Jews together, encouraging much more strict religious observances. This self-conscious reintegration of a group thus repeated in part the experiences of the original Egyptian captivity. Although it is obvious that a great many Jews were far from unhappy in exile, their religious zeal and their sense of special distinction as a "chosen people" were undoubtedly very much heightened. By this time, many of the Jews had undoubtedly come to believe that their destiny was not to be political leadership but rather to provide spiritual leadership as the "suffering servants" of God as Isaiah had preached.[4]

In 538 B.C. after the Persians had conquered Babylonia, Cyrus permitted the Jews to return to Jerusalem and reestablish a colony under Persian jurisdiction but adminis-

---

4 Isa. 53:3-12.

tered by their own governors. The hardships involved in re-establishing the city amidst aliens retarded a rapid return, but, as had happened so many times in Hebrew history, inspired leaders eventually succeeded in bringing many of them back to rededicate the city, rebuild the walls, and erect a second temple to replace the original structure of Solomon.

In 333 B.C. the conquest of Alexander the Great marked the beginning of a process of Hellenization of the Jews. For the first time, they were exposed to a large degree of Classical civilization and culture. Although many of them remained stolidly provincial and strictly orthodox, a general tendency toward increasing worldliness and sophistication was soon noticeable. Many eagerly grasped the opportunity for this new Western learning; many imitated the novelties of Greek dress, manners, and customs. With these new habits there appears to have been a general deterioration in moral tone and spiritual earnestness. Priests became more worldly, more corrupt, and deeply jealous of their prerogatives, and placed more insistence on strict ritualistic observance than on heartfelt piety. Under such conditions many of the Jews migrated to Alexandria and other urban centers of Mediterranean culture, some lured by intellectual, economic, and cultural inducements, others moved by disgust at the deterioration of Jerusalem, which was gradually becoming more of an international city than a sacred shrine. This was the beginning of the dispersion of the Jews throughout the world.

After the death of Alexander in 323 B.C., control of Palestine fell into the hands of a succession of Greek rulers known as the Ptolemies, who were descended from one of Alexander's generals. In 198 B.C. they were succeeded by the Seleucids, descended from another of the generals, who ruled until 167 B.C.

The last political achievement in ancient Jewish history

occurred in the brilliant revolution begun by Judas Mac-
cabeus and continued by his successors of the "Maccabean
dynasty." A religious as well as a national movement, it led
to the purification of the temple in 165 B.C., the complete
overthrow of Greek control in 142 B.C., and the subsequent
annexation and forced conversion of the Samaritans to the
north and the Edomites to the south. After the re-establishment of independence, an inevitable relaxation of fervor
took place and the rift between worldly priests and a strict
religious group known as the Pharisees was widened, but
for seventy-nine years Jerusalem remained free until the
Roman conquest of 63 B.C.

From 40 to 4 B.C., Palestine was ruled by the Roman
puppet king Herod, a half-Jewish and apparently depraved
tyrant whose behavior stimulated a revival of the prophesies
of the coming of a Messiah or Redeemer who would restore
the Jews to at least the glory of the days of Solomon. When
Jesus of Nazareth (probably born in 4 B.C. in terms of our
present calendar) was declared to be the fulfillment of the
prophecy, he was eagerly adopted as the Messiah by throngs
who prepared the way for his triumphal entry into Jerusalem in A.D. 30. Regarded with justifiable suspicion by
Roman authorities and Jewish priests (whom he had attacked for their empty ritualism and worldliness), he was
five days later crucified with the approval of the Roman
procurator Pontius Pilate.

The death of Jesus and his failure to reappear in glory as
a political leader caused the disillusionment of many, or
perhaps most, of his followers. Consequently, while Christianity was beginning its growth to become the dominant
religion of the Western world, most of the Jews rejected
the new faith and returned to the orthodoxy of the past to
await the true Messiah who was yet to come.

In A.D. 66 an unsuccessful rebellion against Rome led,
after a long siege, to the destruction of Jerusalem and the

temple by Titus, son of Vespasian. An estimated million of the Jews were killed, others were enslaved, and the remainder scattered in search of the established Jewish colonies in other parts of the world. The official date of the Diaspora (or dispersion) is thus A.D. 70, when the conquest of Jerusalem was completed. With the priests no longer in power, the Pharisees accepted the leadership of rabbis (teachers or expounders of the law) to preserve the traditions of Hebrew history, learning, and religion, and to keep them isolated from the feared Gentiles.

Although scattered throughout the world, the Jews continued to add to their religious concepts. Rabbi Judah, toward the end of the second century A.D. codified the elaborations of Pharisaic doctrine which had been begun by Hillel under Herod into the *Mishna* ("Doctrine"), a long document containing precise instruction for the conduct of every phase of human life. Before the sixth century, there was added to this a huge, disjointed commentary which, together with the *Mishna,* is known as the *Talmud.*

The long history of Jewish migrations and persecutions has no place in this volume, but a sketchy outline should be added to complete the picture. In the third century, Babylonia provided temporary refuge where schools were founded and where the addition of vowel points to the consonantal text of the scriptures helped clarify basic Jewish writings. Accepted by the Moslems, many Jews migrated to Spain around A.D. 1000. In 1215 the Jew Badge Law imposed by the Church forbade Jews to own land and forced them into a livelihood of business and finance. They were expelled from England in 1290, from France in 1394, from Spain in 1492, from Portugal in 1497. In Germany and Italy they were sequestered in ghettos. Spanish Jews migrated to Turkey, where the Spanish dialect in Hebrew characters was known as Ladino. German Jews who found refuge in Poland and Russia adopted a similar combination

of languages called Yiddish ("Jüdisch"). It was not until
the twentieth century that years of active campaigning for
the establishment of a "Homeland" led to the setting up
by the United Nations of the present Jewish nation of
Israel in 1949.

III. HEBREW RELIGION

The greatest single contribution of Hebraism to Western
civilization was religion. That Christianity was cradled in
Palestine, was originally spread throughout the Western
world principally by Jews, and was built on the solid structure of Hebraic inspiration is simple fact. But of equal
importance is the special quality of religious sensitivity
inherited by the Western world—to the degree that to be
"religious" today implies holding the pious, mystical attitude recorded of the Jewish patriarchs and prophets.

Of the multitudinous religions of the world, that of
the ancient Jews was unique in several important respects.
It was essentially monotheistic, a rare tendency in the ancient world. It was a national religion to the extent that
most Hebrew holidays are commemorations of national
events. It was susceptible to change and growth to meet the
demands of a changing society. It was so all-important and
omnipresent in ancient Palestine that it became the authority for the form of government, for standards of ethics,
customs and behavior, for principles of economics, for sani-
tary codes—in fact, it controlled the entire life of the
individual and produced a completely theocratic state. It
combined standards of personal perfection with broad
social concerns: it sought always to protect the weak and the
poor. It fostered a sense of intimate relationship between
man and God known to no other pre-Christian faith; it was
the only ancient religion, as Frederick B. Artz has so brilliantly pointed out, which offered the concept of "a God
who was seeking man." [5] It created the most humane stand-

[5] *The Mind of the Middle Ages*, p. 62.

ards of ethical conduct, the most severe tests of personal piety, and the deepest religious feeling of the ancient world. Its ultimate achievement is probably best summed up in the two admonitions which the founder of Christianity named the two greatest commandments (Mark 12: 30-31): "Thou shalt love the Lord thy God with all thine heart, and with all thy soul, and with all thy might" (Deut. 6:4) and "Thou shalt love thy neighbor as thyself" (Lev. 19:17).

The Hebraic concept of God was an unusually flexible one, as would be expected of a people who made the study of the nature of God a primary concern of life. Far from being a weakness of the religion, the many revelations of the different and often contradictory aspects of deity offered such a variety of interpretations of the divine nature that any Jew (or Christian) could find at least one concept of godhead to suit his personal spiritual needs. These different interpretations existed side by side, and, because of the uncertainty of dates in early Hebraic writing, it is impossible to do more than speculate about their origins. But a line of probable development may be hazarded.

From an original polytheism, common to all the neighboring religions, there was a pronounced trend toward monotheism, largely the product of a series of extraordinary religious leaders.[6] Probably the earliest "one God" of the Jews was a kind of nature deity, the indwelling spirit of Mount Sinai. Named Yahweh (mistranslated Jehovah in the King James version of the Bible) and true to the volcanic nature of the mountain, this was a god of thunderings, destruction, and fire, a god of wrath who was quick to

[6] As A. C. Bouquet explains in his excellent survey of *Comparative Religion*, nearly all religions tend to contain both monotheistic and polytheistic tendencies. Official Greek religion with its many gods nevertheless revered Zeus as the all-father, and both Plato and Aristotle believed in one God. On the other hand, Christianity, which regards itself as monotheistic, recognizes a trinal godhead, a community of demi-gods (the angels), demonic immortals (Satan and his followers) and, in Catholicism, a Queen of Heaven and a company of saints. A. C. Bouquet, *Comparative Religion,* esp. pp. 60-115.

punish, a jealous god who recognized the existence of other gods but who demanded primacy of worship from his special people. Like the Greek gods, he delighted in sacrifice of animals, birds, or grain and in ceremonials designed to placate his anger. Highly emotional, he gave vent to his wrath by producing such catastrophes as the flood or the destruction of Sodom and Gomorrah and by causing sufferings, enslavements, plagues, famines, and military defeats to visit a recalcitrant people.

The first step toward a more humane idea of divinity was the appearance of an anthropomorphic conception of a deity who talked with Adam and Eve in the Garden of Eden, allowed himself to be bargained with by Abraham, permitted Moses to look upon his back, and loved the sweet savor of burnt offerings.[7] From this rather intimate deity who parallels the gods in Homer, he gradually grows in majesty and remoteness, becoming the sole creator of the cosmos, the universal and only god of mankind with Israel as his chosen people. The God of Moses is no longer an arbitrary oriental potentate but a steadfast ruler who may be best served by keeping his laws, outlined by the ten commandments and all the later additions and elaborations. A summation of this central and most enduring phase of Hebrew religion is contained in the pronouncement, "Behold, I set before you this day a blessing and a curse; a blessing if ye obey the commandments of the Lord your God . . . and a curse if ye will not obey the commandments of the Lord your God but turn aside out of the way . . . to go after other gods." [8]

The record of Jewish religious faith, though probably slanted by priestly editors, is one of constant backsliding

---

[7] Attention should be called to the fact that the order of Hebraic writings in the Old Testament is not the same as the order of the composition of the narratives which are combined in these books.

[8] Deut. 11:26-28.

and of strayings toward other gods. And yet the miracle of the Jews is that, while surrounded by less strict religions and sorely tempted to placate fertility deities who might increase agricultural and human productiveness, they in the main held fast to the arduous worship of a god of law. In the service of this divinity, sacrifice, ritual, and moral conduct were intertwined. Semitic delicacy placed unusual emphasis on hygienic laws, but sin might be almost anything from the breaking of a moral law to the omission of a prescribed ritualistic ceremony. Outstanding in all the piled-up rituals and regulations for nearly every action of human life is the emphasis on observance of the Sabbath as a day of rest, one of the greatest social inventions of all time.

The central concepts of Judaism also included a multiplicity of angels who acted as servants of Yahweh and occasionally as messengers to man. One of the angels, Satan, became identified as the judge of human righteousness. His method of discernment was that of tempting the individual to do evil. He thus became associated with the serpent in the Garden of Eden, and later, influenced by the duality of Persian religious belief in gods of good and evil, he became the fallen angel, now devil, who conducts eternal warfare against God. A symbolic passage in Isaiah describing Babylonia as the star Lucifer was later misinterpreted as the rebellion of Satan against God and was the authority for the story of the devil's fall from heaven to hell. The idea that human beings after death were to be consigned to one of these two regions for eternity was a much later, and principally Christian, development. Ancient Judaism regarded rewards and punishments as principally temporal and material; Sheol, the place of the dead, was a shadowy underworld region even less clearly defined than the Hades of Homer.

During the process of the building of these religious con-

cepts, there appeared also many warmer and closer interpretations of divinity, revealed especially in the Psalms,
and there developed a kind of dual religious leadership
among the Israelites. On the one side were the priests, an
official hierarchy descended from Aaron concerned with
maintaining strict tradition; on the other were the prophets
(or spokesmen) of Yahweh. The prophets were men coming
from any level of society who considered themselves directly
commissioned by God to reveal the divine behests.[9] Some
of them actually prophesied future events, but in our sense
of the word, they were "prophets" only in their habitual
practice of predicting calamity to those who refused to heed
their words. The earliest noteworthy prophet of whom
there is any dependable record was Nathan who boldly
rebuked David for his misconduct and thereafter became
a counsellor of the king, creating a pattern often followed
thereafter. After the division of the two kingdoms in 930 B.C.
the prophets increased in number and in eloquence, probably reaching their highest power and effectiveness during
the period of the Babylonian captivity.

Each of the prophets is distinctly individual. But
although most of them denounced, others pleaded, and a
few were given to mystical visions, they were alike in many
respects. They condemned social injustice, they condemned
empty ritual, they denounced hypocrisy, they emphasized
the closeness of God's spiritual relationship with man, they
rhapsodized on the theme of the glory of God, and some
of them, like Isaiah and the unknown composer or composers of the latter part of the Book of Isaiah, produced the
noblest, the most inspired, and the most eloquent persua-
sions to righteousness that Hebraic writing affords. In a
way the prophets are central figures in a religious faith

---

[9] The best clue to the exact meaning of "prophet" is the scriptural
record that Yahweh appointed Aaron to be his prophet or spokesman
when Moses pleaded his own inadequacy in speaking before Pharaoh.

which stresses the individual calling of man by God to God.

The teachings of the prophets also produced a rift in the Hebrew religious community, a rift which widened as the priests continued to cling to ritual and sacrificial codes of an essentially primitive religion while the prophets, as more advanced spokesmen of Yahweh's will, proclaimed that right living was more important than empty ritual and provided many new interpretations of "the ways of God to man." Many of the priests were revered for their devout piety, but the words of the prophets were recorded and treasured as an especial indication of God's direct communication with his people.

The first literary prophet, Amos (in the eighth century B.C.), was principally concerned with moral behavior and generosity to the poor. Hosea at the same period introduced the highly evocative concept of Israel as the bride of God, a figure adapted by Christianity in describing the Church as the bride of Christ. Isaiah revolutionized the older belief that rewards and punishments were temporal and material by suggesting an after-life of glory for the good and eternal punishment for the wicked. These clues were eagerly taken up by many of the succeeding prophets who became increasingly concerned with Israel's spiritual rather than temporal leadership, and who, in agreement with Persian Zoroastrianism, conceived of a heaven and a hell for the deceased. Heaven is not defined in their writings, but Hell is described as Gehenna, a corruption of "Ge Hinnon," the name of a pagan shrine where children were sacrificed as burnt offerings to a heathen god.

Of utmost importance too are the predictions of many of the prophets of the coming of a Messiah (more fully discussed in Chapter 13) who would confound the wicked and raise the chosen race to their destined place of world leadership. In the darkest periods of their history these predictions enabled the Jews to continue their faith in good hope that purification through suffering would eventually bring them individually to Paradise and nationally to political eminence. The prophet Zechariah added to this concept the teaching that the Israelites were "chosen" as agents for spreading the gospel of the one God throughout the world, another idea eagerly adopted by Christianity.

The total result of the prophetical preachings was to change the Mosaic code "Blessed is he who keepeth the Law" to what many consider the Christian code of "Blessed is he in whose spirit there is no guile." The entrenched priesthood, who clung to the traditions of the past and who were often appointed by the kings, were thus placed in opposition to a new enlightened series of religious ideas. Rival sects within the central framework of Judaism began to appear in the fourth century B.C. By the first century B.C. the Sadducees (party of the priests) were bitterly opposed to the Pharisees and the Essenes who continued to add new interpretations of the law.

The waning of priestly authority was also partly the result of the Babylonian captivity and later dispersions. When the offering of sacrifices in the temple of Jerusalem first became impossible, Jeremiah became the creator of modern Judaism by authorizing the synagogue (or meeting place) as an acceptable place of worship in lieu of the temple. He also stressed the importance of the individual's relationship to God, thereby changing the emphasis of Judaism from a national to a personal religion.

Meanwhile, the concept of Yahweh had been gradually moving away from anthropomorphism. Late in the sixth century B.C., "The Writings of the Unknown Prophet" (II Isaiah) refer to God as an eternal spirit, sole creator of all things, and God of all mankind. Thus late Judaism came to be very close in both doctrine and teachings to the tenets of Christianity. With the destruction of the last temple and the Diaspora, temple worship became impossible, and selected teachings of the Law together with the revelations of the prophets as interpreted by rabbis became the core of Jewish religion.

IV. HEBRAIC WRITINGS

Unlike Greek and Roman literature, the preservation and, in part, the writing of Hebrew literature, were in the hands of priests. The Hebraic literary heritage is the compilation of books which is known to Christians as the Old Testament and to Jews as "The Sacred Writings." As a result, religious writings predominate, but there is little likelihood that much of literary value has been lost. For, in the first place, religious utterances constituted the special genius of the Israelites, and, in the second place, the preservation of such an iconoclastic work as Ecclesiastes, the retaining of such a frankly sensual poem as the Song of Songs, and the failure to edit passages distasteful to both national and religious feeling make it clear that the priestly editors were unwilling to destroy any worth-while expression of the ancient Hebraic heart or mind. The Old Testament Canon (or approved writings), which differs slightly from one religion to another, is made up of thirty-nine books which were divided by the Jews into three sections: the Torah, the Prophets, and the Writings.

The Law, or Torah (the Christian Pentateuch or "five scrolls") is made up of five books traditionally ascribed to Moses and considered as the Word of God by the Jews as early as 400 B.C. In these five books of Genesis, Exodus, Leviticus, Numbers (*In the Wilderness* is the Hebraic title), and Deuteronomy is contained the tremendous undertaking of attempting to describe the entire history of the Jews from the creation of the universe to the invasion of Canaan, including history, biography, religious teachings, laws, rituals, songs, genealogies, legends, short stories, accounts of miracles—in short, nearly everything connected with ancient Jewish tradition and culture. The composition of these books was a long process beginning with ancient legends transmitted for generations by word of mouth until unknown authors finally set them down in writing.

Recent Biblical scholars are generally agreed that the Pentateuch reached essentially its present form in the fourth century B.C. when priestly editors compiled the Torah from at least three previous documents. One of these, the version used in the southern kingdom of Judah, is ascribed to the authorship of an unknown writer or writers identified simply as "J" because of the consistent use of Yahweh (JHVH) as the name of the Deity. The composition of the highly poetical and picturesque series of narratives which made up this document is guessed at as an achievement of the ninth century B.C. A second account known as the E-document because of its author's use of Elohim (the Lord) is more mystical but also more sophisticated and is believed to have originated in the northern kingdom in the eighth century B.C. The writings of J and E were combined by priestly editors together with their own additions (P) into the first four books of the Torah. A third and independent document, the Book of Deuteronomy (Greek for "the second law") appears to have been the work of a group of writers connected with what is known as the Deuteronomic Reform Movement of the seventh century B.C. and was "published" in 621 B.C. All of these were further edited and augmented for the sake of emphasizing religious significance by a line of priestly writers known as "P" who started to work on these records around 500 B.C. and continued to revise until around 250 B.C.

The second section of the Old Testament is known as the Prophets. It contains twenty-one books, six of which (Joshua, Judges, I and II Samuel, and I and II Kings) continue the history from the conquest of Canaan to the Babylonian captivity. The remaining books of the "major" and "minor" prophets are individual accounts and preachings of later religious leaders. The composition of these books dates from their inclusion of orally transmitted fragments from as early as 1200 B.C. to the second-century works of known authors.

Composed in a similar way over a long period of time, the remaining thirteen books, described simply as "The Writings," consist of a miscellaneous collection of history, songs, stories, philosophy, hymns, proverbial wisdom, and an elementary type of drama (in the Book of Job and the Song of Songs).

In contrast to Greek literary production, Hebraic writing is generally simpler, more earthy, more direct, and more spontaneous. It is often poorly organized and shows little regard for form and less for restraint. On the other hand, it speaks most eloquently the language of the heart in its vaulting imagery ("The morning stars sang together"),[10] its imaginative use of simile and metaphor ("The Lord is my shepherd"),[11] its warm humanity in simple and touching stories like that of Ruth, its high emotionalism everywhere present, its disarming frankness about human fallibility, and its unexcelled sense of majesty and grandeur ("Lift up your heads, O ye gates: and be ye lifted up, ye everlasting doors; and the King of glory shall come in").[12]

Largely because of this characteristic of spontaneity, Hebraic writing shows little concern for form in the Classic sense. Much of the prose is as rhythmic and colorful as verse; the poetry relies on rhythm and repetition rather than strict metrical arrangement. Prose and poetry are not strictly differentiated: one flows into the other, and often it is up to the editor to decide which is which. Both poetry and prose make frequent use of similes usually derived

[10] Job 38:7.
[11] Psalm 23:1.
[12] Psalm 24:7.

from nature (to whose inspiration a tremendous amount of later Western literature is indebted) and of a special device known as parallelism. Producing the aesthetic pleasure described by Wordsworth as "the perception of similitude in dissimilitude," parallelism consists in the repetition or almost-exact repetition of a pattern of words, thoughts, or rhythms. Sometimes the same idea is repeated but in different or slightly different words, as in the Song of Deborah: "At her feet he bowed, he fell, he lay down: at her feet he bowed, he fell: where he bowed, there he fell down dead." [13] More often, the rhythmic and grammatical pattern is repeated but the same or a similar idea is presented in different words. "The heavens declare the glory of God; and the firmament sheweth his handiwork" is the opening line of the Nineteenth Psalm, which continues with further additions to the same duplicative pattern. Sometimes a catalog of opposites conforms to a single word pattern as in Ecclesiastes III: "A time to kill, and a time to heal; a time to break down, and a time to build up." The tendency to clothe ideas in such repeated patterns seems to have been almost instinctive among Hebraic writers.

Larger technical forms (like the ode, drama, epic) were unknown among the ancient Hebrews, but many of their writings approximate literary genres created by the Classical world. Although, strictly speaking, there is no Hebraic epic, the historical writings contain (with many interruptions) a single national narrative which might well be called "The Epic of the Promised Land" and which, in its contrapuntal effect of promise, disappointment, and renewed promise to a people seeking a home, is very close in spirit to Virgil's *Aeneid*. The epic begins in Genesis with God's promise to Abraham to make him the father of a great nation. The promise is subsequently repeated to him and to his successors. Fulfillment is impeded by a succession of outer mis-

[13] Judges 5:27.

fortunes and barren wives who conceive miraculously late in life. The significance of this latter phase of the story is often overlooked by modern readers who are not aware of the moral issue involved in the resistance of such barren wives (or husbands to whom the birth of a son was of especial importance) to the inducements of the pagan fertility cults around them. The story with its many heroes is pursued through the Egyptian captivity to the conquest of Canaan, reaches its climax in the fulfillment of the promise in the victorious career of David and the glory of Solomon, and concludes with the final dissolution of the kingdom. In the same way, although the Hebrews had no dramatic literature, the story of Job is both in form and content a philosophical drama which has often been compared with *Prometheus Bound* in profundity.

Sacred and secular poems or songs were a special achievement of Hebraic genius, but the outstanding literary achievement of the ancient Jews is clearly the art of narrative. Story after story, clearly, easily, briefly, and vividly told, fills the pages of the Old Testament. Jonah and Ruth are superb short stories, and the oriental art of story-telling (as witnessed by the *Arabian Nights*) reached the Western world most compellingly through these narratives of the Old Testament.

Two literary modes, the parable and the apocalypse, appear to have been the special inventions of Hebrew genius. The parable is a kind of allegorical preaching which makes its point by reference to some homely, easily understood parallel in everyday life. The earliest recorded parable is that of the trees in Judges IX, but the best and most familiar example is Nathan's parable of the rich man told to David after David had caused Bathsheba's husband to be slain in battle.[14] It is worthy of note that much of the preaching of Jesus took the form of parables.

[14] II Sam. 12.

The other apparently Hebraic invention was the creation
of apocalyptic writings. The term *apocalypse* means "revelation," and the apocalyptic writings (the most notable of
which are the Hebrew books of Ezekiel and Daniel and the
Christian book called The Revelation of St. John) arose
from the fevered dreams of inspired prophets during periods of oppression. They contain visions of strange, fantastic, and utterly inexplicable figures and happenings. Some
of these were (and are) interpretable in terms of events
current at the time of their composition. Others may have
been understandable to an oppressed group who knew a
"code" for the interpretation of these strange imaginings
which their oppressors did not. The most obvious tendency
is the successful attempt to shroud these visions in mystery,
implying perhaps that the revelations of God were beyond
understanding, unless possibly to the elect. Attempts to
decipher these occult messages contributed decisively to the
medieval love of allegory or interest in hidden meanings.

Books of the Old Testament

THE TORAH

Regarded as sacred as early as 500 B.C., the first five books of
the Old Testament are known as the Torah (Law) by Jews and
as the Pentateuch (Five Scrolls) by Christians. Although traditionally ascribed to Moses, they are apparently of multiple authorship, dating in composition from the ninth century B.C. (or earlier
in oral tradition) to perhaps as late as the fourth century B.C.,
with revisions possibly continuing another 150 years. The present
version of these five documents owes much to the Deuteronomic
Reform Movement which began under King Josiah of Judah in
621 B.C. and marked a heightened religious sensitivity which
lasted well into the fourth century B.C.

Genesis (The Beginnings) is the celebrated opening book of the Old Testament and constitutes the first chapter of an extraordinarily ambitious attempt to trace the continuous history of the Jews back to the creation of the world. After a series of stories (regarded as legendary by many scholars), including the Creation, the story of Cain and Abel, the Flood, the Tower of Babel, and the strangely un-Hebraic account of the giants born of sons of God and daughters of men, the "Epic of the Promised Land" begins something like real history with the accounts of Abraham, Isaac, Jacob, and the migration to Egypt at the time of Joseph.

Exodus (The Road Out) is a dramatic and condensed account of the escape from Egypt under the leadership of Moses. It recounts the story of the multiplication and persecution of the Jews in Egypt since the time of Joseph, the struggle of Moses and his brother Aaron to convince Pharoah to permit them to escape, and the journey to Mt. Sinai after the miraculous crossing of the Red Sea. At Mt. Sinai Moses began the creation of a theocratic nation regarded as a kingdom of priests, a holy people. With a basic code of the Ten Commandments and a long series of subsidiary laws, Judges were appointed to be leaders of tribal units, and through a period of some forty years, an organized military, civil, and religious state was painfully created. Aaron and his descendents were named to be the priesthood; the Levites (Aaron's tribe) were to assist with secondary priestly functions.

Leviticus is an elaborate compilation of laws and ritual relating to sacrifices, consecration of the priesthood, distinctions between the "clean" and the "unclean," sex behavior, health, ethics, and admonitions to generosity. Those who break the laws are to be forced to make restitution, to be cut off from the people, or to be put to death. If the laws are not kept, the nation and its prosperity will perish. Buried in a mass of rules and regulations is what Jesus called the second great commandment, "Thou shalt love the stranger as thyself." (19:33)

Numbers is so named because it begins with a census of the tribes. The Hebrew title *In the Wilderness* better describes this continuation of the story of Exodus. The journey into Canaan is resumed, hardships and jealousies provoke frequent rebellions, Joshua is appointed to succeed Moses after his death, and a successful war against the Midianites begins the record of Jewish victories. Interspersed with this strikingly realistic record of triumphs and setbacks are interruptions of the narrative to set forth more tables of ritual and law and also the delightful story of Balaam and the talking ass.

Deuteronomy (The Second Law). This book, or some part of it, seems to be that document which the High Priest presented to King Josiah in 621 B.C. as a newly discovered book of the law. It is represented as a series of speeches delivered by Moses just before his death. Written in a more eloquent style and presenting a considerably more humane and more highly civilized code of behavior than is the norm of the previous records, this body of injunctions and laws represents a high peak of Jewish religious development. The concluding chapters with the promise of multiple blessings for a pious Israel and multiple curses for a faithless Israel are superb examples of the power of the pen. The Deuteronomic Reform Movement of the seventh century B.C. needs to be accounted for by no other stimulus. Along with its central concept of one God for all mankind, with Israel as a "chosen people," it enjoins strict morality, love of God ("with all thine heart and with all thy soul"—the Shema, part of the daily prayer of every Jew and the first commandment of Jesus), and a spirit of generosity and concern for the poor and the stranger that many Christians believe to be unique in their religion.

THE PROPHETS

Following the Torah in the traditional arrangement of the Old Testament are thirty-four books which in turn are divided into the Prophets and the Writings. Of the twenty-one books designated as the Prophets, the first six continue the history of Israel to the Babylonian Captivity and are known as "the Former Prophets." "The Latter Prophets" include three "Major Prophets" (Isaiah, Jeremiah, Ezekiel) and twelve "Minor Prophets." This section of the Old Testament was apparently regarded as canonical by the second century B.C.

The Former Prophets

Joshua, regarded as another compilation of earlier documents completed by 500 B.C., picks up the narrative from the end of the Book of Numbers and describes the conquest of Canaan. Written in a vein of hero-worship, it principally glorifies the all-but-undefeatable leadership of Joshua (a Hebrew name mean-

ing "Yahweh is salvation," of which Jesus is the Greek variant).
Describing the entire conquest as being completed within twenty-
five years (a statement contradicted elsewhere) it is filled with
miraculous events such as the parting of the waters of the Jordan
to permit the passage of the people, the falling walls of Jericho,
and the sun's standing still to allow continued daylight for a
complete victory over five kings.

Judges is one of the oldest books of the Bible. Much of it is
probably close to its original form, and at least one part of it,
"The Song of Deborah," dates back to the twelfth century B.C.
Judges is also the most fragmentary of the historical records. It
begins with a realistic account of the actual situation of the
Israelites in Canaan after the death of Joshua. Apparently on
the verge of disintegration, they were rallied from time to time by
a series of leaders called Judges. The individual stories of several
of these leaders (Deborah, Gideon, and Samson being the most
famous) are woven together to make up the principal substance
of the book. The period described covers approximately the
twelfth and eleventh centuries B.C.

I Samuel is the beginning of what may be regarded as essentially accurate history, recorded shortly after the events or perhaps
compiled later from records made at the time. It describes in
detail the religious leadership of Samuel over a revived Israel,
his selection of Saul and David as Israel's first kings (ignoring the
brief three-year reign of Abimelech over a small area, described
in Judges), and the affecting story of the friendship of David and
Jonathan.

II Samuel opens with the beautiful and moving lament of
David over the deaths of Jonathan and Saul. It is devoted principally thereafter to a brilliant characterization of the many-sided
David. The series of stories of the depth and intensity of his
feelings includes his rapturous dancing before the Ark of the
Covenant when it was brought to Jerusalem, his passionate need
to possess Bathsheba, and his heartbroken lament over Absalom,
his rebellious son. The book also records the spiritual leadership
of the prophet Nathan and one of the best of the Old Testament
parables in Nathan's rebuke to David for the seduction of
Bathsheba.

I Kings. Except for the opening chapters concerning the death
of David and the deeds and glory of Solomon, the remainder of
this history is a pedestrian and confusing account of the secession of the ten northern tribes from the kingdom and the suc-

ceeding kings of Israel and Judah. Effective story-telling is resumed
toward the end of the book with the account of the religious
leadership, prophesies, and miracles of Elijah, certainly one of
the greatest of the Hebrew prophets. The emphasis on Elijah and
the highly moral attitude toward the many different rulers described suggests that this and the following book were written by
priests who used earlier and perhaps official court records as their
sources.

II Kings continues the account of Elijah until his miraculous
ascent to heaven and then describes the miracles and ministry
of his successor Elisha. A further record of the reigns of kings
ends with the capture of Israel by Assyria, the preservation of
Judah's independence by paying tribute, the Deuteronomic Reform Movement, and the final enslavement of Judah by Babylonia. This is the conclusion of an almost continuous historical
record of a people from the time of the pioneer Abraham to the
ironic captive return of his descendants to a region near the land
of his nativity. A much later recasting (c. 300 B.C.) of the materials
of Samuel and Kings makes up the contents of the two books
of **Chronicles** which add the account of the restoration of
Jerusalem under Cyrus.

The Latter Prophets

Although traditionally divided into three major and twelve
minor prophets, a more interesting approach to this compilation
of prophetic writings, which constitute so much of the later
developments of ancient Judaism, is to examine them in their
presumed historical sequence. The utterances of each of the
prophets are individual and timeless in their spiritual purport,
but the conditions of the period in which each lived often illuminate the special character of the pleadings and fulminations
of some of them. Listing them in historical sequence also serves
as a method of following the troubled course of Jewish history
after Solomon.

Amos, one of the most interesting as well as one of the most
broad-visioned of the prophets, was a herdsman living in Judah
in the eighth century B.C. who was inspired with a vision of a
purified and ennobled Jewish state. Apparently aware of the
parlous situation of the northern kingdom, he travelled to Israel
to preach a fiery message of doom unless repentance and a return
to pure worship should occur. A reasonable supposition is that

he was driven back to Judah where he composed the short book which bears his name. Outstanding among his tenets is condemnation of ritual unless attended by moral behavior. He was also a powerful advocate of social justice and of the special concern of Yahweh for the needy and the oppressed.

Hosea, the last prophet of the northern kingdom, follows the general tenor of Amos, his predecessor by a few years, but substitutes a tone of pleading for the violent denunciations typical of most of the prophets. An intense and gifted poet, he describes Israel as a harlot who has forsaken her loving spouse Yahweh. This imaginative allegory became a very popular concept and was repeated by later Jewish and Christian writers, becoming a part of the symbolism of Dante's *Divine Comedy*. The Christian concept of a God of love whose bride is the Church repeats in part this parable which is a far cry from earlier concepts of the thundering deity of Mt. Sinai.

Isaiah is one of the most eloquent, poetic, and idealistic books in the Old Testament. It is actually a combination of at least two groups of inspirational writings. The first thirty-nine chapters, mostly the work of Isaiah himself, are followed by a series of poems composed some two centuries later. This latter part of the book (Chapters 40-66) is sometimes referred to as II Isaiah or "The Rhapsodies of the Unknown Prophet." The spirit of Isaiah is almost identical with what many think of as distinctively Christian. Thundering at his contemporaries, he reiterates the teaching of Amos that a pure heart is superior to ritual and adds the concept of personal immortality (25:8), including the idea of the resurrection of the body (25:19). Intimations of heaven and hell are also indicated in the promise of salvation for "the remnant" (10:21; 28:16-18) and a descent into hell for the wicked (14). In a section interpolated by some later writer, Lucifer (the star used as a symbol of the previous glory of Babylonia) is referred to as contending against God and being cast down into hell (14:12-15), a statement which through misinterpretation may have originated the whole story of the fallen angels best known to English readers through Milton's *Paradise Lost*. Isaiah prophesies the coming of the Messiah in one of the most complete and idealistic of such prophecies (11 and 32). He is the only literary prophet known to have had disciples; he had an especial dislike of frivolous women (by which he may have meant all women); and he appears to have led the kind of ascetic life ascribed to John the Baptist, Jesus, and Saint Paul. The concluding chapters of this book will be described later under the heading of II Isaiah.

Micah, another composition of the eighth century B.C., is a very brief work notable chiefly for its tirade against wealthy and oppressive landowners and its eloquent summation of the finest of the prophetic teachings: "to do justly, and to love mercy, and to walk humbly with thy God" (6:8).

Nahum. Departing from the gloomy tone of most of the prophetical works, the Book of Nahum is actually a brief exultant victory poem occasioned by the Babylonian conquest of Nineveh in 612 B.C., here regarded as the triumph of God over the wickedness of Assyria, Israel's former enemy.

Obadiah, the shortest "book" in the Old Testament, is a bitter reproach of Edom, the province south of Judah, for siding with Babylonia. It would appear, therefore, to have been composed soon after the downfall of Jerusalem.

Malachi, opening with another condemnation of Edom, is a slightly longer anonymous preachment apparently contemporary with Obadiah. It castigates the evils of Judah as well and then turns to a prophecy of the Messiah (here called God's Messenger, "Malachi" in Hebrew) with the interesting additional prophecy that Isaiah would return as a forerunner to that day of judgment.

Jeremiah, the longest of the prophetic works (if Isaiah is correctly subdivided), along with the Book of Lamentations, wrongly though understandably accredited to the same author, has added the word *jeremiad* to our vocabulary because of his lament for the scattering of Israel by God as punishment for the corruption of its priests and its worship of other gods. Living just before and during the early part of the Babylonian captivity, Jeremiah is regarded as particularly the prophet of the exile because he described this calamity as a purifying process, because he emphasized the acceptability of worship in synagogues instead of the Jerusalem temple, and because he taught a doctrine of individual relationship to God (rather than the national responsibility of the "chosen people") which became the cornerstone of later Judaism and Christianity. Building on the figure of Jerusalem the harlot (introduced by Hosea), the Book of Jeremiah abounds in such picturesque and figurative language that it is one of the most quoted of Old Testament works, providing Jesus with his attack on the money-changers in the Temple (7:11), Dante with the three beasts of the *Inferno* (5:6), Poe with the "balm in

Gilead" line in *The Raven* (8:22), and many other writers with memorable phrases.

Zephaniah is a very brief book by one of Jeremiah's contemporaries. It is notable principally because of its vivid prediction of the Day of Wrath which was taken by later religionists as a description of the Last Judgment and made into a famous medieval Latin hymn, the *Dies Irae*.

Habakkuk is another prophetical work written at about the time of the fall of Jerusalem. It adds to the usual interpretation of sin as the cause of Judah's suffering a question concerning the length and extent of God's punishment and concludes with a resolution to live by faith which was made much of by Saint Paul.

Ezekiel. The author and date of composition of this uneven and often baffling book with its strained images and obscure references are still matters of scholarly debate. Its references, however, are to the period of the Babylonian captivity and convey eloquently the kind of leadership which preserved the spiritual community of Israel. Referred to as "son of man," the prophet opens with a mysterious and mystical vision of God, then turns to the traditional denunciations, and concludes with the Messianic prophecy of the Good Shepherd who will restore Israel.

II Isaiah. Chapter 40 in the original Book of Isaiah begins a series of magnificent poems of triumphant joy over the restoration of the Jews to Jerusalem by the Persian Cyrus in 538 B.C. Differences in both style and content have led scholars to attribute this work to an unknown prophet or prophets of that period. But whatever the truth about its authorship may be, it clearly belongs to a different time and temperament than the first thirty-nine chapters, and therefore should be treated as a separate work. Apart from the extremely imaginative beauty of the poetry and the tone of unqualified joy, so rare in Hebraic writing, II Isaiah also gives an inspired and inspiring theory of God and his relationship to his "chosen people." God is held to be an eternal spirit, creator of all things (including evil), who selected Israel to be his "suffering servant." Having been purified through the manifold afflictions of its history, Israel is now worthy to be restored to its position of world spiritual leadership. Christians have found in this book many of the best-known prophecies of the suffering Savior (especially Chapter 53).

Haggai. The event referred to in this brief book is probably of more interest than the work itself. After the restoration of a "remnant" of the Jews to Jerusalem, the temple was not immediately rebuilt, either because of the difficulty of the task or from fear of arousing the anger of the Persian monarch. But a period of internal unrest during the early years of the Persian Darius's reign spurred Haggai to announce boldly that the time was ripe to carry on the Lord's great work. He was so successful in his direct address to Zerubbabel, the royal administrator, and to Joshua, the high priest, that the work was begun immediately in 520 B.C. and completed a few years later.

Zechariah is considerably longer and was composed over a longer period of time than Haggai. The story of Zechariah explains how he, the grandson of a prophet, joined Haggai after two months and added his exhortations for the rebuilding of the temple. Instead of a direct approach, he made use of the apocalyptic style of prophecy and concluded with another Messianic prediction regarded by Christians as foretelling the events of Palm Sunday (9:9-10).

Joel. Entirely uncertain as to date, the brief prophecies of Joel contain almost nothing that is not to be found elsewhere among the prophets, including denunciation of the wicked, prophecies concerning the Last Judgment, and another Messianic prediction of the time when "your old men shall dream dreams and your young men shall see visions" (2:28).

Daniel. This famous apocalyptic and narrative work is usually regarded as having been written shortly after 168 B.C. when the Syrian king Antiochus III attempted to obliterate Judaism entirely. Its mystical visions of the Messiah and the resurrection of the dead together with the accounts of the triumphs of Daniel who kept the laws of Yahweh during the Babylonian captivity must have been of great comfort to a bitterly persecuted people. Although a relatively short book, Daniel is one of the best known principally because of its remarkably good stories of the children in the fiery furnace, the handwriting on the wall, and the casting of Daniel into the lion's den.

THE WRITINGS

The third major division of the Old Testament is called the Hagiographa or Writings, which include the Book of Daniel in the Hebrew canon. These thirteen books, constituting the remainder of the treasures of ancient Jewish literature, include history, poetry, short stories, and books of wisdom.

History

I and II Chronicles (See II Kings).

Ezra, a fifth-century B.C. document, is one of the rare records of Jewish history after the fall of Jerusalem. The first six chapters concern the rebuilding of the temple and the last four are a personal record of the return to Jerusalem of Ezra the scribe to re-establish racial purity and strict observance of the law. Ezra is believed by some to have been also the founder of the synagogue, a meeting place for the reading and interpretation of the law, and to have thus been the originator of modern Jewish religious practices.

Nehemiah is the personal record of the Jewish cupbearer to the Persian Artaxerxes I. It describes Nehemiah's obtaining permission to go to Jerusalem to rebuild the city's walls, the difficulties encountered, and the final success. A companion piece to Ezra, this book also describes Nehemiah's vigorous seconding of Ezra's reform measures when he was made the royal governor of Jerusalem. Written toward the end of the fifth century B.C., this dignified and restrained record sounds more like modern than typical Hebraic writing.

Short Stories

Ruth, the best known of the Biblical short stories, is believed to be a fifth-century composition, written as a mild protest against the racial purity theories of Ezra and Nehemiah. Ruth, the widowed Moabite daughter-in-law of the Jewish Naomi returns with Naomi to Israel and there finds a second Jewish husband. The line of their descendants is then traced to King David with the implication that even he was not of pure Jewish stock.

Jonah is a brilliantly imaginative parable which may have been written as late as 300 B.C. It is important in Jewish religious history because, unlike the exhortations of group-conscious writers such as Ezra and Nehemiah, it teaches the importance of Israel's duty to bring knowledge of the true God to foreigners. Jonah tries to avoid this responsibility, but after the famous episode of the "whale," he does preach to the Gentile city of Nineveh and is further instructed that Yahweh is the God of all mankind.

Esther. Believed to be a composition of the second century B.C., this ingenious and very oriental story of attempted Jewish oppression and of their bloody revenge was incorporated into the Jewish canon probably because of its explanation of the festival of Purim. It remains a very interesting short story because of its details of the operation of an oriental harem and because of the clever dramatic twists in the central situation of intrigue and counter-intrigue.

The Wisdom Literature

Proverbs. This famous collection of aphorisms, ranging from practical sayings to ethical and mystical preachings, was at one time attributed to Solomon. It is now believed to be a gradually-built-up series of wise sayings which reached its present form around the end of the third century B.C.

Ecclesiastes. Written around 200 B.C. and including further proverbs, this is the most cynical, skeptical, and gloomy book in the Old Testament. The preacher (the meaning of the term "ecclesiastes") is an old man who finds no pattern or meaning in life and is aware only that "all is vanity." The inclusion of this non-religious or even anti-religious work in the Jewish canon probably resulted from the fact that it too was originally attributed to Solomon.

Job. Often compared to *Prometheus Bound* as a philosophical drama, the Book of Job has been impossible to date with any degree of accuracy. It seems to be a composition of the fifth or fourth century B.C., but there is no evidence that the Jews were acquainted with the semi-dramatic form in which it is cast until after the Greek conquest, a circumstance which argues for a later date. Attempting to answer the question, perplexing to all religious people, of why the evil are allowed to prosper and the good suffer, the anonymous author conceives of Satan as the tempting angel who gains the Lord's permission to visit all kinds of calamity on the head of Job, a supremely good man. When Job's three "comforters" insist that some iniquity must be the cause of his sufferings, Job refuses to admit his own guilt, insists that the evil often prosper while the good endure hardships and miseries, and accuses God of indifference or remoteness in that suffering man has no way of presenting his case before the Almighty. Thereupon Elihu, a previously silent and unmentioned fourth "comforter" who is distinguished from the others by his youth, rebukes the old men and berates Job for his proud and rebellious spirit, implying that humility is the way to God's favor. At the end of this peroration God, speaking from a whirlwind, draws the contrast between Divine power and human impotence, implies that there is meaning in God's ways but that the mind of man is too small to comprehend Celestial purposes. He then commends Job and repudiates the explanations of Job's friends, thus refuting the older Jewish doctrine of material rewards and punishments and substituting the prophetical theory that earthly trials are a testing process. The most strikingly new doctrine propounded by the author is the right of man to question the intent of God, a right clearly indicated by God's approval of Job's complainings and self-vindication. The fact that the concluding earthly rewards of Job contradict the previous argument has led many to believe that the last seven verses were later additions. The remarks of Elihu are also regarded as probably a later interpolation because he is not mentioned until his speech begins.

Poetry

The Psalms, a collection of 150 sacred songs, comprises the world's finest treasury of religious poems and is the fullest and most condensed expression of Hebraic religious feeling. Composed over a long period of time, the psalms reflect the changing vicissitudes of Hebrew national life and also mark the different personal conceptions of God. The ultimate reputation of this anthology rests upon the fact that in the Psalms may be found expression for nearly every possible mood or human situation. The variety of the poems offers a cross-section in brief of ancient Hebrew civilization.

The Song of Songs. "The Song of Songs, which is Solomon's" is the introductory line of this most unusual book of the Old Testament. It is unusual principally because, although there are other instances of secular poetry scattered through other canonical books, there is no other example of frankly sensual poetry in ancient Hebraic writing. Its nearest analogues are the pastoral poems of late Greek poets like Theocritus (fl. 275 B.C.) whose *Idylls* also give a clue to the unravelling of a series of lines seemingly spoken by individual characters (at least two) and a chorus. If the poem is indeed a Jewish imitation (and a superb one) of Hellenistic pastoral poetry, it could not have been composed earlier than the third century B.C. The editorial assignment of its lines to different speakers depends on whether it is regarded as a composition for a wedding or whether it describes a maiden taken into Solomon's harem but still yearning for a previous shepherd lover as has been ingeniously suggested. Even if read as an unexplained fragment, the poem with its close-packed imagery, exotic and richly evocative, is one of the most memorable and enticing expressions of love ever written.

Lamentations, a collection of dirge-like laments over the fall of Jerusalem, is an extreme expression of Hebraic emotionalism. The translators of the Septuagint fittingly ascribed the authorship to Jeremiah, prophet of the Babylonian captivity, but it seems more likely that one of the laments written soon after the event inspired four successive anonymous composers to add their own expressions of woe to the original.

THE OLD TESTAMENT APOCRYPHA

Meaning "obscure," the term *Apocrypha* is applied to certain other Jewish writings, mostly composed during the second and first centuries B.C. and regarded as not sufficiently inspired or venerable to be included in the canon. Some of them, nevertheless, have historical, religious, or literary importance, or all three. The outstanding books will be briefly noted here.

I Maccabees is an excellent historical account of the regaining of Jewish independence from 166 B.C. to the height of power of the revived state in 135 B.C. **II Maccabees** is a separate account of the years 175 to 161 B.C. with stress on religious interpretation of the events and including the Pharisaic concepts of the after life. **Tobit** is a fanciful short story describing the good offices of the angel Raphael to a distressed Jewish family during the captivity. **Judith** is another narrative of presumably the second century B.C., extolling Pharisaical virtues and centered about the beheading of Holofernes, an enemy general, by the beautiful, bold, clever, and virtuous Jewish widow Judith. The brief and very clever story of **Susanna** and her escape from the machinations of the elders is probably a first-century-B.C. composition. It is an especial delight to the legal-minded because its denouement rests upon the proved unreliability of the pretended eye-witnesses of Susanna's adultery. **Ecclesiasticus** is a long collection of proverbs written in the second century B.C. and very much a favorite among later Jews and early Christians. The **Wisdom of Solomon** is a last century B.C. collection of preachings in which Greek and Hebrew traditions are blended. It was probably the work of an Alexandrian Jew and is an excellent example of the fusion of the two cultures which was taking place and which was further stimulated by the emergence of Christianity.

Jewish Holy Days

Except for the Sabbath, which begins at sundown on Friday and continues until sundown on Saturday, the Jewish Holy Days mainly commemorate historical events, a result of the fact that ancient Judaism was so much a national religion. It is impossible to give exact dates for these occasions, because they are based on the ancient Jewish calendar of lunar months and are consequently, like the Christian Easter, movable feasts.

Rosh Hashanah, the Jewish New Year, is celebrated in the early fall. It ushers in a ten-day period of repentance and soul-searching culminating in **Yom Kippur,** the Day of Atonement.

Sukkot, The Festival of the Tabernacles, occurs on the fifth day after Yom Kippur. As a reminder that the Israelites of the exodus lived in makeshift temporary dwellings in the "wilderness," Jewish custom enjoins that similar booths be built and decorated and lived in briefly as a memorial. The roof of the tabernacle is required to have an opening for a vision of the stars, the same symbols of hope and divine benediction which Dante used to conclude each canticle of the *Divine Comedy.*

Simchas Torah, "Rejoicing in the Law," was intended to be observed at the completion of each cycle of the Sabbath readings of the Torah, on which occasion the last verses of Deuteronomy are followed by the beginning again with the first verses of Genesis, a ceremony symbolizing the infinity of the Law. By prescription of the passages to be read on each specific Sabbath, the festival has been regularized to occur annually on the day following the Feast of Tabernacles.

Chanukah, "Dedication," "The Feast of Lights," usually falls in December and roughly approximates the Christmas season. It commemorates the successful Maccabean revolt and particularly the events of 165 B.C. when Judah the Maccabee conquered Jerusalem, purified the temple, and, according to tradition, found there a single cruse of consecrated oil which burned for eight days. In celebration, successive candles are lighted, one on the first night, and one more on each succeeding night, until the eighth night of thanksgiving and bestowal of gifts concludes the festive period.

Purim, in the month of February or March, is a gay and noisy commemoration of Jewish religious independence, based principally on the Hebrew triumph recorded in the Book of Esther.

Pesach or **Passover** is the great eight-day spring festival in memory of the deliverance of the Israelites from Egyptian bondage. Named for the passing of the angel of death over the homes marked by the blood of a lamb, it opens with the Seder, an evening supper service in the home at which bitter herbs are a reminder of slavery in Egypt, the paschal lamb recalls the deliverance, and unleavened bread (*matzos*) is token of the severe food problems of the "wilderness." The Seder supper was the Last Supper of Jesus.

Shavuos is a harvest festival akin to the American Thanksgiving. It celebrates not only the material gift of the grain harvest but also the spiritual gift of the Torah. The ceremony of Bar Mitzvah or Confirmation often accompanies this holy day.

SUGGESTED READINGS

(Place of publication, when not mentioned, is New York. Other books on the entire Bible will be found on pages 275-6.)

GENERAL

J. M. Adams, *Biblical Backgrounds* (Nashville, 1934); W. F. Albright, *Archeology and Religion of Israel* (1942); M. Arnold, "Hebraism and Hellenism" in *Culture and Anarchy* (1902); J. Baikie, *Lands and Peoples of the Bible* (London, 1932); H. K. Booth, *The Bridge between the Testaments* (1930); H. Creelman, *An Introduction to the Old Testament* (1917); H. T. Fowler, *The Origin and Growth of the Hebrew Religion* (Chicago, 1943); Sir James Frazer, *Folklore in the Old Testament* (1923); I. Goldberg, *Outline of Jewish Knowledge* (1929); A. Hertzberg (ed.), *Judaism* (1962); E. Jacob, *The Theology of the Old Testament* (1958); G. A. Knight, *From Moses to Paul* (London, 1949); L. H. Koehler, *Old Testament Theology* (London, 1957); M. R. Laehr, *A History of Religion in the Old Testament* (1936); J. L. Miller, *Encyclopedia of Bible Life* (1944); I. G. Matthews, *Old Testament Life and Literature* (1923); J. Muilenberg, *The Way of Israel; Biblical Faith and Ethics* (1961); F. B. Oxtaby, *Israel's Religious Development* (1927); L. Powys, *The Cradle of God* (1929); H. H. Rowley, *The Faith of Israel* (London, 1956); H. H.

Rowley, *The Rediscovery of the Old Testament* (London, 1946); R. B. Y. Scott, *The Relevance of the Prophets* (1944); Sir George A. Smith, *The Historical Geography of the Holy Land* (25th ed., 1932).

HISTORY

A. E. Bailey and C. F. Kent, *History of the Hebrew Commonwealth* (rev. ed., 1935); G. A. Barton (ed.), *A History of the Hebrew People from the Earliest Times to the Year 70 A.D.* (1930); S. M. Dubnow, *An Outline of Jewish History* (1925); L. Finkelstein, *The Jews: Their History, Culture, and Religion* (3rd ed., 1960); P. Goodman, *A History of the Jews* (1943); C. H. Gordon, *Introduction to Old Testament Times* (Ventnor, N.J., 1952); H. H. Graetz, *History of the Jews* (1927); A. L. Sachar, *A History of the Jews* (rev. ed., 1953); J. M. Powis Smith, *The Prophets and Their Times* (rev. by W. A. Irwin, Chicago, 1941).

LITERATURE

E. C. Baldwin, *Types of Literature in the Old Testament* (1929); J. A. Bewer, *The Literature of the Old Testament* (1922); W. K. Clarke, *The Story of the Old Testament* (1940); W. Eichrodt, *Man in the Old Testament* (London, 1951); E. J. Goodspeed, *The Story of the Old Testament* (Chicago, 1934); R. B. Henderson, *A Modern Handbook to the Old Testament* (London, 1927); L. B. Langaise, *The Old Testament, Its Form and Purpose* (1945); D. B. Macdonald, *The Hebrew Literary Genius* (Princeton, 1933); G. F. Moore and L. H. Brockington, *Literature of the Old Testament* (rev. ed., Oxford, 1948); L. H. Wild, *Geographic Influences in Old Testament Masterpieces* (Boston, 1915).

chapter 13

EARLY CHRISTIANITY

I. THE FUSION OF HEBRAISM AND CLASSICISM

Prior to the fourth century B.C. the Classical and Hebraic cultures appear to have developed quite independently of each other. That we inherit so much from both of them is attributable principally to their fusion within Christianity, which not only became the dominant religion of the Western world but which also presided over the medieval culture in which our own society is rooted. The spiritual element of the medieval Church was principally Hebraic with some admixture of Hellenic ideas, most of which had already fused with Hebraism before the birth of Christ. But the education of church men and of those they taught was mainly of Classical inspiration.

The first definite and rather dramatic meeting of the two cultures occurred in 333 B.C. when Alexander the Great began the introduction of Hellenism to the whole region of western Asia. Many of the Jews in Palestine and elsewhere eagerly adopted Greek customs and found themselves fascinated by the treasures of Greek learning which were thus opened to them. The creation of a great new cultural center at nearby Alexandria attracted many Jews as it attracted others, and soon a large Jewish colony there was producing such scholars as the Neo-platonist Philo and the translators of the Old Testament into the Greek version known as the Septuagint. Begun in the third century B.C., the Septuagint (Seventy) was so entitled because it was traditionally the work of seventy-two Hebrew scholars. The dissemination of this Greek text made possible the continued reading of the scriptures by Jewish communities now scattered through the Mediterranean and western Asia, where Greek was the universal language of learning. It also opened the way for the conversion to Judaism of Gentiles, many of whom found in Hebraism a more solidly grounded tradition and a higher ethical system than existed elsewhere among the religions of the ancient world.

Simultaneously, the Idealism of Plato provided devout Jews with a more intellectualized version of their own essential beliefs and added very attractive "proofs" of the immortality of the soul. Late Jewish religious writings (contained in the Apocrypha) were inspired by both the prophetic promises of eternal life and the Platonic and Neo-platonic theories. In these ways, and well before the appearance of Christianity, Jews were being educated in the Classical tradition and Classically educated Gentiles were reading the literature of the Jews. Coincidental with the life of Jesus of Nazareth, Philo Judaeus in Alexandria attempted to reconcile Plato with the teachings of the Old Testament. Building on the theory that learned Greeks must have been acquainted with Jewish writings, he made extensive use of allegory to interpret each in terms of the other. Jacob's ladder (Genesis 28), for example, with the angels ascending and descending was renamed the Ladder of Love because it corresponded with the theory in Plato's *Symposium* that love is a mediator between heaven and earth.

Although a meeting of the Classic and the Hebraic was

in these ways taking place, the real fusion was accomplished by the advent of Christianity. Originating as a purely Jewish religious variant, it was soon disseminated throughout the world by virtue of the triple coincidence that the world of that time was more than usually united under the aegis of the Roman Empire, that Jewish colonies in all the major cities provided convenient centers for missionary activities, and that great numbers of people everywhere were apparently yearning for such an otherworldly religion.

When Christianity became, under Constantine, the official religion of the Roman Empire, the entire Hebraic tradition was superimposed upon Classical culture. The completeness of the fusion was made possible by the fact that the early Christian scholars, including the not so early but very influential St. Augustine, were nearly all originally Platonists and infused the new religion with a theology nearly as much Greek as Hebraic and with ceremonies derived often from Roman tradition as well as Jewish temple worship. From that time on, the educated man of the Western world would derive his secular education from Classical sources and his religious training from a combination of Hebraic and Classical roots.

II. THE BEGINNINGS OF CHRISTIANITY

In order to understand the rather sudden conquest of Christianity over all other religions within the Roman Empire, one must take into account the special circumstances under which this new religion was born. Preparations for Christianity may be said to date back to as early as the eighth century B.C. when Amos de-emphasized the importance of temple ceremonial and the endless ritualistic observances of the Law by implying that purity of heart and generous behavior were more acceptable in the eyes of Yahweh than empty formalities. Many of the later prophets took up this theme and, with the destruction of the temple, it became an increasingly dominant aspect of Judaism. The special ethical nature of early Christianity was to be not so much a revolution as a determined emphasis on this aspect of Jewish religion.

The mystical nature of Christianity was simultaneously prepared for by the many predictions of the Messiah (the "Anointed One"). The exact nature of Israel's promised redeemer is usually made rather indefinite in the prophesies. Originally, he was probably thought of as another Moses or David who would be a great spiritual and temporal leader and restore Israel to its former greatness. Soon, however, he is referred to as coming in glory to confound the nations of the earth. Glowing prophetic passages referring to this mighty advent were interpreted by many as references to the Last Judgment. At some undetermined period, the resurrection of the dead was connected with this stupendous event. With the addition of mystical references identifying the Messiah with God (Isaiah 9:6) or describing him as the "son of man" (Daniel 7:13), the groundwork of the Christian religion was completed by at least the second century B.C.

At the time of the birth of Jesus, Palestinian Jews were being sorely oppressed by the Roman puppet Herod. His years of cruel misrule had also accentuated earlier antagonisms among the Hebrews, so that at least four major groups or parties were in existence. The sycophants of Herod and his appointed priests were known as the Sadducees and constituted the aristocratic element in Palestine. The Pharisees set up their own religious teachings (outside of priestly authority) under their own rabbis who interpreted the law and the prophets in synagogues and who were distinguished by strict religious observances and belief in immortality.[1] A smaller group, the Essenes, were in

[1] Although Jesus is described as being in open conflict with the Pharisees because of their emphasis on the letter of the law, the other-

extreme contrast to the luxuriant Sadducees. They lived sternly ascetic lives, practiced celibacy and communal living, and, with their rites of baptism and belief in immortality, foreshadowed many of the characteristics of the Christian faith. The fourth group, known as the Zealots, were fiercely rebellious to Roman domination and pinned their hopes to an extreme degree on the coming of the prophesied Messiah. Their active opposition to Herod accounts in part for his and his successors' concern about the appearance of a new "King of the Jews." According to John, two pretended Messiahs had already been put to death before the crucifixion of Jesus.

Outside of these organized groups were the many ordinary people, referred to scornfully by the Pharisees as "the people of the land," who were sporadically devout but essentially defeatist and lackadaisical in their religious faith. These scattered clingers to Judaism are of importance chiefly because they appear to have been the special objects of Jesus' concern, "the publicans and sinners" of the gospels.

In the midst of such religious tensions and to a distracted majority eagerly awaiting the promised Messiah, Jesus of Nazareth was pointed out by John the Baptist (presumably an Essene) as the fulfillment of the prophecies. The records of his life (c. 4 B.C.-c. 29 A.D. in terms of the present calendar) known as the Gospels [2] appear to have been compiled around the end of the first century A.D. from oral tradition or from previous now-lost written accounts of his birth, ministry, death, and resurrection, or possibly from both.

The authors of this volume have no intention of marring by summary these brief, inspired, and easily accessible gospel versions of the life of the Savior. But in tracing the influence of Judaism on our civilization, it is important to

---

worldly insistence of their beliefs had a great deal in common with the teachings of Christianity.

[2] "Gospel" is variously translated as "Good News" or "Glad Tidings."

point out that all of the recorded events connected with the life of Jesus are closely joined to previous Hebrew traditions. The miraculous birth of John the Baptist ("the voice crying in the wilderness" of Isaiah 40:3) is like the births of Isaac, Joseph, and Samuel. The "Magnificat" of Mary parallels the song of praise of Samuel's mother. The descent of the Holy Spirit and nearly all of the other recorded events of Jesus' life fulfill Old Testament prophecies. The miracles, the teachings, the parables, the group of disciples, the ascetic life, the emphasis on worldly poverty, the casting of the money-changers out of the temple, all have antecedents in Old Testament documents.

At the same time, no one can deny the revolutionary nature of Jesus' life and teachings and his tremendous effect on his followers. As the Christ (the "Anointed"), as son of man and Son of God, he spoke "as one having authority." And although there are inconsistencies and contradictions in the gospel accounts, there is no question about the essential intent of that authority. Eschewing the current Jewish ceremonials (as did so many of the prophets), he substituted for prophetical denunciations the admonition, "Be ye perfect even as your Father in Heaven is perfect." Perfection, he taught, consists in love of God and love of one's fellow men, including even enemies. To be scorned, humble, poor on earth is inconsequential. To follow Christ, even if from afar with right intentions, is to secure eternal life. The Kingdom of God is not the political state of Israel: it exists in the hearts of men.

But what these blank statements of principle cannot convey and what is so much conveyed in the gospels is the spirit of Jesus which is so important to Christianity that a brief and superlative example bears quotation: [3]

And the scribes and Pharisees brought unto him a woman taken in adultery; and when they had set her in the midst, they say

[3] John 8:3-11.

unto him, Master, this woman was taken in adultery, in the very act. Now Moses in the law commanded us, that such should be stoned: but what sayest thou? This they said, tempting him, that they might have to accuse him. But Jesus stooped down, and with his finger wrote on the ground, as if he heard them not. So when they continued asking him, he lifted up himself, and said unto them, He that is without sin among you, let him cast the first stone. And again he stooped down and wrote on the ground. And they which heard it, being convicted by their own conscience, went out one by one, beginning at the eldest, even unto the last: and Jesus was left alone, and the woman standing in the midst. When Jesus had lifted up himself, and saw none but the woman, he said unto her, Woman, where are those thine accusers? hath no man condemned thee? She said, No man, Lord, and Jesus said unto her, Neither do I condemn thee: go, and sin no more.

A coldly external description of the key events of his life would mention his birth in presumably 4 B.C. to the Jewish family of Joseph and Mary in Galilee and his early apprenticeship to the carpenter's trade. His active preachings, which lasted little more than a year, were begun after his recognition by John the Baptist. When John was imprisoned by Herod Antipas (a later puppet ruler than the Herod reigning at Jesus' birth), who feared him as a possible instigator of a popular uprising, Jesus was left alone to preach his doctrine of love. His teachings and miracles attracted great crowds of people who flocked to see and hear him. Going to Jerusalem for the Passover observance, he was greeted by enthusiastic multitudes who strewed his path with palms (commemorated by Palm Sunday). But like John before him, he incurred the suspicion of the government. He also aroused antagonism among Jewish religious leaders, both Sadducees and Pharisees, by his implications concerning the relative unimportance of ritual and by his claim of being the Son of God. Having provoked the enmity of those in power, he was arrested by Pontius Pilate, the Roman military governor, given the semblance of a trial, and crucified as a criminal. (The crucifixion is commemorated on Good Friday.) On the following Sunday (Easter) it was reported that the tomb in which his body had been placed was empty. Later appearances to his disciples convinced them that he had risen from the dead; this together with his later recorded ascent to heaven is the mystical basis of Christianity.

Although many of his immediate disciples were so convinced, others of the enthusiastic Jews who had followed him during his lifetime became disillusioned after the crucifixion and decided that he had been only another imposter, principally because of his failure to come in "glory." But the faithful disciples who remembered his prophecy of a second coming at the Last Judgment began an ardent and successful missionary campaign based essentially on the fundamental doctrine contained in the well-known statement of John, "For God so loved the world that he sent his only begotten son, that whosoever believeth in him should not perish but have everlasting life" (John 4:16). The Book of the Acts of the Apostles records mass conversions, continued miracle workings, and also savage persecution of this particular group by the other Jews. Simultaneously, converts to Jesus as the Messiah were being made in Jewish communities outside Palestine, although there was as yet no apparent idea of forming an independent church, partly because Jesus had remained essentially within the Jewish tradition of temple and synagogue worship and partly because several of his utterances had led his disciples to believe that his second advent was imminent.

The founding of Christianity as a separate religion was largely the result of the missionary activities of Paul. Originally named Saul, he was an ardent religious Jew, born probably shortly after the birth of Jesus, who took an active part in the early persecution of the believers in Christ. Around A.D. 33 he was himself converted to the new faith and undertook at least three remarkable missionary journeys to Asia Minor, Greece, and Italy. Wherever he went, he seems to have left Christian organizations to whom he later wrote letters in which he added a great deal to official Christian doctrine. For the guidance and inspiration of these communities, the letters of Paul and of other Christian leaders were copied and circulated. These, together with the four Gospels, the Acts, and the Revelation of St. John (all apparently written toward the end of the first century A.D.) formed the substance of early Christianity and subsequently became the canon of the New Testament.

The gradual spread of the new religion from these small, principally Jewish communities, together with the groups of Gentiles converted by Paul, is fairly easily understood. The Roman Empire at the time was suffering from a kind of world-weariness and was feeling otherworldly yearnings. Mystery cults (promising immortality to the elect), gnostic cults (offering eternal life to those who could attain a *gnosis* or knowledge of the Platonic Idea), Neo-Platonic groups with similar though somewhat less mystical theologies, and Manichaeism (with its after-lives of heaven and hell) were all making many converts. Official Roman paganism may be briefly described as dead. In the midst of this welter of confused and often dubious religious offerings, the solidity and relatively good sense of the Jewish communities (with their immensely rich background of religious writings) must have looked to many like a spiritual haven in the midst of a sophistic tempest. Early in the second century, the reliable Roman historian Tacitus paid the Jewish colonies the grudging tribute of being "inflexibly honest and ever ready to show compassion" [4] and added that "the Jews have purely mental conceptions of Deity, as one in essence." [5] This doctrine was not official Roman religion, but

[4] *History*, V, 5.
[5] *Ibid.*

it coincided with the teachings of Plato, Aristotle, the Stoics, the Neo-Platonists, and the Gnostics.[6] When the eloquent documents of the New Testament and the examples of Christian martyrs were added to this solid foundation, the appeal of Christianity proved irresistible, especially when it was decided that the new Gentile converts need not become circumcised Jews before being included in the Christian fellowship.

The actual record of these early years is dim, but the tendencies are clear. There were, it is true, sporadic and cruel persecutions, but many new converts from the Gentile world appeared in a steadily increasing stream. Here and there, strictly Judaic religious practices were discarded to be replaced by new ceremonies. Beginning with the simple ceremonies of baptism and commemoration of Christ's last supper with his disciples, Christianity gradually adopted and adapted feast days, vestments, and rituals from many of its rival religions. Similarly, beginning with the Letters of Paul and the Gospel of John, it began to create a theology which owes a great deal to Platonism and Neo-Platonism with its fundamental tenet that Jesus was the incarnate *logos* ("word," the Platonic Divine Essence, the Aristotelian *Nous*, the Stoic *Pneuma*, the Neo-Platonic Idea), the abstract Godhead taking human form. The addition of the Holy Spirit from Hebraic and Gospel sources, as the spirit of God dwelling within man or descending from God to the elect, completed the Christian Trinity, which concept of three as being one had the authorization of Neo-Pythagorean and Neo-Platonic philosophies. For reasons such as these, some scholars have described Christianity as an eclectic religion. It would be more properly described as a continuation and variation of Judaism, to which non-Jewish

[6] Gnosticism seems to have originated before Christianity, but it continued to flourish during the early Middle Ages, when it incorporated much of Christian doctrine into its own theology.

and Hellenized Jewish converts added their own interpretations and ritualistic observances.

In the fourth century A.D., at a time when Christianity and Mithraism were contending for religious leadership, the emperor Constantine selected Christianity as the official Roman religion. This development was simultaneously helpful and harmful to the Christian cause. It was clearly helpful to the prestige of the Church, but the addition of masses of hypocritical "converts" undoubtedly diminished the spirituality of the Christian community. The Church had already built a fairly solid organization: each local capital was presided over by a bishop, archbishops controlled the larger provinces, and at the head of the Church were the patriarchs in Rome, Constantinople, Jerusalem, and Alexandria. But scholarly churchmen up to that time had often been in heated argument about matters of doctrine (a tendency to be repeated later in the Protestant Reformation), which condition encouraged a freedom of intellectual activity like that of the Classical world and very much unlike that of the inquisition movements to come. With Constantine's calling of the Council of Nicaea in 325 for the formulation of official Christian doctrine, Christianity became the authoritative faith of the Middle Ages.

Intellectually, one may quarrel with this authoritarian development. At the same time it is arguable that the solidity of Roman Catholicism is all that held Europe together after the Gothic invasions. The solidity of the Church was further enhanced by the proclamation of the Roman bishop Leo I in 451 that the bishop of Rome was the successor of Peter, the chief disciple of Jesus. The Papacy was thus established at Rome in imitation of the High Priesthood of Jerusalem's temple, and when Roman power declined in the West, the Church became its inevitable successor, not only because it was the only remaining well organized, educated institution but also because it possessed a document known as the "Donation of Constantine" (proved to be a forgery in 1440) by which Constantine supposedly had conferred upon Pope Sylvester I sovereignty over the western portion of the Roman Empire.[7]

Apart from political interests engendered by this growing power, the Church was inevitably prompted to exert its authority by renewed emphasis on the terrors of the Last Judgment as depicted in the Revelation of St. John. Repeating thereby much of the story of the priesthood of Judaism after official sanction and selection of priests by kings, Christianity during the early Middle Ages was turned into a kind of negative religion with emphasis on punishment for those who disobeyed the edicts of pope and priests.

The record, *in toto,* is that of diminishing spirituality and increasing worldliness. But, again paralleling the record of the days of Judah's corrupt priesthood, many truly devout Christians removed themselves from the world by setting up monastic orders in emulation of the ascetic lives of the Essenes or hermits of other faiths, or the pattern of the original disciples including, presumably, Paul. In the fourth century these organizations began to impose upon their members definite rules of communal and devotional living. The most famous monastic regimen was the work of Benedict of Nursia (c. 480-550) who founded the monastery of Monte Cassino, where a daily schedule of routines of prayer and work, together with explicit regulation of food and clothing, was put in force. The monasteries, though not exempt from the corrupting influence of the times, acted as a striking symbol of the Christian ideal of the saintly and contemplative life. From the ranks of these and other sincere Christians was drawn a line of scholars who continued to write commentaries, defenses, and interpreta-

[7] After the establishment of the papacy in 451, earlier bishops of Rome were recognized as previous popes.

tions of the new religion, culminating, in the early years of Christianity, in the brilliant works of St. Augustine (354-430). Most important historically is the fact that, however corrupt, the early Christian church became sufficiently organized and solidified to preserve the cores of Classicism and Hebraism through the dark ages that followed the Gothic invasions.

III. CHRISTIAN THEOLOGY

The basic structure of Christian theology was completed during the early centuries of the church in the midst of discussions, controversies, and earnest searchings into the full significance of Christ's mission on earth. Fortunately for the continuation of a unified Christian tradition, a series of church councils culminated in several documents which still represent the essential dogmas of the Christian religion.

The most important of these early statements of principles is the Nicene Creed, adopted by the Council of Nicaea in 325, amplified at the Council of Constantinople in 381, and approved by the Council of Chalcedon in 451. It formulates the fundamental beliefs of Christianity as follows:

We believe in one God the Father All-sovereign, maker of heaven and earth, and of all things visible and invisible; and in one Lord Jesus Christ, and only-begotten Son of God, Begotten of the Father before all the ages, Light of Light, true God of true God, begotten not made, of one substance with the Father, through whom all things were made; who for us men and for our salvation came down from the heavens, and was made flesh of the Holy Spirit and the Virgin Mary, and became man, and was crucified for us under Pontius Pilate, and suffered and was buried, and rose again on the third day according to the Scriptures, and ascended into the heavens, and sitteth on the right hand of the Father, and cometh again with glory to judge living and dead, of whose kingdom there shall be no end; and in the Holy Spirit, the Lord and the Life-giver, that proceedeth from the Father, who with Father and Son is worshipped together and glorified together, who spake through the prophets; in one Holy Catholic and Apostolic Church. We acknowledge one baptism unto remission of sins. We look for a resurrection of the dead, and the life of the age to come.

In 529 the Council of Orange approved of the doctrine of sin and redemption which was formulated by St. Augustine, the heart of which may be seen in the following canons:

Through the sin of the first man, free choice was so warped and weakened that thereafter no one is able to love God as he ought, or believe in God, or do anything for God that is good, without the grace of God's mercy.

After grace has been received through baptism all the baptized, with the aid and coöperation of Christ, have the power and the duty to perform all things that pertain to the soul's salvation, if they will labor faithfully.

We do not believe that some have been predestined to evil by the divine power.

To these essential theological principles, a few important elements of medieval Christian tradition are here appended:

The Attributes of the Trinity: Power (the Father), Wisdom (the Son), and Love (the Holy Spirit).

The Sacraments: The rituals whereby the Christian partakes of the fellowship of Christ by symbolic tokens which have spiritual significance, "the outward and visible sign of an inward and spiritual grace." These are:

1. *Baptism:* Immersion in or sprinkling on of water, denoting the washing away of original sin and incorportion into the body of the church.
2. *Confirmation:* The laying on of hands to signify the adult acceptance of the Christian responsibility conveyed at baptism.
3. *Penance:* Confession of sins in the presence of a priest;

absolution by the priest, acting in God's name, of sins committed after baptism. Thus the baptised person who strays from the Christian fellowship by sin is periodically reunited to fellowship with Christ by confession, contrition, and usually some sort of retribution involving self-abasement for the wrong committed.

4. *Holy Eucharist* or *Communion* or *Lord's Supper:* The partaking of bread and wine which have been blessed in commemoration of Christ's last supper with his disciples, and signifying the mystic reception by the communicant of the body and blood of the crucified Lord.

5. *Holy Orders:* The rite of ordination into the ministry.

6. *Holy Matrimony:* The blessing of the life-long monogamous union of a man and woman.

7. *Extreme Unction:* Anointing with an especially consecrated oil of a dying person by a priest to confer grace and to beg remission of sins.

Last Judgment: The court at the end of the world at which all men, living and dead, will be judged by Christ, and a final separation made of the good and the evil.

Heaven: The dwelling place of God beyond the farthest stars, inhabited by angels and the souls of the redeemed.

Hell: The place of eternal punishment for the damned and the abode of Satan, situated within the earth, believed to be composed of fire, darkness, and unimaginable torments.

Purgatory: A condition of temporal punishment after death as satisfaction of sins not otherwise absolved. The duration of the punishment is in proportion to the sins committed, and those suffering in Purgatory can be aided by the offering of prayer and the Mass by the living.

The Mass: The formal ritual of the Church service, consisting of a series of rites of preparation, a symbolic enactment of the crucifixion, observance of the Eucharist, a general thanksgiving, and the final dismissal. It has four progressively simpler forms: Pontifical, Solemn, High, and Low. Low mass is spoken; the others are chanted throughout.

The Seven Virtues of the Christian were made up of the four "cardinal virtues" of Plato and the Stoics (Prudence, Temperance, Fortitude, and Justice), to which were added the three "theological virtues" (Faith, Hope, and Love).

The Seven Deadly Sins are Pride, Envy, Anger, Sloth, Avarice, Gluttony, and Lust. These are "venial" or forgivable sins, as distinguished from the "mortal" sins of Idolatry, Murder. and Adultery. Venial sin does not alienate the sinner from God, but the commission of mortal sin subjects the sinner to excommunication and requires extreme penance for reinstatement into the body of the Church.

The Saints: Deceased persons who because of unusual holiness in life have been declared by the Pope to be regarded as already enjoying Heaven. A patron saint is one chosen by a person or an organization to be a guardian and special intercessor with God.

Holy Days: Every Sunday and, by the twelfth century, thirty-six special festivals such as Christmas (birthday of Christ), Palm Sunday (the triumphant entry of Jesus into Jerusalem), Good Friday (the crucifixion), Easter (the resurrection), and Pentecost (seventh Sunday after Easter, commemorating the descent of the Holy Spirit). Lent or the Lenten Season is the forty-day penitential period from Ash Wednesday to Easter eve (omitting Sundays).

Excommunication: Partial or total expulsion from the Christian community, usually attended by loss of civil rights as well as the implication of eternal damnation.

Books of the New Testament

The New Testament is a collection of twenty-seven documents or "books" which are the memoirs of early Christianity and which were all written during the second half of the first century or early in the second century. The language of the earliest manuscripts is Greek, but these may be translations from Aramaic, the common speech of Palestine during this period. Having nothing like the extent or range of Old Testament literature, these books include the four rather brief memorials of the life of Jesus known as the Gospels, a book called The Acts of the Apostles which describes early Christian missionary activities, the apocalyptic work known as The Revelation of St. John, and a series of short letters circulated among early Christian communities. In spite of its comparative brevity, however, the New Testament is nearly always eloquent and almost completely consistent in preaching its message of God's good will to men.

The Gospels. The New Testament opens logically with a series of accounts of the high points in the life and teachings of Jesus known as the four gospels. Of these, the first three of Matthew, Mark, and Luke are known as synoptical ("seen with the same eyes") because of their many parallels. The most sensible explanation is that Mark is the earliest of the three and that the other two are based on Mark and other now lost sources. The fourth gospel of John is a separate account with qualities peculiarly its own.

Mark, believed to be the earliest of the gospels, is a brief, direct, and unornamented account of the principal events in the life of Jesus. Although it is not as poetic as the other gospels, it is vivid, fast-moving, and dramatic. Omitting the birth and early years of Jesus, it begins with his baptism by John the Baptist. In a mounting crescendo, it then describes the arrest of John, the subsequent preaching of Jesus, his calling of disciples and performance of miracles. The drama is intensified by the growing enmity of the Pharisees on the one hand and the oppressive crowding of enthusiastic followers and frantic invalids on the other. Inserted into the midst of this wave of adulation, the description of the death of John serves as a prelude to Jesus' triumphant entry into Jesusalem, his cleansing of the temple, his betrayal by Judas, his trial and crucifixion, and the resurrection. Early tradition ascribed this book to John Mark, based on oral reminiscences of the apostle Peter. Recent scholarship finds no evidence of definite authorship and assigns A.D. 75 as a probable date of composition.

Matthew. The author of Matthew adds considerably more detail, is more thoughtful, and is interested in correlating events in the life of Christ with Old Testament prophecies. He traces the genealogy of Joseph to David, adds the virgin birth, the appearance of the wise men, the flight into Egypt to avoid Herod's wrath, the temptation of Jesus by the devil, and many other memorable details, such as Christ's prophecies of his approaching death and resurrection. He also includes many more parables and five important sermons. The fact that Matthew repeats large portions of Mark and that many of the additions exactly parallel material in Luke has caused scholars to believe that Matthew and Luke were both derived from Mark and from some other now-lost document possibly entitled "The Sayings of Jesus." Dated around A.D. 90, Matthew appears to be the work of a Christian Jew designed to convert other Jews to the new faith.

Luke seems to have been written at about the same time by the Greek physician who accompanied Paul on some of his missionary journeys. It is the most beautiful and poetic of the synoptics, with its elaborate accounts of the birth of John, the *Ave Maria* of the angel Gabriel, the *Magnificat* of Mary, the child in the manger, the appearance of the angels to the shepherds at the beginning, and the walk to Emmaus at the end. It also adds a few highly effective parables to the accounts of Matthew and Mark, and, as might be expected of a Gentile author, presents Jesus as a Savior of the world.

John, the fourth gospel, although it repeats much of the same material, presents Jesus as a more majestic personality. It also differs from the other gospels in a number of details regarding the events of Jesus' ministry. It is principally distinctive in its Neo-Platonic identification of Jesus with the *Logos,* "the incarnate word," and in its almost argumentative insistence that Jesus was indeed the fulfillment of the messianic predictions. Originally ascribed to John "the beloved disciple," this gospel has aroused endless interest and controversy in attempts to decide its probable authorship. A considerable body of internal evidence suggests an early second-century date of composition: the combination of insistence on the messiahship of Jesus, the mystical presentation of an exalted Christ, and the philosophical expositions suggests a development of Christian doctrine definitely subsequent to the simpler presentation of the other gospels.

The Acts of the Apostles is an invaluable direct and graphic account by Luke, as a sequel to his gospel, of Christian missionary activities immediately after the death of Christ. After a kind of prologue referring to the ascent of Jesus to heaven after forty days of communion with his disciples, it describes the descent of the Holy Spirit upon the apostles at Pentecost and continues with the miracles, mass conversions, and persecutions that followed. The book is of great religious importance, because it substitutes the presence of the Holy Spirit, the *paraclete* or "comforter," for the visible presence of Jesus. It also describes the building of a definite religious organization with financial contributions from new converts and tells of occasional suspicions, jealousies, and controversies among the leaders. The latter part of the book is devoted essentially to the missionary journeys of Paul (who considered himself especially an apostle to the Gentiles) until the time of his Roman imprisonment. The narrative breaks off abruptly, leaving the last years of Paul a matter of mystery and speculation.

The Epistles. Following the narratives of early Christianity in the usual arrangement of the "books" of the New Testament are the twenty-one epistles or letters written by Paul and other early Christians to individuals or to early church organizations. They are remarkable records of early Christian thinking and the development of peculiarly Christian laws and customs, and some of them unwittingly provide clear characterizations of some of the early Christian leaders. The dates and order of composition of many of the letters are very dubious, and so the customary arrangement of these brief documents will be followed here.

Romans is one of the longest of Paul's letters, written around A.D. 58 to an already established church in anticipation of his own hoped-for visit. More formal than most of his other correspondence, it states a number of Paul's basic tenets, including his arguments for the admission of uncircumcised Gentiles to the Christian fellowship, the doctrine of original sin through Adam and its vicarious atonement through Christ (for "the wages of sin is death"), the rejection of the physical to illuminate the life of the spirit, and the explanation that the ten commandments of Moses are summed up in the second commandment of Jesus, "Thou shalt love thy neighbor as thyself."

I Corinthians (c. A.D. 54) is the first of two letters by Paul to the church in Corinth, where he spent eighteen months and for which he was apparently much concerned because of the temptations toward worldliness offered by a wealthy city. Sharp reproof and eloquent statements of faith are mingled as he pleads for unity, counsels excommunication of the wicked, pauses for ceremonial details such as the prescription that women should worship with the head covered and men with head uncovered, adds the three theological virtues (faith, hope, love) to Christian tradition, and rises to lyric heights in his description of the exaltation of the spirit coincident with baptism, in his famous glorificaton of love (13), and in his doctrine of the resurrection of the dead in a "spiritual body."

II Corinthians. The tone of rebuke is paramount in this second letter (c. A.D. 56) to the same congregation. The letter is interesting principally because of Paul's mention of his persecutions and his undefined physical infirmity and because of the fact that it contains the earliest extant references to the church as the bride of Christ (11:2) and to the three persons of the Trinity (13:14).

Galatians is a short Pauline letter written around A.D. 52 to churches in the Roman province in Galatia, which were apparently being torn by the "circumcision controversy." Paul firmly establishes his status as missionary to the Gentiles by telling of his past ministry and then boldly announces that not only is circumcision unnecessary for Christians but that the Christian is free from the Mosaic code and requires only faith in Christ for salvation. This theory of "justification by faith" was to be of prime importance later in Martin Luther's Protestant doctrine.

Ephesians is still controversial as to date, authorship, and even its intended recipients. It bears the impress of Pauline ideas in its concern for the subordination of wives to their husbands and was possibly intended as a kind of circular letter to reinforce Christian doctrine wherever needed. Among its general admonitions for moral living and strength in the faith, it presents a central and important doctrine of a unified church which is to be the authorized representative of God on earth.

Philippians, containing many eloquent lines which have made this letter a perennial favorite in supplying texts for sermons, was seemingly written by Paul from the Roman prison (c. A.D. 61-64) to the first church which he had organized in Europe (at Philippi, a Roman colony in Macedonia). The most noteworthy passage

(2:5-11) applies the prophetic idea of Israel as the "suffering servant" to Jesus and reinforces the doctrine of the incarnation presented in John.

Colossians, also written from prison, is a brief letter to the church in Colossae in refutation of a growing tendency there to incorporate gnostic and other ideas into the Christian tradition. Paul reiterates that Jesus, the incarnate God, is the only and eternal creator and ruler of the universe.

I Thessalonians, written by Paul around A.D. 51, is believed to be the earliest extant Christian document. Composed on the occasion of Timothy's report of the continued faithfulness of one of the earliest of Paul's churches (at Macedonian Thessalonica), it expresses the author's great pleasure, adds several typical Pauline preachments, and promises the reward of the rising of the dead at the Last Judgment.

II Thessalonians continues the discussion of the Last Judgment, pointing out that it will not come until after the appearance of an anti-Christ (pretending to be God) who will be destroyed by Jesus. This letter may mark the beginning of the concept of a Christ of majesty and wrath, repeated in the Revelation of St. John.

I Timothy is the first of three "pastoral letters" written to other church leaders about administrative matters and codes of ethical conduct. Originally ascribed to Paul, these letters are now usually held to be the compositions of a later church leader and are dated at about A.D. 100 because they assume a rather advanced stage of church organization. The first letter describes the contrast between the old Mosaic dispensation and the new doctrine of grace, discusses the necessity of submissiveness in women, gives rules for the conduct of bishops, deacons, and elders, warns against straying after gnostic creeds, and includes the often quoted maxim, "the love of money is the root of all evil" (6:10).

II Timothy seems to be an earlier and much more personal Pauline epistle which contains the good advice to be firm in the faith and to continue preaching the gospel. Highly personal are its premonitions of Paul's death, his plea to Timothy to come soon, his statement that Luke is with him, and his request for books, cloak, parchments, and the company of Mark.

Titus is addressed to a follower of Paul who remained in Crete to organize a church there. The letter emphasizes the importance of "sound doctrine" and sober living for Christian men and women.

Philemon, less a letter than a note, is an extremely personal appeal from Paul in prison to forgive and accept into Christian fellowship Onesimus, one of Philemon's slaves who had fled to Rome and been converted there by Paul. Apart from this personal matter between Paul and his friend, the letter mentions Paul's own hopes for freedom and his expectation of visiting Philemon in the near future.

Hebrews was originally ascribed to Paul, but recent scholarship dates it as later than A.D. 90. Apparently written during Roman persecution of the Jews of the Diaspora, it contains appropriate reminders of scriptural passages concerning Jesus who brings the Sabbath of rest, emphasizing a Hebrew and Christian idea of the seven ages of the world. It also describes Christ as an eternal High Priest offering a new covenant to be solemnized by such rituals as ablution and the laying on of hands. This new High Priesthood is to culminate with the resurrection of the dead at the Last Judgment. Chapter XI is a much quoted and eloquent peroration on faith, and Chapter XIII is the origin of the well-known quotation concerning entertaining angels unaware.

James was apparently written near the end of the first century by a vigorous and practical church leader, who had little regard for "faith without works" and who preached a forthright doctrine of godliness in anticipation of the second coming of Christ.

I Peter seems to have been composed around A.D. 96 by an unknown Christian leader who counsels submission to Gentile rulers, urges good conduct and purity of heart as marks of the true Christian, and repeats Paul's matrimonial advice. Of especial interest is his allegory of Noah's flood as a premonition of Christian baptism, a suggestion expanded by later Christian writers and one of the several instances of the use of allegory in the New Testament.

II Peter, believed to be among the last-written epistles, mentions the story of the fallen angels and comforts those who are worried about the delay of the Second Coming by explaining that one day is as a thousand with the Lord.

I John, quite probably composed by the author of the fourth gospel, emphasizes the doctrine of love and the forgiveness of sins through Christ who came to destroy the works of the devil. It also mentions the approaching advent of the anti-Christ and the imminence of the Last Judgment. It was apparently written as a counterattack against the growing tendencies of early Christians to include gnostic elaborations in their dogmas.

II John, a very personal letter of a few paragraphs, proffers love and comfort to an unknown lady.

III John, another personal note, is directed to one Gaius in rebuke of a gnostic or some other heretical doctrine which was gaining favor.

Jude, by an unknown author, is a brief but authoritative sermon on keeping the true faith and avoiding the lures of heretical doctrines which have "crept in unawares."

The Revelation of John is the last and most extraordinary book of the New Testament. An apocalypse like the Old Testament Book of Daniel, it was apparently written around A.D. 96 in the midst of Roman persecution. Since John is such a common name, its authorship has been the subject of endless and unresolved theorizing. Its mysterious symbolism, allegorizing, and elaborate schematizations built on the number seven, its visionary and ecstatic poetry, its prophecy of the victory of a god of wrath over his enemies—all these piled-up utterances set it apart from the usually direct and relatively plain statements of other early Christian writers. Whatever its origin, it is an extraordinary and all-but-unique masterpiece of imaginative literature. It is so difficult, however, for the uninitiated reader and so much quoted and referred to by later writers that it will be described here in a brief chapter-by-chapter commentary.

Chapter I, to the seven churches in Asia by John on Patmos, promises a vision of what will soon take place. The beginning of the vision describes Jesus surrounded by seven lampstands (the seven churches) holding in his right hand seven stars (angels of the seven churches). In his mouth a two-edged sword, the first suggestion of a Christ of wrath, is a prelude to his warning that he holds the keys of death and of hell (basis of the doctrine that Jesus descended to hell between the crucifixion and resurrection). Chapters II and III interrupt the main stream of the narrative with special counsels and rebukes to each of the seven churches. Chapters IV and V return to the vision of a throne (of God) surrounded with twenty-four thrones of elders (twelve sons of Israel plus twelve apostles). Before the throne are seven torches of fire (gifts of the Holy Spirit from the Book of Isaiah), and around the throne are four creatures, a lion, an ox, a man, and a six-winged eagle (suggested by Isaiah and interpreted later as the authors of the four gospels). On the right of the throne is a scroll with seven seals which are successively broken by the Lamb (Jesus).

The breaking of the first four seals reveals the famous "four horsemen of the Apocalypse" (symbolic of the disasters to overtake Rome). The first is a white horse and a crowned rider headed for conquest (possibly the Parthians who menaced Rome). The second is a red horse and rider, symbolic of internal discord. The third is a black horse and rider with scales to weigh food, symbol of famine. The fourth is a pale horse whose rider is Death, symbol of plague. The breaking of the fifth seal presents the contrasting view of Christian martyrs in glory. The breaking of the sixth seal prophesies earthquakes and prophetically warns against terrors to come. In Chapter VII, an angel from the East (locale of the seven churches) orders the four horsemen to desist until the 144,000 of the faithful from the twelve tribes are sealed (twelve tribes times twelve apostles multiplied by thousands to include the total number of the Elect). Chapter VIII describes the opening of the seventh seal which foretells the events of the Last Judgment.

In this prophecy seven angels are given trumpets. The first trumpet call is the signal for the scorching of a third of the earth. At the blowing of the second trumpet, a mountain hurled into the sea destroys a third of marine life. At the third trumpet a star falls from heaven, poisoning a third of the earth's fresh water. At the fourth trumpet one-third of the celestial bodies are darkened. In Chapter IX the fifth trumpet is prelude to the falling of a star (Lucifer) to earth which opens hell and releases a plague of "locusts" to torture unbelievers. The "locusts" are a composite of human, animal, and bird, and are ruled by Apollyon. At the sixth trumpet four angels from the Euphrates (the four rivers of Eden) release "twice ten thousand times ten thousand" supernatural cavalry who slaughter one-third of mankind.

Chapter X describes another mighty angel holding a scroll. Seven thunders sound and a voice from heaven tells John to seal up the message of the seven thunders in secrecy and to eat the angel's scroll and prophesy. Accordingly, Chapter X foretells that nations will trample upon the holy city (the community of Christians) for forty-two months (three and a half years), that two witnesses (Christian leaders) will have power to prophesy 1266 days (the same period, seemingly referring to the active persecution of Christians by Nero after the fire of A.D. 65) before Satan (imperial Rome) kills them, and that after three and a half days (in memory of the three and a half years?) they will rise from the dead and ascend to heaven. The concluding seventh trumpet brings a vision of the coming of the Kingdom of God.

Chapter XII originates a new series of symbols referring to past Christian history. Adapted from a primitive sun myth, a woman "clothed with the sun" (Mary), crowned with twelve stars (tribes of Israel) appears in child-labour. A red dragon with seven heads and ten horns (Rome) is to devour the child (Jesus). The woman bears the child which is rescued by God (the resurrection), whereupon the woman (persecuted Christianity) flees to the wilderness (Christians seeking safety) for 1266 days (the same three and a half years). Then is described the war in heaven and the downfall of Satan who pursued the woman (early Christianity) who was given wings to fly (make an escape) for "a time and times and a half a time" (the same three and a half years). Added to this is the repeated figure of the dragon (Rome) which warred on Christians and stood on the seashore (of Asia Minor?).

Chapter XIII describes a beast from the sea (Rome) who received power from the dragon (Satan and Rome are interchangeable in this allegory) and who warred on Christians for forty-two months (the same three and a half years). Thereupon a second beast, adjutant of the first (the adjutant priests of Nero attempting to enforce emperor worship?), arose from earth bearing the mysterious number 666. (By the numerical "science" of gematria this number can be made to fit the name of Nero, but no really convincing solution of its meaning has been offered.) In Chapter XIV the Lamb (Christ) is envisioned as standing on Mount Zion with the 144,000 Elect. An angel proclaims the Last Judgment, a second angel announces the fall of Babylon (Rome), and a third angel ordains wrath for the worshippers of the beast (Roman pagans). The chapter concludes with a vision of Christ with a sickle to reap the harvest of souls and another angel to reap the unholy for the winepress of the wrath of God.

Chapters XV to XVIII describe the last seven plagues culminating with the fall of Babylon the Harlot (Rome). Chapter XIX is a vision of the Last Judgment. In Chapter XX an angel hurls Satan to the bottomless pit and chains him for a thousand years, after which he is to be loosed a little while to prelude the judgment of the living and the dead for their places in heaven or hell, only the martyrs having been raised to glory before this time. Chapter XXI is a vision of the new heaven and new earth, a glorified Jerusalem, and the concluding Chapter XXII is a glowing description of the river of life flowing from God through the celestial city. The revelation concludes with the warning that the time of the fulfillment of these prophecies is near.

Editions and Translations of the Bible

The collection of the sacred writings of the Jews and Christians seems to have been first named the Bible (*Biblia,* meaning "books") in the second century A.D. The canon of the Old Testament was authoritatively decided on by a rabbinical council in A.D. 100, and the Christian canon was authorized in A.D. 367. No early manuscripts, however, exist, and present versions are accordingly based on comparisons of later copies of earlier texts. The oldest extant Old Testament Hebrew manuscripts of any size are ninth- and tenth-century copies. The earliest Greek versions of the Bible are second-, third-, and fourth-century documents. Earlier fragments of both Hebrew and Greek editions have been discovered from time to time and are valuable for scholarly comparison with later texts.

The Old Testament was originally composed in Hebrew. The New Testament was written in a popular form of Greek known as the Koiné. Among early translations into other languages, the two most famous are the Septuagint and the Vulgate. The Septuagint, meaning "seventy," is so named because it was traditionally the work of seventy-two Hebrew scholars living in Alexandria who began in the third century B.C. to translate the Old Testament into Greek. The work was probably not completed until the first century B.C. The Vulgate, so designated because of its common use in medieval European churches, is a translation of the entire Bible into Latin, the twenty-five year labor of St. Jerome in the fourth century. This edition as revised in 1592 (the Clementine edition) is the authoritative Bible of Roman Catholicism.

The Reformation was the occasion for many more (Protestant) translations into modern European languages. In English the Tyndale-Coverdale translation of 1535 set the tone for the most famous English Bible, the King James or Authorized Version which was the work of some fifty scholars commissioned by James I. The completion of their three years of work in 1611 gave to the world one of the most eloquent, poetic, and beautifully cadenced writings in the English language.

An important Protestant revision, the Revised Version, was completed in 1895, principally notable for its modernization of Elizabethan words which had become archaic. An American variation of this edition known as the American Revised Version appeared in 1901 and embodied readings preferred by American Biblical scholars.

Meanwhile, the first Catholic English translation of the Vulgate, the Rheims-Douai Bible, was published in 1610. A revision by Bishop Challoner in 1750 is the standard English Bible still approved by Catholicism.

Recent ameliorations of the theory of the sanctity of any given version or translation have led to movements in the twentieth century to produce more readable, more accurate, and more up-to-date translations. New translations of the Bible in modern English have appeared, notably those of Moffatt (1935) and Smith and Goodspeed (1931). A new Revised Standard Version, often referred to as the Nelson Bible (1952), is the work of American Protestant scholars whose aim was to correct the "inaccuracies and errors" in former editions. To make the Bible more accessible, *The Bible Designed to be Read as Living Literature* (1936) was a notable departure from most previous editions in its omissions of repetitious, genealogical, ceremonial, and other unliterary materials. It also carefully distinguished verse from prose, eliminated the numbering of the verses, and provided the attractive large typeface and page layout of most modern secular publications. An improvement on even this fine venture produced the Dartmouth Bible in 1950, a magnificent publication which adds to the aforementioned features excellent introductory and explanatory materials, copious and easily accessible notes, and many other kinds of useful aids for either scholarly or casual comprehension of what Biblical authors really meant. The Dartmouth Bible, the result of years of scholarly research and thoughtful arrangement by Roy B. Chamberlin and Herman Feldman, to whom the authors of this volume are deeply indebted, is a monument to the best in American scholarship, good sense, and good taste.

SUGGESTED READINGS

(Place of publication, when not mentioned, is New York.)

RELIGION

H. Betterson (ed.), *Documents of the Christian Church* (1947); A. C. Bouquet, *Comparative Religion* (3rd rev. ed., London, 1950); M. Burrows, *An Outline of Biblical Theology* (Philadelphia, 1946); S. C. Carpenter, *Christianity* (London, 1953); E. C. Colwell, *The Study of the Bible* (Chicago, 1937); V. D. Macchioro, *From Orpheus to Paul* (1930).

HISTORY

C. K. Barrett (ed.), *The New Testament Background* (1961); D. M. Beck, *Through the Gospels to Jesus* (1954); G. Bornkamm, *Jesus of Nazareth* (London, 1960); C. T. Craig, *The Beginning of Christianity* (Nashville, 1943); F. R. Crownfield, *A Historical Approach to the New Testament* (1960); W. D. Davies, *Christian Origins and Judaism* (Philadelphia, 1962); M. Dibelius, *Paul* (1953); M. S. Enslin, *Christian Beginnings* (1938); F. J. Foakes-Jackson, *The Life of St. Paul* (1926); G. H. Gilbert, *Greek Thought in the New Testament* (1928); T. R. Glover, *The Jesus of History* (1921); J. Klausner, *From Jesus to Paul* (1943); S. Madeleine and J. Lane Miller, *Encyclopedia of Bible Life* (1944); A. C. McGiffert, *A History of Christianity in the Apostolic Age* (1912); A. T. Olmstead, *Jesus in the Light of History* (1942); J. W. Parkes, *The Foundations of Judaism and Christianity* (London, 1960); A. Robertson, *The Origins of Christianity* (1962); W. Walker, *A History of the Christian Church* (1959).

LITERATURE

A. E. Barnett, *The New Testament: Its Making and Meaning* (1946); A. C. Culler, *Creative Religious Literature* (1930); C. A. Dinsmore, *The English Bible as Literature* (1931); F. C. Eiselen, E. Lewis, and D. G. Gowney (eds.), *The Abingdon Bible Commentary* (1929); R. H. Fuller, *The New Testament in Current Study* (1962); F. C. Grant, *Ancient Judaism and the New Testament* (1959), F. C. Grant, *The Gospels: Their Origin and Their Growth* (1957); H. H. Halley, *Pocket Bible Handbook* (Chicago,

1946); J. Hastings (ed.), *Dictionary of the Bible* (1942); M. E. Lyman, *The Christian Epic* (1936); J. L. Price, *Interpreting the New Testament* (1961); F. B. Rhein, *An Analytical Approach to the New Testament* (Great Neck, N.Y., 1966); D. W. Riddle and H. H. Hutson, *New Testament Life and Literature* (Chicago, 1946); J. H. Ropes, *The Synoptic Gospels* (Cambridge, Mass., 1961); E. F. Scott, *The Literature of the New Testament* (1932); W. O. Sypherd, *The Literature of the English Bible* (Oxford, 1938); E. R. Tratner, *Unraveling the Book of Books* (1929).

Chronology for Part II

ANCIENT JEWISH HISTORY

(All dates are B.C. except where indicated otherwise.)

Pioneers from the Arabian desert area move into Canaan and Egypt (2000-1700); prosperous years in Egyptian territory of Goshen (1700-1500); enslavement in Egypt (1500-1290); exodus under Moses and conquest of Palestine (1290-1225); troubled years in Canaan under rule of Judges (1225-1025); rule of Saul, anointed by Samuel as Israel's first king (1025-1005); reign of David, Jerusalem the new political and religious capital (1005-970); glory of Solomon, building of palace and temple (970-930); civil war under Rehoboam and secession of northern kingdom (930-925); conquest of both kingdoms by Assyria, limited independence accorded Judah (733); Assyrian deportation of "the ten lost tribes" (721); beginning of Deuteronomic Reform Movement under King Josiah (621-608); Nebuchadnezzar deports leading Jews to Babylonian Captivity (597); destruction of Jerusalem, and many more added to the Captivity (586); Cyrus conquers Babylonia and permits Jews to return to Jerusalem (538); second temple completed (516); Greek rule of Palestine under Alexander (333-198); dynasty of Ptolemies governs Egypt and Palestine (323-198); Palestine ruled by the Seleucids (198-167); the Maccabean Revolt (167-142); resurgence of Jewish state under Maccabean Dynasty (142-63); Roman control of Palestine (63 B.C-A.D. 66); Jewish revolt against Rome (A.D. 66); Roman destruction of Jerusalem and the Diaspora (A.D. 70).

Part III

THE
MEDIEVAL
FUSION

chapter 14

THE GOTHIC CONTRIBUTION

I. EFFECTS OF THE GOTHIC INVASIONS [1]

We have seen how the Classical and the Hebraic cultures blended to create the new Christian civilization of the fourth century A.D. The continuation and growth of this composite culture was rather abruptly halted by the Gothic or Germanic invasions of the fifth century. The immediate effect of these migrations was the widespread destruction of past achievements of every sort and the degeneration of European civilization to a crude, chaotic, and almost tribal condition. Knowledge of Greek gradually disappeared and even the ability to read Latin become rare; books were destroyed, abandoned, or hidden away and forgotten; schools all but ceased to exist. Quite appropriately named the Dark Ages, the fifth, sixth, and seventh centuries mark one of the lowest ebbs in European development.

In spite of the general cultural aridity of the age, a thin

[1] These invasions are more properly referred to as Germanic, but since the Goths were the most active and destructive of the tribes and since their name is so much associated with the Middle Ages, as in Gothic architecture, the present authors have used this somewhat inaccurate designation in preference to running the risk of causing confusion with later Germany.

trickle of learning survived in the Church, the only remaining organization with a solid past tradition. Church rituals alone remained a binding link to and a reminder of the past, and even though the level of ignorance was high among Churchmen, Latin services continued to be spoken, if necessary by priests who had memorized the words with little understanding of their meaning. Naturally, superstition flourished and the true sense of Christianity was often weirdly distorted, but the Church nevertheless preserved a thin substratum of learning. Chiefly in the monasteries, a few revered pagan books, a few elementary textbooks based on Classical sources, and a considerable body of Christian writings were preserved and copied. There too, in the main, sufficient education continued to exist to produce even a few Christian writers like Gregory the Great (540-604) and Isidore of Seville (d. 636).

The Goths, being semi-barbarous, had little to contribute to Western culture in the usual sense of the word. They were slowly assimilated, civilized, and adopted into the main cultural stream which was rejuvenated in the Middle Ages. But a few sharp differences between pre-Gothic Christian Europe and post-Gothic medieval society indicate the novelties in attitudes and traditions introduced by the Goths. That these novelties were probably of Gothic origin is indicated by the early observers of the Germans, Julius Caesar and Tacitus. Caesar noted their peculiarities in his *Gallic Wars,* and some two centuries later Tacitus, perhaps the most eminent and most reliable of Roman historians, devoted a book to the description of these potential invaders of the Roman Empire.

Of the Gothic attributes so recorded, the most striking is the emphasis on activity. The history of Gothic migrations is an indication of a kind of intense ethnic restlessness which seems to imply a love of motion for its own sake. Tacitus implies that this was their only form of self-expression. Characterizing them as having "fierce blue eyes, red hair, huge frames, fit only for sudden exertion," [2] he concludes, "Inaction is odious to the race." [3] Speaking of their generals, he adds, "If they are energetic, if they are conspicuous, if they fight in the front, they lead because they are admired." [4] Caesar had earlier made a similar observation in remarking that "their whole life is occupied in hunting and in the pursuits of the military art; from childhood they devote themselves to fatigue and hardships." [5] Gibbon in his *Decline and Fall of the Roman Empire* sardonically observes that the ancient Germans had essentially only two states of being, lethargy and violent activity, and that the activity was a necessary release from the boredom of constant laziness. There may well be considerable logic in these remarks, but since Caesar and Tacitus were principally impressed by the Germanic interest in energetic pursuits, and since the Germanic ideal of an after-life was an eternity of days of fighting and nights of carousing, it seems fair to assume that action was their positive ideal, just as godliness was a Hebraic characteristic and intellectualism a Classical quality, in spite of the many recorded failures of each culture in the service of these ideals.

An immediate effect of this passion for violent action, which usually took a belligerent direction, is observed in the individual knight-errantry and mass knight-errantry (the Crusades) of the succeeding Middle Ages. It appears also in the medieval tournaments and the continued eruptions of local wars and personal feuds in the Middle Ages and Renaissance. More subtly, it is reflected in medieval epics and *chansons de geste* ("songs about deeds"), and in the restless lines and ornamentations of Gothic architec-

[2] *Germany*, 4.
[3] *Ibid.*, 14.
[4] *Ibid.*, 7.
[5] *Gallic Wars*, VI, 21.

ture, which are far removed in spirit from classic serenity. The inactive and non-belligerent "trimmers" in the third canto of Dante's *Inferno* are castigated for "never having been alive" and are scorned by the author as "hateful to God and to the enemies of God." The love of activity in later Western civilization can scarcely be held to be the sole product of Gothic inheritance, but it is worth pointing out that Dante's paradise (unlike former similar conceptions) is in incessant motion, that Goethe's Faust in his Gothic study translated the opening lines of the Gospel of John as "In the beginning was the Act," that the literary progeny of intervening writers like Rabelais, Cervantes, and Lesage are very restless heroes, and that the German philosophies of Kant, Schopenhauer, and Nietzsche make the power of reason subservient to some more active principle. Recent social critics have gloomily observed that the passion for action, usually unaccompanied by thought, is one of the most salient characteristics of twentieth-century life.

Another outstanding trait of these primitive peoples was their love of independence. Tacitus emphasized this quality in his wonderment that they had no cities and did "not even tolerate closely contiguous dwellings." [6] Independence was cherished in different ways by both Hebraism and Classicism, yet after centuries of submission to imperial Rome, this quality required the stimulation of the invaders to produce immediately a stubborn refusal to bow tamely before the authority of the medieval Church, although the Church, with its monopoly on education, religion, and accepted tradition, was seemingly in a position to enforce absolute obedience. Medieval Europeans accepted the tenets of Church doctrine in spite of recurrent heresies, but there was little disposition to succumb to the Church's ambition to delegate to itself the total sovereignty of the

[6] *Germany,* 16.

previous Roman Empire. More recently, the same kind of stubborn independence played its part in creating the democratic tradition of the Western world.

A third Gothic characteristic which had a decisive effect on European civilization was the Germanic respect for women. One important tribe, the Langobardi, worshipped not a male deity but Mother Earth (a concept revived in *Faust*). Another group regarded a woman, Veleda, as a deity, and, as Tacitus summed up this, to him, peculiar attitude, "the sex has a certain sanctity." [7] Medieval worship of Mary and the chivalric regard for women, although probably influenced too by Moslem idealogy, are thus rooted in Germanic tradition, to which we also seemingly owe current ideas of the romanticizing of women, ideas which are scarcely products of either Classicism or Hebraism.

A rather less certain Gothic contribution seems to have been a fascinated interest in the grotesque, the strange, and the mysterious. Cathedral shadows and gargoyles, Dante's figure of Minos in the *Inferno*,[8] terrifying and haunting ghosts, witches, and goblins appear to have been products of primitive imaginations which feared the terrors of an unknown and antagonistic world and created strange imaginary monsters as the expected products of the dark forests, treacherous bogs, glaring snow, and violent storms of northern Europe. In the *Grettir-Saga*, the fearful rampages of Glam's ghost, which made houses creak and had baleful effects on whole communities, were the subject of an apparently favorite bedtime story.

In brief, the Goths contributed no written literature, no art forms, no ornaments of culture. But certain basic qualities of their nature (love of action), of their attitudes

[7] *Ibid.*, 8.

[8] Canto V. Compare this grotesque judge of the underworld with the original Minos in the *Odyssey*, Bk. XI.

(independence, veneration of women), and of their imagination (creation of the mysterious) had an immediate and
often a lasting effect on Western life and thought.

II. THE GOTHS AND OTHER GERMANIC TRIBES

The Goths were the most violent and the most active of a
group of tribes who are described by Caesar and Tacitus as
the "Germans." But when one speaks of the ancient Germans, it is imperative that he eliminate from his mind the
boundaries of modern Germany. In history, the designation
"German" covers a vast amount of territory and includes
much historical ferment only very remotely connected with
the direct ancestors of the Reich. For the most part, England, the Low Countries, Austria, France, and Switzerland
can claim to be as "German" as Germany itself, and Scandinavia and Iceland are even more so. Furthermore, there
are large German elements in the Baltic countries, central
Europe, Italy, Spain, Portugal, and even in North Africa.
The large majority of citizens of the United States are also
of Germanic background. Sometimes the term "Barbarians"
is used by historians to apply to the ancient Germanic
tribes, but this term is even less satisfactory, since it is also
used freely to apply to other groups of non-Germanic origin
(e.g., the Gauls and the Huns), and since it suggests a more
savage state of culture than actually existed.

The earliest known habitat of the Germans was the west
shore of the Baltic Sea, in what is now East Prussia, Denmark, and lower Scandinavia. However, references to a
great migration between 1000 and 500 B.C. suggest an even
earlier home, possibly in eastern Germany or Poland. Since
these primitive peoples did not possess the art of writing
until the second century of the Christian era, there are no
records of their early life. The first account of their civilization was written by Julius Caesar when he was governor of
Gaul in 58-51 B.C. By the time of Caesar, the Germans had

migrated south as far as the Rhine, occupying all of modern Western Germany and the Low Countries.

Though always warlike and far from stagnant, the Germans apparently needed the challenge of Roman expansionism to rouse them from mere inter-tribal warfare to large-scale military activity and political development. The appearance of Caesar's legions in Gaul stirred new apprehensions in the Germans, and when Caesar conquered the Celtic Gauls he found that he had far fiercer enemies to deal with along the Rhine. Roman fortifications at Coblenz, Cologne, Mainz, and other Rhineland cities succeeded in containing the Germans for many generations at that point, though elsewhere the tribes continued to move southeastward. Eventually Roman fortifications stretched 228 miles along the Rhine and Main and an additional 108 miles across country to the Danube, but the aggressive spread of the Germans was not to be halted; by A.D. 200 they covered all the territory from the mouth of the Rhine to the Black Sea, and were pressing irresistibly on the borders of the Roman Empire.

A. *The Goths*

The most warlike and dynamic of the Germans were the Goths, the easternmost of the tribes, who occupied the land along the southern Danube basin and the Black Sea. They were divided by the Dniester River into Ostrogoths (East Goths) and Visigoths (West Goths), and were actually two independent groups speaking a common language and following similar customs. The Visigoths were the most migratory of all the German tribes. About A.D. 200 they moved into what is now the Ukraine, north of the Black Sea. From there they were pushed southward by the Huns, until by 395 they were occupying Athens and Corinth. At the opening of the fifth century they started moving northwest toward Italy; in 410 they deviated to sack Rome (the occasion for Augustine's composition of the *City of God*) and then, turning northwest again, crossed Gaul from whence they headed south into Spain. Here they consolidated and set up a strong kingdom, attained a high degree of civilization, and eventually were assimulated into the Roman culture already established in Spain. Their rule continued until overthrown by the Moors in the early part of the eighth century, by which time they had lost their language and their legal code, together with other orient tribal traditions, and had become indistinguishable from the Latin elements in the Iberian peninsula.

The Ostrogoths were only slightly less travelled. They moved across the Balkans into Italy, defeated in 493 a rival Germanic prince, Odoacer, to gain control of the entire peninsula and the island of Sicily. Here they ruled until they were defeated by the armies of the Emperor Justinian and absorbed into the Byzantine Empire in 555.

B. *The Franks*

Unlike the Goths, the Franks were among the least migratory of the Germans and the most durable in their culture. They remained close to their home in the western Rhineland, imitated the Romans in government and military organization, and gradually took over Gaul as the Roman occupation dwindled in strength. Their leader Clovis, who ruled 481-511, overpowered the Romans of northern France and then continued his aggression against the Ostrogoths until he controlled all the territory between the Rhine and the Pyrenees. Several other powerful leaders developed among the Franks, the most famous being Charles Martel (714-741) and Charlemagne (768-814).

C. *Other Germanic Tribes*

Among the other Germanic tribes were the Angles, Saxons, and Jutes, who moved from the channel coast into

England (449-547); the Burgundians, who settled in eastern France and were dominated by the Franks, though the territory did not become an official province of France until 1678; the Alemanni, a minor tribe along the central Rhine, of interest chiefly because they gave their name to the modern French designation for Germany; and the Vandals, a ruthless and bloodthirsty lot who eventually settled in North Africa.

D. *The Gauls*

Early history makes so many references to the Gauls that a few words concerning them will not be amiss here. The Gauls were not Germans but Celts, with no proved racial kinship to their Teutonic neighbors. The original habitat of the Celts is as mysterious as that of the Germans, but we know that as early as the fourth century B.C. they were living in southern and western France and were strong enough to carry out a successful sack of Rome. Celtic civilization was also established in the western Iberian peninsula, along the channel coast, and in the British Isles. In the last-named place they were called Britons; thus Britain and French Brittany were named from their early Celtic inhabitants, as is Belgium, from a tribe known to every high-school Latin student as the Belgae. Culturally, the most interesting contribution of the Celts is the *Mabinogion,* a collection of Celtic myths and legends compiled in Welsh in the fourteenth and fifteenth centuries from older materials.

SUGGESTED READINGS

See end of Chapter 15 for suggested readings.

GERMANIC RELIGION,
MYTHOLOGY, AND LEGEND

Like the Greeks, the ancient Germans had an elaborate theogony of gods and goddesses, a vast body of nature myths, and a fanciful theory of the creation of the world. Also like the Greeks, they behaved rather casually toward their deities, deferred to them politely but without either awe or deep conviction, and founded their real values on more worldly ethical considerations. However, in tone and spirit Greek Olympian religion was brilliant sunshine to the Northman's cold and gloomy night. The Greek gods were a set of lively, all-too-human Olympian playboys whose antics did not interfere with Greek love of life and its pleasant custom of reducing the concept of virtue to an ethical principle of *sophrosyné,* or moderation. Northern religion, on the other hand, was based upon the joyless nature of both heaven and earth and upon the bitter, endless, and hopeless struggle of good against overpowering evil. It is no wonder, then, that the Germans were among the first converts to Christianity, which presented them with a belief in a Redeemer of Mankind and the possibility of a happy life to come. In 341 Bishop Ulfilas came as a missionary to the Goths, translated parts of the Bible into

Gothic, and converted his flock even before Christianity became the official religion of Rome. Other tribes were converted by later contact with Christian Romans. This early acceptance of the Gospel accounts for the many Christian elements in a mythology obviously pagan in origin.

Our sources for much material concerning northern religion are the *Eddas,* of which the *Elder Edda* was set down by an unknown poet about A.D. 1050 and the *Younger,* or *Prose Edda,* was composed by one Snorri Sturluson about 1230. The material in both *Eddas* is somewhat similar, and obviously originated many centuries before it was set down in writing.

The *Eddas* tell us that originally the Universe was a bottomless deep called Niflheim, with a world of mists suspended somewhere above. The only sign of life in this world was a fountain from which flowed twelve cold rivers, the ice from which gradually filled the chasm beneath. Just below the world of mists lay Muspelheim, the world of light, warm winds from which blew against the ice and formed clouds. From these clouds were born Ymir, the Frost giant, his cow Audhumbla, and a number of anonymous frost-maidens. Audhumbla found sustenance by licking salt from the ice, and by this strange means of nourishment inadvertently created the first god. One day, while she was licking a block of ice, the god's hair appeared; the second day, the entire head emerged, and the third day the body. This new-formed deity lost no time in mating with one of the frost-maidens, who in due course presented him with three sons, Odin (variously called Odin, Woden, or Wotan), Vili, and Ve. On reaching maturity, the three boys turned against Ymir and slew him by pinning him under a huge ash-tree called Ygradasil. From his body they made the earth, from his blood the seas, from his hair the trees, from his bones the mountains, from his skull the heavens, from his brain the clouds, and from his eyebrows a great wall surrounding a portion of earth called Midgard, the home of man. Sparks from Muspelheim formed the stars and the planets, and as the sun shone on the newly-created earth, vegetation sprang forth and flowers bloomed. The whole structure was supported by the ash-tree Ygradasil, whose three roots extended to Asgard, the home of the gods, Jötenheim, the abode of powerful giants, and Niflheim, the realm of darkness and cold. The root leading to Asgard was tended by the three Norns, Urda, Verdandi, and Skuld, who sat beside the Well of Fate and oversaw the past, present, and future respectively; the root leading to Jötenheim was securely fastened by the Spring of Wisdom, but the Niflheim root was constantly gnawed by the adder Neidhogge, or darkness. Consequently, the tree was in constant danger of collapsing and bringing the universe down with it. Thus the three supports of the tree represent allegorically, the spirit, wisdom, and ignorance. Four harts, representing the winds, constantly ate the buds from the tree, and occasionally the remains of Ymir, pinned under the tree, stirred and caused great earthquakes.

After the formation of the physical universe, the gods created Aski, the first man, from an ash-tree and gave him a mate in Embla, whom he fashioned from an elm. They also created the Dwarfs, superb craftsmen who lived under the earth, and the Elves and Sprites, who tended the flowers and streams. To man, Odin gave life and soul, Vili reason and power of motion, and Ve the five senses. Thus equipped, our original ancestors were left to hew their own dubious course in an unstable world.

The gods themselves were no less insecure. To the Germans, the divinities were not all-powerful, but were rather forces for good struggling against the superior odds of the evil giants of Jötenheim. Eventually, the giants would triumph and the gods would go to destruction in a monumental *Götterdämmerung;* thus would the powers of brute force eventually overcome those of wisdom and the spirit. The gods themselves realized that their ascendency was but temporary, and sat in their domain at Asgard sternly and joylessly awaiting Ragnarok, or the day of doom.

The enmity of the giants had been incurred while Odin was constructing the fortress Valhalla. Valhalla was both a stronghold for the gods and a heaven for warriors slain in battle. There Odin sat with his ravens Hugin and Munin (who brought him daily tidings from the world of men) perched on his shoulders. There also were the Valkyries, warrior-daughters of Odin who visited the battle fields and brought back a choice selection of the slain to live among the gods. The heroes banqueted all night and spent each day in battles in which they hewed each other to pieces and then were magically made whole at nightfall; a monotonous and exhausting sort of heavenly reward, of which the happy warriors apparently never tired. This dubious paradise had been built by the giants who were promised Freyr, goddess of love and beauty, as payment. When the task was completed, Odin refused to carry out his share of the bargain. In the argument that ensued, Thor, the thunder-god, killed one of the giants with his hammer. From that time onward the giants were mortal enemies of the gods who, creatures of light and wisdom as they were, were through their cupidity responsible for their own eventual downfall. Against such a depressing conception of the universe, where the very gods bring about their own destruction, Christianity must have come to the Northmen as a great light, and their ready acceptance of its doctrines is easily understood.

The northern hierarchy of gods, goddesses, and other superhuman beings was as elaborate as that of the Greeks, but for our purposes a few notes on the leading inhabitants of Asgard will suffice. The most important of the gods was, as we have seen, **Odin,** a joyless and tortured deity who nevertheless tried sincerely to bring good to mankind. He had given up an eye in exchange for a drink at the Well of Wisdom, had hung nine nights impaled by a spear to a wind-rocked tree, in order to learn the mysteries of the Runes, or Germanic alphabet, and had stolen from the Giants the skaldic mead, a draught of which would make any man a poet. Unlike Zeus, he did not seek to hoard these powers to himself but passed them freely on to mankind. Despite his good-will, however, he was capable of stooping to covetous and unethical deeds, and his morals among beautiful women, both of the heavens and the earth, were about on a par with those of his Greek predecessor.

Odin's wife was called **Frigga** or **Fricka** and, like the Greek Hera, she was a rather literal-minded, shrewish character whose divine function as preserver of the sanctity of marriage and the home was sorely tried within her own household. Frigga's sister was called **Freyr,** goddess of love and beauty. In addition to being the inspiration of lovers, she cultivated the golden apples the gods ate to preserve their eternal youth, though in some legends this latter function was entrusted to a minor goddess named Iduna. The most important of Odin's children was named **Thor.** Thor was the god of thunder and the strongest of all inhabitants of Asgard. He owned a hammer which he used with rather too frequent abandon against his enemies, a belt of strength which doubled his muscular powers, and a set of iron gloves which rendered his aim with the hammer infallible. He was the "front man" for the gods and, like the Greek Hermes, was entrusted with most of the difficult jobs of diplomatic relations. His brother **Frey,** god of fertility, governed the sunshine and rain, while a third brother, **Tyr,** was god of war.

The most beloved of all the gods was **Baldur the Good,** who was a Germanic combination of Apollo and Achilles. Baldur was supposedly invulnerable, and the gods used to amuse themselves by throwing all manner of deadly missiles at him and watching them bounce tamely from his body. Only the fire-god **Loki,** the official mischief-maker and nuisance in Asgard, knew that the beloved Baldur was vulnerable to the seemingly harmless mistletoe, and one day he induced one of the gods to pelt Baldur with a twig of this plant. Baldur was instantly pierced to the heart, and, despite all the efforts of the gods to save him, went to **Hela,** the realm of the dead.

The most constant reminders of Germanic mythology in our lives are the names of the days of the week. Except for Saturday, which is derived from the Roman god Saturn, all the days are named for northern divinities: the sun, the moon, Tyr, Odin (Woden), Thor, and Freyr. In literature the most important works springing from German myths and legends are the previously mentioned Eddas, the many *Heldensagen,* or hero-stories concerning such figures as Grettir the Strong, Jal, Sigurd, and Beowulf, and the great thirteenth-century epic, the *Nibelungenlied.*

The Legends of Charlemagne

The large body of legend surrounding the Frankish king Charles the Great, who ruled what is now France from 768 to 814, presents a complicated literary problem which can be given only the most superficial treatment here. Like all legendary material growing out of the career of an actual historical personage, the Charlemagne story has a fundament of fact which poets and story-tellers, most of whom remain anonymous, have used as a springboard for their most fantastic flights of imagination. As in the case of the King Arthur legends, which the Charlemagne stories somewhat resemble, many versions of the same incident often exist, all of them usually far removed from actual historical happenings. To make matters more complicated, story-tellers seem at times to have confused the rule of Charlemagne with that of his grandfather, Charles Martel, who as Mayor of the Palace was actual, if not nominal, king of France from 714 to 741.

Most of the Charlemagne legends hinge upon that noble

warrior's championship of Christianity against the powerful attacks of the Saracens across the Pyrenees. The Moslems, after the death of Mohammed in 632, had spread rapidly from Arabia through Asia Minor, Egypt, and North Africa. In 711 they entered Spain, where they began to cross the Pyrenees for murderous raids on the Franks, and for nearly a century thereafter they remained a primary danger to Frankish security. In 725 the Saracen general Anbessa captured the town of Carcasonne, and in 732 they captured Bordeaux and spread so menacingly over southern France that drastic action to check their advance became immediately necessary. In October of that year Charles Martel, aided strategically by King Eude of Acquitaine, overwhelmed the Saracens at Tours and checked their advance for all time, and in 759, at the battle of Narbonne, Charles' son Pepin destroyed Islamic power in France completely. Thus, when Pepin's son Charlemagne came to the throne in 768 there were no longer any Moslem forces north of the Pyrenees, nor did Charlemagne ever fight Saracens on French soil, though he did campaign against them incidentally in Spain. The famous battle of Roncesvalles, where in 778 Charlemagne's rear-guard under the legend-magnified Roland was wiped out to the last man, was fought not against Mohammedan armies as the *Song of Roland* has it, but against a small force of Gascon mountaineers. Incidentally, the poem presents Charlemagne as having attained the impressive age of two hundred at the time of this battle; actually he was about thirty-five.

The germ of most of the Carolingian legends is therefore not unvarnished history. Rather it is a Latin chronicle, *De Vita et Gestis Caroli Magni*, formerly attributed to the Archbishop Turpin, a contemporary of Charlemagne. According to legend, Turpin died heroically in the battle of Roncesvalles, but he really died of natural causes about the year 800. Actually the work has little to do with history and nothing to do with the Archbishop, but much to do with the wealth of folk and literary epics of Charlemagne that appeared in great profusion from the eleventh century onward. The *De Vita et Gestis* makes Charlemagne a white-bearded patriarch of supernatural powers, served by noble knights conceived in the best traditions of medieval chivalry. Outstanding among his followers are the twelve Peers or Paladins who, as noble companions of the king and dauntless champions of the right, greatly resemble the Knights of Arthur's Round Table. The most famous of the Paladins is Charlemagne's nephew Roland (or Orlando, as he is called in Italian), who is the central figure of the French medieval epic, the *Song of Roland*. Other well-known Paladins are Roland's cousin Rinaldo, Florismart, Roland's close friend, Ogier the Dane, Ganelon the Treacherous, Oliver the Wise, and the brave Archbishop Turpin.

Later poets of the Renaissance enjoyed allowing their fancies to play with the imagined deeds of these remote and shadowy heroes. Luigi Pulci (1432-1484) strung together a series of adventures in a serio-comic style in his *Morgante Maggiore*. Boiardo (1434-1494) used the same material for the composition of his unfinished but elaborate romantic epic *Orlando Innamorato,* a revision of which by Francesco Berni (1490-1536) also became immensely popular. It remained for Ariosto (1474-1533) to complete Boiardo's work in the most elaborate of all the versions, the *Orlando Furioso.*

SUGGESTED READINGS

(Place of publication, when not mentioned, is New York.)

J. B. Bury, *The Invasion of Europe by the Barbarians* (1963); E. S. Duckett, *The Gateway to the Middle Ages* (1938); V. Gronbech, *The Culture of the Teutons* (Oxford, 1932); M. L. W. Laistner, *Thought and Letters in Western Europe 500-900* (London, 1931); H. S. Moss, *Birth of the Middle Ages 294-815* (Oxford, 1935); E. K. Rand, *Founders of the Middle Ages* (2nd ed., Cambridge, Mass., 1929); H. O. Taylor, *Classical Heritage of the Middle Ages* (1925); B. Thorpe, *Northern Mythology* (London, 1851).

chapter 16

THE HEIGHT
OF THE MIDDLE AGES

I. COMPLETION OF THE CULTURAL FUSION

The period in European history known as the Middle Ages is that broad interval between the end of ancient civilization and the beginning of the modern world. It is often described, therefore, as being bounded by the fall of Rome in the fifth century and the fall of Constantinople in the fifteenth. Principally as a result of the Gothic invasions, the earlier medieval centuries were largely confused and chaotic. The concluding fourteenth and fifteenth centuries remained medieval throughout most of Europe, but striking indications of the new Renaissance attitude were becoming apparent in Italy. Particularly when surveying history from the literary viewpoint, which usually sees fourteenth-century Petrarch and Boccaccio as Renaissance authors, we find it useful to think of the Renaissance as beginning in the fourteenth century and to treat the three preceding centuries of cultural revival and cultural stability as the culmination of the medieval state of mind.

From this point of view, the height of the Middle Ages marks the recovery of civilization from the chaos and ignorance of the five preceding centuries and particularly from a series of disastrous raids by Vikings, Slavs, Magyars, and Moslems in the tenth century. It also represents the fusion of the three cultural heritages—the Classical, the Hebraic, the Gothic—and a relatively equal balance of the three in the creation of a new kind of culture which was as clearly neither decadent Roman nor early Christian as it was certainly not primitive Gothic. In the earlier centuries, immediately following the Gothic invasions, the semi-barbarians had gradually adapted themselves to the Christian tradition, but except for the elements of Classical thought already in Christianity, the world of Classical learning was very much in the discard, being represented only by a sparse scattering of elementary texts and uncritical compendiums of Greek and Roman intellectual achievements.

The beginnings of a Classical renaissance were made by Charlemagne in his effort to revive secular scholarship in the early years of the ninth century. With the added stimulus of the reintroduction of Greek thought by the Moslems in Spain beginning in the eleventh century, Gothic energy began to make itself felt in an attempted mental expansion, a direction quite new to it and foreign to its antecedents. As a result, both the secular and the religious aspects of life became more uniform, more intellectualized, and more humanized. Although the era remained full of confusions, conflicts, and glaring imperfections, a relative stability was nevertheless achieved. A civilization still dominated by Christianity emerged; but the three co-equal attributes of the Christian Trinity—Power, Wisdom, and Love—are interesting symbols of a near-equal regard for the three merged cultural strains. Power (energy, action) was the Gothic contribution. Wisdom was a dominant ideal of the Classical world. Love was the hallmark of Hebraic emotionalism with its concepts of the Good Shepherd and Loving Father as images of deity, originating among the prophets and carried over into the Christian tradition. Man creates God in his own image at least in the sense of conceiving of deity in terms of humanity's own highest aspirations. The medieval tri-unity of cultural heritages thus produced a conception of deity which embraced all three.

II. ORIGINS OF THE LATER MIDDLE AGES

The first definite beginning of the new movement toward order and higher standards of education was the Carolingian Renaissance. Building on the monarchical foundations of his ancestors of the Carolingian dynasty, Charles the Great assumed the throne of the Frankish Kingdom in 771. A series of successful wars gradually increased the size and power of the Frankish Empire until Charles became the undisputed strong man of Europe. In 800 Pope Leo III anointed him as Emperor of the West, thus originating the new Holy Roman Empire, an act which in itself indicated a strong desire to return to the stable *Pax Romana* of the past. Although this new Carolingian empire did not long outlast the death of its founder in 814, it made clear the possibility of higher standards of civic administration, social organization, and enforceable codes of law. It also acted as an impetus to learning because of Charles's rejuvenation of the Palace School to which he imported the best European scholars available. He also directed the founding of other schools in connection with cathedrals and monasteries, and so stimulated a general revival of intellectualism and the preservation and copying of Roman classics. This renewed interest in learning continued, though with considerable abatement, during the later weakening of Charlemagne's political structure. The most interesting facet of this rather minor "Renaissance" is the spectacle of a Frankish or Germanic state reaching out to assimilate the riches of the Roman Classical and the Christianized Hebraic culture, one aspect of which is depicted much later by Goethe in Faust's rescue of Helen of Troy.

A second stimulus to greater enlightenment came from the reintroduction of Hellenic learning through the Moslems, who had preserved and translated many Greek writings (which had survived in the Byzantine East) into Arabic. When the Moslems swept into Spain in the eighth century and established a new center of learning in Cordova, Jewish scholars penetrated the barrier between Christian Europe and Moslem Spain to reintroduce the Greek inquiring and scientific spirit to the Western world. They were soon followed by Christian explorers into this new world of learning. By the eleventh century Greek and Moslem works began to circulate in Christendom; in the twelfth century a Christian school for translators was established at Toledo, which had been captured by Christians in 1085. Graeco-Arabic mathematics, science, and philosophy constituted the cores of the new knowledge so disseminated, and the two outstanding commentators on Aristotle, Avicenna (960-1037) and Averroes (1126-1198), became revered as authorities second only to the Bible itself. The stimulation of Moslem thinkers was largely responsible for the achievements of the medieval intellectual movement known as scholasticism and for the growth of such cathedral schools as Paris and Chartres into the first great modern universities.

It must be borne in mind, however, that these new incitements to learning were not forced upon the inhabitants of medieval Europe. On the contrary, it required deliberate effort to surmount geographical, national, religious, and linguistic barriers to reach them. We must conclude, therefore, that the medieval revival was principally the result of the sheer human instinct to advance and that the imported enlightenment of foreign scholarship was partly an incentive but partly also only a means to that end. But regardless of cause and effect, new contact was established with Classical learning by gradual degrees, and when Constantinople fell to the Turks in 1453, fleeing Greek scholars seeking refuge in Europe found a warm reception for their intellectual wares.

III. CHARACTERISTICS OF THE LATE MIDDLE AGES

The most striking characteristic of this new upsurge of civilization was its yearning for order. After centuries of chaos, an orderly society was not easy to achieve and, in fact, was not achieved; but the medieval mind abounded in neat diagrammatic arrangements which it sought, with very limited success, to impose on society. Two models of organization were readily available: the model of Church organization and the civic pattern of the Roman Empire. St. Augustine in his *City of God* had distinguished between the City of Man (originating in Greek civilization and culminating in the Roman Empire) and the City of God (originating in Hebraism and culminating in Christianity). Augustine had argued that the new Christian city should supplant the old, and the medieval Church naturally sought to impose this point of view. In supporting this claim to temporal domination, the Church also possessed a document known as the "Donation of Constantine" (see p. 248) in which the Emperor Constantine had supposedly conferred upon Pope Sylvester I sovereignty over the western portion of the Roman Empire. But strong civil units, dating back to Germanic tribal organization and potentially as strong as the Carolingian Empire, held the Church to a very limited realization of its temporal ambitions. In the daily lives of men, in the worlds of learning and discipline, the Church became unquestionably supreme. But in government and society the two states of St. Augustine existed, and the two outstanding kinds of medieval architecture, cathedral and castle, stood as monuments to the dual nature of medieval life.

In civil life the desire to impose order upon chaos resulted in the feudal system. Whether traced back to the Roman social arrangement of nobleman and dependents or to the similar Germanic tribal organization of leader and subordinates, feudalism resulted from the natural desire of the weak to rely on the strong, particularly in times of stress. In return, the strong could command service and obedience from those who required protection. From this simple situation there gradually emerged two distinct classes of society, noble and peasant. The aristocracy owned all the property, were professional fighters and rulers, and enjoyed sufficient leisure to create a courtly society with all its ramifications of rank and ceremonial. The peasant, serf, or vassal rendered the many services required for the maintenance of himself and his overlord, his principal responsibilities being to obey commands and pay due homage to his superiors. The two classes became increasingly remote from each other, intermarriage between them was unknown, and there developed a feeling among the aristocracy that the peasant was actually a different kind of being, born to be ignorant, coarse, and subservient, and probably not endowed with even the same kind of blood that coursed through noble hearts.

Meanwhile, the growing wealth of the Roman Catholic Church (which in 1054 had broken off from the Eastern organization, since known as the Greek Orthodox Church) had attracted the attention of feudal noblemen and ordinary adventurers who saw in Holy Orders many an easy and lucrative means of livelihood. From simony (the selling of Church offices) at the top to the peddling of pardons and exhibition of holy relics at the bottom, the Church was shot through with the varieties of venality so thoroughly excoriated in Dante's *Divine Comedy* and laughed at in Chaucer's *Canterbury Tales*.

Yet, amidst all these collusions and confusions of religious and secular lives, the ideal of order remained clear, whether it was argued that a politically supreme Church should rule (the Guelf position in twelfth-century Italy) or that a revived Holy Roman Empire should dominate (the Ghibelline theory) or that a revived Holy Roman Empire and a purified Church should each be supreme in its own sphere, as Dante believed. Since none of these goals was realized or apparently realizable, the medieval idealist found satisfaction for his desire for order by organizing in theory what usually refused to be organized in fact. The models, as we have noted before, were the organizations of the Christian Church and the Roman Empire. Since both of these were authoritarian organizations with a supreme head at the top and successive ranks below, order and hierarchy came to mean essentially the same thing. Aristotle and Plato had also posited a supreme God from whom lesser creations had emanated, Hebraism had believed in an omnipotent deity with angels as intermediary powers—all authority, in short, held that the immutable law of the universe proceeded from a supreme head through a chain of successively dependent hierarchies.

In imitation of this absolute archetype of order, the Church elaborated the many ranks of the clergy descending from the supremacy of the pope. Theologians arranged the angels in a descending scale of nine ranks from seraphim and cherubim at the top to archangels and angels at the bottom. Astronomers envisioned the heavens as arranged in nine concentric circles in imitation of the angelic hierarchy. The feudal lords set up their own elaborations in assigning relative supremacy to the different levels of nobility. On paper, at least, medieval society and medieval ideas were beautifully arranged down to the most minute detail. The macrocosm (the universe) and the microcosm (human society) theoretically moved in clearly defined hierarchical grooves: in the heavens from Primum Mobile to Earth, in the Church from pope to lay worshipper, in the State from

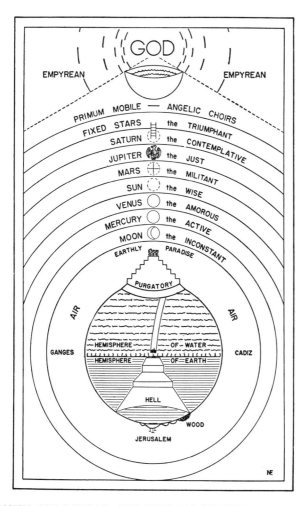

HEAVEN, PURGATORY, AND HELL (AS VISIONED BY DANTE)

king to peasant. The elaborate architectural structure of the *Divine Comedy* is a supreme testimonial to the medieval love of order—and the chaotic scenes of the *Inferno* are the mirror of the disorder which actually existed. It is by no means a new observation that seldom in history was the human ideal so high and human performance so low.

The new, more civilized spirit of the age, with its idealizing tendency, also had important effects on Christian religious concepts. For in spite of the scandalous venality which flourished behind the facade of Christianity, the common people and many uncommon people remained devout and upright. For such as these Christianity became more humanized, more spiritualized, and more intellectualized.

The humanization of Christian doctrine took the form of gradual abandonment of the concept of deity as the awful Judge of the Revelation, allowing the God of love and the suffering Savior to re-emerge from the shadows where the Dark Ages had hidden them. Even so, the reminders of the Day of Wrath were not easily eradicated, and it required the introduction of a novelty to change the stress in religious teaching. This novelty was the worship of the Virgin Mary, known as Mariolatry. Intellectualized concepts of the Trinity were too abstract to generate much warmth of heart, the image of Christ as the Eternal Judge was difficult to forget, but the mother of Jesus who had suffered the pangs of childbirth and who had seen her Son hanging on the cross presented a vivid human appeal. One could pray to Mary, knowing that she would understand, and beg her to intercede with her Son. The worship of Mary was undoubtedly stimulated by remembrances of Germanic woman-worship, by Moslem influences, and by Neoplatonic theories which held that love of earthly beauty was the first step in the ladder of love by which one could ascend to a comprehension of celestial beauty. Whatever the factors of its composite origin, the result of Mariolatry was the ennoblement of all women as sisters of Mary, witnessed in the chivalric regard for women and apotheosized in Dante's adoration of Beatrice which led him ultimately to a vision of Mary as Queen of Heaven and thence to the vision of God as "the love that moves the sun and other stars."

Henry Adams, in his brilliant examination of this phase of medieval life (*Mont Saint-Michel and Chartres*) ascribes the renewed spirituality of the Middle Ages entirely to this new phenomenon of devotion to Mary. It is undoubtedly true that Mariolatry had a great deal to do with it, but the original human need for an object of devotion must also be taken into account, and the humanizing of the Christian faith in a more civilized era was inevitable if Christianity was to survive at all. The results of this renewed religious devotion are clear in any case. The Crusades (1095-1270), undertaken to free the Holy Land from the Turkish infidels, provided an outlet for the energies of the feudal lords, but they also indicate strikingly the new religious incentives to action. The building of the great cathedrals, massive and intricate structures difficult to be equalled by the best modern machinery, was accomplished by the tedious hand labor of earnest multitudes, described by the Archbishop of Rouen as halting only to offer prayers to God.

A similar indication of the new spirit was the growth and expansion of the monastic and mendicant orders, the former composed of monks who gave themselves to ascetic retirement from the world by joining the newly formed Cluniac, Cistercian, or Carthusian Orders and the latter of friars who devoted themselves to simple pastoral work and teaching, begging their bread, and living in poverty in imitation of the simple way of life of the original disciples. Outstanding among these mendicant orders were the Augustinians, Carmelites, Dominicans, and Franciscans. The latter two became especially prominent and, as their size, wealth, and power increased, they also became susceptible to the corruption which was omnipresent in Church organization. The origin of these orders was nevertheless spiritual, and, however corrupted, they continued to produce outstanding scholarly and religious leaders.

One of these leaders, the great Franciscan Bonaventura, calls attention to another phase of medieval spirituality: the emergence of a number of men and women known as mystics. The most prominent of these were St. Bernard (1090-1153), Hugh (1096-1141) and Richard (d. 1173) of Saint Victor, Hildegard of Bingen (1098-1179), and Bonaventura (1221-1274). Inspired by apocalyptic and Neoplatonic modes of thought, the mystics sought to identify themselves with the spirit of Godhead, proceeding by gradual degrees of visions and raptures from earth to heaven.

Although most of the prominent mystics were highly intelligent men and women, the principal intellectual revival of the Middle Ages took the form of that reasoned exposition of the fine points of Christian theology known as scholasticism. The origin and method of scholasticism are accredited to Abelard (1079-1142) who in his famous *Sic et Non* ("So and Not" or "Yes and No") proposed 158 theological problems for discussion. Instead of the previous dogmatic approach of earlier theologians, Abelard listed the opinions of past authorities on both sides of each question and left the final decision to the reader. This lucid presentation of the idea that theological doctrine could be open to controversy was revolutionary enough, but the implication that reason could be a final judge between diverse opinions stimulated the minds of other thinkers to examine and weigh much more closely than heretofore the conclusions of previous Christian authorities.

The next development of scholasticism took the form of the *Sentences* of Peter Lombard (c. 1100-1164), who attempted to harmonize conflicting opinions by his own reasoning. Apart from highlighting theological problems, these "sentences" pointed out to inquiring minds basic philosophical conclusions about Christian doctrine. It was a touchy matter to imply that there could exist different non-heretical conclusions about any point of Christian theology; it therefore became a major function of scholastic philosophy to harmonize the dicta of the major respected authorities of the past. With the renewed interest in Greek thought introduced by the Moslems, an even graver problem was posed in the attempt to reconcile Greek and Christian philosophy.

From the many thinkers who struggled with this problem, two great schools of Christian philosophy emerged. The first, known as Realism (derived from Plato's theory that reality exists only in the mind), acknowledged the intellectual leadership of Bonaventura who continued the tradition of Plato and St. Augustine (a Platonist converted to Christianity), and created an elaborate mystical philosophy which was especially venerated by the Franciscans. The Dominicans, on the other hand, preferred the Nominalism (derived from Aristotle's position that Plato's "absolutes" were merely names imposed upon observed phenomena) of their own two great intellectuals, Albertus Magnus (1206-1280) and Thomas Aquinas (c. 1224-1274), both of whom were essentially Aristotelian. The greatest achievement of scholasticism is the massive *Summa Theologica* of Thomas Aquinas with its patient inquiry into the most minute of religious problems, its elaborate listings of pros and cons, and its closely reasoned conclusions. Aquinas resolved the basic dilemma of the frequent opposition of faith and reason (Hebraism and Classicism) by premising two varieties of truths: one available to man by the use of his God-given faculty of reason; the other knowable by revelation alone.

The fact that Platonic Realism and Aristotelian Nominalism could co-exist in the Middle Ages and that a scholar-poet like Dante could admire and find meaning in them both seems superficially contradictory to the medieval belief in the necessity of authoritarian regimentation of thought. The resolution of this difficulty was provided by both scripture and Aristotle. All agreed that there was indeed only one ultimate truth, but there were at least two different ways of approaching that truth as indicated by the Thomistic distinction between reason and faith. The way of reason was identified with Aristotle's approval of the Active Life in his *Ethics;* faith coincided with his definition of the Contemplative Life. Leah and Rachel in the Old Testament, Martha and Mary in the New were authoritative scriptural symbols of God's approval of both mundane and spiritual lives.[1]

Examples of Medieval Hierarchy

Celestial	Spiritual	Ecclesiastical	Feudal
Empyrean	God	Pope	King
Primum Mobile	Cherubim	Patriarch	Duke
Stellar Heaven	Seraphim	Archbishop	Baron
Saturn	Thrones	Bishop	Knight
Jupiter	Dominions	Priest	Bachelor
Mars	Virtues	Deacon	Squire
Sun	Powers	Subdeacon	
Venus	Principalities	Acolyte	
Mercury	Archangels	Exorcist	
Moon	Angels	Lector	
		Doorkeeper	

[1] Leah bore Jacob many children; the sterile Rachel, better loved, finally produced the dreamer Joseph. Martha busied herself about the housework in entertaining Jesus while Mary sat at Jesus' feet. Thus Leah and Martha were interpreted as symbols of the active life, Rachel and Mary as symbols of the contemplative life, simultaneously dramatizing the two great Christian commandments, love of neighbor and love of God.

It must also be observed that Plato and his pupil Aristotle were actually not very far apart on basic principles, and that the task of reconciling Greek and Hebraic thought was facilitated by the circumstance that early Christianity had been built up as a blend of the two. The most important achievement of scholasticism, from the viewpoint of its general effect on Western culture, was its encouragement of mental activity and speculation, even though within somewhat limited fields. We still speculate within the limited fields of our cultural heritage; the principal restriction on medieval thought was the impossibility of reaching a conclusion opposed to any article of Christian dogma.

Allegory

Of the literary modes of the Middle Ages, the most foreign to modern minds is the device known as allegory. Allegory in a work of art means the deliberate insertion by the artist of a secondary or hidden meaning, usually conveyed by symbols which may be either fairly obvious or deeply concealed. In most instances this hidden meaning is more important than the easily comprehensible surface, since it usually defines the intent, purpose, or ideas of the artist.

The origin of allegory is evident in both Hebraic and Classical cultures. In Hebraism the parable was a story with a concealed meaning. In Nathan's parable, the rich man was meant to be David, the poor man was Bathsheba's husband, and the sheep was Bathsheba. In early Greek story-telling, the fables of Aesop were built on similar lines except that animals were usually employed as symbols of human character traits. Greek plays also made use of allegorical figures, like Might and Force in Aeschylus' *Prometheus Bound;* and insofar as any piece of writing implies a meaning beyond the compass of its own restricted stage setting, nearly all literature might be regarded as allegorical in nature.

Formal allegory, however, appears to have originated at that stage of mental development when primitive religious myths and rituals could no longer be seriously accepted in a literal sense. Custom dictated that their venerable sanctity rendered them invincible to destruction. To be preserved, they must be explained as symbolic of eternal truths. In Greece from the fifth century B.C. on, particularly among the later Stoics, the seemingly irresponsible doings of the Olympian gods were explained as having allegorical significance. Similarly, educated Jews like Philo Judaeus explained primitive Old Testament events in allegorical terms. The considerably greater urgency of oppressed Jews and early Christians to communicate secretly with each other led to extensive use of allegory not only in the apocalyptic documents but even in common oral intercourse: in early Christianity, for example, the word "fish" meant *Christ* from the coincidence that the letters of *Ichthus,* Greek for "fish," stood for "Jesus Christ, God's son, Savior." The connection of the fish living in water with baptism and the story of Christ's miraculous feeding of the multitude added to the associational value of the word.

The appeal of the allegorical method was great during the early Christian centuries. Theologians examined word by word the pages of scripture, reconciling Old and New Testament doctrines and finding endless new hidden treasures. The author of the first epistle of Peter, for example, finds the salvation through flood of Noah's family a premonition of the salvation through baptism of the Christian family (3:20-21). St. Augustine, who remarked that "the hidden meanings are the sweetest," elaborated this suggestion into the following allegorical commentary, here reproduced only in part:

That Noah, with his family, is saved by water and wood, as the family of Christ is saved by baptism, as representing the suffering of the cross. That this ark is made of beams formed in a square, as the Church is constructed of saints prepared unto every good work: for a square stands firm on any side. That the length is six times the breadth and ten times the height, like a human body, to show that Christ appeared in a human body.... That it is 300 cubits long, to make up six times fifty; as there are six periods in the history of this world ... that it is thirty cubits high, a tenth part of the length; because Christ is one height, who in his thirtieth year gave his sanction to the doctrine of the gospel, by declaring that He came not to destroy the law, but to fulfill it. Now the ten commandments are known to be the heart of the law; and so the length of the ark is ten times thirty. Noah himself, too, was the tenth from Adam....

That clean and unclean animals are in the ark; as good and bad take part in the sacraments of the Church.... That Noah, counting his family, was the eighth; because the hope of our resurrection has appeared in Christ, who arose from the dead on the eighth day, that is, on the day after the seventh or Sabbath day.... That the flood came seven days after Noah entered the ark, as we are baptised in the hope of future rest, which was denoted by the seventh day.... That it rained for forty days and forty nights; as the sacrament of heavenly baptism washes away all the guilt of the sins against the ten commandments throughout the four quarters of the world....[2]

Just as Old and New Testament teachings were harmonized by allegorical devices, so revered Classical writings had to be made susceptible to Christian interpretation. Virgil was revered, and almost sainted, because his *Fourth Eclogue* seemed to predict the

[2] *Contra Faustum*, XII.

coming of Christ. His *Aeneid,* on the other hand, was a distinctly pagan composition in its literal sense. But by allegory, it could be made clear that the destruction of Troy meant the destruction of Jerusalem, that the pious Aeneas was the apostle Peter, that the migration from Troy to Rome portended the transfer of the Holy City from Jerusalem to the Seat of the Papacy.

So stimulated, creative writers elaborated on the parable-fable-apocalypse-commentary tradition by writing allegories of their own. The revered work of Boethius, *The Consolation of Philosophy,* is an extended allegory; even a very prominent textbook on the seven arts by Martianus Capella was compiled in allegorical form as *The Marriage of Philology and Mercury.* By the Middle Ages allegory had become so common as to be almost a way of thinking. Christian sermons were essentially allegorizing on a given scriptural text. More than that, the medieval intellectual knew that all things were closely related to each other. All had proceeded from the mind of God and so must necessarily reflect the unity of the Divine Concept. Therefore the Macrocosm (the "great world"—the universe) and the Microcosm (the "little world"—man) must have features in common. An individual's character was believed to be determined by the stars that presided over his nativity. (Did astrology require better authority than the special star over Bethlehem at the birth of Christ?) The stars were moved by angelic intelligences. The angels were emanations from the mind of God. All spirits, all things, all people thus reflected the eternal plan and were believed to be but the manifold details of a single divine pattern.

The literature of any age is inevitably a mirror of its period, but seldom have writings been so obviously a reflection of a specialized habit of thought as the allegorical mode of the French *Romance of the Rose* or the Italian *Divine Comedy.*

SUGGESTED READINGS

(Place of publication, when not mentioned, is New York.)

H. Adams, *Mont Saint-Michel and Chartres* (1904); F. B. Artz, *The Mind of the Middle Ages* (1953); M. Bloch, *Feudal Society* (tr. L. A. Manyon, Chicago, 1963); N. F. Cantor, *Medieval History: The Life and Death of a Civilization* (1964); M. H. Carre, *Realists and Nominalists* (Oxford, 1946); G. G. Coulton, *Medieval Panorama* (Cambridge, England, 1939); C. G. Crump and E. F.

Jacob, *The Legacy of the Middle Ages* (1926); S. J. Curtis, *A Short History of Western Philosophy in the Middle Ages* (London, 1915); H. W. C. Davis, *Medieval Europe* (2nd ed., 1960); E. G. Gardner, *Dante and the Mystics* (1913); E. Gilson, *The Spirit of Mediaeval Philosophy* (1936); E. Gilson, *Reason and Revelation in the Middle Ages* (1938); G. H. Haskins, *The Renaissance of the Twelfth Century* (Cambridge, Mass., 1927); G. H. Haskins, *Studies in Medieval Culture* (1929); G. H. Haskins, *The Rise of Universities* (1923); B. J. Hawkins, *A Sketch of Mediaeval Philosophy* (London, 1946); F. J. C. Hearnshaw, *The Social and Political Ideas of Some Great Medieval Thinkers* (1923); F. J. C. Hearnshaw, *Medieval Contributions to Modern Civilization* (1922); R. Klibansky, *Continuity of the Platonic Tradition during the Middle Ages* (London, 1939); R. P. McKeon, *Selections from Medieval Philosophers* (1929); J. T. McNeill, *Makers of Christianity* (1935); S. H. Mellone, *Western Christian Thought in the Middle Ages* (Edinburgh, 1935); S. Painter, *A History of the Middle Ages* (1953); E. K. Rand, *Founders of the Middle Ages* (1957); H. Rashdall, *The Universities of Europe in the Middle Ages* (1895); R. R. Steele, *Medieval Lore* (1924); J. L. Stocks, *Aristotelianism* (1925); H. O. Taylor, *The Classical Heritage of the Middle Ages* (1901); H. O. Taylor, *The Medieval Mind* (4th ed., 1927); J. W. Thompson, *The Middle Ages* (1931); A. S. Turberville, *Medieval Heresy and the Inquisition* (London, 1920); K. Vossler, *Medieval Culture* (1929); H. B. Workman, *Christian Thought to the Reformation* (1914); M. de Wulf, *History of Mediaeval Philosophy* (1953); M. de Wulf, *Medieval Philosophy, Illustrated from the System of Thomas Aquinas* (Cambridge, Mass., 1922); M. de Wulf, *Philosophy and Civilization in the Middle Ages* (Princeton, 1922).

Chronology for Part III

THE EARLY MIDDLE AGES

I. FOURTH CENTURY

Emperor Constantine presided over the first council of the entire Christian world, the Council of Nicaea, which formalized official Christian doctrines (325); France invaded by the Franks (326); birth of St. Augustine, most influential of early Church writers, whose *City of God* stated the Christian as opposed to the classical ideal (354).

II. FIFTH CENTURY

Height of barbarian aggression in Europe: Rome captured by Visigoths (410); Attila the Hun repelled by Franks and Visigoths (451); Rome sacked by Vandals (455); Franks becoming powerful under Clovis (481); Theodoric the Ostrogoth became King of Italy (493).

III. SIXTH AND SEVENTH CENTURIES

Goths expelled from Italy by Roman Emperor Justinian (555); North Italy conquered by Lombards (565); Mohammed born (570); Byzantine fleet defeated by Moslems (655); Franks united under Pepin of Heristal (687).

IV. EIGHTH CENTURY

(By 700, "Roman" means region around Rome; in Gaul the Franks speak Gallic-Latin or French, in Italy Lombards and Goths modify Latin into various Italian dialects, in Spain and Portugal Latin is becoming Spanish and Portuguese.) Spain invaded from Africa by Moslems (711); Moslems defeated in France by Charles Martel (732); Charlemagne crowned king of the Franks (Franco-Germany) (771); attack on Charlemagne's rear-guard at Roncesvalles, commemorated in *The Song of Roland* (778).

V. Ninth and Tenth Centuries

Charlemagne crowned by Pope Leo III as Emperor of the West, now renamed "The Holy Roman Empire" (800); Charlemagne succeeded by Louis the Pious (814); collapse of the Carolingian Empire at death of Louis the Pious (843); Otto I, King of Germany, crowned Holy Roman Emperor (962).

THE LATER MIDDLE AGES

I. Eleventh Century

Avicenna died (1037); Church split into Eastern (Greek Orthodox) and Western (Roman Catholic) divisions (1054); conquest of England by William of Normandy (1066); reform movement imposed upon the Church by Pope Gregory VII (1073); Carthusian Order founded (1084); Toledo wrested from Moslems by Christians (1085); First Crusade summoned by Pope Urban II (1095); Cistercian Order founded (1098); Jerusalem captured by Godfrey of Bouillon (1099).

II. Twelfth Century

Lisbon captured and the Christian kingdom of Portugal founded by Second Crusade (1174); Jerusalem recaptured by Saladin, Sultan of Egypt (1187); Third Crusade wins right of pilgrims to enter Jerusalem untaxed (1192); Averroes died (1198).

III. Thirteenth Century

Fourth Crusade attacked the Eastern Empire (1202) and captured Constantinople, reuniting Eastern and Western Churches under Western domination (1204); failure of the Children's Crusade (1212); Dominican and Franciscan Orders approved by Church (1216); failure of the Fifth Crusade, aimed at conquest of Egypt (1221); part of the Kingdom of Jerusalem secured by Frederick II of Sicily in Sixth Crusade (1228) and recaptured by Sultan of Egypt (1244); Seventh Crusade against Jerusalem failed (1250); Constantinople recaptured by the Greeks (1261); travels of Marco Polo begun (1271); Carmelites recognized by Church (1274); Pope Boniface VIII held great Papal Jubilee, attracting multitudes of pilgrims to Rome (1300).

Part IV

THE
MODERN
SPIRIT

chapter 17

THE RENAISSANCE

I. THE REBIRTH OF SECULARISM

The cultural movement known as the Renaissance originated in Italy in the fourteenth century, continued there in full tide until the mid-fifteenth century, and then gradually spread to the other European nations, where it reached its height in the sixteenth century. Although called a "rebirth," it was actually an acceleration of the same kind of impetus that had created the medieval revival; the only aspect of life that was actually reborn was the Classical emphasis on secular rather than religious activities. The causes of this change in basic attitude, although numerous, are not hard to find. It so happened that the weakening of the authority of the Church coincided with renewed contact with the pagan world and with the offering of broader opportunities for mundane enjoyment.

The decline of the prestige of the Church was the direct result of the increasing worldliness and corruption of that powerful medieval institution. As Dante so bitterly pointed out in the *Divine Comedy,* where the three popes of his day find places in hell, the servants of God on earth had become seekers after political power, wealth, and luxurious enjoyment. Even the great Dominican and Franciscan Orders, founded to inject new spirituality into the fabric of Christianity, had been engulfed in the flood of greed, unable to resist the temptations which medieval ecclesiastical power so readily proffered. The precise mind of Dante was capable of distinguishing between Christianity as a body of exalted doctrine and the Christian leaders temporarily (he hoped) in control of Church organization. But most people, not capable of such logical refinements, began to see Christianity itself as being essentially a powerful worldly institution. If there remained any doubt of the political nature of Church activities, that doubt was dispelled when Philip the Fair of France ensured the election of Clement IV as pope and removed the Papal See to Avignon in 1305, where it remained until 1377. In 1378 the Christian world was treated to the unedifying spectacle of two popes, Urban VI in Rome and Clement VII at Avignon, each claiming to be God's sole representative on earth.

Serious religious thinkers continued to cling to the Christian faith, either attempting, like Erasmus, to reform the Church from within or else breaking completely with the existing institution and attempting to return to the simple faith of the apostolic age, a movement which had stimulated the Waldensian Heresy of the twelfth century. In the fourteenth century, the seeds of complete revolt from papal authority, which was to culminate in the Reformation, began to appear in various more or less underground movements like that of John Wycliffe (c. 1320-1384), who denounced the authority of the pope and began the translation of the Bible into English. John Huss, who preached Wycliffe's doctrines, was excommunicated in 1412. Pope Martin V proclaimed a crusade against the Wycliffites and Hussites in 1420. In 1517 Martin Luther posted his theses at Wittenberg as a kind of official manifesto of the German Reformation, that remarkable revival of Hebraism whose

strong, religious current paralleled that of the more powerful revival of non-mystical Classicism which is associated
with the Renaissance.

But while serious Christians, chiefly in the north, continued their earnest spiritual struggles, the majority of
Europeans apparently lapsed into varying degrees of cynicism, usually paying lip-service to Christianity and perfunc-
torily attending its rituals, but showing little trace of it in
their daily lives. The story-tellers of Boccaccio's *Decameron*
desist from their amusements on Friday in commemoration
of the crucifixion, but one of the fashionable narrators is
also permitted the remark that Heaven would indeed be
heaven if lovers were there permitted as much enjoyment as
they had experienced on earth. Petrarch and Boccaccio, a
generation later than Dante, both suffered tortures of
conscience but were really more interested in literary immortality than in any other kind. Rabelais advised gour-
mandizing the experiences of this life; Montaigne was
frankly skeptical of the possibility of attaining any kind of
final truth.

Enjoyment of earthly things became the mode even
among Churchmen. Pope Pius II wrote an improper novel
and wished to be known primarily for his "eloquentia" or
skill in Latin. Leo X is said to have remarked, "Let us enjoy
the Papacy since God has given it to us." Popes Pius II,
Nicholas V, and Sextus were all zealous patrons of secular
learning. The Borgias, Alexander and his son Cesare, were
capable and brilliant, but also sensual, perverted, and
avaricious monsters who openly sold Church appointments
and had their critics assassinated. The ebullient zest for
living, which encouraged the lawlessness of a Benvenuto
Cellini as well as that of the Borgias, was coupled, as in
these two instances, with an intense passion for beauty.
Renewed interest in the human form and in all the color-
fulness of earthly life created the new schools of art which

produced the masterpieces of Michelangelo, Raphael, and Leonardo da Vinci, to name only the giants of the inspired art and architecture of the period.

If the decline of spirituality turned men's minds to mundane interests, there were also offered new opportunities for secular satisfaction. The renewed medieval contact with Classicism was the opening of a door through which the treasures of pagan learning and literature continued to flow in increasing volume. The Crusades had introduced Europe to oriental luxuries, and the growing medieval towns with their industries and commerce not only provided increased monetary wealth and luxuries to spend it on but also signified the origin of a new middle class, the bourgeoisie (town-dwellers) whose independence and ability to live in comfort contrasted favorably both with the medieval serf in his squalid hut and with the feudal baron in his splendid but chilly castle. The dominant spirit of the Renaissance thus turned from otherworldliness to worldliness, from the spiritual fount of Hebraism to the frank acceptance of the offerings of mundane life which had characterized Greek and Roman Classicism.

II. THE EMERGENCE OF NATIONALISM

The revival of trade, the increase of monetary wealth, and the appearance of an independent bourgeoisie all spelled the doom of the feudal system. Feudalism first lost its strength in Italy, where traders, townsmen, and bankers flourished; more gradually a similar weakening appeared in northern Europe. The Babylonian Captivity of the papacy was an overt manifestation of the bankruptcy of the authority of the Church. Dante in his *De Monarchia* had argued for an independent Church to be man's spiritual guide and a revived Roman Empire to rule man's temporal life, but the failure of Henry VII of Luxemburg through his death in 1313 to make good his attempted revival of the

Holy Roman Empire constituted the end of any important movement to recreate the kind of world order which had been the medieval dream. As a result, smaller political units began to develop. In Italy the peninsula was cut up into numerous city-states like those of ancient Greece, and those who lived in them were not "Italians" but citizens of Rome, Naples, Venice, Ferrara, Perugia, and other lesser "nations." Florence and Venice were the only "republican" states, and they were usually controlled by influential families or patrician groups. The others were outright despotisms, the court of Ferrara being almost oriental in its ceremonials and homage to the reigning duke. Each state developed its own court and courtly society. Wealthy and often highly talented rulers rivalled each other in an attempt to reproduce the grandeur as well as the accomplishments of the Golden Age of the Roman Empire. Through a renewed sense of patriotism they became, like the emperor Augustus, patrons of poets, scholars, artists, musicians, and men possessed of any talents that might add to their fame, "fame" having become what "beatitude" had been in the Middle Ages. In France Marguerite of Navarre and her brother Francis I set up sixteenth-century courts in imitation of these earlier Italian examples.

Outside of Italy in countries where the feudal system was more deeply entrenched, this political movement more usually took the form of the gradual strengthening of the power of the monarch and the concurrent weakening of the feudal nobles. With this transition, popular loyalties shifted from homage to overlord to national patriotism, so that when in 1430 the English were driven from France through the inspired leadership of Joan of Arc, they were defeated not so much by feudal knights as by a peasant girl who fought for her country rather than for bishops or lords. France, England, and Spain were the most prominent of the new nations. Their pillaging of the treasures of the

New World was symptomatic of the growing importance of money and the slackening importance of land. The new individualism of persons, of cities, and of nations acted in each instance as a stimulus to creative activity in the arts,

WORLD MAP BY MACROBIUS
Published in Venice in 1500.

energizing the imaginations of the brilliant galaxy of Renaissance painters, sculptors, and writers who glorified mortality and, who like Petrarch, thirsted for the heady wine of earthly fame.

III. EXPLORATION

With the revival of secularism and its concomitant urge to seek out the treasures of the universe, the spirit of exploration which had been characteristic of Hellenism reasserted itself. Geographical exploration went by way of both land and water: land routes to the Orient were developed by pilgrims, missionaries, and traders like Marco Polo; sea routes to America and India were charted by explorers like Columbus, Vespucci, Diaz, and Vasco da Gama. Exploration into the physical universe brought about a revival of science which was the immediate beginning of the scientific achievements of our own age. Particularly at the University of Paris, the fourteenth century abounded in new theories of physics, chemistry, medicine, mathematics, and astronomy, theories that contributed in later centuries to the extraordinary achievements of men like Newton and Galileo. While scientists, conducting independent research, were contradicting the authority of Aristotle and Holy Writ and coming to a more exact formulation of natural laws, they were also opening the way for speculation and research which bore practical results in invention and solidified the structure of pure science. The notebooks of the many-sided Leonardo da Vinci (naturalist, anatomist, engineer, and artist) are filled with sketches and descriptions of bridges, derricks, lamp chimneys, canal locks, implements of warfare, and even an airplane. In such researches and inventive plans, the new spirit of individualism began the creation of the modern world, gradually freeing itself (but very gradually) from the reverence for what had formerly been believed to be the eternal truths of Hebraic and Classical writers. Practical results of these researches were soon apparent in the invention of all kinds of new mechanisms designed to free man from the drudgery of slow and painful manual labor. The most revolutionary of these was the invention of printing. In 1446 the first books were printed in Haarlem by Coster, and after 1500 numerous editions of the classics and contemporary works were published, thus making the wider dissemination of the new knowledge readily available.

IV. THE REVIVAL OF CLASSICISM

The order in which these principal facets of Renaissance culture have been presented bears no relationship to their temporal sequence. They all occurred at the same time and mutually stimulated each other. The rediscovery of Aristotle was, as we have seen, an important factor in stimulating further investigation and exploration. Similarly, the urge to explore created a group of manuscript hunters who ransacked the monastic repositories of forgotten books to bring to light again many lost treasures of Classical writing. Literary scholarship turned to compilations of Classic myths and legends like Boccaccio's *Genealogy of the Gods.* Creative writers attempted to imitate Classic subjects and modes of composition. In education, this revival of interest in man known as humanism added to an essentially religious curriculum studies of Classical literature and philosophy together with more extensive study of the seven liberal arts.

Particular enthusiasms broke out here and there, most notably the Neo-Platonic revival which occasioned the founding of the Platonic Academy at Florence under the patronage of Cosimo de' Medici. The aim of the Academy was to enlarge the knowledge of Plato and to reconcile Platonism with Christianity. Neo-Platonism was based on the concept of the ladder of love by which the initiate mounts by successive rungs from the contemplation of earthly beauty (as in women) to the ultimate comprehension of Celestial Beauty. The theory is best known to English readers through Spenser's *Fowre Hymnes* and to

European readers through Marguerite of Navarre's *Heptaméron* (based on her own Neo-Platonic circle) and Castiglione's *Courtier* which concludes with a discussion of Platonic love.

The prevailing atmosphere of Classical imitation was particularly prominent in those urban centers where fashionable courts could afford the luxuries associated with Greek and Roman paganism. The Renaissance princes lived in magnificent palaces, surrounded by sumptuous tapestries, painting, and furnishings. Highly cultivated men and women made up the courts, and professional painters, poets, and musicians were well paid to entertain them. In Florence, a prominent banker, Cosimo de' Medici (1434-1492), became the popular head of the government. Both cruel and generous but with a great zest for learning and elegance, he attracted grammarians, manuscript hunters, connoisseurs, translators, scholars, and authors to encourage the study of Italian, Greek, Latin, Arabic, and Hebrew. His son, Lorenzo the Magnificent, was a many-sided genius who was not only a great patron of the arts and learning but practiced them himself. Boccaccio attained an ambassadorship at Florence because of his literary ability rather than his knowledge of practical affairs. Artists were signally honored by celebrations given in their honor, and poets were invited by bishops, Roman senators, and university rectors to be crowned with laurel wreaths in recognition of extraordinary achievements.

In consequence, while serious scholars and scientists were transferring the concerns of research from the next world to this, poets, novelists, playwrights, artists, and musicians were mainly interested in offering elegant entertainment. Tragedies and comedies were written on Latin models, to be played in sumptuously decorated settings with solid elaborate scenery painted by the best artists of the day and accompanied by choral dances and music. Poets aspired to walk in the footsteps of Virgil; prose writers attempted to recapture the elegant periods of Cicero. Both aimed at the entertainment of an immediate sophisticated audience by public readings of their works. Under these circumstances, fashionable "novella" writing and light romantic "epics" satisfied a popular taste that preferred pleasure to profundity.

As may well be inferred from the foregoing, the Classical revival was necessarily rather superficial. Knowledge of ancient pagan civilization was very partial; the centuries of Christian culture were not to be easily shaken off; the most obvious aspects of Classic writing were those most immediately imitated. The Latinity of Cicero and Virgil was often more highly regarded than the contents of their writings; the fanciful myths of paganism were more commonly admired than the wisdom of the ancients. Greek principles of human conduct were largely ignored. Instead, cleverness (not wisdom) and boldness (not moderation) seem to have been the new virtues most admired by early Renaissance writers such as Boccaccio, Cellini, and Machiavelli; later authors like Rabelais and Montaigne were more thoughtful and richer in meaning. But the latter were products of France which was both more serious (the nation of Calvin) and more remote from immediate reminders of the surface of Roman paganism. In Italy Roman monuments were restored, and Greek and Roman statuary was recovered. In imitation of the triumphal processions of Roman emperors and victorious generals, "triumphs" were instituted, in which symbolic figures on foot or in chariots or floats represented current events, ecclesiastical doctrines, or gods and goddesses of ancient mythology. Castiglione's *Courtier,* which set the standards of polite behavior, does indeed point out that the ideal courtier should be useful as well as ornamental, but the substance of the book is much more concerned with aristocratic skills and deportment than with statesmanship.

The most significant development of the whole period was the new spirit of individual inquiry which had begun in medieval scholasticism. From a mental attitude that forbade disagreement with any of the revered authorities of past or present, these imitations of paganism were declarations of liberty from medieval restrictions. Their reminders of a culture other than the Christian served as a spur to the independent investigation of the truth of authoritarian conclusions by comparing them with observable facts. The new spirit is given excellent expression by Machiavelli when, in *The Prince,* he remarks, "It has seemed wiser to me to follow the real truth of the matter rather than what we imagine it to be."

V. THE REFORMATION AND COUNTER-REFORMATION

Although the revival of secularism was one of the most striking and obvious aspects of the Renaissance, strong religious currents continued to be in evidence. In the midst of a growing skepticism, many like Dante, Michelangelo, and Erasmus were possessed of an intense and living faith. From similarly deeply religious men who could not reconcile their belief in Christianity with their horrified awareness of the corruption of the Church was born the Protestant Reformation of the sixteenth century in which a growing tidal wave of dissatisfaction reached its crest. In *The Divine Comedy* Dante, although unwavering in his basic Catholicism, had consigned three contemporary popes to hell, and his embittered criticisms had been echoed and amplified by prominent Christian leaders like the English John Wycliffe (1320?-1384), the Bohemian John Huss (1369-1415), and the Italian Savonarola (1452-1498). Simultaneously, there was widespread resentment of the immense wealth of the Church and its heavy financial demands upon the populace. Politically, the monolithic power of the Church clashed with the new impetus toward nationalism. As a result, the growing religious revolt attracted many for non-religious reasons and acted as the stimulant for largely secular rebellions such as the bloody and violent conflicts of the Peasants' War in Germany (1524), the revolt of the Netherlands against Spanish rule (1568), and the civil wars which disrupted France during the second half of the sixteenth century.

The Protestant Reformation as such began at Wittenburg University where Martin Luther was a professor of Biblical literature. He had given much thought to the question of human salvation and was formulating his doctrine of "salvation by faith" in opposition to the Catholic doctrine of "salvation by sacrament and good works" when the Dominican friar John Tetzel was commissioned to sell indulgences to raise money for the building of St. Peter's Church at Rome. The buyer of an indulgence was assured easement of punishment for his sins on the theory that the donation of money to the Church fell in the category of "good works."

In 1517 Luther made an official announcement of his disagreement with the sale of indulgences and several other practices of the Church in the form of Ninety-five Theses which he posted on the church door at Wittenberg. The Theses were printed, widely circulated, and became the center of heated argument. In a debate with the Catholic theologian John Eck, Luther admitted that his belief in man's direct relationship to God was like that of the heretical John Huss and, protected by Frederick the Wise, Elector of Saxony, he divorced himself from the Church and published three treatises in which he elaborated on his theory of salvation by faith and encouraged German rulers to confiscate Church property and remove themselves from Roman jurisdiction. Luther proceeded to organize his own reformed church which was enthusiastically supported by the upper and middle classes who found Lutheranism a welcome relief from "foreign" taxation and control.

In 1525 Huldreich Zwingli inspired the founding of a Reformed Church in Switzerland which came under the leadership of John Calvin in 1536, the year of publication of his extraordinarily popular and influential work *The Institutes of Christian Religion*. Thus was begun the proliferation of sects which spread Protestantism rapidly through Germany, Switzerland, England, Scotland, Hungary, Poland, the Low Countries, Scandinavia, and France, and even made a faint impression on Italy and Spain. Calvinism itself was the religion of the French Huguenots, and it acted as the inspiration of the Presbyterian Church in Scotland and the Dutch Reformed Church of the Netherlands.

Although every sect formulated its own doctrines and practices, it is possible to generalize about Protestant innovations. Retaining nearly all the essentials of medieval Christianity, including belief in the sanctity of the Bible, the novelties of Protestantism were aimed against the authoritarianism and what were regarded as the corruption and superstition of Roman Catholicism. The new emphasis was on direct relationship between man and God, eliminating the necessities of a mediating priesthood, veneration of relics and images, pilgrimages to holy places, and most of the elaborate Catholic rituals. Protestants emphasized the Bible as the ultimate fixed authority, replacing the varying dogmas of the Church fathers, and introduced starker forms of worship in comparatively bare and unadorned churches.

Calvinism was particularly austere in its belief in the essential sinfulness of man and in its doctrine of predestination, which held that God had "elected" some to be saved and others to be damned. The "elect" could be identified by their conspicuously moral behavior and that repugnance for worldly pleasure popularly associated with the adjective *puritan*. (A byproduct of this condemnation of

aesthetic satisfaction was general disapproval of art, literature, and especially drama. Most Protestant writings were
confined to matters of religion, whether inspirational, theological, didactic, or controversial.) Sex was regarded as
especially sinful, and morality was popularly associated
with sexual abstinence, countenancing at most marital sex
relations for the propagation of children.

An important compensation, particularly for the rapidly
growing middle class, was Calvin's approval of industry
and thrift which was broadly interpreted to mean that the
successful business man was an eminent member of the
"elect." Catholicism had discouraged the profit motive, but
Protestantism gave its blessing to the accumulation of
wealth and allowed its doctrine of individualism to include
most forms of business enterprise.

The Protestant threat to Catholicism was met by the
Church at the international assembly known as the Council
of Trent, convened in 1545 for the purposes of extirpating
Protestantism, clarifying Church doctrine, and correcting
ecclesiastical abuses. This council of the Counter-Reformation met intermittently until 1563. It reaffirmed the doctrine of salvation by faith and good works, it confirmed
papal absolutism, it banned Protestant translations of the
Bible and authorized only the medieval version known as
the Vulgate. It also instituted the continuous Papal compilation of the Index, or list of forbidden books. The
effects of this Counter-Reformation were felt everywhere
but particularly in Spain and Italy where the oppressive
measures of the Spanish Inquisition, instituted to eliminate Moors and Jews but now principally directed against
Christian heretics, imposed strict censorship. The most obvious literary result of this religious conflict was the renewed interest in religious subject matter, evidenced in the
production of such Christian epics as Tasso's *Jerusalem
Delivered* and Du Bartas' *The Week*.

VI. THE RENAISSANCE IN SPAIN

While partaking of the general characteristics of rebirth and new birth found elsewhere in Europe, the Spanish Renaissance was attended with phenomena not to be found elsewhere on the continent. Some of the differences can be accounted for by the relative isolation of the Iberian Peninsula from the rest of Europe with the Pyrenees acting as a barrier to easy communication. But the principal distinctiveness derives from the peculiar nature of earlier Spanish history.

The Iberian Peninsula, inhabited originally by Celts and Iberians, was invaded by Rome at the time of the Second Punic War and became part of the Roman Empire. The Roman philosopher and playwright Seneca and the poet Lucan were both born in Spain, as Renaissance Spaniards enjoyed reminding themselves.

In 409, the year of the sack of Rome by Alaric, Spain was overrun by the barbarians. In 415 a Visigoth kingdom was established. The Visigoths were quickly converted to Christianity and became the most zealous of European Catholics, savagely intolerant of heretics and unbelievers—and early in the seventh century so cruelly oppressive of the Jews that even some members of the clergy apparently tried to intercede. In 711, the Visigoth Kingdom collapsed before the waves of the Arab invasion.

The Moslem conquest of Spain, though it endured for over seven hundred years, was never complete. Large Christian communities persisted, and even in Moslem-ruled areas Christians continued to survive. A noteworthy Moslem achievement was the founding of centers of learning where Arabic translations of the works of Aristotle were studied and soon reintroduced into the rest of medieval Europe (see Chapter 16). But the principal chronicle of medieval Spain is a record of battles between Christians and Moors, conquests, defeats, reconquests. Spaniards seldom figure in the records of the Crusades because they were carrying on their own crusade at home. By the end of the thirteenth century this persistence had regained all of Spain for Christianity except for Granada, which did not capitulate until 1492.

During this period Spain resembled the rest of Christian Europe in being composed of a number of individual states. The marriage of Isabella of Castile to Ferdinand of Aragon in 1469 paved the way for a union of these two powerful states and marked the emergence of Spain as a nation. When Navarre was annexed in 1512, the entire peninsula was Spanish with the exception of Portugal.

Beginning with the voyages of Columbus, Spain became a great and wealthy world power principally by pillaging the gold of the New World. The revolt of the Netherlands in 1581 and the failure of the Spanish Armada in 1588 contributed to the collapse of Spanish glory, which had been purchased at the terrible price of a disastrously unsound economy and the desperate impoverishment of the common people.

Strangely enough, the so-called Golden Age of Spanish Literature had its heart at the end of the sixteenth and beginning of the seventeenth century when Spain was enduring its ruinous decline. Most of the peculiar characteristics of this cultural Renaissance can be traced to events in Spain's highly individualized medieval past. As a result the Spanish Renaissance is quite a different phenomenon from that of the rest of Europe.

A. *Christianity*

The creeping skepticism which was generally characteristic of the Italian Renaissance and the genial humanism of most of Renaissance Catholicism are scarcely perceptible in Spain. With roots in Visigoth religious intolerance and a history of conflict against the Moslems, it was obviously patriotic in Spain to be a Catholic. It is not surprising that the Holy Office of the Inquisition was established in Spain in 1478 and that Charles V, proclaimed Holy Roman Emperor in 1519, vigorously pursued persecution of heretics in his capacity of "Defender of the Faith." Censorship was the rule during the Spanish Renaissance, and religious plays, *autos sacramentales,* remained in vogue long after they had diminished in popularity elsewhere in Europe.

B. Insularity

Partly because of the barrier of the Pyrenees, but principally because Spain was so preoccupied with her own problems, Renaissance impulses which flowed northward from Italy penetrated only fitfully into Spain. This remoteness, coupled with a general lack of patronage for artists and writers, produced what has been called "a literature without a literary tradition" intended for a wide audience rather than aristocratic connoisseurs. An early work popularly known as the *Celestina* is divided into acts like a play, but is a curious combination of narrative prose and dramatic dialogue; it therefore defies being categorized as a play or a novel or any other recognizable literary type. The picaresque novel, a new genre aptly described as "the romance of roguery," had its origin in *Lazarillo de Tormes* (1554). Lope de Vega, an incredibly prolific playwright, said that he "locked up all the rules with six sets of keys" in producing his immensely popular three-act tragicomedies.

C. Españolismo

In addition, there are a number of highly individualized traits of temperament which are vividly reflected in Spanish Renaissance literature. The Spaniard prided himself on his stoicism and physical courage. He was fiercely individualistic, often to the point of egotism, and had the greatest disdain for the foreigner. He took pride in the formalities of etiquette, delighted in grandiose behavior and grandiloquent language (the apex of this elegance is Don Quixote). He made a point of personal courtesy, and his extreme tenderness about "points of honor" resulted in his preoccupation with this theme in his literature. He was particularly sensitive about the honor of his women. A girl who was known, or perhaps merely reputed, to have been seduced had only the alternatives of marriage and the nunnery. Her father, brothers, and other relatives were duty bound to seek revenge, a tradition which gives especial point to Tirso de Molina's *Trickster of Seville*. Most of these characteristics are exhibited in the works embodying the two most famous Dons of Spanish Renaissance literature. The larger-than-life figure of Don Quixote is the personification of the national refusal to come to terms with reality. Don Juan's scorn for women, convention, and even death highlights Spanish individualism, rebellion against the mundane, and passion for living one's life with a flair.

SUGGESTED READINGS

(Place of publication, when not mentioned, is New York.)

R. H. Bainton, *The Reformation of the Sixteenth Century* (Boston, 1952); J. Burckhardt, *The Civilization of the Renaissance in Italy* (Phaidon ed., London, 1937); E. Cassirer and others (eds.), *The Renaissance Philosophy of Man* (Chicago, 1948); R. T. Davies, *The Golden Century of Spain 1501-1601* (rev. ed., London, 1958); W. Durant, *A History of Civilization in Italy from 1304-1576 A.D.* (1953); E. Emerton, *The Beginnings of Modern Europe* (1917); W. F. Ferguson, *The Renaissance in Historical Thought* (Boston, 1948); M. P. Gilmore, *The World of Humanism 1453-1517* (1953); F. P. Graves, *A History of Education during the Middle Ages and Its Transition to Modern Times* (1925); H. J. Grimm, *The Reformation Era, 1500-1650* (1956); B. Hathaway, *The Late Renaissance in Italy* (Ithaca, N. Y.,

1962); D. Hay, *The Italian Renaissance in Its Historical Background* (Cambridge, 1961); E. M. Hulme, *The Renaissance, the Protestant Revolution, and the Catholic Reformation in Continental Europe* (1914); H. Kamen, *The Spanish Inquisition* (1965); H. S. Lucas, *The Renaissance and the Reformation* (2nd ed., 1960); J. O. Riedl (ed.), *Catalogue of Renaissance Philosophies, 1350-1650* (Milwaukee, 1940); N. A. Robb, *Neoplatonism of the Italian Renaissance* (London, 1935); R. Roeder, *Man of the Renaissance* (1933); F. Scheville, *The First Century of Italian Humanism* (1928); F. Scheville, *A History of Florence* (1936); E. Sichel, *The Renaissance* (1914); J. A. Symonds, *The Revival of Learning* (3rd ed., London, 1897); J. A. Symonds, *History of the Renaissance in Italy* (1935); H. O. Taylor, *Thought and Expression in the Sixteenth Century* (1920); J. N. Thompson and others, *Civilization of the Renaissance* (Chicago, 1929); W. T. Waugh, *A History of Europe from 1378 to 1494* (1932); W. H. Woodward, *Vittorina da Feltre and Other Humanist Educators* (Cambridge, England, 1897).

chapter 18

Neo-Classicism

I. THE NEW CLASSICISM

As its name implies, seventeenth-century Neo-Classicism was a self-conscious effort to restore the atmosphere of the Classical world. The enthusiasm for the Greek and Roman civilizations which had characterized the Renaissance continued into the following centuries without abatement and prompted deeper penetration into the writings of the ancient Greeks, opening a rich vein of literary and philosophical treasure which had only begun to be mined during the preceding period. To the seventeenth-century scholars, the Greek emphasis upon form and reason in both art and life seemed to suggest unsurpassable ideals of human perfection, ideals worthy of revival in a world given new energy and hope through the humanistic developments of the Renaissance. On the other hand, it must again be pointed out that it was the rational orderliness of Hellenism that impressed the Neo-Classicists; the spirituality and the deep thoughtfulness of Greek literature had apparently made little impression on the Renaissance, and made little more on the seventeenth century.

Simultaneously, the scientific impetus of the Renaissance

flowered in a remarkable group of intellectual giants like Galileo, Kepler, Newton, Descartes, Pascal, Halley, Hobbes, and Locke. Each of these made new discoveries or at least presented new theories about the nature of man and his universe. The fact that these new theories were usually described as "laws" was partly the result of humanity's need to be assured of an orderly world, but was also the reflection of the spirit of the age which was determined to envision the world as a rational and well-organized system. Previous concepts of God began to be replaced by an "enlightened" realization that the Deity should be understood as the remote and inaccessible Creator of the laws of nature, the operation of which would never be changed for the accommodation of any personal desire. The new intellectuals therefore discarded as fictitious past or contemporary accounts of miracles and were generally dubious about supernatural manifestations of any kind.

Because of this desire to restore Classical concepts of order and to find new principles of order in the physical universe, individual idiosyncrasies or aberrations were frowned upon by society. Correctness, together with the formulation and maintenance of standards, became a new ideal to be applied to everything from human conduct to the composition of verse. Emotions and passions became suspect; wit and debonair sophistication were admired. The strong tendency toward the formation of "academies" of science and the arts to act as arbiters of correctness is the most striking manifestation of the desire for regimentation. This scorn of individualism was reasonable enough in view of the conclusions of the new intellectualism that there must be one best way of doing anything and that human reason was as capable of discovering the best principles of human conduct as it was of ferreting out the universal principles of natural law.

This quest of the "universals" produced a literature in

which society rather than the individual was the object of study. And since the search for the highest standards of behavior was a serious matter, literature usually attempted to teach a moral lesson. Thus, satire, which involves both cleverness and a didactic purpose, became a popular mode of expression. And since novelty in form, thought, and material was regarded with suspicion by the custom of the time, it was through subtlety, neatness of phrasing, wit, and polish of form that the artist sought to outshine his rivals. The fact that the French are outstanding in their love of formalism and precise distinctions is the probable reason for their literary leadership of Europe during this period. Instead, therefore, of continuing a general discussion of tendencies generally characteristic of seventeenth-century Europe, it will be more profitable to examine the peculiarities of the age as they exhibited themselves in the aristocratic *beau monde* of France.

II. THE GOLDEN AGE OF FRANCE

The French counterpart of the Age of Pericles in Athens and the Elizabethan Age in England is the seventeenth century, known in France as the *Grand Siècle*. Under the guidance successively of Richelieu, Mazarin, and Louis XIV, the government of France became an absolute monarchy, boasting the most sumptuous, elegant, and scintillating court in Europe. Simultaneously, the French nation became the leading political power in the Western world.

The trend toward nationalism and absolutism had been growing since the closing years of the Hundred Years' War when the inspired leadership of Joan of Arc (in 1430) had driven the English out of France, created a spirit of nationalism among the people, and weakened the prestige of the nobility. Common soldiers had succeeded where the panoplied knights had failed, and these soldiers had fought for France and the king rather than for their feudal overlords. Taking advantage of the heightened prestige of the throne, Louis XII, in the early sixteenth century, began the process of removing government of the provinces and collection of taxes from the hands of the nobles and entrusting them to paid government officials drawn from the upper middle class. Since this new official class was dependent entirely on the favor of the sovereign himself, government policies fell increasingly under the dictatorship of the king. Subsequently, the highest of these paid officials became the king's ministers. An unfortunate effect of this trend was that direct imposition of taxes on the people, to support the increasing splendor of the court, split France essentially into two nations. The nation of workers and taxpayers came to be regarded as a grubby half-civilized horde whose existence was justifiable only on the grounds that it provided the luxuries of Court Society which meant only itself when it spoke of "France." The long-term result of such flagrant disregard of the common good was the French Revolution (1789).

The era of magnificence really begins with Henry IV (1589-1610), who brought peace and stability to France. With the aid of his minister, Sully, he concluded an expensive war with Spain, ended religious conflicts, and inaugurated a series of plans and reforms designed to bring general prosperity to the nation. When he was assassinated by a religious fanatic in 1610, his successor, Louis XIII, was only nine years old. The government fell for a time into the hands of his mother, Marie de' Medici, whose administration was so inept that, in 1614, a meeting of the Estates General was called. The event is notable principally because it was the last meeting of that representative body until the Revolution. When Louis came of age, he banished his mother and placed the conduct of the government in the extraordinarily capable hands of Cardinal Richelieu.

Richelieu destroyed Protestantism as a political factor,

ended the few remaining powers of the feudal lords, and labored incessantly to make the monarchy absolute and to heighten the power and prestige of France. He insisted on efficiency in the various departments of the government, made France militarily unassailable, and directly encouraged art, science, and scholarship. Consequently, while Germany was caught in the turmoil of the Thirty Years' War, while England was being torn by revolution, and while Spain was attempting to support its tottering empire, France assumed the leadership of Europe and French became the international language of diplomacy.

When Richelieu died in 1642, he was succeeded as Chief Minister by Cardinal Mazarin, another remarkable statesman who continued the same general policies. Louis XIII died in 1643, leaving the throne to Louis XIV, whose seventy-two-year reign marked the full flowering of the Golden Age. When Mazarin died in 1661, Louis XIV announced that he would be his own Prime Minister. Regarding himself as God's representative on earth, he was not exaggerating if he really made the statement attributed to him, *"L'Etat, c'est moi"* (colloquially, "The State, that's me"). Like Richelieu before him, he was an enthusiastic patron of the arts and a worshipper of splendor. Continuing to load the burden of taxation upon the common people, using bribery as an instrument of statecraft (Charles II of England was in his pay), he devoted himself to making his great palace at Versailles the admiration of the world and his luxurious court the apogee of gracious and sophisticated society. Surrounded by all the arts and refinements of living, the court gentlemen with powdered wigs, dressed in silks and laces, tottered on high heels (with the support of long thin canes) and bowed to the court ladies, whose towering headdresses and billowing skirts (suspended on wire) were in keeping with the ornamentation of their exquisite conversation.

Absolutism and elegance in the state were reflected by absolutism and elegance in the French language and literature of the period. The individualism and exploratory impulse of the Renaissance were replaced by a concerted effort to set up and maintain rigid standards. Originality was considered *gauche* in a society that sought to attain the heights of absolute perfection in language, behavior, art, and literature. Under such impetus, the importance of subject matter was often relegated to second place in comparison to perfection of form. Literary standards were based on the critical dicta of Aristotle and Horace, together with their Italian Renaissance followers, Scaliger and Castelvetro. Veneration for the wisdom and literature of Greece and Rome was still so universal that it was assumed that everything of value had been said. Because of this studied imitation of Classical form and subject matter, the period is well named the Neo-Classic Age. As in Classic art, permissible subject matter was limited to universals of human nature and social behavior. (It was not difficult for the Society of the court to consider man as primarily a social animal.) At its best, the object of Neo-Classicism came to be the presentation of human truth in perfect form. Truth, moderation, proportion, fitness, harmony, and beauty characterize the best literary productions of the age. The second-rate authors of the period often lost themselves in strained involutions of expression which they considered the acme of sophistication, nonchalance, and elegance.

The quest for perfection, which became the ruling passion of Society, had its genesis in the most distinctive institution of the century, the *salon*. In 1628, Catherine de Vivonne, an Italian by birth who was married to the Marquis de Rambouillet, found court society too uncivilized to suit her taste. Consequently, she withdrew from court to her own house near the Louvre, and there entertained a select group of artists and intellectuals. Until 1648, the *Hôtel de Ram-*

bouillet was frequented by the leading figures of French culture. Since drawing-rooms were then unknown, these celebrated receptions were held in the Blue Chamber, the bedroom of Mme de Rambouillet. She sat on the bed while her guests occupied chairs or stools or stood in the spaces surrounding the bed. These spaces were known as *ruelles;* hence *"ruelle"* became a synonym for a *salon* or reception.

At the *salon,* only intellectual or witty conversation was welcomed, and the social graces were assiduously cultivated. One of the aims of these conversation-fests was to make the French language a more delicate and precise instrument for conveying shades of thought and feeling. Shrinking from the common or the vulgar, these self-designated *Précieux* and *Précieuses* ("Exquisites") coined such euphemisms as "the furniture of the mouth" for "teeth," "children of the air" for "sighs," and "sustenance of life" for "bread." Some words were struck out of the language because of their vulgarity. *"Poitrine,"* the French word for "breast," was banished because "breast of veal" was an expression used by butchers. A debate is said to have raged for weeks about the propriety of admitting the common word *"car"* ("because") to polite conversation.

Along with much that appears nonsensical and frivolous to a later generation, these *salons* contributed a great deal to the sharpening of wit, clarification and purification of language, creation of formal artistic standards, and the production of a special brand of light sophisticated verse for which the French term, *vers de société,* has no exact equivalent in English. The *salon* of Mme de Rambouillet remained essentially intelligent and sensible; the *salons* of her imitators like Mlle de Scudéry, Mme de Sablé, and Mme de Lafayette carried preciousness to the extreme that made it a fit subject for ridicule by Molière in his *Précieuses Ridicules (Highbrow Ladies)* (1659).

The impetus that created the *salon* took another direction in the formation of The French Academy. In 1629, under Louis XIII, eight literary men formed a club to discuss matters of common interest. Richelieu proposed that they become an unofficial body under state authority. In part, the Prime Minister undoubtedly intended to extend the absolutism of the crown to the world of intellect and culture, but he was also motivated by a sincere love of French language and learning. In 1634, accordingly, a constitution was drawn up and the number of members was fixed at forty. In 1637, the organization was ratified b' Parliament under the official name of the *Académie Française*. By 1671, the Academy had become such a national institution that the meetings were opened to the public, and in 1672, Louis XIV gave the organization an apartment in the Louvre. It was also Richelieu who suggested that the Academy compose a dictionary to standardize and purify the language. Plans were drawn up in 1638, but it was not until 1694 that the *Dictionnaire de l'Académie* made its appearance. The peculiarity of this dictionary lay in the selection of words to be included. Instead of listing all words and usages, the editors gave space only to those which were considered correct. Through the Academy, the French man of letters became an influential person, almost a member of the government. In the *salon* and at court, he was received on an equal footing with members of the nobility. The Academy officially sanctioned or condemned writings of the period and became sovereign over national taste in language, art, and literature. It has continued ever since to exert a conservative influence on French creative genius and to crystallize that love of form which is a national characteristic.

Meanwhile, another aspect of the social world, the theatre, had its inception in this atmosphere of formality and elegance. Only troupes of Italian players and undistinguished French companies had been known in Paris until 1628 when the *Comédiens du Roi* (King's Comedians) established themselves permanently at the Hôtel de Bourgogne. The chief playwright of the company, Alexandre Hardy, based his plays on Greek tragedy, omitting the chorus and attempting to introduce more action and spectacle. Although in no sense a literary man, he paved the way for Corneille and Racine by concentrating plot on a central issue after the manner of Greek tragedy instead of dramatizing the entire event in the Shakespearean fashion. The Neo-Classic veneration for Aristotle together with the current delight in formality led to scrupulous obedience to the principle of the Unities, absence of action on stage, and the other rigidities of Greek drama. Before long, three theatres were flourishing in Paris. In 1643, Molière and nine others organized another theatre company, *L'Illustre Théâtre,* which hired a tennis court and began to produce tragedies. The venture bankrupted Molière in 1654, and the company toured the provinces for twelve years. But in 1658, Molière returned to Paris, having become a seasoned actor, director, playwright, and producer. Invited to perform at the Louvre, he so impressed Louis XIV that his company was sanctioned under the title, *Le Troupe de Monsieur,* and permitted to share the theatre used by the Italian players.

A great deal of seventeenth-century French literature appears trivial, strained, and superficial as an inevitable result of the accent on form and style. Much of it also achieved the effect of flamboyance rather than elegance. But innate vivacity, intelligence, imagination, and wit are distinguishable no matter what restricting costumes they may wear. The brilliant cynicism of Rochefoucauld and the infectious sparkle of Mme de Sévigné were encouraged by the intellectual climate of the age and require no apology. The observations on human nature made by La Fontaine, Racine, and Molière are intelligent and often penetrating; and even the artificial formalism in which their writings are cast is worthy of admiration and appreciation. The man on the flying trapeze gets nowhere, but his grace and agility in accomplishing a difficult feat is itself sufficient justification for his performance. Humanity is seldom so civilized as when it deliberately eschews the easy and the obvious to subject itself, by act of will, to the rigid discipline of formal standards. Criticism of the *Grand Siècle* can find no fault with its philosophy of perfectionism. Not the setting of standards but the limited, artificial, derivative, and snobbish nature of the specific criteria which it adopted mark the age as one of frequent perversion of talents that might have been more worthily employed.

SUGGESTED READINGS

(Place of publication, when not mentioned, is New York.)

J. Boulenger, *The Seventeenth Century in France* (Magnolia, Mass., 1963); E. Cassirer, *The Philosophy of the Enlightenment* (Princeton, 1951); A. Cobban, *In Search of Humanity: The Role of the Enlightenment in Modern History* (1960); G. R. Cragg, *Reason and Authority in the Eighteenth Century* (1964); Lester G. Crocker, *An Age of Crisis: Man and the World in Eighteenth Century French Thought* (Baltimore, 1958); Otis Fellows and Norman Torrey, *The Age of the Enlightenment* (1942); A. Guerard, *The Life and Death of an Ideal: France in the Classical Age* (1957); C. Hastings, *The Theatre: Its Development in France and England* (1901); George Havens, *The Age of Ideas* (1955); Paul Hazard, *The European Mind: The Critical Years (1680-1715)* (New Haven, 1953); Paul Hazard, *European Thought in the 18th Century* (New Haven, 1954); W. H. Lewis, *The Splendid Century* (1954); D. Ogg, *Europe in the Seventeenth Century* (3rd ed., 1938); H. Peyre, *Le Classicisme Français* (1942); L. Rothrug, *Opposition to Louis XIV: The Political and Social Origins of the French Enlightenment* (Princeton, 1965); A. E. Shipley, *The Revival of Science in the Seventeenth Century* (Princeton, 1914); S. G. Tallentyre, *The Women of the Salons* (1926); H. O. Wakeman, *The Ascendency of France* (London, 1897); B. Willey, *The Seventeenth-Century Background* (London, 1934); C. H. C. Wright, *French Classicism* (Cambridge, Mass., 1920).

chapter 19

RATIONALISM AND ROMANTICISM

I. THE BEGINNING OF SKEPTICISM

The eighteenth century can best be characterized as an age of revolutions. In France and in the Thirteen Colonies there were political upheavals whose repercussions were felt throughout the western world; in England, and later on the Continent, an Industrial Revolution was changing the shape of world economy by elevating middle-class industry to a position of supreme power and importance. But behind political and industrial developments lay a third and still more far-reaching phenomenon: the Intellectual Revolution. Deeds are but the enactment of ideas; in order to understand the full significance of eighteenth-century political and economic revolt, it is necessary to examine the forces that catalyzed this great upheaval.

The new interest in science which had originated in the Renaissance gradually bore fruit in a series of fundamental discoveries about the nature of the universe. Ever since Copernicus in 1543 shook the faith of the Christian world by showing that the earth was not the center of the universe, men had become increasingly concerned with natural phenomena, and such important developments as Harvey's discovery of the circulation of blood (1628), Boyle's law of the expansion of gases (1660), and Newton's law of gravitation (1687) had served to intensify that interest. As man discovered more about the natural laws that governed him and his universe, he was drawn less and less to a theological and "unscientific" explanation of the phenomenon of life. Gradually the authority of the "Ancients" began to break down; man was realizing that he was capable of extending his understanding through far different means than those employed by the great minds of the past.

Religion itself began to lose its hold in an age of growing scientific enlightenment. As more and more mysteries of the universe were revealed from the laboratory rather than from the pulpit, it became increasingly difficult from some thinkers to accept the concept of a mystical, anthropomorphic God. Since Copernicus, scientists had shown clearly that nature was governed by changeless laws which were not beyond the understanding of man. It is only natural that a school of thought should develop which would conceive of God in rational terms and would consider the examination of natural laws a form of divine worship. This philosophy, known as Deism, first developed in England with the writings of Baron Herbert of Cherbury (1583-1648).

The Deists conceived of God as a First Cause, rather than as a ubiquitous, omnipotent Deity. God in his benevolence had created reason, natural law, and an impulse to progress, and had then been replaced as a governing force by the phenomena he had created. He was no longer regarded as an all-powerful perpetrator of miracles; rather he instigated the laws by which the universe is governed, after which he allowed man to work out his own destiny subject to those laws. To worship God, then, man should study nature, the rational aspects of life. Historic Christianity is acceptable insofar as it coincides with reason, but in its belief in the Virgin birth, the divine nature of Christ, the Resurrection, and other miracles it is irrational and hence unacceptable. So ran Deistic thought, and its impact upon the eighteenth century was both shattering and dramatically propulsive.

II. FRENCH ENLIGHTENMENT

The impetus for French revolutionary thought came not from within France itself but from England. Until the opening of the eighteenth century, the French had been so absorbed in the study of the Classics that they had completely ignored England as an intellectual force. Even Milton and Shakespeare were virtually unknown to most Frenchmen. However, the revocation of the Edict of Nantes (1685) ended the toleration of Huguenots in France and caused many Protestant Frenchmen to flee to England and Holland, where they came into contact with Deism. Many of these exiles kept journals or wrote propaganda tracts embodying Deistic ideas, and gradually their writing filtered slowly into France to arouse a burning interest in the new thought. From Holland, Peter Bayle's *Critical and Historical Dictionary* (1697) searchingly set forth the irrationality of most orthodox religious beliefs and formed a landmark in the rise of religious skepticism. In 1700, Locke's *Essay Concerning Human Understanding* was translated and published in France and added fuel to the fires of the Enlightenment by denying the existence of innate ideas and stating that all of man's reactions, including his religious responses, are the result of worldly experience alone.

The first Frenchman to publish important skeptical work was Voltaire. Long an admirer of Bayle and an outspoken critic of the French court, Voltaire in 1726 was exiled to England for ridiculing the king's ministers and the Regent of France. While in England, the witty philosopher came directly under the influence of Lockeian thought and wrote his *Letters on the English,* which are filled with Deistic concepts transmuted by the vitriolic sarcasm of Voltaire's pen. Though suppressed by the French government, the *Letters on the English* had a powerful effect on French thinkers. By praising such English institutions as parliamentary government, religious tolerance, and civil liberties, Voltaire called attention to the lack of similar institutions in France and made all liberals fume at the feudalistic repressiveness and reactionary bigotry of Court and Church. Voltaire followed this bombshell by vast numbers of pamphlets, plays, and satirical novels attacking political, religious, and philosophical conservatism and upholding the scientific belief in reason and natural law. His wit made Frenchmen roar with laughter, and with their laughter he destroyed his enemies.

Following Voltaire, France was inundated by a flood of radical writing, most of which was far more extreme in thought than that of the "laughing philosopher." Condillac, in his *Traité des Sensations,* agrees with Locke that man at birth is a blank page, without innate instincts or preconceptions, and thus is molded by the experience of the senses only. Though a priest, he rejected the orthodox idea of man's natural propensity for evil and thus laid the groundwork for later beliefs in the perfectibility of the human race. Far more radical than Condillac was his disciple Helvétius, who in his *De l'Esprit* first applied his master's ideas to social and political life. Starting with the premise that all reaction is the result of sensation, Helvétius shows that man is solely concerned with self-interest. He seeks his own pleasure and comfort and abhors all that pains or confines him. Man is served through his ego; he is "virtuous" only insofar as it flatters his sense of self-importance to be so. Government, therefore, must cater to man's desire for comfort and individual stature. It must grant him freedom of action, must foster his sense of dignity, and must raise the general level of intelligence by widespread public education. Only by doing this will the state act as a positive force for universal good. On the other hand, he concluded, any government seeking to deny man his natural desire to serve his own comforts is anti-social and should be over-thrown. One may well imagine the furor caused by such revolutionary ideas in the coercive and absolutist France of 1758; it is little wonder that Helvétius' book was publicly burned and its author forced to flee the country.

But perhaps the most important agency in disseminating radical thought was the *Encyclopaedia*. Published in seventeen volumes between 1751 and 1765, the *Encyclopaedia* was a compilation of knowledge in all branches of learning, with special emphasis on science and philosophy. The tone of the work was extremely rational, and its views on such subjects as war and peace, religious intolerance, and penal codes, as well as upon religion and government, were well in advance of the times and presented a ringing challenge to all progressive minds. Among the contributors to this monumental work was a group of thinkers, known as the *Encyclopaedists,* whose ranks included Diderot (general editor of the work), De la Mettrie, Montesquieu, Condorcet, D'Alembert, and Holbach. Of these, it was Holbach who caused the greatest sensation and made the most violent attack upon existing institutions. Holbach was a wealthy nobleman of German extraction whose home was always open to the advanced philosophers and artists of the day and whose sincerity and dignity earned the respect of even those who disagreed violently with his extreme opinions. In his *Système de la Nature* (1770), Holbach denied the existence of any sort of God, even a God of Nature, and reaffirmed Helvétius' belief that man is prompted solely by self-interest. He attacked the Church as being founded on superstition and stated that orthodox religion caused men to waste valuable energy in trying to adjust themselves to the capricious will of a non-existent supernatural being.

Man is really governed not by a set of theological commandments and prohibitions but by mechanical natural laws which know no soul or divine spirit. Morality must follow natural laws, not the arbitrary and often unnatural standards of church and government. If man is evil, he reasoned, it is because these institutions make him so. To bring about universal good, government must encourage the natural equality and dignity of the human race. Even more imperatively the Christian Church, with its feudal attitude and unscientific superstitions, must be completely eliminated.

Of the leading Encyclopaedists, only Condorcet lived to see the Revolution, but the fire of their beliefs lived on for many years and fed much of the scientific and naturalistic thought of the nineteenth century. Rational, hard-headed, unsentimental, sincerely equalitarian, they gave much to the great democratic movement in Europe and America. As calmer reflection and the passage of time softened some of their more extreme views, particularly in matters of religion, they emerged as prophets of the materialistic realism of the present age and as pioneers in the history of liberal democracy.

III. JEAN-JACQUES ROUSSEAU: A TRANSITIONAL FIGURE

The greatest firebrand of the eighteenth century was Jean-Jacques Rousseau. A fascinating and somewhat revolting character, Rousseau, with his brilliant pen and his simple, sentimental ideas, earned the scorn of the rationalists but won the hearts and the enthusiasms of the people. The Encyclopaedists, in their radical pronouncements, reached the intellectual minority, but it was Rousseau's political manifestoes that inflamed the masses and supplied the emotional impetus leading to the French Revolution.

Rousseau first gained a name for himself by writing his anti-intellectual *Discourse on the Arts and Sciences* (1750), in which he stated that scientific study, far from making man happier, merely complicates his life and leads to further corruption. Man in a primitive state was happy, he said, and learning has only served to confound his natural goodness. Furthermore, the arts have made him conscious of luxury and thereby selfish and greedy. All of this has led to social inequality, the greatest single cause of human unhappiness. Therefore, "our minds have been corrupted in proportion as the arts and sciences have been improved"; man has tried to find in scientific laws the guidance he could gain much more easily by heeding his own nature.

Virtue! Sublime intuition of simple minds, are such industry and preparation needed if we are to know you? Are not your principles graven on every heart? Need we do more, to know your laws, than to examine ourselves, to listen to the voice of conscience . . . ?

From this point Rousseau, in his *Discourse on Inequality* (1755), went on to glorify the "state of nature," where the fruits of the earth are available to all, and man, a "noble savage," is ignorant, satisfied, and perfectly free. It is only when private property is introduced that man begins to enslave himself and to lose his natural goodness. Government is an institution to protect private property, and thus has its origin in evil and exists to promote inequality. It is only when government is destroyed and man returns to a state of nature that equality can be restored.

Naturally, Rousseau realized that the "state of nature" was only a philosophical abstraction and that man could never "return" to it save in a relative sense. In his most important work, *The Social Contract* (1762), Rousseau advanced his practical solution to the problem by advocating a democratic form of government which will function only as servant of the people and will derive its authority from the consent of the governed. Sovereignty rests inalienably in the people, he pointed out; coercive and absolute government is contrary to the law of nature and should be overthrown. The best form of government is that in which all people participate, but since in large states this procedure is impossible, the next best form is government by representatives responsible to the people and chosen by popular election. Thus, government should be a contract between the people and the governors, in which the former hire the latter to run the state and keep order for the consideration of a portion of their natural freedom. But at no time do the people surrender their sovereignty, and at no time is the government more than a public servant subject to discharge if its actions are contrary to the general welfare.

The Social Contract struck the potential revolutionaries with a blinding and almost messianic light. More than any other document, it raised the banner of human rights and eventually ignited the ready fuse of the French Revolution.

Rousseau is generally regarded as the "father" of Romanticism and, as such, the direct antithesis to the rational Classicism of the Encyclopaedists. Certainly in his emotional approach to life, in his distrust of reason and learning, and in his sentimental belief in the "natural" goodness of man, he was at an opposite pole from the Enlightenment, and yet in many other respects he found himself on common ground with his antagonists. Like them, he venerated the Classics and often pointed to Sparta or the Roman Republic as models in state organization; like them he was a political revolutionary with a deep and bitter hatred for monarchies in general and for the Bourbon monarchy in particular. Furthermore, though he shuttled back and forth between Protestantism and Catholicism, his true point of view throughout his life was as Deistic as that of Voltaire or Diderot, and his attacks upon the priestly hierarchy almost as intense. Later Romantics, while retaining a strong political liberalism, discarded the Classicism and replaced Deism with far more mystical religious beliefs. Thus, it would be more accurate to consider Rousseau not as "father" of the Romantic movement but as a transitional figure, a bridge over the two streams of Enlightenment and Romanticism which during the eighteenth century flowed side by side and which, despite many contradictory twistings and turnings, tried ultimately to reach the same ocean.

IV. THE RISE OF ROMANTICISM

When Rousseau died in 1778, an unhappy, half-demented old man, nobody could say that he had lacked a hearing or that he was wanting in disciples. Though his last years had been spent in voluntary isolation from society, the emotional appeal of his ideas had won him an enthusiastic following among all sorts of people in every social category. Political societies adopted him as their patron saint; philosophers such as Hume, Kant, Herder, and Thomas Paine made him their mentor; writers, including St. Pierre, Chateaubriand, Goethe, Schiller, Boswell, and innumerable others imitated his style and projected his themes. At the other extreme, the light-headed took up his cry of "back to nature" and pretended to admire the simple pastoral life; even Marie-Antoinette particularly fancied herself in the role of Arcadian shepherdess in a sylvan setting complete with bucolically disguised courtiers, a rustic hut or two, and plenty of servants to do the work.

And yet the new "Romanticism" did not for many years eliminate entirely the spirit of rational Classicism. Throughout the Revolution and the era of Napoleon, the disciplined Classical tradition maintained its strength both in ideas and in popular taste. The Revolution was dominated by Classical motifs and rational thought, and during the Reign of Terror Christianity was temporarily disestablished in favor of a religion of nature, with Reason as its goddess. Classical painting, sculpture, and architecture flourished throughout the Napoleonic era, and the transition from Classical to Romantic tradition in music was not noticeable until Beethoven "took a new path" with his Eroica symphony in 1804.

It is now high time for us to attempt to define Romanticism. Loose and general term as it is, Romanticism, in all of its many manifestations, has its common denominator in the idea of *freedom,* as against the Classical attitude of *disciplined* thought. Using freedom as a basis, then, let us enumerate some of the principal aspects of Romanticism with a view to defining the larger concept in terms of its most prominent attributes.

A. *Individualism*

The Romanticists regarded the welfare of the individual, not of the state or group, as the primary object for consideration and sought a society which would allow the most complete freedom of action, both political and social. The serious aspect of this doctrine is found in the equalitarian feeling (also shared by the Encyclopaedists) which "sparked" the revolution; the absurd side is seen in the egotistical posturings of persons, especially literary and artistic persons, who felt that the accentuation of individual differences, even to the point of eccentricity, was a sign of genius.

B. *Emotionalism*

Romantic philosophy puts a high premium on the emotions of man as opposed to his rational responses. This attitude grew largely from the concept of man's innate goodness stifled by the corrupting influence of society. Neo-Classical society regarded the display of emotions as "low" and attempted to restrain this natural manifestation of man's inner promptings. Since freedom from restraint was the soul of the Romantic movement, obedience to and even a display of emotions was considered by the Romantics a sign of one's independence and superiority.

C. *Worship of Nature*

We have seen that Rousseau regarded the "state of nature" as ideal and virtuous and the state of civilization as corrupt and wicked. By extension, all forms of nature became a symbol of the beautiful and the good, whether they be found in the free emotional responses of the individual or in a beautiful landscape. Along with this belief went a rather silly veneration for the "noble savage" and a worship of the American Indian or the South Sea Islander as the embodiment of all that was most heroic in humanity. At the same time man's newly-awakened awareness of nature aroused much more serious responses which inspired some of the most beautiful paintings, poems, and musical works ever written, and which gave rise to some of his most sublime flights of philosophical thought.

D. *Exoticism*

The veneration for nature and natural man, plus the distinction attached to novelty, led many Romantics to seek the exotic in life, to glorify strange lands and colorful peoples, to become absorbed in the occult and the supernatural, and even rather morbidly to adopt bizarre habits in diet, dress, occupation, and social pleasures. It also took the form of *antiquarianism,* and examined the history, customs, and particularly the folk literature of the medieval past as a reaction against the Classicist preoccupation with Greece and Rome.

E. *Nationalism*

Partly as a corollary to the political nationalism which held the nineteenth century in a crushing grip, and partly out of its interest in colorful antiquarianisms, nineteenth-century Romantics took every opportunity to develop peculiarly "national" themes in literature, art, and music.

Folk songs and dances were transmuted into symphonic music; plays and operas became ringing patriotic manifestoes; and poets and philosophers wept for countries whose political and ethnic independence had been forfeited to a foreign oppressor. National independence was seen as a necessary prerequisite to individual freedom, and many an idealistic young Romantic eagerly left his own country to fight for the independence of Greece, Italy, or even the Confederate States of America.

F. *Disillusionment*

With the coming of the nineteenth century, the attitude of the Romantic turned from its optimistic belief in the natural goodness of man to deep, frustrated disillusionment. At the outbreak of the Revolution most intellectuals, whether Classicist or Romantic, had believed in the Enlightenment of modern man, but as the Revolution degenerated into the Reign of Terror followed by the momentary glory and subsequent defeat of the Napoleonic era, the sensitive Romantic began to despair of man's potentialities even in an enlightened world. Reason had been tried and found lacking; civilization had exerted its decaying influence too long for man ever to return to a more natural and noble existence. Nothing seemed ahead but further suffering, and it is little wonder that many sensitive young Romantics fled to the New World or the South Seas, or renounced society to take refuge in impotent dreams or, worse still, gave up all hope and committed suicide.

Thus we see that Romanticism was a tapestry of many strands. From these six characteristics and their several combinations arose innumerable political, social, religious, and artistic movements. Some were utopian, some mystical, some medieval, some supernatural. Such diverse enthusiasms as nature worship, the glorification of patriotic heroism, or "art for art's sake" were currents in the Romantic stream. All of these activities transformed the nineteenth century, sometimes thought of to-day as being so staid, into the most conglomerate welter of intellectual activity in history. Some of this activity was "crackpot," but most of it found man at his highest creative pitch. Certainly no movement which, in addition to men already named, produced Kant, Hegel, Wagner, Brahms, Wordsworth, Shelley, Byron, Emerson, Thoreau, Whitman, Hugo, Gogol, or Poe could be denied its place as one of the most abundant eras of creative art since the Age of Pericles.

The Revolutionary Era (1770-1815)

THE FRENCH REVOLUTION

The French Revolution, though a logical and even inevitable outcome of the radical ideas previously described, did not break out solely as a result of intellectual manifestoes. Enlightened thought, after all, was well disseminated throughout Europe, and advanced political theories were voiced by Englishmen, Germans, Italians, and others, as well as by Frenchmen. And yet only in France was there actual revolution at this time.[1] Ideas alone seldom cause concrete action; conditions must be favorable for the growth and acceptance of those ideas. The seeds of the Enlightenment, sown indiscriminately throughout Europe, sprouted most rapidly and vigorously in France because only in France did they fall on soil already well prepared to yield the fruits of rebellion.

Actual political and social conditions in France were

[1] Democratic upheavals occurred in other European countries, of course, but at much later dates. Germany, for example, had her "revolution" in 1848, Italy had hers in 1870, and Russia hers in 1917. Other nations, such as Great Britain and the Scandinavian countries, managed to develop democratic institutions peacefully by the slow course of political evolution.

hopelessly behind the prevailing thought of the period. The "Old Regime" of the Bourbon dynasty was feudal in thought and corrupt in practice, and the church in its policies had hardly advanced a step since medieval times. The class system was still firmly established and was regarded, as it had been in the Middle Ages, as part of the Divine Order of the universe. For any man to attempt to rise above his class was to fly in the face of Providence, and to talk of a relaxing of class distinctions and class privileges was to utter near-blasphemy. The aristocrats assumed their favored position with an arrogance born of many centuries of unquestioned superiority and neglected their responsibilities with the flippancy of the eternally secure. Paying no taxes themselves, they supported their increasing extravagances by making heavier and heavier financial demands on the lower orders. At the same time, following the example of the Bourbon kings Louis XIV and Louis XV in their constant pursuit of extravagant pleasures, they utterly abandoned their traditional duty of furnishing responsible leadership and adopted instead a life of vicious and unmitigated hedonism. It is said that in one year alone Louis XVI, who compared to his Bourbon predecessors was almost penurious in his personal habits, nevertheless managed to spend over $70,000,000 of the people's money entirely at his own discretion and without any responsibility for a public accounting.

The peasants, of course, were bled white. What with the land taxes (the *taille*), church tithes, poll taxes, required labor on the roads (the *corvée*) and in the landlords' fields, indirect imposts such as the *gabelle* (required annual purchases of salt from the government salt monopoly at prices ten times the product's worth), and crops shared with the landlord, it is estimated that over four-fifths of the individual farmer's produce and labor was annually extracted from him through taxation. To make matters worse, the

French peasants, though seldom serfs as were their counterparts in other continental nations, were nevertheless tied to their rapidly declining lands by the traditional "open field" system of agriculture. This system forced them to plant only prescribed crops in prescribed places, thereby frustrating any soil-conserving methods of crop rotation, and to let their stock run with the common village herd, thereby preventing any effective system of disease control or of scientific breeding. If an individual peasant wished to leave his lands to seek greener pastures in another locality, he would have to pay an exorbitant quit-rent which few peasants could afford, and thus he remained chained to his exhausted plot as effectively as if he were still a bondsman.

For all his burdens, however, the French peasant was more fortunate than his fellows in other countries. Paradoxically enough, it was probably this factor of relative well-being that made him an effective rebel. He was still sufficiently well off economically to understand comfort and to desire a really fair share of the produce he raised, and despite the tyranny of his government he had not yet sunk to the brutalized impotence to which most European farmers had been reduced by their oppressive governments and landlords. Furthermore his land, though depleted after years of unscientific cropping, was still sufficiently fertile to furnish him an opportunity for decent living if only he could have been relieved of bearing the burden of the pleasures of the rich. Thus he became a rebel not because his lot was hopeless and his future black, but rather because he saw that there was yet something to fight for.

Even more potentially favorable was the lot of the *bourgeoisie,* or urban commercial class. Trade and commerce, which had been developing since the age of discovery and which had received a tremendous impetus through the Industrial Revolution, had drawn many ambitious young men from the farms to the cities, where some of them had achieved a quick prosperity in market place and factory. With this prosperity came a sense of power which was hardly to be contained by the outmoded feudal patterns of the Bourbon regime. Dynamic and spurred on by the success of British middle-class capitalism, the ambitious French *bourgeoisie* of the late eighteenth century were ready to fight for any social or political reforms likely to give them a freer hand to grasp the opportunities they felt to be rightfully theirs. More prosperous and better educated than the peasants, the *bourgeoisie* eagerly read the pronouncements of the revolutionary *philosophes* and enthusiastically led the struggle for reform. The fact that these proposed reforms could at one and the same time stir their idealism and open up greater opportunities for their individual prosperity made the enlightened middle class into formidable enemies of the Bourbon passion for preserving the *status quo*. It is significant that when the time finally came for talk to be translated into action, it was not the peasants but rather the *bourgeoisie* who, together with a few enlightened nobles, lit the first fires of rebellion.

The greatest single source of irritation leading to the inevitable revolt was the utter chaos of French government finances. There was traditionally no budget, no fiscal plan, no distinction between the king's money and that of the nation. Taxes were collected haphazardly and tax money was spent as soon as it was collected. No accounts were kept, and public officials from the king on down were completely ignorant as to the state of national finances until, like those imprudent housewives who write checks indiscriminately, they had to be told that there was no more money in the treasury with which to honor their extravagant drafts. Throughout the eighteenth century, the French financial situation had been acute. For decades after the death of Louis XIV in 1715, France had been drained dry to pay the costs of the sun-king's expensive warfare. Conditions were rendered even more dangerous by the prodigal wastefulness of the self-indulgent Louis XV, and by the time that monarch had the patriotic decency to die, the most important legacy he could deliver to his twenty-year-old grandson, Louis XVI, was a bankrupt treasury, together with the cynical statement that the new king, financially speaking, would have to look out for himself.

Louis XVI, fortunately, was not the flippant wastrel his grandfather had been. Though not overburdened with intelligence, he was at least sober and well disposed, and for a time it looked as though his finance ministers who succeeded one another with bewildering frequency might be able to avert fiscal catastrophe. But capable and efficient as several of these ministers were, they could not do the impossible. Clearly the only way to save France was by taxing the nobles, and the nobles were quite unwilling to consent to this unprecedented move. As a result, the government could resort only to loans which became harder and harder to obtain and each one of which, when obtained, only pushed the tottering treasury nearer to the brink of utter disaster. By 1786, the national debt had reached the unprecedented figure of $600,000,000 and the annual deficit was $25,000,000 and growing. Louis XVI in desperation called an Assembly of Notables (1787) for the purpose of consenting to the taxation of aristocrats, but the Assembly was not so altruistic and contented itself with a reduction of the *corvée,* a sop to the peasants which only reduced the amount of tax income and left the situation worse than before.

Finally, faced with threats of open revolt, Louis had no recourse but to heed public demands to reconvene the Estates General, an advisory body comprised of the three "Orders" of nobles, clergy, and commoners, which had not been called into session since 1614. In times past, kings had convened the Estates General largely as a polite formality, the commoners had been consistently outvoted by the combined voices of the nobles and clergy, and the king had been able with impunity to accept or reject the recommendations of the body as he saw fit. But this time things were different. The Third Estate was a social order much altered from its modest status of 1614. Prosperous, aggressive, and fighting mad, it was a force to be reckoned with, and to have its representatives present in an official government body was to lay the groundwork for unprecedented and even violent reform. When the Estates General were convened in May, 1789, the Third Estate immediately demanded that voting be done "by head," that is as individuals instead of by the traditional method of voting "by order" or social class. Since the representatives of the Third Estate equalled the combined vote of the nobles and clergy, and since some of the upper orders themselves favored reform, the conservatives of the Assembly for weeks stalled the proceedings by violently refusing to consent to the new method of voting. The king did nothing to resolve the squabble and finally, on June 17, 1789, the Third Estate met separately, proclaimed itself a National Assembly, and invited the other two Estates to join with it in the cause of reform. When the upper orders responded to this invitation by locking the Third Estate out of the convention hall, the by now thoroughly roused commoners proceeded to the tennis court, where they swore a solemn oath never to adjourn until a constitution had been drawn up for France. The "Oath of the Tennis Court" was the real beginning of the French Revolution; with it the principle of divine right of kings had been repudiated and Bourbonism notified of its impending doom.

Louis XVI nevertheless stubbornly refused to read the handwriting on the wall. He openly moved French troops from outlying provinces to the neighborhood of Versailles and Paris, and the Parisian public, outraged by the king's hostility to the National Assembly on July 14, 1789, stormed the arsenal of the Bastille, a former prison which symbolized Bourbon persecution of political opposition. Here the mob massacred the garrison of Swiss mercenaries and appropriated its store of ammunition for the National Guard, a people's army which proceeded virtually to take over the government of the city of Paris. A few months later, angered by rumors of an extravagant banquet given for royal reinforcements arriving from Flanders, the women of Paris, together with men dressed as women, marched to Versailles, broke into the royal palace and forced the king and his hated queen, Marie-Antoinette, to return with them to the capital where they were subsequently ensconced in the palace of the Tuileries, so that their movements could be more closely watched than they had been at Versailles.

The die was now cast, and it was evident to everyone that the royal power had been destroyed. Nobles and clergy, anxious to salvage what they could out of the wreckage of the Old Regime, joined in desperate eagerness with the Third Estate in abolishing class privileges, oppressive taxation, and all the remaining vestiges of feudalism and Bourbon autocracy. The result was proclaimed the "Declaration of the Rights of Man," an enlightened document establishing the sanctity of the individual and guaranteeing him rights of "life, property, security, and resistance to oppression," together with rights of free speech, a free press, and freedom of worship. In addition, in 1791, a National Constitution was adopted, establishing a limited monarchy in which the king occupied an executive position subject to the will of the legislature and, ultimately, to that of the people themselves. The spirit of Rousseau and the *philosophes* had triumphed: France in 1791 had a Social Contract, and the liberation from tyranny and injustice seemed, for the moment, to be established and complete.

But unfortunately for the peace of France, to establish a

constitutional monarchy was not to root out all traces of
the Old Regime. Even as early as the Bastille, reactionary
nobles had begun to leave the country. As the National
Assembly increased in strength, the stream of emigration
flowed ever faster, until by 1791 a sizeable army of these
"émigrés" had assembled along the northern and eastern
frontiers. From here they harassed the revolutionary government with floods of propaganda and constant political
intrigue while awaiting a propitious moment to strike
against the new order with armed force. Within France also
there were many who sympathized secretly with the émigrés
and who constituted a steady threat to the revolutionaries.
The royal family was strongly suspected of being among
the internal reactionary sympathizers, and in June 1791
these suspicions became open fact when the king, with his
queen and his children, attempted to flee the country to
join the émigrés. Halted at Varennes, near the border, the
royal fugitives were brought back to Paris virtually as prisoners and with whatever small popularity they had enjoyed
among the people now completely dissipated.

The attempted escape of the royal family brought about
a new tone in French politics. The radical element, using
the counter-revolutionary activities of the émigrés as a
pretext, now began to agitate powerfully for a complete
eradication of the upper orders and the establishment of a
people's republic. Most outspoken in these radical activities
was a group known as the Jacobin Club, which had been
organized as a moderate society favoring the constitution
but which had quickly transformed itself into the voice of
extreme republicanism after the attempted "treason" of the
fugitive king. Among the most influential members of the
Club were Marat, Danton, Desmoulins, and Robespierre,
all of whom played roles of great importance in the developments to come.

Meanwhile, from the first meeting of the Legislative

Assembly in October, 1791, the constitutional government had found itself in trouble. It was hampered in its work by the king, who, though held under palace custody, still stubbornly insisted in using his veto powers to embarrass the legislature. Furthermore, it was harassed from within by a peasant revolt in La Vendée and by the threatening complaints of an impoverished Parisian proletariat. On the border the émigrés were awaiting a propitious moment to strike, and there were discomforting indications that Britain, Prussia, and Austria were preparing for war against the revolutionary government. By April, 1792, these indications had become a dead certainty, and France, taking the initiative, declared war on Austria and Prussia.

But the initiative proved to be of little advantage to the French armies, and as defeat followed defeat and Paris itself was threatened, the people took action. In August, 1792, the Parisian radicals, led by Danton, invaded the royal palace, seized the king after he had appealed to the Assembly for protection, and forced the terrified legislature to dissolve itself in favor of a National Convention which was to prepare a new republican constitution. On September 22, following a long-awaited French victory against the invading forces of the Duke of Brunswick, the National Convention enthusiastically resolved that from this date on royalty was abolished in France, the émigrés were forever banished, and Year I of the Republic had begun. With the establishment of the Republic, Louis XVI had but few weeks to live. In December, 1792, he was brought to trial and condemned to death by a close vote. On the following January 21 he was executed, and within a few months Marie-Antoinette and other members of his family followed him to the guillotine.

The beheading of Louis XVI marked the end of the bourgeois phase of the French Revolution. From here on, the proletariat took over, bringing with it the Reign of

Terror during which the streets of Paris were drenched with blood. For the next year and a half, more than five thousand "enemies of the people" were guillotined in Paris alone and at least three times as many more met their death in the provinces. The National Convention itself abdicated in favor of a dozen radical leaders who styled themselves the Committee on Public Safety and who exercised absolute powers over the administration of the entire nation.

Having established themselves in power by killing or imprisoning their political enemies among the royalists and moderates, the radicals now began to squabble among themselves. By the middle of 1794 Marat had been assassinated and Danton, Desmoulins, and even Robespierre himself had gone to the block. The death of the last named marked the end of the Reign of Terror, and in 1795 France put into effect a new constitution establishing a republican Directory, in which the executive and appointive functions of government were to be assumed by five Directors elected by the legislature.

The Directory lasted only until 1799 and was beset with difficulties from the beginning. The Directors themselves were political weaklings, unable to control the destructive political factionalism within their regime and apparently unwilling to stem the internal graft and corruption which kept the government on the verge of bankruptcy. And at the same time that government revenues were being diverted into the pockets of venal officials, the Directors had to respond to the mounting expenses of foreign wars by issuing paper *assignats* which inflated the currency and later had to be repudiated.

These costly foreign wars, however, were ironically enough the only happy factor in the gloomy regime of the Directors. Thanks to the efforts of a hitherto inconspicuous commander named Napoleon Bonaparte, the French armies had waged successful campaigns in Italy and Egypt, and under other leaders had made progress along the Rhine. Napoleon had been rebuffed in Syria and had lost a naval battle against the British admiral Lord Nelson at the mouth of the Nile, but so successful was the brilliant general in his public relations that he was able to minimize these defeats and make himself into the hero of the day.

By 1799, enthusiasm for the Corsican general had reached a fever pitch and he was able to make his great *coup d'état*. Surrounding the legislature with loyal troops, Napoleon intimidated the Assembly into overthrowing the Directory and instituting a new constitution under which he became First Consul of the French Republic. Thus, within a decade France had gone nearly full cycle from a feudal kingdom through constitutional monarchy, popular republicanism, committee demagoguery, before sinking finally into the lowest form of all—a military dictatorship. Within a few years the cycle was to be completed by a return to royalism, first in the form of the Empire, and then in the "legitimate" re-establishment of the Bourbons. But before that ultimate catastrophe, France was to regain for a brief period all of her former glory and to rise with dizzy swiftness to world leadership through the intoxicating genius of Napoleon Bonaparte.

THE ERA OF NAPOLEON

During his five years as First Consul (1799-1804), Napoleon performed miracles of administration as sensational as any of his victories on the field of battle. He cleaned out the noisome corruption within the national government, eliminated legislative shilly-shallying by taking over most of the law-making duties himself, and highly centralized his rule by virtually eliminating elective officers within the cities and departments and placing his own appointed officials in their stead. In short, he soon transformed France into a smooth-running dictatorship which contrasted dramatically with the chaos of former days. By outwardly professing himself a champion of the revolutionary ideals of liberty, equality, and fraternity, and by continuing the revolutionary policy of eliminating class privilege, Napoleon was able to increase his already overwhelming popularity and at the same time add to his personal power. After a decade of increasingly disastrous attempts at popular rule, France was quite willing to entrust her hard-won political and social liberty to the sole charge of the one man who seemed able to make the machinery run.

Once securely established in his role as ruler, Napoleon was able to make reforms of every sort. He revised the tax structure, instituted much-needed economies in public expenditures, and climaxed his fiscal rehabilitation by establishing the Bank of France, which has remained ever since one of the soundest financial institutions in the world. He re-established the Catholic Church (though he kept control over many of its activities), instituted an effective system of public schools, promoted public works of all sorts, patronized arts and letters and, above all, consolidated and clarified the welter of contradictory laws into the famous Code Napoléon, which became the legal model for most of Europe and for much of the New World. All of these reforms, while springing from the ulterior motive of centralizing government functions and thereby enhancing Napoleonic power, nevertheless were effected with an enlightenment that far transcended the opportunism of the moment and resulted in their permanent retention as basic institutions of French life.

In international affairs, Napoleon was no less successful. In 1800-1801 he campaigned successfully against Austria and forced her to sign the Treaty of Lunéville. In 1802 he also concluded a truce with England in the Treaty of Amiens, which left France still strong and at peace for the first time in a decade. Riding on the crest of these successes, he held a plebiscite which made him First Consul for life. From this position, it was only a short step to making the office hereditary and changing his title to that of Emperor. Taking that step with the arrogant assurance that characterized his every move, Napoleon on the second of December, 1804, in the presence of Pope Pius VII, placed the crown on his own head and proclaimed himself Napoleon I, Emperor of the French.

Little change in French life was noticeable by this alteration in title, but Napoleon, now certain of maintaining his influence even beyond the grave, moved with even greater boldness and ambition than before. War had been resumed against Great Britain in 1803, and in 1805 Austria, Russia, and Sweden joined the British in the so-called Third Coalition, with the avowed objective of eliminating Napoleonism once and for all from the European scene. The ten-year history of the First Empire is one of continuing and deepening warfare. With the details of its campaigns, its alliances and counter-alliances, and its confusing and quickly-terminated treaties, we will have little to do here. Suffice it to say that Napoleon, though occasionally defeated, rose higher and higher in power and prestige and by 1808 found himself ruler of an empire that stretched from Italy to Denmark, from Gibraltar to Warsaw. Within this territory only Portugal and Prussia were independent of French rule. Members of the Bonaparte family were on the thrones of Spain, Naples, Holland and the small state of Lucca, and outside his Empire Napoleon counted the rulers of Denmark and Russia as his friends and supporters. Austria and Prussia had been reduced to third-rate powers; only Great Britain remained adamant against the European colossus.

The end of the story is a theme for Greek tragedy. The last six years of the Empire witnessed the *hubris* of the seemingly invincible Bonaparte, the loss of his allies, the disaffection of his supporters within France, the catastrophic collapse of his marvellous army, and, most subtle of all, the slow physical and mental degeneration of the great hero himself. The strain of years of one-man rule over an Empire comparable to that of Rome in its glory and the anxiety attendant upon the holding of the fruits of victories won solely by military strength took their inevitable toll. The vibrantly energetic thirty-year-old genius, who in 1799 had seized the position of First Consul, by 1808 had become old at thirty-nine, fat, self-indulgent, physically depleted, with an egotism and insatiable thirst for ever more power bordering on outright insanity.

Not content with being master of continental Europe, Napoleon from his earliest years as Emperor had directed his efforts to overthrow England as mistress of the seas. British naval victories on the Nile (1798), off Copenhagen (1801) and Trafalgar (1805) had ultimately frustrated his nautical ambitions and had led him to substitute an economic boycott of Great Britain known as the Continental System. Under this system British goods were barred from the Continent, thereby depriving Britain of her richest export market. The plan was not so simple as it seemed, however. Many European coastal towns depended strongly upon British shipping for their existence. Furthermore, British manufacturing, being technologically more advanced than that of the Continent, was able to produce goods cheaper and better than its rivals and therefore attracted more consumer interest than did the products of the mainland. In attempting to enforce the Continental System, Napoleon had to reckon not only with Britain, but also, more important, had to keep his own subjects and allies from secretly encouraging the desirable and often critically necessary British trade.

Naturally, Britain did not take the continental boycott lying down. She responded with the "Orders in Council" which declared all vessels trading with France as subject to search and seizure and which further stipulated that under certain conditions neutral vessels would have to touch at a British port before proceeding to their destinations. The British rebuttal made as much ill feeling among neutrals as did the Continental System among European shippers and was a direct cause of the War of 1812 with the United States, but it also imposed great privation upon the peoples of Europe and added fuel to the increasing fires of disaffection for Napoleon. In the long run, it was the impossible Continental System as much as declining military fortunes which caused the First Empire to fall apart.

In addition to his losing struggle with the forces of economics, Napoleon was beset with increasing military frustration against Spain and Portugal. In 1808 the Spanish arose against their Bonapartist king, Napoleon's brother Joseph, forced him to flee the country, and successfully induced the British to send an army under the Duke of Wellington to help expel the French forces from the Iberian peninsula. After five years of extremely bloody war, in which the rugged Iberian terrain and the ruthless Spanish guerilla tactics constantly hampered Napoleon's armies, the Emperor finally had to concede defeat. At the same time, Austria struck for freedom and, though unsuccessful, diverted considerable French military energy from the problem of Spain. In Prussia too a resurgent nationalism was arising which proved increasingly embarrassing to the Emperor of the French. But most costly of all was the rupture with Russia in 1812 which led Napoleon to turn the main strength of his Grand Army against his erstwhile ally Czar Alexander. Employing a "scorched earth" policy, the French swept triumphantly into Moscow, which they set in flames by their own carelessness. Subsequently, with their potential food supplies destroyed by their own actions, the Grand Army, in the face of starvation, guerilla raids, and the Russian winter, was forced to make the long and terrible retreat back home over the same devastated route by which it had come. It was one of the most completely shattering military disasters in history.

Napoleon's prestige had been severely curtailed and his Grand Army decimated by the retreat from Moscow; it now remained only to destroy his pride. This took a considerable amount of doing. On his arrival in Paris after the defeat of 1812, Napoleon had immediately recruited a new army and with characteristic resilience had proceeded to gain temporary victories against a coalition of Russians and Prussians at Lützen and Bautzen in May, 1812. He scored another success at Dresden in August, but finally at Leipzig on October 16-19 the tide turned against him and he went down to decisive defeat in the "Battle of the Nations," which cost him 70,000 casualties and forced his precipitate retreat across the Rhine. After Leipzig, it was a question only of mopping up. Napoleon fought like a cornered animal, but the issue was never in doubt. On April 13, 1814, the harassed Emperor was forced to sign the treaty of Fontainebleau, by which he renounced his throne in return for an annual pension and sovereignty over the small island of Elba. His place as ruler of France was taken by a fat, futile Bourbon, Louis XVIII, brother of the beheaded king.

In the fall of 1814, the allies met in the Congress of Vienna to set about the overwhelming task of restoring order and dividing the spoils. In February this international poker game, which was still proceeding at a snail's pace, was suddenly thrown into a state of frenzy. Bonaparte had returned! With seven hundred loyal supporters, the irrepressible former emperor one dark night had sailed from the island, had landed without opposition on the coast of France, and before the news of his coup had reached Paris or Vienna, had raised a sizeable army by merely uttering the magic name of Napoleon.

The Allies acted swiftly. Forgetting their differences of the conference table, they once again took up arms and stormed toward France. After a few minor actions, the rival armies on June 18 met in full scale action at Waterloo. Here, in a battle that has been immortalized in just about every form of the written word from bare military history to heroic poetry, Napoleon went down for the last time. His electrifying Hundred Days, which had never had the remotest chance of bringing about his permanent restoration, were over. A prisoner of the British, he was exiled to the small island of St. Helena, off the coast of Africa, where he lived in nostalgic dreams of better times until death took him on May 5, 1821. His death found him already a legend, his overwhelming ambition and his bloodthirsty campaigns forgotten in his new incarnation in fancy as the heroic child of the people. Meanwhile the poker game of Vienna was over, and a Bourbon once again ruled on the throne of France.

SUGGESTED READINGS

(Place of publication, when not mentioned, is New York.)

F. A. Aulard, *The French Revolution* (1910); I. Babbitt, *Rousseau and Romanticism* (1919); J. Bainville, *History of France* (1926); J. Barzun, *Classic, Romantic, and Modern* (2nd ed., Boston, 1961); C. L. Becker, *The Heavenly City of the Eighteenth-Century Philosophers* (New Haven, 1932); E. Cassirer, *The Philosophy of the Enlightenment* (tr. by F. C. A. Koelln and J. P. Pettergrove, Boston, 1955); A. Cobban, *In Search of Humanity: The Role of the Enlightenment in Modern History* (1960); W. and A. Durant, *The Age of Voltaire* (1965); W. and A. Durant, *Rousseau and Revolution* (1967); H. N. Fairchild, *The Romantic Quest* (1931); P. Gay, *The Enlightenment: An Interpretation* (1966); F. C. Green, *Eighteenth Century France* (London, 1929); F. C. Green, *Minuet* (London, 1935); A. Guerard, *France: A Modern History* (Ann Arbor, 1958); G. R. Havens, *The Age of Ideas* (1955); C. J. H. Hayes, *A Political and Cultural History of Modern Europe* (1932); P. Hazard, *The European Mind: The Critical Years (1680-1715)* (New Haven, 1953); J. C. Herold, *The Age of Napoleon* (1963); R. Z. Lauer, *The Mind of Voltaire* (1961); G. Lefebre, *The Coming of the French Revolution* (Princeton, 1947); H. Nicholson, *The Age of Reason, 1700-1798* (London, 1960); J. H. Rose, *The Revolutionary and Napoleonic Era* (1895); J. J. Rousseau, *Confessions;* H. M. Stephens, *European History from 1789 to 1815* (1893); H. M. Stephens, *The French Revolution* (1902); R. N. Stromberg, An *Intellectual History of Modern Europe* (1966); H. Taine, *The Ancient Regime* (1875-1885); J. M. Thompson, *The French Revolution* (1943); A. A. Tilley, *The Decline of the Age of Louis XIV* (1929); A. R. Viney, *History of French Literature in the Eighteenth Century* (Edinburgh, 1854); A. Young, *Travels in France* (1792).

chapter 20

GERMAN ECLECTICISM (1740-1870): THE SEARCH FOR A NATION

I. THE FRENCH PERIOD (1740-1770)

While France was undergoing her long, frustrating search for a stable political order to replace the feudal decay of Bourbonism, the German states were experiencing an equally protracted struggle for unification. From the treaty of Westphalia (1648) to the treaty of Frankfurt (1871), the multitudinous kingdoms and petty principalities which had once formed the nucleus of the Holy Roman Empire struggled with one another for supremacy, made and broke alliances, combined and separated with a frequency seemingly without pattern or reason and as utterly confusing to European political life at the time as it has subsequently been to students of European history. The Holy Roman Empire (which, to use a time-worn cliché, was neither holy, Roman, nor an empire) at the end of the Thirty Years' War consisted of some three hundred independent Germanic cities and states. It had a Diet which met occasionally for purely formal purposes; it even had an emperor, usually an Austrian Hapsburg whose imperial title was held purely by courtesy. And although the inhabitants of this fantastic "empire" held a common bond of language and culture, it was not until the nineteenth century that there developed any real desire to combine this mishmash of first-rate powers and comic-opera principalities into anything resembling a unified German nation.

For a century following the end of the Thirty Years' War in 1648, the German states existed in a stupor of political and intellectual stagnation. The petty princes took advantage of this inertia to exercise despotic power over their helpless subjects, to milk the land dry for their pleasures, and to intrigue for personal power within the moribund Empire. The once prosperous burgher class had been ruined by the Thirty Years' War, and any social or intellectual stimulus which should normally have emanated from this group was nullified by the economic prostration of German middle-class capitalism.

It is no wonder, therefore, that little German literature of consequence should have appeared during this period or that what did appear was essentially imitative. In the first half of the eighteenth century, with the various court aristocracies trying to outdo one another in imitating the splendors of Louis XIV at Versailles, there was little interest in truly German culture. French dress, architecture, and interior decoration were assiduously aped. The artificial seventeenth-century French wit was carefully cultivated, and the exquisite refinements of French vice eagerly adopted. The very language of the courts was often French, with German being regarded as a tongue suitable only for burghers and peasants. The writers who gained court favor, therefore, were those who, like Christian Gottsched, most consciously imitated French models. These literary lights, without necessarily abandoning their native German, shone through their ability to approximate the stiff Neo-Classicism of Racine or Corneille or the sharp wit of Molière or La Fontaine. Since neither the German mind nor the German language is particularly well adapted for these

peculiarly Gallic forms of expression, it is not to be wondered that little of worth was produced during the "French"
period of German literature.

The most famous of the many "little Versailles" within
Germany was the court of Frederick the Great, king of
Prussia, who reigned over that state with distinction and
political resourcefulness from 1740 to 1786. By the time of
this famous monarch, some order had begun to develop
from the political chaos which had followed the Treaty of
Westphalia. Four German states, Bavaria, Saxony, Austria,
and Brandenburg-Prussia, had emerged as political entities
of considerable importance, with the last two holding particular weight in the European balance of power. Frederick,
who came to the throne the very same year as his arch rival,
Maria Theresa of Hapsburg, devoted most of his long reign
to political intrigue and frequent warfare against his great
Austrian enemy. There were many wars involving many
nations in the eighteenth century, and Frederick never sat
one out when participation would mean additional prestige
for Prussia. In the War of the Austrian Succession (1740-
1748) and the Seven Years' War (1757-1763), as well as in
the First Partition of Poland (1772), he scored signal successes over Austria and placed Prussia in the front rank of
European nations.

In addition to this career of warfare and intrigue, however, Frederick also led the life of an enlightened despot.
He instituted economic and agricultural reforms, improved
the Prussian system of education and, above all, encouraged
the development of science and the arts. A man of considerable musical and literary talent himself, he made his
court into a grand salon to which the leading philosophers,
artists, writers, and musicians of Europe were frequently
invited guests. Most of these visitors were French (Voltaire
himself was a visitor for a while), and their presence only

added to the prevailing mania for French art forms. But as time went on, French writings shed the cold formalism of the Golden Age and became more enlightened and socially conscious. The presence of ideas emanating from a country about to enter into a period of revolution could not but stimulate German nationalistic consciousness. Furthermore in Frederick the Great, despite his lack of interest in German art, German thinkers had a national hero around whom they could rally as a symbol of nascent Germanic culture.

Thus the court of Frederick the Great was of great service in stimulating national self-expression. Although the time had not yet arrived for German writers to cease their borrowings from the culture of other countries, it had at least advanced to a point where these writers had developed self-respect and the desire to attain higher planes of cultural unity and nationalistic glory. As a result, by the third quarter of the eighteenth century, German literature at last began to show national individuality and to make its presence felt in European intellectual life.

II. THE ENGLISH INFLUENCE (1750-1770)

Although the court of Frederick the Great had strongly favored French ideas and forms of artistic creation, the strongest impetus in the revival of German literature was given by the English. Even in the first half of the eighteenth century, minor German poets had been imitating Pope, Thomson, Prior, and Gay, and the works of the last two had been translated frequently into German. Defoe's *Robinson Crusoe* (1719) was a great favorite with German novelists and was copied widely over the next hundred years.[1] The sentimental romances of Samuel Richardson

[1] There were "Robinsons" for nearly every country within Germany —a *Saxon Robinson,* a *Thuringian Robinson,* a *Swabian Robinson,* and

were also inordinately popular and German bookstalls bristled with minor imitations of *Pamela* and *Clarissa Harlowe*. Much more important was the somewhat belated recognition of Milton and Shakespeare. With the Miltonic *Messias* of Friedrich Klopstock, finished in 1773 after more than twenty-five years of creative effort, German literature achieved its first great modern epic, while the Shakespearean translations of C. M. Wieland (1762-1766) and, later, those of A. W. Schlegel (1797-1810) made the Stratford playwright as influential and well-beloved in Germany as in the English-speaking world.

The English influence in German literature is best exemplified by the career of Gotthold Ephraim Lessing (1729-1781). A great critic and dramatist in his own right, Lessing had early recognized that a German national drama, if it were to develop at all, would have to do so after English forms and not after the stilted French Neo-Classicism of the *Grand Siècle*. His own early play *Miss Sara Sampson* (1755), subtitled *Ein bürgerliches Trauerspiel* (a tragedy of everyday life), was an imitation of the drama of common life established by the British dramatist George Lillo in his *Merchant of London* (1731).[2] Such was the popularity of *Miss Sara Sampson* that it virtually with one blow destroyed interest in the French aristocratic tragedy and turned playwrights to the creation of *bürgerliche Trauerspiele,* until plays of common life became a well-established genre in the dramatic literature of Germany. Lessing's own *Minna von*

---

so forth. There was a *Spiritual Robinson,* a *Medical Robinson,* and even a *Girl Robinson.* Most of these were the cheapest of catch-penny romances, but the four-volume *Albertus Julius* (1731-1743) was a Robinsonian work that ranked as the most popular of all German novels throughout the century. Most famous of all was Wyss' *The Swiss Family Robinson* (1812-1827), whose popularity remained undimmed until well into the twentieth century.

[2] The lachrymose plot of *Miss Sara Sampson,* however, was probably suggested by Thomas Shadwell's *Squire of Alsatia* (1688).

Barnhelm (1767) has been recognized as being among the dramatic masterpieces of all time, and his *Laokoon* (1766) and *Hamburgische Dramaturgie* (1767-1768) among the first works of literary criticism. As director of the short-lived but important German National Theatre of Hamburg, he was able to give practical expression to his British-inspired theories of dramaturgy and to take his place as the leading influence of the early days of the German literary renaissance. Later, in *Emilia Galotti* (1772) and *Nathan der Weise* (1779) it can be said that Lessing outgrew his dependence upon English models and achieved examples of a truly national drama. Altogether, by bringing the drama out of the Classical cloudlands, Lessing opened the way for the remarkable theatrical renaissance that eventually culminated in the magnificent productions of Schiller and Goethe and gave Germany its greatest claim to literary fame.

One other example of the English influence upon German writing must be mentioned. This was the pseudo-Celtic epic poetry of Ossian which after its "discovery" and "translation" by the Scotchman J. W. Macpherson in 1762 swept both Europe and America like a prairie storm and did much to induce the early stages of the romantic movement.[3] Translated by the Austrian M. Denis in 1768-69, the poems became immensely popular and, along with Shakespeare and Milton, acted as the chief influences of the *Sturm und Drang* (Storm and Stress) period of German literature.

---

[3] Macpherson claimed to have discovered ancient manuscripts containing poems by the third-century Irish epic bard, Ossian. Accused of being a fraud by no less a critic than Dr. Samuel Johnson, Macpherson took refuge in blustering threats of lawsuits but never showed his manuscripts. It has long been accepted that such documents were fabricated and that the Ossianic poems were by and large created by Macpherson himself. But genuine or no, the poems had a powerful influence upon literary developments of the next half century.

III. STURM UND DRANG (1770-1790)

It is interesting to note how the quickening of the arts in Germany coincided with the resurgent periods in European political life. The rise of Prussia and Frederick the Great had started the literary pot simmering; the rise of democratic idealism in America and France brought it to a boil in the youthfully exuberant movement known as *Sturm und Drang*. Later, the Napoleonic Wars coincided with the flowering of German Romanticism, the stormy period between the French July Rebellion of 1830 and the general wave of Continental uprisings in 1848 manifested itself in the Young Germany movement. Subsequently, the rise of Bismarck and the final unification of Germany were marked by an optimistic though often ruthless literary nationalism that produced such unique work as the philosophy of Frederick Nietzsche. With the possible exception of the last, all of these stages of German Romantic writing were characterized by the energy and freshness of youth. Young poets, novelists, and dramatists, sensitive to the electrifying intellectual currents of a world in transition, sought to break with the literary forms and traditions of the past and strove for new media of expression to accompany the intoxicating new ideas springing from an era of enlightened revolution. It could well be argued that most of this literary energy between 1770 and 1870 sprang from the slow but certain metamorphosis of Germany into a unified nation, from the self-confidence that accompanied the growth of a sense of national destiny. The only flaw in the pattern lay in the irony that when German unity was finally achieved under Bismarck, most of the energy of the German literary renaissance had already been spent.

Sturm und Drang, the first of these periods of youthful impulsiveness, dates from the winter of 1770 in Strassburg, where the minor writer J. F. Herder preached to a coterie of poets (which included the young Goethe) the greatness of Shakespeare, the emotional sensibility and the enlightened social thought of Rousseau, and the vast wealth of literary beauty lying fallow in the folk literature of the German people. Almost overnight the movement sprang into flame. Collections of German *Volkslieder* began to appear in profusion, poets by the dozens composed verses in the simple affecting style of the folk song, sentimental novels and plays involving the lives of simple folk appeared at every hand, and emanating from all was the Rousseauistic spirit of humanitarianism, sentimentality, love of nature, and faith in the intuitive goodness of simple hearts. Most notable of such books was Goethe's *The Sorrows of Werther* (1774), a cloying, sentimental tale of frustrated love which took Europe by storm and caused an entire generation of young men to imitate Werther in dress, and in his agonies of hopeless passion, and caused some of them—to an alarming degree—even to seek his final solution in suicide.

In addition to following the lead of Rousseau, the man of "sensibility," the *Sturm und Drang* writer, also followed Rousseau the revolutionist in calling for social justice against the entrenched privilege and decadent tyranny of priest and king. Notable among such writings were Goethe's *Götz von Berlichingen* (1773) and *Egmont* (1788) and Friedrich Schiller's violently individualistic *Die Räuber* (The Robbers) (1781), in which sentimentally noble leaders struggled in the name of liberty to free the common man from the bonds of feudal oppression. As can readily be imagined, much of this writing, while touched with inspired genius, was at the same time excessive, fatuous, and even anti-social. But at the same time it was irresistible, and its surging vitality carried its followers to new heights in literary expression and to new depths of penetration into the spirit of a great people.

IV. ROMANTIC CLASSICISM (1790-1800)

One of the most interesting aspects of German literary borrowing from other nations is the element of Classicism that for a brief period crept into the works of Goethe, Schiller, and other *Sturm und Drang* writers. The lure of ancient Greece and Rome is also manifest in the literature of other nations during the Romantic period, but it takes the form of admiration for Greek forms of government (Rousseau professed especially to a love for Spartan life) or, more often, it dissolves into a morbid and often escapist antiquarianism. At one point in the Romantic Movement, it became very fashionable to affect a love of ruins, and Greece and Italy were much frequented by poetic young men who visited the Coliseum or the Parthenon and brooded darkly and lyrically over the transitory nature of fame and glory. Goethe was such a traveller, and from his journey to Italy (1786-1788) dates his emergence as a poet of world stature. His journey to Classical lands not only furnished the direct inspiration of such works as *Iphigenie auf Tauris* (1787) and *Torquato Tasso* (1790), as well as of many parts of *Faust* and *Wilhelm Meister,* but it also matured him as a poet and gave him a clear perspective of his literary mission. From the fusion in Goethe's subsequent work of the hot inspiration of *Sturm und Drang* and the dignity, restraint, and enduring beauty of Classicism sprang the loftiest utterances of the German spirit.

Schiller too, though never attaining the serenity of Goethe at his best, was also matured by the touch of Classicism, and in his *Wallenstein* trilogy he attempted with considerable success to combine the characteristics of Greek and Shakespearean tragedy. The same happy combination is achieved, though a bit less impressively, in his later dramas *Maria Stuart* (1800) and *Die Braut von Messina* (1803). After that, Schiller abandoned his fruitful experiment. He wrote to Goethe: *"mit den griechischen Dingen ist es eben eine missliche Sache auf unserm Theater"* (freely translated, "The concern with Greek forms has been an unfortunate thing for our theatre") and devoted himself thenceforth to works of unabashed Romanticism.

While the Classical interlude in German literature affected few writers beyond the giants Goethe and Schiller, its influence was far-reaching. Not only did it prove to be the maturing ingredient in the poetic growth of the two greatest writers, but it also led to the most successful merging of the Classic and the Romantic in any European literature. Furthermore, it opened the way for an understanding and appreciation of the Classics as such by divorcing them from the stiff, artificial Neo-Classicism of the *Grand Siècle*. After Goethe's tribute to Greece in the Helen of Troy scene in *Faust,* Part II, the culture of ancient Hellas no longer needed the refining dogmatism of the French Academy to shine forth in its truest glory.

V. THE HEIGHT OF THE ROMANTIC MOVEMENT (1780-1850)

It has already been pointed out that the various phases of German literature are usually closely tied with political developments on the European scene. Thus it is to be expected that the career of Napoleon would have been of particular significance in shaping the literary forces of the early nineteenth century into the movement known as Romanticism. The tenets and salient attributes of this movement have already been described in Chapter 16, and we have seen how many of these phenomena were already manifested in the *Sturm und Drang* phase of German literature. The principal effect of the Napoleonic Wars on literature in Germany, therefore, was to concentrate these forces already at large and to focus them on a common enemy. Because of the extreme despotism of the individual German states, writers within those confines had always been severely limited in their opportunities for political expression. With revolution in the air, German writers of the late eighteenth century could deliver themselves of only the most personalized or the most vaguely general of revolutionary sentiments for fear of stern reprisal on the part of their governments. Part of the excessive emotionalism of the *Sturm und Drang* is readily attributable to the frustration of authors burning to be more specific, forceful, and local in their sentiments for freedom and political reform, and being unable to do so for fear of the ever-present hand of censorship.

With the coming of Napoleon all this was changed. In the face of the ever-expanding French Empire, patriotic nationalism in Germany was no longer questionable. Napoleon became the villain who threatened to extinguish German life and could be used as the scapegoat for all the hitherto repressed political feelings of socially conscious writers.[4] After the final defeat of the French emperor at Waterloo, it became evident to everyone that Europe was entering a new era in which the national reorganization of the continent was to be the principal order of business.

After the scourge of Napoleonism was removed and new political horizons were in the making, a new spirit of emotional freedom swept over Europe, bringing with it many significant developments in the other creative arts. Not all of this creation was specifically political, to be sure, but it partook of the spirit of expanding political horizons to reach new heights of intellectual and emotional expression. The most important of these developments took place in the fields of literature, philosophy, and music.

[4] It must not be thought, however, that Napoleon was universally hated within Germany. At the beginning of his career he had many friends and supporters who, like Goethe, made the common mistake of regarding him as being a true son of the French Revolution. It was only after his ruthless ambition became obvious that he became generally hated and feared.

A. *Romantic Literature*

The Classical interlude in late eighteenth-century German literature proved to be just a brief calm between two Romantic storms. With the opening of the nineteenth century came a new surge of Romantic writing, less rebellious and unfocused than the outpourings of the *Sturm und Drang,* but no less individualistic and emotionally unfettered. Flagbearer of the new Romanticism was the Berlin *Athenaeum,* published by August W. and Friedrich Schlegel. The brothers Schlegel, the elder of whom had made the most distinguished translations of Shakespeare's plays to appear in any language, acted as the critics and high priests of the movement, and their *Athenaeum* became the bible of all aspiring writers of the time. Not the least worthy achievement of the magazine was its transcending of the limits of mere critical evaluation to develop the art of interpretive writing. By its lucid and penetrating analyses of literary works, the *Athenaeum* did much to bridge the gap between author and reader and to make the literate public more acquainted with the aims and methods of the creative artist.

Although the general materials and characteristics of German Romantic literature were little different from those of France, there are certain literary forms that are characteristically German and which must have brief mention here. Most distinguished of these was the *Lied* (or short lyric poem), which is somewhat differentiated from the lyric poetry of other nations by its folkloric simplicity and its almost inevitable wedding with musical expression. Springing directly from the eighteenth-century revival of interest in folk poetry and spurred by the collections of *Volkslieder* of Arnim and Brentano from 1805 to 1808 in *Des Knaben Wunderhorn (The Youth's Cornucopia),* the *Lied* was perhaps the most satisfying of all the aspects of German

Romanticism. The *Lieder* of Goethe, Heine, Eichendorff, Mörike, Chamisso Müller, Heyse, and dozens of others have an emotional poignancy and a subtlety-in-simplicity that is entirely unique in the field of lyric poetry. Wedded to the music of Schubert, Schumann, Brahms, or Hugo Wolf, these *Lieder* constitute an aesthetic experience unsurpassed by anything in the field of creative art.

Another literary form closely related to the *Lied* was the *Märchen,* or folk story. A *Lied* in prose, the *Märchen* found its most effective expression in the writings of J. L. Tieck and the famous fairy tales of Wilhelm and Jakob Grimm. A later development of this taste for the folk tale was the reawakening of interest in ancient and medieval Germanic legend as expressed in *Lohengrin, Tannhäuser,* and *The Ring of Nibelungs* of the composer Richard Wagner.

Influential in its effect on other literatures was the German Gothic tale. Though the form itself was one of the many eighteenth-century importations from England, it was given a considerable fullness of development in nineteenth-century Germany. The Gothic tale is one which is based upon the elements of the weird, the suspenseful, the fantastic, and often the horrible. It had its most characteristic expression in the hands of E. T. W. Hoffmann (1776-1822) and the so-called Heidelberg school, whose writings often found imitation in the short stories of Edgar Allan Poe.

Finally, there was the German drama which, having been revived during the *Sturm und Drang,* now reached its apex in the later work of Schiller and Goethe. In Schiller's *Die Jungfrau von Orleans* (1801), a play concerning the life of Joan of Arc, and his *Wilhelm Tell* (1804) we have the highest expression of the drama of political idealism, while in Goethe's monumental *Faust* is found the greatest of philosophical plays. In its combination of the Classical and the Romantic, of the political and the individual, of the sublime and the folkloric, *Faust* achieves in a single work a lofty exegesis of the entire Romantic Movement.

The latter days of German Romanticism, following the death of Goethe in 1832, were marked by the reawakening of the revolutionary spirit in a movement known as Young Germany. Fired by the July Rebellion of 1830 in Paris and continuing through the People's Uprisings of 1848, the Young Germany movement can be interpreted largely as being the literary manifestation of a widespread and deepening desire for German national unity. For a while after the defeat of Napoleon in 1815, it had seemed as though this long-cherished dream of One Germany might be achieved, but as time went on and the conservative policies of the wily Prince Metternich continued to keep Germany in a state of divided impotence, a feeling of patriotic restlessness developed which finally resulted in the abortive and frustrating rebellions of 1848.

Much of the literature emanating from this generation of political tensions was professedly anti-Romantic. It ridiculed the sentimental nature worship and the self-absorbed individualism of earlier days and turned its attention to social reform, to polemic journalism, and to political philosophizing. Much of what was produced was ephemeral and mediocre, but since it also prompted some of the best writings of Heinrich Heine and since it led also to the maturing of the young Richard Wagner, it cannot be written off as a totally sterile period in the annals of German art.

B. *Romantic Philosophy*

A second great development of German Romanticism was its philosophy. For the most part individualistic and moral in tone, German Romantic philosophy both spurred the prevailing desire for freedom and at the same time exuded a spirit of moral idealism which kept that individualism from degenerating into selfish license. First and greatest of the German idealists was Immanuel Kant (1721-1804), whose writings formed a transitional link between the Enlightenment and Romanticism. A product of eighteenth-century rationalism, Kant was a distinguished physicist and physical geographer as well as a philosopher, and it was his long career in the laboratory which convinced him that God was to be understood more clearly through the medium of natural phenomena than through the dogma of theology. But as a man of science, he also had to concede that God was simply an hypothesis, and that man in his rational worldly experience could never have direct proof of the existence of a Deity. What we cannot prove, therefore, we must accept by intuition. Man's moral sense, his innate sense of goodness, his striving for values greater than those in the realm of the five senses indicate the existence of a Higher Law which operates within man as a "categorical imperative," tempering his purely material and selfish urges and subordinating them to moral and spiritual considerations.

Kant's lofty idealism was followed by the patriotic individualism of J. G. Fichte (1762-1814), who saw his master's "categorical imperative" as being not merely an intellectual principle but also a dynamic force compelling man, as an individual, to drive himself toward ever higher achievement. An ardent patriot, he applied this principle of dynamic propulsion to the Germanic spirit itself and thereby did much to encourage the resurgence of German nationalism which accompanied the wars against Napoleon.

While Fichte was transmuting the ideas of Immanuel Kant into a fiery nationalism, Friedrich W. J. Schelling (1775-1854) was developing them into a quiet, contemplative philosophy of nature. Like Spinoza and Kant, with their concepts of an all-pervading Higher Law, Schelling believed in a *Weltseele* (World Soul) which embraced all things and which is most clearly demonstrable in the world of the senses by the visible phenomena of nature. He furthermore saw an absolute identity between the individual and nature, both being partial manifestations of the World Soul which embraces and unifies all phenomena. In this mystical nature philosophy we see mirrored much of the pantheistic spirit of nineteenth-century Romanticism, and it is not surprising to find that the writings of Schelling were as influential outside of Germany (especially on such writers as Coleridge, Shelley, and Emerson) as they were in their own land.

Equally idealistic but somewhat less ethereal was the thought of Georg Wilhelm Friedrich Hegel (1770-1831). One of the most influential philosophers of the nineteenth century, Hegel proclaimed a system of historical evolution that perfectly complemented the studies in the origin of species of his day and helped pave the way for such definitive later evolutionists as Charles Darwin and Karl Marx. The heart of Hegelian metaphysics lies in his concept of progress through struggle. Each force (thesis) in the universe has its counter-force (antithesis). From the clash of these opposing forces comes a new element (synthesis), which combines the stronger and better aspects of the erstwhile antagonists. Thus society, like individual organisms, is in constant turmoil, but this ferment leads not to chaos and disintegration but rather to the survival of the best and the destruction of the undesirable. It is clear that such a view of man's progress through the ages must be highly optimistic, but it is equally clear that, in its acceptance of struggle as natural and in its equation of the survival of the strong with the survival of the good, it does much to destroy the moral idealism of the earlier Kantians in favor of an acceptance of evil as a necessary propulsive in the relentless evolution of society toward ever more exalted levels of existence.

Quite different from the Hegelian optimism is the gloomy thought of Arthur Schopenhauer (1788-1860). A Kantian in that he accepts the hypothesis of a universal moral spirit which transcends the values of reason and the visible world, Schopenhauer goes on to show that the conscious world, the world of the intellect, is but a poor shadow of the real world, which exists in the Will. All perceptions and reactions actually proceed from within, from the Will, and all external processes are but the rationalizations of the desires of subconscious forces. The Will is unalterable; man cannot change his basic nature by reason—he can only slightly temper or alter the outward signs of his inner promptings. Furthermore, the promptings of the Will spring from its own sense of inadequacy and suffering; a perfectly satisfied inner nature would remain serene and in a state of complete rest. Therefore, the urges of men must always spring from suffering, and since man's reason and his conscious existence are powerless to alter these basic urges, it is evident that man must be forever unhappy until his will is satisfied by that perfect peace which can arrive only in death. Although attracting little attention until after the middle of the nineteenth century, the philosophy of Schopenhauer ultimately became one of the most important sources of modern pessimistic thought. Its influence is particularly evident in the work of Sigmund Freud, whose psychological theories have exerted so powerful an effect on twentieth-century life, while its impact upon the arts is best seen in Richard Wagner's great music-drama *Tristan und Isolde* and in the monumental novels of Thomas Mann.

C. *Romantic Music*

Perhaps the most satisfactory of all the developments of Romanticism in Germany was its music. From the time when Beethoven, in composing his Eroica symphony (1803), deliberately took a "new path" of musical expression, German symphonic and operatic writing veered sharply from the Classical formalism of Haydn and Mozart and took on the unmistakable characteristics of Romantic individualism. The brooding introspection of the late Beethoven string quartets, the folkloric themes in the nationalistic operas of Weber, and the exquisite *Lieder* of Schubert are as different in atmosphere and expression from the music of the eighteenth-century Viennese composers as the latter had been from the baroque contrapuntal style of Johann Sebastian Bach.

Nor did the stream of colorful, intensely personal music show any signs of slackening with the second or third generations of Romantic composers. Schumann and Mendelssohn had none of the profundity of Beethoven and only partly matched the phenomenal lyric gifts of Schubert, but their symphonies and songs formed a pleasant, ingratiating interlude between the early Romantics and the giants Brahms and Wagner. And even after the generation distinguished by the powerful symphonies of the former and the towering music dramas of the master of Bayreuth, the Romantic current still flowed fully in the works of Richard Strauss, Hugo Wolf, and the young Arnold Schönberg. Furthermore, German music acted as the leading influence upon composers in other countries, so that it can be said that virtually all of the Western music of the nineteenth century has its deepest roots in German soil. All in all, Germany can look with pride upon the music of its Romantic composers as being among the very few creations of man "not of an age, but for all time."

VI. THE TRIUMPH OF NATIONALISM (1848-1870)

The period between 1848 and 1870 was a slack one in German literature and, to a large extent, in the kindred arts. The revolutionary days of 1830 and 1848 had not established liberal principles in government after all, nor had they brought about the national unity the great mass of the German people so earnestly desired. Under the circumstances, the optimism of early Romanticism became thoroughly dissipated, and the urge to create great works seemed to have fled.[5] It was not until after the successful termination of the Franco-Prussian War (1870-1871) that the German creative spirit took renewed confidence and began once again to function with any suggestion of the fertility which had obtained before 1848.

Politically, however, the period was more productive of decisive activity. Though liberalism had suffered a serious setback in Germany in 1848, nationalism (which was prevalent among both conservatives and liberals) was far from being a dead issue. By 1860 Prussia, under Wilhelm I, had begun to take steps toward establishing its ascendancy among German nations, and in 1862 made a long stride toward the achievement of that end with the installation of Otto von Bismarck as chief minister (and virtual dictator). Bismarck, though a conservative, nevertheless took an aggressive policy from the beginning. What Germany needed, he announced, was not the program of patriotic speeches and pious resolutions that had resulted in the fiasco of 1848, but rather a policy of "blood and iron" that would obtain by force what intellectual abstractions had formerly failed to produce.

Accordingly Bismarck, following the principle that the end justifies the means, built up a large and highly efficient army, and waged brief but fruitful wars against Denmark (1864) and Austria (1866). The former resulted in an extension of Prussian territory, the latter in the crushing of the

[5] A major exception to this statement is found in Richard Wagner, whose greatest music dramas were conceived during this period. It is significant, however, that with the exception of *Die Meistersinger von Nürnberg*, these intensely nationalistic compositions all reflect the deepest pessimism.

greatest foe of Prussian supremacy. The next step was the incorporating of some twenty-five important German states into the closely knit North German Confederation (1867), which left only Austria, Bavaria, Württemberg, Baden, and Hesse-Darmstadt as independent entities. Then, in 1870-1871 came the war against France, which enlisted the unincorporated south German states as allies of Prussia and, save in Austria, broke down the spirit of inter-Germanic jealousy in a surge of patriotic feeling fed still further by complete victory over the French.

The final step was made on January 18, 1871, when King Wilhelm I of Prussia was proclaimed Emperor of Germany. The long struggle for unification was over. That unification was not complete, to be sure, for Austria still remained outside the Empire, and some of the southern states, though part of the federation, yet retained the fiction of independent monarchy. But for all practical purposes, the more than three hundred autonomous political units of the eighteenth century had finally been gathered together under one strong, practical government. The long-cherished dream of poets and philosophers had been realized: there was a united Germany at last. But that Germany under the imperial banner of the Hohenzollerns was far from being the liberal brotherhood of their hopeful dream. Furthermore, by the time union finally did come about, most of these literary dreamers were already dead, and with them had passed the Golden Age of German creative art.

SUGGESTED READINGS

(Place of publication, when not mentioned, is New York.)

E. K. Bennett, *A History of the German Novelle* (Cambridge, England, 1934); J. Bithell (ed.), *Germany, a Companion to German Studies* (London, 1937); W. A. Braun, *Types of Weltschmerz in German Poetry* (1905); W. H. Bruford, *Germany in the Eighteenth Century* (Cambridge, England, 1935); E. M. Butler, *The Tyranny of Greece over Germany* (Cambridge, England, 1935); K. Francke, *A History of German Literature* (1916); G. P. Gooch, *Germany and the French Revolution* (1920); J. H. Hayes, *A Political and Cultural History of Modern Europe* (1936 et seq.); C. Hentschel, *The Byronic Teuton: Aspects of German Pessimism, 1800-1933* (London, 1940); L. W. Kahn, *Social Ideals in German Literature, 1770-1830* (1938); G. Lichtheim, *Marxism: An Historical and Critical Study* (1961); G. Mann, *The History of Germany since 1789* (1968); K. Popper, *The Open Society and Its Enemies: Hegel and Marx* (1926); A. W. Porterfield, *An Outline of German Romanticism, 1766-1866* (Boston, 1914); H. S. Reiss, ed., *Political Thought of the German Romantics 1793-1815* (1956); J. G. Robertson, *A History of German Literature* (1925); J. J. Saunders, *The Age of Revolution* (1949); W. Silz, *Early German Romanticism* (Cambridge, Mass., 1929); O. Walzel, *German Romanticism* (1932); R. M. Wernaer, *Romanticism and the Romantic School in Germany* (1910); G. T. Whitney and D. F. Bowers, eds., *The Heritage of Kant* (1962); L. A. Willoughby, *The Classical Age of German Literature, 1740-1805* (1926); L. A. Willoughby, *The Romantic Movement in Germany* (1926).

chapter 21

POST-NAPOLEONIC FRANCE: THE RISE OF NATURALISM

I. THE NATURALISTIC ATTITUDE

In contrast to the burning idealism of the French Revolution, with its faith in democracy, its hopes for eternal human progress, and its inspiring slogan of *Liberté, Egalité, Fraternité,* post-Napoleonic France presented a picture of almost unrelieved pessimism and despair. With the return of the ineffectual Bourbons, the hopefulness of the early Romantics soured rapidly into a frustrated *Weltschmerz* (world-sorrow), which became more and more cynical and neurotic as the century progressed. By the eighties this spirit of defeatism had driven some of the more extreme intellectuals into the bitter and quite unromantic movement known as literary naturalism.

In contrast to the sentimental hopefulness of Rousseau or Chateaubriand or to the Encyclopaedists' faith in eternal progress through human reason, the literary naturalists came to view man as being only a helpless creature of chance, a mere chemical phenomenon in a chaotic and meaningless universe. They conceived of man's existence as being without form, without ideals, without morality, and even without God. The wretched human animal finds himself blown about meaninglessly, like a tumbleweed on the desert, by natural forces over which he has no control. A victim of the inscrutable complexities of heredity and environment, he flounders about helplessly in a world which regards his bewildered struggle with complete and utter indifference. His life is at most a chance series of biochemical responses to stimuli he cannot understand save in the deceiving language of theology. He tries to give himself importance by talking in terms of his soul, his immortality, and his anthropomorphic God. To the naturalist, this attempt to give life spiritual significance is madness; as Zola put it, "Nothing is occult; men are but phenomena and the conditions of phenomena."

The cause of this attitude of pessimistic determinism in Europe lay clearly in the continued failure of the democratic experiment in France and in the simultaneous, but unrelated, rise of scientific inquiry, with its especially disturbing developments in the field of evolutionary biology. It will be necessary to examine both of these factors in some detail in order to understand the complex ramifications of literary naturalism.

II. FRANCE AFTER NAPOLEON

The pessimistic attitude out of which naturalism grew can be traced back to the downfall of Bonaparte in 1815. After the Napoleonic dream of empire had turned into the nightmare of the Hundred Days and Waterloo, France found herself in desperation turning backward to the sticky mess of Bourbonism. The glorious revolution had been an abortive shambles; Napoleon, "the saviour of the people," had turned out to be a brilliant destroyer. Since the 1812 rout of the Grand Army in Russia, realistic thinkers had been shaking their heads and predicting a bad end. Now their worst fears had been realized in the restoration of the monarchy under Louis XVIII, a timid and intellectually vacuous Bourbon even less inspiring than his deposed brother Louis XVI.

The new king had sense enough, however, to realize that even a defeated and spiritually bankrupt France would not tolerate another royal despot. He thereupon insisted upon a constitutional monarchy that seemingly preserved some of the ideals of the Revolution while restoring the traditional prestige of a ruling family. But this concession on Louis' part did not satisfy the liberals. The symbol of monarchy was intolerable in any form, and the Bourbons in the past had shown themselves to be the most ineffectual of rulers. To add to this feeling of disaffection, the Napoleonic legend began to grow apace soon after the former Emperor had been deported to St. Helena. Sentimental liberals began to identify him with the spirit of 1789, to forget his opportunistic despotism, and to sheathe him in an aura of sentimental mysticism as a martyr to the cause of human freedom. Such legends flourish mightily in defeated countries, and France, fallen from a pinnacle in the European family of nations, became more and more restive under the plodding mediocrity of Louis XVIII and his reactionary successor Charles X. Particularly incensed were the young intellectuals who, unborn during the Revolution and too immature to remember the Empire, blew up the Napoleonic myth to absurd proportions and became increasingly voluble and aggressive in demanding a change. They clamored for a re-establishment of French honor by reannexing the lands lost to the allies in 1815, and when Charles X in 1830 tried to still the uproar by a pointless diversional campaign against Algeria, the insurgents took possession of Paris and forced the king to abdicate.

Once victorious, the rebels made the oft-repeated mistake of dissipating their victory in factional dispute. While the Bonapartists and the Republicans were engaged in cutting each others' throats, the moderate constitutional party created a successor to Charles X in another Bourbon, Louis-Philippe. Louis-Philippe, Duke of Orleans, came from a more bourgeois and liberal branch of the family than his cousin Charles X. He had favored the Revolution of 1789, and in 1830 he tried hard to capture the liberals by paying lip-service to their ideals. He set himself up as king of France "by the grace of God and the will of the nation," restored the revolutionary tricolor as the national flag, encouraged industry, and proclaimed that as king he would "reign but not govern." But no amount of good intentions and righteous proclamation could obscure the fact that Louis-Philippe was a weak and plodding mediocrity, a muddle-headed symbol of the outmoded institution of Bourbonism. His policies were popular only with the wealthy industrialists. Old-line legitimists found him too bourgeois and revolutionary, while on the other end of the scale Republicans and the growing Socialist element found him too conservative and undemocratic. Reformers considered him unprogressive, and chauvinistic Bonapartists regarded his "peace at any price" policy as an insult to the national honor. Altogether, the compromise regime of this well-meaning Bourbon succeeded only in antagonizing nearly every political group in the country.

In 1848 Parisian restlessness came to a head. On February 22 and 23, a crowd of students and workingmen rioted in the Place de la Concorde. Imprudently, the king's minister, Guizot, ordered troops to fire on the crowd, and twenty-three persons were killed. This rash act so fanned revolutionary fervor that on February 24 Louis-Philippe decided he had had enough and abdicated. The Second French Republic was proclaimed the same day.

The most violent and effective group in the "revolution" of 1848 were the Socialists, under Louis Blanc, and once the Second Republic was established it was Blanc's party which assumed direction. An elaborate program of social reform was instituted with such features as universal manhood suffrage and co-operative industrial associations sponsored by the government. The latter experiment failed from the outset because of concerted opposition from private business; the former backfired when the first general election returned a National Assembly composed largely of moderates. Then, in the first presidential election in December, 1848, the people overwhelmingly acclaimed as chief executive Prince Louis-Napoleon, nephew of the Emperor. The magic name of Bonaparte had dazzled France once more; a return to former days of glory was eagerly anticipated. No one in 1848 realized that within three years the newly-elected messiah would, like his uncle before him, betray the Republic and proclaim himself Emperor of the French.

Prince Louis-Napoleon, one of the slipperiest and easily the most vilified of all nineteenth-century politicians, had led a career of brazen opportunism before he was elected to the presidency in 1848. Exiled by the restoration of the Bourbons in 1815, "Napoleon the Little," as Victor Hugo ungraciously called him, had kept the Napoleonic legend alive by writing flamboyant books and pamphlets in exile, and by noisily but ingloriously joining the revolutionary Carbonari movement in Italy in 1831. Twice he also tried unsuccessfully to re-enter France during the regime of Louis-Philippe. On the second occasion he was imprisoned in the fortress of Ham, from which he escaped disguised as a workingman and made his way to England. Here he managed to keep his name before the public as an avowed symbol of "law and order," and in June, 1848, while still in England, he was elected to the National Constituent Assembly as a tribute to the Napoleonic legend he himself had done so much to foster. From there it was but a step to election as president.

In his three years as chief executive, Louis-Napoleon tried to appear democratic while carefully taking every means to foster reaction. He flattered the workingman with speeches but favored the employer with laws; he turned the schools back to the Catholics; he fought a law which disenfranchised one-third of the electorate by playing on democratic fear of a very possible monarchist reaction. When the monarchist-dominated assembly refused to repeal the election law, Louis-Napoleon on December 2, 1851, executed a daring *coup d'état* by proclaiming himself temporary dictator pending a plebiscite authorizing a revision of the constitution. On December 21, the electorate overwhelmingly supported the president, who was thereby enabled to institute a government which gave him sweeping executive powers. On December 2, 1852, exactly one year after his *coup d'état,* Louis-Napoleon proclaimed the Second Empire with himself as emperor under the name of Napoleon III. And so history had repeated itself, and the second French experiment with republican government had ended in an imperial *coup d'état* by a pseudo-democrat named Napoleon. Further resemblance between the regimes of the two Napoleons is found only in France's humiliating downfall eighteen years later; the power and military glory of the Little Corporal was almost ridiculously absent in the decadent era of Napoleon III.

In the eighteen years of the Second Empire France became, according to a current phrase, "a sickroom in which people spoke with lowered voices." Making the usual conciliatory democratic gestures, "Napoleon the Little" nevertheless turned France into a police state with the usual apparatus of secret police, wholesale political imprisonment, and abrogation of civil rights. His foreign affairs were even more unfortunate. To divert attention from the sorry conditions at home, Napoleon miscast himself in the unrewarding role of military leader, expanded the French Empire in Algeria and the Far East, supported Britain and Turkey in the successful but unsensational Crimean War, and meddled in Italian affairs by aiding liberal agitation for a unified Italy. This last adventure was a great mistake, for it lost Napoleon his Catholic support and also antagonized liberals by resulting in an Italy that, while unified, was no freer than before.

In the face of growing dissatisfaction at home, Napoleon continued to blunder abroad. He tried to install a puppet, the Archduke Maximilian of Austria, as "Emperor of Mexico" (1862-1867) and succeeded only in infuriating the United States and lowering French prestige in the eyes of the world. Then when Prussia triumphed over Austria in 1866, Napoleon's diplomatic intrigues to gain Belgium for France resulted only in his contemptuous defeat at the hands of the Prussian premier Bismarck. Finally, in 1870, came the greatest humiliation of all: Bismarck cynically provoked France into declaring war on Prussia. Theoretically, it should have been an easy thing for France to defeat her enemy, who ranked at the time as no better than a second-rate power. But Bismarck realized, as most of the world did not, that France was in a state of somnolent decadence. Her army was weak, her spirit was dead, her allies non-existent, and her moral stamina dissipated with long years of Napoleonic backstairs intrigue. Defeat came rapidly at Sedan on September 4, 1870; a defeat which was to hang heavy on France for more than a generation to come. Napoleon III was made a German prisoner, the Second Empire was declared finished, while the war dragged on to an anti-climactic close. By January, 1871, the Prussians were in Paris and, after nearly a century of experiment in the cause of political liberty, France had reached the nadir of humiliation and despair.

III. THE GROWTH OF SCIENTIFIC INQUIRY

Though the political misfortunes of nineteenth-century France were enough in themselves to dissipate all romantic hopes, the pessimism of the intellectuals was further deepened by the growing spirit of scientific inquiry, particularly in the matter of evolution. During the Enlightenment of the eighteenth century, such philosophers as Locke, Diderot, Helvetius, and Holbach had pointed out the similarity between man and animal, and such natural historians as De Bonnet and Lamarck had gone still further in showing evidences of mutation and development in animal species, validating the assumption that profound changes take place over the course of many generations and even suggesting that all animal forms had a common organic origin. We often think of Darwin as the "father" of evolution; actually the publication of *The Origin of Species* in 1859 served largely to crystallize and popularize scientific ideas that had long been promulgated.

Of fundamental importance in Darwin's work is the theory of "natural selection." This theory maintains that, in the struggle for existence, survival is most likely for those organisms which deviate from the norm toward a greater adaptation to their environment. Through this adaptation, these exceptional organisms develop characteristics which they pass on to their posterity and which give their particular species superiority—and even possible mastery—over bodies less well adapted to the battle of life. Thus, in a highly competitive universe, only the fittest survive, and this survival is dependent upon the outstripping of rival organisms even to the point of eliminating them from the race altogether.

The impact of this mechanistic, amoral, predatory conception of man's relation to the universe upon received standards of Christian theology was, of course, devastating. Not since the time of Copernicus had any scientific theory so profoundly disturbed the faith of the Western world. Darwinism became the battleground of the Great Debate of the nineteenth century. The details of this controversy need not be examined here; it will be sufficient to note that from the welter of acrimonious discussions, manifestoes, and overheated polemics arose an entirely new body of thought on the phenomenon of man. Eventually, of course, all but the most fanatic on both sides modified their positions to admit the possibility that religious and scientific truths could be coexistent, but not before many new and arresting concepts of man's nature and responsibilities had been added to the treasury of human thought.

One of the most influential thinkers on this subject was Auguste Comte (1798-1857). Even before Darwin, this brilliant French philosopher had been attempting to reconcile the age-long controversy between reason and faith by advocating that the two be combined to form a new theology of Positivism, with mankind as its God. Comte demonstrated that the history of man's thinking has shown an evolutionary tendency to adapt itself increasingly to the needs of human existence. Thought has passed through three stages, he pointed out: the *theological,* in which man's ideas and reactions are governed by *authority;* the *metaphysical,* in which man begins to speculate abstractly and independently; and finally the *positivistic,* in which all speculation finally can be based upon demonstrable, scientific fact. In the first stage, man attributes all universal phenomena to supernatural forces—a god or a multiplicity of anthropomorphic gods—which represent to him the summation of power, wisdom, and authority. In the second stage, he discards the idea of gods in human form and looks upon the universe as being motivated by natural laws or by undefined natural forces. With the third, or positivistic, stage, however, nothing further is left to speculation. Mysticism, superstitions, and even shrewd assumptions disappear as man arrives at a knowledge of the universe that is exact, demonstrable, and predictable. The very causes of all phenomena will be understood in scientific terms and with mathematical precision.

Although Comte felt that it was unlikely that man would soon reach the positivistic stage in all branches of knowledge, he did not doubt that such development would finally be attained. Some sciences, he pointed out, have already reached this ultimate state: mathematics, astronomy, physics, chemistry. Biology is approaching positivism. Only the science of everyday living is seriously laggard. Man has as yet but little exact knowledge of his own habits, environment, prejudices, and taboos. Until such matters are studied and understood with laboratory accuracy, humanity will remain groping in the dark, ignorant of the very phenomena which affect it most directly. In advocating such a study, Comte laid the groundwork for what has come to be known as "social science," and it is entirely appropriate that he has since been generally recognized as the "father" of sociology.

In literature, two of the most important disciples of Comte are Charles Augustin Sainte-Beuve and Hippolyte Taine. The former, a critic of great stature and influence, introduced the method of viewing an author's work against his biographical background and thereby presented social environment as an important factor in evaluating literary ideas and imagination. Taine, in the introduction to his *History of English Literature* (1864) held that literature cannot be divorced from the age in which it was written and that, like the age itself, it is conditioned by "race, moment, and milieu." More and more as the evolutionary idea developed, it became apparent that literature to be worthy of serious consideration must be based upon a thorough study of social forces.

Another powerful voice to influence literary naturalism was that of Karl Marx. A radical greatly disappointed by the failure of the democratic revolution of 1848 in his native Germany, Marx worked out a social theory called "dialectical materialism" based partly on the Hegelian system of *thesis, antithesis,* and *synthesis* and partly on a concept of continual social evolution. To Hegel, all reality evolves from the clash of two directly opposite forces (thesis and antithesis) producing a new force (synthesis). Marx applied this formula to society, holding that only from a clash between the "haves" (bourgeois capital) and the "have-nots" (proletarian labor) can the ultimate good of mankind be produced in the form of a classless, unpropertied world in which society as a whole and not the individual is the common unit. Only in an international collectivist society, he held, can complete social equality be attained. Government, which exists only to protect private property, can therefore be abolished, for there will be no private property to protect. The state will belong to all the people, nations will disappear, and throughout the world all men will labor side by side, in universal brotherhood, gaining satisfaction not in accumulating a personal fortune but in the joy of working for the common good.

Naturally, Marx was not such a sentimental Utopian as to believe this blissful synthesis could be attained by proclamation. Rather, a long spiral of social evolution had to be worked out. The first step was to foster an industrialized society with a consequent strong capitalist bourgeois class. This would automatically result in the reciprocal creation of a proletariat, or working class, who would be depressed and exploited by the forces of bourgeois capital until they were ripe for rebellion against their masters. Step two called for a successful world-revolt of the workers, followed by a dictatorship of the proletariat, during which time all private property and all individualistic activity would be ruthlessly suppressed. When this struggle of *thesis* and *antithesis* had ended, the result would be a synthesis of a classless and propertyless world without government, nationalism, or class distinctions.

If the ultimate stage in Marx's dialectic convinced relatively few persons, it nevertheless had a profound influence in focusing attention upon the struggle between capital and labor and in elevating the study of economic forces to an important position in the process of furthering man's understanding. The working class, in particular, took on an unprecedented importance in social thinking, and the concept of life as being a struggle based on economic factors permeated the consciousness of even the most conservative minds. Marxian influence was felt particularly in literature, where the economic aspects of life could no longer be ignored and the lives of the poor could no longer be dismissed patronizingly as "short and simple annals." Literature is essentially a record of struggle, and in Marx's projection of the war of the classes most nineteenth-century authors saw new seas to be explored, seas in which some writers fancied was forming the wave of the future.

IV. NATURALISM IN LITERATURE [1]

In the previous sections of this chapter we have outlined the political reverses of nineteenth-century France and the simultaneous growth of the scientific attitude toward society. The result of both of these developments upon French literature was to produce an attitude of the deepest gloom. To the destruction of the romantic concept of man's ultimate rise to perfection in a democratic world, science added her assurance that man was but an animal still in a relatively early stage of societal evolution. That men like Comte and Marx saw an eventually happy dénouement (though for different reasons) in man's struggles made little impression upon the writers. The important consideration to them was the present, and man in the present was preda-

---

[1] The following section has been excerpted from Rod W. Horton and Herbert W. Edwards, *Backgrounds of American Literary Thought,* Chapter XI, with the permission of the publishers, Appleton-Century-Crofts.

tory, depressed, and bewildered. He had lost all of his theological and most of his metaphysical props and found himself, a creature of still unpredictable chemical action and reaction, adrift in a world governed by still undefined natural forces. Furthermore, he discovered he was engaged in class warfare, a ruthless and cynical economic struggle. That the natural forces would eventually be defined and the economic struggle resolved was small comfort; the battle between what Zola called "the Fat and the Thin" left little taste for a contemplation of the millennium.

It is difficult to say just when the spirit of naturalism began to creep into French literature; perhaps it was with Balzac and his celebrated preface to his *Comédie Humaine* (1842). Taking his cue from natural history, Balzac suggested that human beings, like animals, are the products of their environment and develop individual characteristics according to the life around them. The materials of a good novelist lie therefore in society.

French society is the real historian, and I have merely tried to guide its pen. By taking an inventory of its virtues and vices, selecting the most important of social occurrences, and forming types by the combination of several similarly constituted characters, I have perhaps managed to write the history of morals which so many historians have forgotten to do.... The immeasurable scope of a plan which embraces not only a history and criticism of society, but also an analysis of its evils and an exposition of its principles, justifies me, so I believe, in giving my work the title ... *The Human Comedy.*

Flaubert too, in his correspondence with George Sand and in his *Madame Bovary* attempts to take the "scientific" approach. An artist ought not to appear in his work, he says; he should observe his characters objectively, try to get inside their souls and see them as they are. *Madame Bovary* was to be composed

without a single agitated page, and not a single observation of the author.... No lyricism, no observations; personality of the author absent. It will be dismal to read; there will be atrocious things in it—wretchedness, fetidness.

The brothers Goncourt also conceived of the novel in terms of science. "The novel of today is made with documents narrated or copied from nature, just as history is made with written documents," they declared in their journal in 1865, and they proceeded to put this principle into practice by gathering voluminous information upon the life of the Second Empire, showing a marked favoritism toward the sordid and the sensational.

But the first thoroughgoing exponent of "scientific naturalism" was Emile Zola. Fascinated by the Darwinians, Comte, Marx, and Taine, Zola enthusiastically presented himself as an evolutionist, a positivist, and a materialist. For the artist to paint life, he must first seek the explanation of life in science and the "natural evolution of things." He proclaimed the "Experimental Novel" in which the author is a laboratory scientist, studying the reactions of his characters against the background of heredity and social environment. "We take man from the hands of the physiologist solely to solve scientifically the question of how men behave in society," he declared. In the volumes of his Rougon-Macquart series he studied the history of an unpleasant family during the period of Louis-Napoleon. Many critics at the time and since have regarded this series as cheap sensationalism for its own sake; actually the experiment was a sincere attempt to portray the decay of the bourgeoisie and the struggles of an emerging but brutal proletariat. The protagonist was society itself, from salon to coal mine, from mansion to brothel. There is no sentimentalizing, no promise of ultimate Utopia; the picture is one of unrelieved decadence, of an unregenerate middle-class society riding to political and moral destruction.

In this outline of the genesis of naturalism, we see anatomized the prevailing pessimism of the present age. Naturalism symptomizes the loss of individual dignity in a world grown smaller, more mechanized, more collectivistic; it removes from mankind most of the spiritual belief that formerly had served as a bulwark in times of adversity; it paints for the distant future only the most academic and improbable Utopias. In the late nineteenth century Matthew Arnold saw himself "standing between two worlds: one dead, the other powerless to be born." Henry Adams in 1905 looked sourly upon the dynamo and saw in it a symbol of Infinity, of a crazy, impersonal God leading the world into centrifugal chaos. So men have always thought at the end of an historical era, and yet the supposed death-throes of humanity have turned out to be the birth-pangs of another age. The world-spirit which fostered literary Naturalism may have been but a statement of temporary despair, or it may have been simultaneously the closing of an epoch and a step forward into a new and unpredictable cycle of world history.

SUGGESTED READINGS

(Place of publication, when not mentioned, is New York.)

FRENCH HISTORY AND THOUGHT

F. B. Artz, *France under the Bourbon Restoration* (1931), *Reaction and Revolution, 1814-1832* (1934); J. L. Dubreton, *The Restoration and the July Monarchy* (1929); C. J. H. Hayes, *A Political and Cultural History of Modern Europe* (1936 *et seq.*), *The Historical Evolution of Modern Nationalism* (1931); H. Laski, *The Rise of European Liberalism* (London, 1936); G. Ruggiero, *The History of European Liberalism* (1927); J. J. Saunders, *The Age of Revolution* (1949); F. A. Simpson, *The Rise of Louis Napoleon* (1909); F. A. Simpson, *Louis Napoleon and the Recovery of France* (1923); R. Soltau, *French Political Thought in the Nineteenth Century* (1931).

DARWINISM, MARXISM, NATURALISM

J. Barzun, *Darwin, Marx, Wagner—Critique of a Heritage* (1947); O. Cargill, *Intellectual America* (1941); J. Dewey, *The Influence of Darwin on Philosophy* (1960); R. Dumesnil, *Le Réalisme et le Naturalisme* (Paris, 1963); G. Himmelfarb, *Darwin and the Darwinian Revolution* (Gloucester, 1962); S. Hook, *Toward the Understanding of Karl Marx* (1936); S. E. Hyman, *The Tangled Bank: Darwin, Marx, Frazer, and Freud as Imaginative Writers* (1962); M. Josephson, *Zola* (1931); F. Meirung, *Karl Marx* (1936); H. B. Parkes, *Marxism: An Autopsy* (Boston, 1939); V. L. Parrington, *Main Currents in American Thought*, Vol. III (1932); G. Saintsbury, *History of a French Novel* (1919); P. B. Sears, *Charles Darwin* (1950); Robert Shafer, *Christianity and Naturalism* (New Haven, 1926); H. Taine, *History of English Literature* (1873).

chapter 22

RUSSIA

Because of its enormous area, the geography and climate of Russia can be briefly described only as an immense array of diversities and contrasts, from the bitter cold of the arctic plains to the balmy subtropical atmosphere of the regions bordering on the Black Sea. But most Russian authors whose works include references to environment have tended to concentrate on the bleaker aspects of the many provincial areas where treeless plains, poor soil, and rigorous winters have made life desperately difficult for the poor and depressing even for the upper classes. The desire "to go to Moscow," a leitmotif in Chekhov's *The Three Sisters,* is a dream of escape from the melancholy aspects of country life which this play presents.

The many rivers rise in the large marshes which have been Russia's best defenses from invasion as well as places of refuge for the oppressed. Three big river systems fostered commerce in early Russian history as well as the broad sociability for which Russians are noted. They also encouraged centers of commerce, four of which grew into the most prominent of the few cities in the country: Kiev on the Dnieper, Moscow on the Volga, and Novgorod and St.

Petersburg on the Volkov-Neva river system. In the main, the Russian population lives in small villages where agriculture is the principal means of livelihood. Communal land tenure dates back to the earliest days. In each village, sections of good, medium, and poor lands were parcelled out annually to each family in accordance with the number of "working hands." The prevalence of poor soil and bad management led to periodic famines which often lasted three years at a time.

The experience of living in a harsh and open country which is home to so much of the population seems to account for the peculiarities of the traditional Russian temperament. Necessarily hardy and used to suffering, the Russian is apt to be fatalistic about the troubles that befall him, and takes a kind of pride in his ability to withstand suffering. "Vynoslivost" is a commonly heard Russian word, which means "lasting a thing out." The Russian is also accustomed to space in his physical world and enjoys spaciousness in his thinking. He loves talk, especially of a philosophical sort, and conversation is more apt to consist of individually expressed thoughts and opinions than discussions in the European manner of individual contribution to a topic which concerns the entire group. He loves to wonder about the unknown, and is fascinated by theories of learning and science; but his mind is ultimately more spiritual than practical, more dreamy than exact. He dislikes being pinned down. His enjoyment of equivocation and inexactness has led Russia to be called "the country of evasion." His mind is very active but lacks a sense of proportion. Like the climate, he is given to extremes, and his violent moments of gusty and excessive enjoyment are counterbalanced by moods of dejection, gloom, and "black thoughts." In this combination of emotionalism and love of speculation lies "the Russian soul," which is both the preoccupation and one of the major appeals of Russian writers.

The early years of Russian history (865-1240) were dominated by European and Christian influences under the autocratic rule of a family of Viking ancestry.[1] From 1240 to 1480, the country was overrun by the Asiatic invasions of the Tartars, during which the feudal system was introduced. As a willing alternative to being carried off into slavery by the invaders, the peasants submitted as serfs to the control, taxation, and government of officer-squires. It was during this period that Moscow became the central capital by reason of the fact that it was entrusted by the Tartars with the general collection of tribute from the villages or communes, which were taxed as a whole. In each commune an elected elder was in charge of distribution of the land and collection of taxes, but he acted mainly as a manager for the king. Many of the peasants revolted from serfdom and migrated to the south where, as soldier-workers, they successfully resisted the Tartars. These so-called Cossacks ("piece-workers" in translation) set up a loose democratic government, which was converted during warfare to the dictatorship of the elected chief or Hetman.

The organization of Russia under a single ruler was solidified during the long rule (1547-84) of Ivan the Terrible. In 1547, he rejected the control of the nobles or boyars and was crowned as Czar (or Tsar), a Slavonic form of the Latin Caesar. An extremely intelligent and energetic man, he summoned the first elected national assembly, set up an office for petitions, instituted a system of local self-government, led a crusade against the Tartars, and began the conquest of Siberia. The death of his wife, whom he believed to have been poisoned, appears to have been the cause for the alteration of his character which made him "terrible." He revoked his previous liberal measures, set up a despo-

[1] Converts to Christianity increased in number from the tenth century on. Greek Orthodox Catholicism gradually became the dominant religion, and the fall of Constantinople in 1453 left the Russian Church as the leading Christian influence in the East.

tism, and committed a long series of cruelties and atrocities. His death was succeeded by a period of violence, palace intrigues, and civil war, during which occurred the vigorous but hectic six-year rule of Boris Godunoff, brother-in-law of Ivan's eldest surviving son. Accused of the murder of one of the princes, who should have succeeded to the throne, and forced to contend with a pretender to the throne, who was backed by the Polish nobles, Boris nevertheless managed both to strengthen the power of Russia and to renew the tradition of the supreme authority of the Czar.

His sudden death, probably by poison, opened the way to a Polish assault upon Moscow which enthroned the pretender in the Kremlin and left the treasury and the city open to plunder by the Poles. Finally, an army recruited from the peasants drove the Poles from Moscow and elected Michael Romanoff as Czar (1613). Under his rule, the serfs, who had gained considerable independence during the preceding turmoils, were rigidly bound to their lands, and all who had fled were forced to return except for the Cossacks, who were too powerful. In 1649, the register of serfs was begun. This record of the names of all peasants and children born to them constituted the official legal recognition of the bondage of the peasants, a census which provided the skeleton plot of Gogol's *Dead Souls*.

It was Peter the Great (1682-1725) who was mainly responsible for Europeanizing Russia. An absolute monarch who regulated everything, he started the army and the navy, forced all of the jobless into state service, created Russian industry and appointed its directors, established an intricate system of indirect taxation, reformed the alphabet, and edited the first newspaper. He travelled throughout Europe, married off his children to European princes, and instituted the contact with Europe whereby French gradually became the elegant language spoken by the nobility to distinguish them from the vulgar peasant.

Russian authors soon began to imitate the writers of Europe, with France as the principal source of inspiration

After Peter's death, a series of weak Czars allowed the nobility great privileges but granted exemptions from state service. In the eighteenth century, the serf became the complete property of his master, who had no obligations to him. Peasant families were broken up at will; serfs were sold or exchanged for horses and could be sent arbitrarily to Siberia as punishment. In the latter half of the eighteenth century, Catherine II (1762-1796) attempted a reformation, but was unable to enforce her will on the nobles. She was enthusiastic about such liberals as Diderot and Voltaire, did some writing herself, and encouraged the translation of French literature, which, in turn, stimulated further creative literary activity in Russia. This contact with French liberalism, which was increased by Russia's partial occupation of France after the Napoleonic wars (1814), stirred a ferment of social thinking among many of the noblemen. Secret societies were organized to plot the assassination of the Czar and set up a constitution. One such group, containing many of the most remarkable men of the time, failed in an attempted rebellion. Five of their leaders were executed, and many others sent to Siberia. The conspirators were known as the Decembrists from the month of their uprising in 1825.

This was the last attempted revolution to be led by members of the nobility. From 1825 to 1855, Nicholas I introduced minor reforms but imposed a rigid censorship and ruled with an iron hand. In spite of this, talk of social reform was heard everywhere, particularly among the middle class. The universities were largely attended by sons of poor parents. These students supported themselves by translating, tutoring, or performing manual labor in order to find enlightenment. The writings of European social philosophers, including those of Karl Marx, were translated, read, and discussed. The appearance of such writers as Pushkin, Turgenev, Dostoievsky, and Tolstoy testifies to the vitality and richness of this underground current of thought and speculation. That most of the agitation centered about social as well as political reform was the natural result of the existing conditions.

The movement known as Nihilism, which appears to have taken its name from Turgenev's novel *Fathers and Sons,* became the heart of the propaganda and revolutionary activities of the nineteenth and early twentieth centuries. As preached by the hero Bazarov of Turgenev's novel, it apparently originated as a philosophy of extreme individualism, denying the rights of state, church, or family to impose obligations on the individual. It soon turned into a liberal movement in the cause of liberty with equality of women, emancipation of serfs, and the establishment of constitutional government as its principal goals. Turning from oral agitation to terroristic violence, it resulted in waves of strikes, conspiracies, and revolts that culminated in the Revolution. In its early phases Nihilistic propaganda, coupled with the preachings of European liberals, bore fruit in the emancipation of the serfs in 1861 by Alexander II. Under this act, the peasants were given personal liberty and came under the direct supervision of the state in the commune system. An elected local government, the Zemstvo in the county and the Duma in the town, had theoretical control over such things as taxation, education, and public health, but actually governmental matters remained under the rigid control of the provincial governor who represented the Czar. Furthermore, both the local police and the secret police were federal officers. The emancipation of the serfs brought about an inevitable economic upheaval. High rents of land charged by ruined noblemen sent peasants thronging to low-wage-paying factories. Less land was cultivated, and famine and poverty became more prominent than before. Incipient revolutions and guerrilla warfare became frequent until one such rebellion culminated in the murder of the Czar Alexander II and ended all reforms from 1881 to 1904.

Liberalism reappeared in 1904 under Nicholas II, who instituted a national assembly or Soviet which set about creating a program of conservative reform. The new reform movement was only beginning to accomplish results when it was interrupted by the outbreak of the first World War. Russia fought effectively during the first fourteen months, but then its war effort dwindled, partly because of a deficiency in munitions and food but mainly because the emperor relinquished the government and transferred it to the empress and her adviser, the peasant mystic Rasputin. In November, 1916, Rasputin was assassinated by members of the imperial family. With food riots constant among the civilians and the army weak and disaffected, the military commanders insisted on abdication of the royal house on March 16, 1917. In the ensuing chaos, the battle for control of the government between the Bolsheviks and the Mensheviks resulted first in the triumph of the Bolsheviks under Lenin. There followed the attempted intervention of the allies, the treaty of Riga which ceded large portions of land to Poland, and the ultimate emergence of the U.S.S.R. (Union of Soviet Socialist Republics) ruled by the Communist party under the leadership of Stalin.

SUGGESTED READINGS

(Place of publication, when not mentioned, is New York.)

M. Baring, *Landmarks in Russian Literature* (1910), *Outline of Russian Literature* (1914); E. Crankshaw, *Russia and the Russians* (1948); H. von Eckardt, *Russia* (1932); J. G. Fletcher, *The Two Frontiers* (1930); M. T. Florinsky, *Russia: A History and an Interpretation* (1953); N. K. Gudzii, *History of Early Russian Literature* (1949); I. F. Hapgood, *A Survey of Russian Literature* (Chautauqua, 1902); R. Hare, *Russian Literature from Pushkin to the Present Day* (1947); P. Kropotkin, *Ideals and Realities in Russian Literature* (1915); T. G. Masaryk, *The Spirit of Russia* (1919); P. N. Miliukov, *Outlines of Russian Culture* (Philadelphia, 1942); D. S. Mirsky, *Contemporary Russian Literature* (1926); H. Muchnic, *An Introduction to Russian Literature* (1947); B. Pares, *Russia* (8th ed., 1953); W. L. Phelps, *Essays on Russian Novelists* (1916); S. F. Platonov, *History of Russia* (1925); B. J. Stern (ed.), *Understanding the Russians* (1947).

chapter 23

Fin de Siècle:
The Eve of World War I

I. PRAGMATIC NATIONALISM

At first glance, the more than four decades from the end of the Franco-Prussian War to the outbreak of World War I seem to have been merely a continuing and an intensifying of tendencies already related in previous chapters. There is apparently the same nationalism, except that the rivalries between nations are more acute; there is the same profusion of political liberalism; and there is the same interest and wonder in the amazing discoveries and developments of science. But upon closer analysis, we can discern striking differences between the half-century succeeding the treaty of Frankfurt and that following the Congress of Vienna. Only the theatre is similar; the actors have changed parts, and the drama has been altered from romantic dream-play to brooding tragedy. Prussia, a supporting player in the first piece, has usurped the star part from France, and new actors, in the form of the Slavic nations, have been introduced to complicate the plot. The pace has been quickened and the conflict sharpened. Furthermore, much of the moral and patriotic idealism has been removed from the script to be replaced by lines reflecting only hard-bitten realism and cynical selfishness.

While it is true that there was still considerable talk of peace, democracy, and the rights of the masses, and that at least some of this talk resulted in definitive gains for the ordinary citizen, the tone of the period was pragmatic rather than idealistic, and the principal forces in the development of history were nations, not men. As the period advanced, there was a growing realization that nineteenth-century nationalism was developing into a Frankenstein monster which ultimately would destroy its creators. Among intellectuals in particular there arose a sense of foreboding which gradually spread from the ivory tower to permeate the entire population. Half aware that it was sowing the wind, Europe after 1870 anxiously, restlessly awaited the coming of the storm.

In the race for national greatness, it was Germany who set the pace. Proud in her newly-achieved unity and flushed with her relatively easy victory in the Franco-Prussian War, she continued to develop in military power until she possessed the most efficient, mobile, and formidable army in the world. By the turn of the century her navy, too, was developing to proportions which gave anxious moments even to Great Britain, while her boastful determination to gain "a place in the sun" through an aggressive imperialism kept all of Europe under arms in self-defense. With the genius of Bismarck to direct her diplomatic activities and a superb military machine to enforce respect, Germany soon found herself in the driver's seat in European politics and apparently on her way to achieve her dream of dominating the trade and commerce of the world.

Actually, the German chancellor did not want war. Despite his belligerent gestures, he much preferred to follow the slower means of diplomacy, at which he was a past master. In such a game, he found the mighty German army a powerful persuader by its very existence, but he hoped to be able to avoid its actual use, at least until Germany had become strong enough throughout the world to be certain of victory in any armed conflict. Had Bismarck been allowed to pursue this policy of "persuasion" for a few more years, it is quite possible that a substantial part of his objectives might have been realized. But in 1888 Wilhelm II succeeded to the throne of Germany, and the Iron Chancellor soon found that he had a stubborn and highly opinionated rival for the diplomatic spotlight.

Wilhelm II was a ruler of great energy, overwhelming egotism, and a discouraging lack of true statesmanship. Unable to share the stage with another, he soon found himself at odds with his chancellor. In 1890 he announced that henceforth he would tend personally to the making of German policy and thereby elicited Bismarck's resignation. By this act of "dropping the pilot," Wilhelm II discharged the one man who had done more for the political prestige of Germany than anyone else in the history of the nation, and at the same time he served notice upon a nervous Europe that from here on force, not diplomacy, was to be the keynote of German policy. He boasted that with the help of God (he was always generous in including the Creator as an active partner in his plans) and his unbeatable army, he would soon achieve for Germany the high position for which she had been chosen by destiny. Despite his high-stomached speeches, however, the policies of Wilhelm II were little different from those of Bismarck. Nevertheless, his brash arrogance, his constant sword-rattling, and his mercurial changes in attitude kept all of Europe in a froth of apprehension for the entire twenty-eight years of his reign.

With Germany riding the crest, France was reduced to a secondary position in European affairs. Badly defeated in the Franco-Prussian War and isolated from her potential allies by Bismarck's post-war policies, she quickly sank into a state of political instability and intellectual disillusionment. From 1871 to 1914 she had no fewer than fifty different ministries, in addition to two abortive insurrections which fell far short of their intended objective of achieving full-scale popular revolution. Materially, however, France prospered. Her industry developed with phenomenal speed, and during the period between the wars, she increased the machine horsepower of her factories from 870,000 to 8,600,000. Great fortunes were made, foreign investments increased fourfold, many colonies were added, and the national wealth was augmented by 50 per cent. Gradually this increased prosperity both at home and abroad enabled France to escape from the net Bismarck had closed around her and to elevate the more progressive middle class to a position of power in domestic affairs to replace the tired conservatives left over from the days of the Second Empire. It also intensified the bitter hatred of Germany and increased the determination to avenge the treaty of Frankfurt, with its "rape" of Alsace and Lorraine and its stunning blow to French national pride. By 1914 France, without actually desiring war, was nevertheless both psychologically and physically as ready as Germany for that moment of reckoning the Germans had designated as *Der Tag.*

In social morale, however, France had lost much during the period from 1870 to 1914. The rise of industry had darkened her cities with smoke, had created a miserable proletariat living under the most depressed slum conditions, and at the same time had elevated the *nouveaux riches,* their fortunes and prestige swollen with quick and easy profits, to a position of power in French affairs. The scramble for wealth, the crass materialism of social values, and the ugliness of the industrialized cities gave a sordid and cynical tone to the entire life of the period and contributed to an attitude of despair and disillusionment among those persons sensitive to moral standards. In a society in which vulgar and ostentatious luxury walked side by side with vice and misery, it is small wonder that intellectuals should have become adherents to the bitter cult of literary naturalism (see Chapter 21). And the fact that the disenchanted *fin de siècle* attitude which produced a Zola should have spread quickly to other nations, including the United States, was ample evidence that the disease of "soulless materialism" was endemic throughout the world and was everywhere rapidly approaching its critical stage.

A less negative by-product of the rise of industry in France and elsewhere was the intensification of proletarian movements. Though stemming from the inflammatory teachings of Karl Marx (see pp. 398 f.) and the radical pronouncements of the international labor movement, socialism in the last two decades of the nineteenth century had become both moderate and reasonably respectable in most of the countries of Europe. Splinter groups, such as the Anarchists and Syndicalists, occasionally sent shivers up industrialist spines by threats of the "red terror," but the usual form of proletarianism was that of social democracy, which strove to improve the lot of the working man without waving the flag of revolution. By following a policy of moderation and gradual reform, the Labor movement gained considerable strength throughout Europe in the days before World War I and through its efforts did much to rectify the economic dislocation and social inequities brought about by the quick rise of industry. Furthermore, this policy of mild evolution seemed to have achieved permanency in problems of labor-management relations. Had it not been for the extreme injustice of the position of peasants and workers in Russia following the fiasco of that nation's participation in the World War, it is probable that the name of Marx, with all that it implies, would today hold only a historical significance in the annals of international affairs.

II. THE WHITE MAN'S BURDEN

Of even greater importance than the practical materialism of the European domestic scene was the program of pragmatic nationalism through colonial expansion. Although colonialism had long been a familiar factor in European politics, the expansionist activities of the late nineteenth century differed from those of earlier times in several respects. First, their purpose was almost entirely industrial. Whereas in earlier times nations had annexed territories in undeveloped sections of the world for settlement and military purposes as much as for trade, the colonial race in the half-century preceding World War I was undertaken mainly to secure raw materials or markets for the products of industry. Trade, the theory went, follows the flag, although so hectic was the competition for colonies and protectorates in remote parts of the world that it sometimes was difficult to discern whether it was the trade or the flag which was doing the following. In the rush to add territories, nations often annexed places of dubious value, encumbering the national budget and the national defense with chronically unprofitable lands simply in order to prevent their going to a rival country. Since most of these acquisitions were in remote parts of Asia, Africa, or Oceania, the problem of their defense was an acute one and the life line of empire often proved a tenuous one indeed.

Another distinctive feature of this latter-day colonialism was the welter of racial mysticism it engendered among the avowed disciples of Darwin, to whom the predatory scramble represented merely an example of the survival of the fittest. There was much highfalutin talk of white supremacy over the "lesser breeds without the law," of the moral obligation of the Caucasian peoples to "bear the white man's burden" and to bring the benefits of their superior culture to the "backward" or "colored" nations of the world. Learned tomes, such as de Gobineau's *The Inequality of the Human Race* (1853) and Houston Stewart Chamberlain's *Foundations of the Nineteenth Century* (1899) were regarded as almost Biblical authority to support the theory of racial differences. Chamberlain's book was particularly influential in establishing the myth of "Aryan" supremacy over the races of southern Europe and fostered much of the ethnic prejudice which later spawned such monstrosities as Nazi Germany. In the mixed atmosphere of patriotism, hypocritical altruism, and frank racial chauvinism, the commercial imperialists, bolstered by the findings of "science," blandly encouraged the march of the flag.

Few nations of any size abstained from the race for colonies. By 1900 virtually all of Africa, East Asia, and Oceania were in European hands or under European control, with Great Britain, France, The Netherlands, and Belgium holding the richest prizes. Italy, Spain, and Portugal held lesser territories and Germany, entering the contest belatedly, caused much anxiety among other nations by announcing her intention to use her military and naval might to gain her "place in the sun." In other parts of the world, Japan and the United States embarked upon similar acquisitive programs, though in the latter nation imperialism encountered considerable opposition and was soon abandoned in favor of a more subtle and less expensive "dollar diplomacy."

To the sensitive eyes of a few intellectuals and men of good will, the spectacle of the Western world engaged in a territorial free-for-all was anything but edifying and elicited bitter reactions even beyond the sweetening power of the racial moralists, but for the most part the period between 1870 and 1914 was one of imperialism triumphant, marked by an energetic and constantly increasing patriotic jingoism which formed a ready fuse for the igniting fires of Sarajevo. And yet, when that fuse was finally lighted by the assassination of an unimportant Austrian archduke and his wife in that obscure Bosnian town, only Germany was ready for the explosion which immediately followed. Despite all of the sword-rattling, the marching and countermarching, the race for empire, and the still acute hatreds left over from the Franco-Prussian War, most of the nations of Europe had been too busy enjoying their industrial prosperity, their improved standards of living, and their dreams of future greatness to concern themselves with the powder kegs resting on their very doorstep. Inwardly, they had long realized that general war was inevitable, but they had persisted in telling themselves that it couldn't possibly happen for a long time to come. True, after 1900 there had been serious outbreaks in Morocco, in Turkey, and throughout the Balkans, and in Asia, Russia and Japan had, for a year and a half, been at one another's throats, but these actions had seemed hardly more than local disturbances at the time, isolated events of no significant relationship to the European scene as a whole. Furthermore, they had been ended by that spirit of enlightened arbitration which had lately come to characterize international relations. Since the late years of the nineteenth century, there had been much talk of international co-operation and many instances of friendly intervention by disinterested nations to end dangerous disputes. Societies for international peace had been formed to spread the doctrine of pacifism, and in 1899 and again in 1907 the great nations of the world had attended peace conferences at The Hague with a view toward limiting armaments and fostering international understanding. With such civilized talk and activity under way it was easy to overlook the fact that the peace movements and international conferences themselves had accomplished little and that bitter competition among nations still constituted the dominant pattern of the times. Besides, conditions of general prosperity have a way of making even the most transparently wishful thoughts assume the appearance of positive truth.

And so world war, the first in a century, burst upon a morally unready world. Even after hostilities had started, it was hard for people to understand the real nature of the conflict. Everybody believed that it would all be over in a matter of weeks or months; that the enlightened spirit of modern, pragmatic society would, through its various governments, find a ready solution to stop the carnage. Only after the Kaiser's armies had ripped triumphantly through Belgium and northern France and stood at the very outskirts of Paris did some observers begin to realize that this was in truth *Der Tag*, the time of reckoning after a full century of free-wheeling nationalism.

In that century, it is true, much had been achieved. Science had taken giant strides toward that positivism of which Comte had dreamed. The average individual was healthier, more comfortable in his physical surroundings, freer, and more prosperous. Thanks to labor-saving machinery, he worked less strenuously and, thanks to mass production, he personally enjoyed more of the goods he created. If he was still receiving relatively little formal education, he at least, through improved communications and widened interests abroad, was coming to know more about the rest of the world.

Still, there were some who felt that in gaining these advantages, man had paid dearly. Max Nordau, in his sensational treatise *Degeneration* (1893) pointed to the palpable decay in European moral fiber, the loss of idealism and dignity. Democracy, he felt, had not brought peace; industrialism had merely substituted one form of slavery for another. Science had destroyed spiritual values and had become more dogmatic and tyrannical than any clerical orthodoxy. Friedrich Nietzsche looked at the liberal humanitarianism of his time and saw in it only a quest for self-advantage. "Distrust all those who jabber about justice," he said; "when they call themselves good and just, do not forget that they fall short of the Pharisee in one thing only: Power." Revolted by the selfishness and mediocrity of materialistic Europe, he preached the necessity of surpassing man, of attaining the next higher step in the evolutionary process: the Superman. And in England Matthew Arnold was disgusted by the new "Philistines" whom he described as principally given to money making, devoid of culture, and indifferent to art.

SUGGESTED READINGS

(Place of publication, when not mentioned, is New York.)

C. E. Black, *Twentieth-Century Europe* (1966); E. Brandenburg, *From Bismarck to the World War* (1927); G. Brandes, *Main Currents of the Nineteenth-Century Literature* (6 v, 1901-1905); H. S. Chamberlain, *The Foundations of the Nineteenth Century* (2 v, 1911); G. L. Dickenson, *The International Anarchy, 1904-1914* (1931); A. de Gobineau, *Essay on the Inequality of the Human Race* (1915); J. L. and B. Hammond, *The Rise of Modern Industry* (1925); Q. Howe, *A World History of Our Times* (v. 1, 1949); J. S. Kittie, *The Partition of Africa* (1895); H. Kohn, *Nationalism and Imperialism in the Near East* (1932); W. Millis, *The Road to War* (1935); L. Mumford, *Technics and Civilization* (1934); M. Nordau, *Degeneration* (1895); O. Pflanze, *Bismarck and the Development of Germany* (Princeton, 1963); S. H. Potts, *History of French Colonial Policy* (2 v, 1929); C. G. Robertson, *Bismarck* (1918); J. J. Saunders, *The Age of Revolution* (1949); B. E. Schmitt, *The Coming of the War* (2 v, 1930); W. M. Simon, *Germany in the Age of Bismarck* (1968); R. Soltau, *French Political Thought in the Nineteenth Century* (1931); M. E. Townshend, *The Rise and Fall of Germany's Colonial Empire* (1930); A. Toynbee, *The Industrial Revolution* (1912).

chapter 24

THE COLLAPSE OF EUROPE: BETWEEN WORLD WARS

I. WORLD WAR I

The war which ushered in what has been called "The Century of Total War" was a new kind of conflict in that it absorbed the total energies of the populations engaged in it and was fought to the point of exhaustion, with fearful destruction of lives and property of every kind.

Its roots can be traced back to the beginning of the century and even earlier in the efforts made by the Hapsburg monarchy to suppress Balkan nationalism, the growing opposition of German and Russian territorial ambitions, and the dynamic German drive to gain her "place in the sun" after she had been allowed only the most minor role in the nineteenth-century grab for colonies. Simultaneously, the nineteenth-century movement toward international socialism and international labor organization was gradually eroded by new patriotic nationalisms and alliances between the military and right-wing business elements in the increasingly industrialized and mechanized nations.

The murder in Serajevo of the heir to the Austrian throne, Archduke Francis Ferdinand, and his wife on June

28, 1914, was the culmination of a series of terrorist activities by the Black Hand, a Serbian secret society, directed against Austria and aimed at enlarging Serbian territory and power. Austria reacted by sending an ultimatum demanding that Serbia halt anti-Austrian activities and punish all persons connected with the assassination. The Serbian response was conciliatory but evasive. On July 28, 1914, Austria declared war on Serbia.

Russia, because of her Slavic interests, immediately began to mobilize. Germany reacted with an ultimatum to Russia to halt mobilizing or face war. Because of the Franco-Russian alliance, the German military had devised the so-called Schlieffen plan, whereby in the event of war with either of these powers, Germany would strike a decisive blow against France and then concentrate on Russia because Russian mobilization would be slower and her communications less efficient than either the French or German. But the success of this plan depended on speed, and therefore, having received no reply to her ultimatum after twelve hours, Germany declared war on Russia on August 1 and on France on August 3. To evade French fortifications, the German troops violated the territory of Belgium to attack France from the north. Britain, bound by a treaty to defend Belgium, declared war on August 4. Turkey then joined the Central Powers (Germany and the Austro-Hungarian Empire) in October, followed by Bulgaria in 1915. Japan, Italy, Greece, Rumania, Montenegro, and Portugal joined the Allies (Great Britain, France, and Russia). In Europe only Spain, Switzerland, the Netherlands, Denmark, Norway, and Sweden remained neutral.

The German plan for the rapid destruction of France encountered unexpectedly stiff resistance by Belgian and British troops. The Germans' defeat at the Battle of the Marne stopped their advance toward Paris, and both sides on the western front confronted each other from a huge

network of trenches whose lines remained almost unchanged throughout the war.

On the eastern front the Central Powers were more successful, although the necessity of maintaining two fronts
placed a severe strain on manpower and resources. Russian
troops were gradually driven back, and in March, 1917, the
outbreak of the Russian revolution further demoralized
Russian resistance and caused the Czar to sue for peace the
following November.

The stalemate on the western front made it increasingly
clear that an Allied blockade was the only device to force
capitulation of the enemy. Britain had clear superiority on
the seas, and the desperate German attempt to counter
British naval strength by engaging in unrestricted sub-
marine warfare resulted in the United States' declaring war
on Germany on April 6, 1917. The addition of vast American resources ensured an Allied victory, and on November
11, 1918, the armistice was signed.

Apart from the huge destruction of men and resources,
the war was a prelude to World War II in its use of scientific and mechanical devices: submarines, tanks, airplanes,
poison gas, to name a few of the most obvious military
novelties. The manpower provided by the United States
was important, but even more important were the military
supplies which were brought to bear against the depleted
resources of the blockaded Central Powers.

The American entry into the war also brought with it
Woodrow Wilson's idealistic statement of war aims, designed to restore the earlier nineteenth-century trends
toward democracy and peaceful internationalism. He proclaimed "a war to save the world for democracy," announcing that victory would bring a lasting peace on the basis
of his Fourteen Points which included self-determination
of nations, "open covenants openly arrived at," freedom of
the seas, reduction of tariff barriers, general disarmament,

and the formation of a "general association of nations."

The Treaty of Versailles established a German Republic, stripped Germany of her colonies and the Saar coal mining region, reduced her military forces to a minimum, returned Alsace-Lorraine to France, and imposed reparations of an unspecified amount. Austria and Hungary lost considerable areas of territory, Rumania was enlarged, and the new nations of Poland, Lithuania, Czechoslovakia, Estonia, Latvia, and Jugoslavia were created.

The League of Nations was established, but while it enjoyed considerable success in social and economic areas, its principal function of insuring peace was vitiated by America's repudiation of Wilson and refusal to become a member, and by the lack of real commitment by the European powers on basic political problems.

II. THE 1920s

The cost of the war in terms of human life has been estimated at 10,000,000 dead and 20,000,000 wounded. In Europe this amounted to the elimination of almost a total generation of men in their prime. Many of those who survived suffered from a psychological estrangement from society, popularly described as "shell-shock," and nearly all the combatants relived in dreams the nightmare ordeals of the trenches, described in such war novels as Erich Maria Remarque's *All Quiet on the Western Front* and Henri Barbusse's *Under Fire*. The German psyche nursed the additional wounds of having been the loser, not to mention the corruscating sense of injustice resulting from the imposed Treaty of Versailles—Germany was not represented at the conference table—with its assumption that Germany had been solely responsible for precipitating the war.

Both winners and losers were concerned about the possibility of the spread of communism from the Russian Revolution, but European Communist parties (strongest in Italy,

Germany, and France) did not in fact achieve notable size or political power, and the transition from wartime to peace economies was generally accomplished with a minimum of displacement and personal suffering. European economies remained relatively stagnant, but the necessary retooling of manufacturing concerns meant modernization of equipment and a rise in the standards of living, together with distinct advances in technology and agricultural production. Medical science also made enormous strides and is estimated to have saved as many lives as were lost during the war. Coupled with the new democratic idealism of Wilson and the vaguely euphoric existence of the League of Nations, this new sense of stability, peace, and progress made the 1920s a generally optimistic period. Even Germany, after suffering a disastrous inflation encouraged by the government to avoid payment of reparations, made a rapid recovery following the financial arrangements embodied in the Dawes Plan of April, 1924.

In the intellectual world, the impact of Sigmund Freud, whose *Three Essays on the Theory of Sexuality* had been published in 1905, and of Albert Einstein, whose *Theory of Relativity* had made its bow in the same year, was added to the already established non-religious and pragmatic attitudes of the early years of the century. Freudian psychology, as popularly interpreted, implied that the individual was not responsible for his behavior; personality was the result of inherited characteristics and childhood influences; sex was exalted as the quintessence of the libido, that vaguely understood "life-force" and powerhouse of the individual. Scarcely anyone understood Einstein, but his theory of relativity was widely accepted as an indication that there existed no "objective correlative," as Eliot called it, no definite yardstick of any kind by which to measure values. This philosophical relativism found its outstanding expression in the novels of André Gide and the plays of

Luigi Pirandello. Divorced from the comfort of relying on either mystical or scientific certainty, most artists and writers tended to go their own individual ways, exploring the subconscious mind, naturalistically recording a meaningless world, or building highly personalized fantasies.

Departing from the popular movements of the latter nineteenth century, art tended to become esoteric and reserved for the aesthetic elite. "Metaphysical painting" in Italy, Marc Chagall's dream fantasies, and the Vorticist School in England during the war were forerunners of the Dadaist movement, which originated in Switzerland and which consisted of a nihilistic attack on any theories of artistic order or restraint in art or culture. In 1924 André Breton wrote the first Surrealist Manifesto, glorifying unfettered imagination: "The marvelous is always beautiful, in fact only the marvelous is beautiful." The naturalistic treatment of social themes in literature was replaced partly by the epic attempts of Proust and Mann to explore the region of inner man and partly by the expressionism of André Gide. Psychological exploration was also the forte of Alberto Moravia of Italy, Jean Anouilh of France, and Hermann Hesse of Switzerland. Exoticism and fantasy mark the works of the French Antoine de Saint-Exupéry and Jean Cocteau. Symbolism, expressionism, and psychology are combined in the uncanny world of the German-Czech Franz Kafka; expressionism and surrealism are united in the poems and plays of the Spanish García Lorca. Many writers who attempted to survey their contemporary world tended to be pacifists like Jean Giraudoux or Marxists like André Malraux and Ignazio Silone. Experimentation (and difficulty) in poetry was the hallmark of most European poets, often composing in the shadows of Ezra Pound and T. S. Eliot.

III. THE U.S.S.R.

The Union of Soviet Socialist Republics, whose revised

constitution was adopted in 1936, represented a striking social innovation. Its basic principles were stated in Article 12 of the constitution: "He who does not work, neither shall he eat." "From each according to his ability, to each according to his work." The origin of the Soviet Union stems from the revolution led by Lenin which erupted in November, 1917, and which developed into a civil war lasting through 1919. In 1918 the treaty of Brest-Litovsk took Russia out of the war and the "Red Terror" brutally exterminated enemies or suspected enemies of the new regime, including the royal family itself. In 1919 the Comintern (or Communist International) was formed to direct communist activities in all foreign countries, whereby Russia became the "mother country" and all communist parties were given to understand that their first duty was the "unreserved support of Soviet Russia."

The attempt to convert a huge country into an entirely new kind of society met with intense peasant resistance which, when coupled with a drought which took the lives of some four million Russians in 1921-22, caused a temporary retreat to a more traditional capitalist-oriented economy. When Lenin retired from active party leadership in 1922, disagreement on essential communist aims grew between his two most powerful successors, Leon Trotsky and Joseph Stalin. Trotsky wanted to devote communist energies to inspiring a world revolution; Stalin more realistically preferred the solidification of a prosperous Russian Communist regime as the first step. By strong-arm tactics and much underground chicanery, Stalin succeeded in having Trotsky demoted in 1926, exiled in 1929, and murdered in Mexico in 1940. By a succession of purges he eliminated those who disagreed with him and made himself an undisputed dictator over the Party, and hence the government, by 1928.

In that year he instituted the First Five-year Plan aimed at creating a modern industrial state which Stalin realized was a first essential for the recognition of the Soviet Union as a world power. Goals were set, quotas assigned to individual units, and workers, pawns of the state, were rewarded or punished according to their productivity. In 1929 an attempt to force the peasantry into collective farms was met by violent resistance, but the revolt was put down by bloody military counter measures, and by 1939 collectivization had become the agricultural norm.

The "Stalin Constitution" of 1936 codified the one-party rule of the state. Universal suffrage was guaranteed, but the slate of candidates was to be selected by the Party. The constitution provided for a bicameral legislative body known as the Supreme Soviet, consisting of an upper house, the Supreme Council, and a lower house, the Council of Nationalities. The Council of People's Commissars, a kind of cabinet, was to be chosen by the Supreme Soviet. Members of the Supreme Soviet were to be elected by provincial soviets of the different republics; these soviets in turn were to be chosen by soviets at the local level.

Actual control over the government was invested in the Communist Party, representing principally industrial workers, with an extremely limited membership estimated at 3 per cent of the total population. The Party was made up of local cells which were directed by higher organizational levels culminating in the Presidium, a small central committee. Stalin, as General Secretary, held close to dictatorial powers.

Cultural achievements under Communism consisted principally of universal education (and indoctrination) and great advances in science. In contrast, censorship was rigid, news was controlled by a party press, religion was discouraged, political deviationists were at the mercy of the secret police. All art and literature were supposed to be channeled into the service of the Party, glorifying the spirit of Russian socialism. Many hopefully independent Russian authors were purged, but some like Boris Pasternak managed to publish abroad, and a few were able to adapt themselves to the new socialist realism, notably Boris Pilnyak and Mikhail Sholokhov.

Despite the activities of the Comintern, the Soviet Union was too preoccupied with internal problems to be much concerned with the rest of the world during the years between world wars. A series of violent purges between 1934 and 1938 eliminated groups who might oppose the existing regime of Stalin. Nervousness about Japanese aggressiveness and Hitler's rise to power in 1933 caused Stalin to join the League of Nations and seek alliances in the West, but he was both feared and distrusted by European governments, and the U.S.S.R. remained virtually divorced from Europe until World War II. Inside the Soviet Union the new gods were Science, Atheism, Mechanization, and Education for Production and for the State.

IV. THE 1930s

The mild optimism of the 1920s was replaced in the 1930s by the pessimism and spiritual panic emanating largely from the great economic depression of the early part of the decade. In the United States a mania for investment in a rapidly rising stock market had grossly inflated the prices of securities. The resulting unhealthy condition, together with concomitant overexpansion in agriculture and industry and a perilous overextension of credit, led to the stock market crash of 1929 and a severe American depression whose effects spread throughout Europe. The industrial nations like England, France, and Germany were hardest hit, but no European country escaped the wave of unemployment and collapsing credit. World production decreased by 42 per cent between 1929 and 1932, and world trade was diminished by 65 per cent. The financial structures of Germany and Austria crumbled in 1931.

In literature the depression revived the novel of society, notably in Jules Romains' *Men of Good Will* in which he used a new technique labeled "unanism," focussing on an entire culture rather than on a single individual. There was also great nervousness about Russian Communist inspiration and infiltration, and outstanding writers like Romain Rolland and André Gide were overtly sympathetic. Actually, Communism achieved no practical political triumphs outside of the U.S.S.R., but it made a strong appeal to the lower and middle classes, fearful about their economic insecurity, and an even stronger appeal to intellectuals who found ideological security in a doctrine which seemed to promise domestic concord, social justice, and international harmony.

The most obvious prevailing mood of the period was the sense of despair and loss of direction reflected in such novels as Louis-Ferdinand Céline's *Journey to the End of the Night*. The strikingly bizarre fantasies of the surrealist artist Salvador Dali, while seemingly designed to shock middle-class sensibilities, caught the popular fancy partly because of the immediate impact of their technical virtuosity and extraordinary combinations of familiar objects like watches and telephones strangely juxtaposed, misshapen, or fluid. But his principal appeal probably lay in his Freudian sexual symbolism and his nightmare depictions of limp watches, suggestive of Einstein's relativity, draped on ossified logs or leafless twigs in the midst of immense hollow desert landscapes, reflecting an arid world suggestive of T. S. Eliot's "Waste Land" where familiar realities had lost their comforting solidities and were isolated and alien.

An extraordinary prediction of what was to occur during the decade to come was made by José Ortega y Gasset in *The Revolt of the Masses,* published in 1930 in Spain. He pin-pointed the origin of this revolt in the demoralization of Europe because of the loss of power it formerly exercised over the rest of the world. By the "masses" he meant Europe's middle classes whose state of mind feared the unusual and glorified the commonplace. It was his contention that when minority group opinions divide a society, the empty space left by the absence of a predominant public opinion will be filled by brute force. In essence, this is exactly what happened. With a rise of some 50 per cent in unemployment, a pervasive fear of labor uprisings coupled with nervousness about Bolshevist terror activities caused increasing reliance by upper and middle classes on governmental powers and paved the way for the series of dictatorships which characterized the period.

In Italy the failure of a leftist revolution in 1920 had already led to the counter-revolution of fascism. Fearing communism, the army and business interests combined to make Benito Mussolini prime minister in 1922. In 1924 Il Duce became dictator of what was called a corporative state, a one-party fascist government controlling industry and labor as well as assuming all the other functions of the state.

An even deeper discontent with depressed conditions in Germany created the Nazi party which elevated Adolf Hitler to power through a similar coalition of the military and big business. Condemning Communists, Jews, and the Versailles treaty, Hitler preached the purification of the Aryan super race and promised the union of all Germans and *Lebensraum* (living space) for the German *Volk*. On February 27, 1933, the Reichstag building in Berlin was destroyed in a mysterious fire which Hitler's lieutenant, Herman Göring, blamed on the Communists. In the resulting panic the Nazi party received 44 per cent of the votes in the next election. In 1934 Hitler became both chancellor and president of the Third Reich, a new government established by general election in 1933. Through public works, rearmament, and energetic youth organizations, as well as through exerting his extraordinarily hypnotic personal magnetism to create a prevailing atmosphere of mass hysteria, Der Fuehrer convinced most Germans that the long-delayed and richly deserved day of glory for Germany had at last arrived, a day he had already described magniloquently in his autobiography, *Mein Kampf.*

Coincident with the rise of dictatorships elsewhere in Europe, Spain from 1936 to 1939 underwent a devastating civil war which concluded with the triumph of another dictator, General Francisco Franco, representing a coalition of the Catholic Church, the army, and the upper classes. Poland under Pilsudski and Hungary under Horthy also traded democracy for dictatorial governments.

Thus did Wilson's dream of a democratic and cooperative European society of nations collapse, to be replaced by a nightmare of fiercely nationalistic states, each concerned more with the power of the state than with the rights and welfare of the individual, and all of them essentially militant in nature.

V. WORLD WAR II

If World War I had come as a surprise, World War II was the foreseeable and virtually inevitable result of two basic phenomena: the deadly rivalries of the power-hungry European dictatorships and the moral collapse of the democratic nations in allowing these dictatorships to rise to power in the first place.

In 1933 Hitler withdrew from the League of Nations. In 1935 he recovered the Saar by a plebiscite and announced a policy of German rearmament. In the same year Mussolini conquered Ethiopia despite economic sanctions imposed on Italy by the League. In 1936 the Rome-Berlin axis was created and an Anti-Comintern pact was concluded with Japan. In 1938 Austrian Nazis took over their government and announced union (*Anschluss*) with Germany. The powerful industrial area of Czechoslovakia known as the Sudetenland was principally inhabited by Germans. On the grounds of self-determination of peoples, Hitler massed troops on the border in September, 1938 and demanded independence for Henlein's Nazi-led Sudeten population. A conference was hurriedly called involving Hitler, Mussolini, Daladier of France, and Chamberlain of England. Hitler was given his way, and Chamberlain returned to England, announcing that he had secured "peace in our time." In March, 1939, Hitler swallowed the remainder of Czechoslovakia, finally making it clear to Britain and France that their policy of appeasement had been a mistake. At this point Britain and France guaranteed the defense of Poland, but Hitler, playing on the Soviet desire to expand in eastern Europe, signed an alliance with the U.S.S.R. and invaded Poland on September 1, 1939, beginning a war for which only Germany was at all prepared.

Poland was quickly subdued and was partitioned between Germany and the Soviet Union. Britain and France declared war on September 3 but were not in a position to do anything but attempt to build their armaments. In April, 1940, Hitler's fast armored divisions, supported by air power, launched a successful *Blitzkrieg* on Denmark and Norway, then Belgium, the Netherlands, and France. British troops were evacuated from Dunkirk between May 27 and June 4. Italy meanwhile attacked France from the south, and Hitler entered Paris on June 14. France signed a peace treaty with the Axis on June 22, leaving two-fifths of the country under a French government which agreed to pay the occupation costs of the German forces in the remainder of the nation. Within the conquered countries Hitler permitted medical experiments on the helpless subdued peoples and attempted the extinction of European Jewry by extermination camps. An estimated six million

Jews were killed in the course of this diabolical campaign.

As a preliminary to the invasion of Britain, now alone against the Axis, Hitler turned to an aerial attack which was met so successfully by Britain's Royal Air Force that the invasion plan was abandoned. After a quarrel over domination of the Balkans, Hitler attacked Russia on June 22, 1941, where his invasion was halted before reaching either Leningrad or Moscow.

During the war the United States had remained neutral but was sympathetic to Britain and, as "the arsenal of democracy," had been supplying many of England's war needs. Meanwhile, the growing tension between the United States and Japan on account of the Japanese invasion of China had reached a critical point because of the American embargo of August, 1941, of exports to Japan of scrap iron and petroleum. When Japan launched a surprise attack on the naval base at Pearl Harbor on December 7, 1941, the United States entered the war. In Europe the British-American strategy of invasion from the south (Africa to Sicily to Italy) and separately into France at Normandy, accompanied by persistent air raids on Germany, finally brought about a German surrender on May 8, 1945. A similar campaign of Pacific island-hopping toward the Japanese mainland exhausted the Japanese economic and military resources and brought about the overthrow of the Imperial wartime cabinet. The succeeding government attempted to sue for peace, but was unwilling to accept Allied demands for unconditional surrender. As a result, America dropped the first atom bomb[1] on Hiroshima on August 6 and a second on Nagasaki on August 9. Japan thereupon had no choice but to accept American terms; the papers of surrender were signed on September 2, 1945.

[1] Theories for splitting the atom had been developed in Weimar Germany and England. But Nazi Germany apparently did not realize the wartime potential of these theories, and the creation of the atomic bomb took place in America in the mysterious Manhattan Project.

Despite a number of conferences during the war, almost no agreement had been reached on the disposition of the European nations after victory should be secured. It was agreed that a world organization, the United Nations, should be set up and that the nations of Eastern Europe were to have provisional governments until free elections could be held. In point of fact, nearly all these nations fell under Soviet domination, notably Poland, Czechoslovakia, Hungary, Romania, and Bulgaria. Germany was divided, with East Germany controlled by the Soviets. Berlin, 110 miles inside East Germany, was divided into four zones to be separately administered by the Soviet Union, France, Britain, and the United States.

The conclusion of World War II saw Europe exhausted, leaving the United States and the U.S.S.R. to confront each other as the only remaining great world powers. The price of achieving this situation has been estimated at 22,000,000 in loss of life of combatants and civilians and $3,000,000,-000,000 in military expenses and property damage.

SUGGESTED READINGS

(Place of publication, when not mentioned, is New York.)

L. Albertini, *The Origins of the War of 1914* (tr. and ed. by I. M. Massey, 3 v, London, 1952-1957); R. Aron, *The Century of Total War* (Boston, 1955); G. Barraclough, *Introduction to Contemporary History* (1965); J. Barzun, *Darwin, Marx, Wagner* (Boston, 1941); C. E. Black and E. C. Helmreich, *Twentieth Century Europe: A History* (2nd ed., 1963); A Bullock, *Hitler, a Study in Tyranny* (Evanston, Ill., 1964); H. Butterfield, *The Origins of Modern Science* (1952); E. H. Carr, *A History of Soviet Russia* (1951); W. S. Churchill, *The Second World War* (6 vols., 1962); I. Deutscher, *Stalin: A Political Biography* (1949); A. Eddington, *The Nature of the Physical World* (1929); J. E. Edmonds, *A Short History of World War I* (London, 1951); A. Einstein, *The World as I See It* (1949); E. Eyck, *A History of the Weimar Republic* (2 vols., Cambridge, Mass., 1963);

H. Feis, *Churchill, Roosevelt, Stalin: The War They Fought and the Peace They Sought* (Princeton, 1957); E. Fischer, *The European Age* (rev. ed., Cambridge, Mass., 1948); J. K. Galbraith, *The Great Crash, 1929* (Boston, 1955); K. Heiden, *Der Führer* (Boston, 1944); Q. Howe, *A World History of Our Own Times* (v. 2., 1953); H. S. Hughes, *Contemporary Europe: A History* (Englewood Cliffs, N.J., 1961); G. Hugnet, *Fantastic Art, Dada and Surrealism* (1949); I. Kirkpatrick, *Mussolini: Study of a Demagogue* (London, 1964); H. Kohn, *The Twentieth Century* (1950); A. W. Levi, *Philosophy and the Modern World* (Bloomington, Indiana, 1959); E. Lyons, *The Red Decade* (Indianapolis, 1941); A. J. May, *Europe and Two World Wars* (1947); R. B. Nowat, *The Concert of Europe* (London, 1930); L. Mumford, *Technics and Civilization* (1963); B. Nelson (ed.), *Freud and the Twentieth Century* (1957); E. Nolte, *Three Faces of Fascism* (tr. by L. Vennewitz, 1966); R. R. Palmer and J. Colton, *A History of the Modern World* (1956); E. A. Peers, *The Spanish Tragedy, 1930-1936* (1936); R. Pipes, *The Formation of the Soviet Union* (rev. ed., Cambridge, Mass., 1964); C. Sforza, *Contemporary Italy* (1944); W. L. Shirer, *The Rise and Fall of the Third Reich: A History of Nazi Germany* (1960); L. L. Snyder, *The War: A Concise History, 1935-1945* (1960); H. Thomas, *The Spanish Civil War* (1961); A. J. Toynbee, *A Study of History* (1947); D. Treadgold, *Twentieth-Century Russia* (Chicago, 1964); A. B. Ulam, *Lenin and the Bolsheviks* (London, 1966); F. P. Walters, *A History of the League of Nations* (1952); D. C. Watt, F. Spencer, N. Brown, *A History of the World in the Twentieth Century* (1968); A. N. Whitehead, *Science and the Modern World* (1925); C. Wilmot, *The Struggle for Europe: World War II in Western Europe* (1952); B. Wolfe, *Three Who Made a Revolution* (1948).

chapter 25

EUROPE SINCE 1945

I. A NEW ERA ?

During World War II it was standard conversational practice to affirm solemnly, after admitting that nobody could really win a modern war, that the world which would emerge from the conflagration would be different from anything we had ever known or imagined. For once a facile cocktail-party ploy intended merely to dazzle turned out to be the understatement of the modern era. Even as late as the beginning of August, 1945, with the forces of Hitler and Mussolini long since defeated and those of Hirohito in their last stages of island resistance, what amateur political expert could have asserted that within a few years Germany, Italy, and Japan would find themselves on terms of close alliance—and even friendship—with the United States and the nations of Western Europe? And, although few if any really expected the Western alliance with the Soviet Union to survive the war, how many fully understood the depth of the cleavage between East and West which would follow 1945? Who could have guessed the degree to which Western Europe would be reduced to the role of a pawn in the power struggle between the United States and Soviet Russia? Or the economic boom of the fifties which, despite her political downgrading, would bring virtually all of Western Europe to a state of business prosperity and private affluence unprecedented in history? Above all, what drawingroom pundit could have foreseen the implications—or even the fact—of the atomic age: the bomb, the cold war, the exploration of space, the landing of men on the moon?

In its relatively short period of recorded history, the world has frequently been shaken by events and discoveries which have radically changed man's understanding of himself and his universe. Somehow it has adjusted to such considerably spaced phenomena as Confucius, Christ, Columbus, and Copernicus. It handled Newton neatly, perhaps all too neatly. It took only a generation to place Darwin in his proper perspective; it even began to understand Einstein—in theory. But when the implications of relativity and quantum physics began to be felt on the factual level and tangible results of these theories appeared with accelerated frequency as headlines in the daily newspapers, the effect was, as the expression has it, to boggle the mind. When astronauts Armstrong, Aldrin, and Collins returned from the moon, President Nixon stated flatly that theirs had been the greatest deed since the Creation. At first hearing, this remark could have been attributed to political glibness and to the familiar preference for superlatives common to public men. And yet there was somehow a sense that a new frontier had been passed. If man now possessed the technological sophistication to launch a totally successful moonshot, what limits were there to his potential for the direction and application of that knowledge to the betterment—or destruction—of the problem-ridden planet on which he lived?

II. THE COLD WAR

After the shooting stopped in August, 1945, predictions

of a war without a winner materialized into reality with dismaying promptness. Even earlier, during the joint occupation of Berlin by the Allies at the end of the European phase of the conflict, tensions had developed between the Soviets and their Western allies. For more than two decades, while the so-called Iron Curtain descended between the West and Soviet Union and her satellite states of Eastern Europe, a divided Berlin served as a tragic, living example of the Cold War, the practical, chilling demonstration of the effect of a ruthless power struggle on the everyday lives of ordinary beings, of the everpresent danger of a resumption of hostilities in which both antagonists were equipped with increasingly powerful weapons of mass annihilation. In early 1947 President Truman announced the policy of the United States "to support free peoples who are resisting attempted subjugation by armed minorities or by outside pressures." Although this policy, which immediately became known as the Truman Doctrine, referred at the time only to Greece and Turkey, it was well understood by everyone that its ultimate application was worldwide. Furthermore, it was no empty formula, as subsequent events in Berlin, Korea, Laos, Viet Nam, and elsewhere were to demonstrate. The first major confrontation of rival powers following this declaration arose out of the decision of the Western nations to found a West German government without waiting for a settlement among the former allies (in particular, the U.S.S.R.) as to the terms and conditions for the reestablishment of a united Germany. The Russians responded to this action by cutting off all ground access to Berlin in an attempt to literally starve the two million inhabitants of the Western zones of that city and bring about a capitulation to Soviet demands for a complete Western withdrawal from the Berlin area. Having already seen Hungary, Bulgaria, Rumania, and Czechoslovakia fall into Communist hands, the West was not in any mood to take another tactical and ideological defeat. They countered the blockade with the famous "Berlin airlift," which for nearly a year flew approximately two and a half million tons of food, coal, medical supplies, and other necessities into the beleaguered city before the Communists tacitly acknowledged their defeat by ending the blockade.

The Berlin crisis demonstrated to the Western allies the necessity for cooperation against the threat of communism, cooperation on a far larger scale than hastily, though brilliantly, improvised responses to isolated emergencies. They realized there must be full preparation, both military and political, to forestall further Soviet aggression, and, even more important, there must be economic rehabilitation of the war-devastated European nations still outside the Communist orbit. The result was the Brussels Pact of 1948, creating the justly celebrated Marshall Plan, which established a defensive alliance among Britain, France, and the Benelux nations and set up the machinery for their economic rehabilitation (the Point Four Program). In April, 1949 the United States, Canada, and ten European nations formed the North Atlantic Treaty Alliance to provide military defense and necessary technological skills to be applied to European reconstruction and Communist containment. The first steps toward the old Briand dream of a United States of Europe had been taken, not so much out of a relaxation of traditional nationalistic rivalries as the result of the demonstrated need for maintaining a united front against the Soviet policy of sequestration and absorption of adjacent economically and militarily distressed areas.

The death of Josef Stalin in 1953, though undoubtedly touching off considerable backstage maneuvering in the Kremlin, did not bring about any perceptible change in Soviet foreign policy, and in the ultimate assumption of party leadership by Nikita Khrushchev in September, 1953,

the Soviet peoples found a strong leader with as great public impact as the departed Stalin. For the next decade,
Khrushchev was to prove a formidable foe to Western security, an aggressive and resourceful strategist whose ability
to engineer unpleasant surprises exceeded that of any Soviet
leader in history. His most disagreeable—and potentially
most dangerous—tactic was the erection of the Berlin Wall
in August, 1961.

Traffic among the various occupied sectors of Berlin had
been at best only loosely controlled during the fifteen years
following the close of World War II. Approximately fifty
thousand inhabitants of the Russian zone were employed
in Western areas of the city and passed daily from one sec-
tor to another as a matter of course. Sometimes, abandoning home and property, they chose not to return and were
generally received as repatriated citizens of West Germany.
Not only East Berliners, but inhabitants of all of East
Germany took part in this migration; it is estimated that
between 1945 and 1961, some 3,350,000 persons defected
from the Russian-occupied territories. By July, 1961 the
flow of escapees reached 2,600 a day, and Chancellor Adenauer of West Germany declared, perhaps imprudently,
that the Communists were in a "panic" and that East
Germany was rapidly becoming "depopulated."

On the night of August 13, 1961, the Communists responded with the most dramatic action of the postwar
period. The frontier between East and West Berlin was
closed, in open violation of the Four Power agreement
guaranteeing free movement throughout the city. In a
matter of days, with tension mounting and rumors of
World War III on every tongue, the Communists constructed a wall twenty-six miles long separating East and
West Berlin. Subsequently, this was fortified with barbed
wire and pillboxes, and no Germans were allowed to pass
from one area to another. Foreigners could make the transi-

tion, at the risk of unpleasant delays and possible incidents, through only one gate, dubbed by the Americans "Checkpoint Charlie." The widest gap in the Iron Curtain was now effectively sealed. In the succeeding months, a few freedom-loving spirits managed to escape through the barbed wire or by swimming the river separating the two sectors, but far more who made the attempt fell victims to the bullets of the sentries in the pillboxes. Fortunately, open war was averted, but Western prestige suffered as a result. The Communists had turned the slow defeat of migration into a quick propaganda victory; they had with impunity defied the Four-Power Treaty. Western standing throughout the world was at a very low ebb indeed.

Nevertheless, in winning this momentary victory, the Communists placed themselves in a position of eventually losing the cold war. The closing of the frontier, separating families and friends, depriving individuals of employment, and shutting off all but the most vital economic connections with the more prosperous West, struck most persons outside the Iron Curtain as being an action of unparalleled cruelty, one which revealed fully the cynicism and tyranny of the Kremlin mind, as it was later to be demonstrated in Czechoslovakia in 1968 when the liberalized communism of Dubcek came into conflict with the more austere policies of Moscow.

III. THE FRAGMENTATION OF EMPIRES

While the Soviet Union was systematically attempting to reduce its satellites to complete submission, the Western European nations were steadily, if not always enthusiastically, terminating the history of their one-time extensive colonial adventures. In 1942 Winston Churchill made the public statement that, as prime minister of Great Britain, he had no intention of presiding over the liquidation of the British Empire, and yet almost within his own term of office such liquidation became a virtual fact. India achieved her independence in 1947, Gold Coast (Ghana) in 1956, South Africa in 1961, followed by many other of the African states in subsequent years. Since 1948 all citizens of British dominions have become full British subjects. Membership in the British Commonwealth, with its obvious economic and military advantages, became a purely voluntary association, and several former British colonies, after a spell of association with the Commonwealth, have elected to break the ties and go it alone.[1] The great days of the British Colonial Office were over; the spirit of Lucknow, Ladysmith, and Mafeking seemed as remote as that of the Crusades, and the ghosts of Sir Cecil Rhodes and Sir Joseph Chamberlain melted quietly into the ectoplasm of the barely remembered past.

On the continent, the same process had been taking place among the one-time imperialist nations. Germany, of course, had lost her overseas territories as a result of World War I, and Mussolini's grand attempt to expand the Italian Empire had ended in the assassination of that dictator and his mistress in September, 1943. Belgium suddenly withdrew from the Congo in 1960, thereby causing a political upheaval in that vast territory that is still far from settled despite nearly a decade of bloodletting. The Dutch were finally forced to recognize the independence of Indonesia in 1946 and relinquish all sovereignty in 1949. Since 1961, the Portuguese have been carrying on an expensive struggle to retain control of their African provinces of Angola, Guinea, and Mozambique. The French colonial empire which in the early days of the century had rivaled

1 By the decade of the 1960s, England found herself in the position of having to accept her former colonies as equals in the Commonwealth without retaining the power to compel them to remain members of that body should they decide in favor of complete independence, as many of them eventually did.

that of Great Britain went through a similar process of erosion. Forced out of Syria, Lebanon, and Indochina, ejected ingloriously from Morocco and Tunisia, France found the last shreds of her overseas prestige placed in the balance by the Algerian crisis of the late 1950s.

So traumatic was this Algerian experience and so profound its effect upon the whole course of French culture during the period that a brief outline of its events is called for, even within the narrow confines of a volume devoted primarily to literary backgrounds. France's involvement with Algeria began in 1827, when the Turkish dey in Algiers became incensed at the French consul and struck him with a fly swatter. In a somewhat belated response to this insult to Gallic honor, the French government in 1830 sent a punitive expedition which occupied the territory and ended by staying indefinitely. It was not until 1847 that the native Moslem forces were reduced to a state somewhat resembling passive sufferance; and, in fact, at no time during the ensuing century were the French ever made to feel that their presence in North Africa was anything but an unwelcome intrusion.

Moslem hostility notwithstanding, the French *colons* fell in love with Algeria and persuaded themselves that the benefits of French civilization they had bestowed on the area more than compensated for any inconvenience to the nine million native Arabs, whose contact with that civilization was limited generally to an indifferent and uncomprehending view from well outside the pale. In the 1950s, the long-smoldering fires of Moslem resentment began to show signs of increasing incendiary potential. With European prosperity growing, the affluence of the million and a quarter French inhabitants of Algeria formed a sharp economic contrast to the more than seven million Arabs who lived entirely outside the European economy (nearly one million of these being chronically unemployed), or even the two million who operated on the fringes of that economy as small shopkeepers, minor public officials, or as household servants.[2]

Underground Moslem resistance organizations had always existed during the period of French occupation and, since 1927, agitation for Algerian independence had become increasingly embarrassing. Suggested French solutions for the resultant "Algerian problem" ranged the entire gamut from forceful military repression to complete French withdrawal, but the most popular course, at least in lip service, was that of slow assimilation of the natives to French patterns of culture. In 1943 General Charles de Gaulle, as leader of the French forces in exile, offered French citizenship to members of the Moslem "elite" (former Army officers, holders of university degrees, civil servants, state employees) and, when he found the response less than enthusiastic, expanded his offer to include high-school graduates and army veterans of all ranks. Such an offer, of course, accorded with the assimilationist solution. Moslems, who felt that they had a culture of their own, established through centuries of living in the region, simply were not interested in becoming Frenchmen; they pointedly ignored the de Gaulle largesse and continued more and more insistently to press for independence.

On May, 13, 1958, during a Memorial Day service, open revolt broke out in Algiers. A mob of 100,000 Moslems attacked the Governor General's palace, determined to expel the French once and for all. This action served to divide

[2] In 1954 only seven thousand Moslems were enrolled in schools above the primary level, and not more than one-fifth of the boys and one-sixteenth of the girls were in school at all. Only 6 per cent of the Moslem men and 2 per cent of the women were literate in French. In contrast, the *colons,* as the French Algerians were called, lived on a scale comparable to that enjoyed by continental Frenchmen. Roy C. Macrides and Bernard E. Brown, *The de Gaulle Republic* (Homewood, Ill., 1960, Supplement 1963).

the European defenders into two antagonistic groups, one favoring repressive military action and the other advocating diplomatic negotiation. In the resultant Parisian cabinet crisis, the Paris government of Pierre Pflimlin, which favored negotiation, fell and was succeeded by one headed by de Gaulle, who was supported by the Army and was generally believed to favor the more forceful solution. The change of government for a time quieted what could have been a three-cornered Algerian civil war, with the *colons* against the Parisian government and the Moslems against all Europeans. But only for a time. Before long it became apparent that, much to the disgust of old army types, de Gaulle also was willing to negotiate, a fact which enraged the right-wing *colons,* who felt betrayed by the leader they had supported. In January, 1960 these "ultras," as they were known, defied their government and entered into open conflict with the FLN, the native independence army, and de Gaulle found himself in the middle taking the blows from both sides. Valiantly, he tried to make proposals which would grant concessions to each extreme, but found neither in a mood to compromise. Finally, in November, 1960 the imperturbable General proposed a cease-fire to be followed by negotiations to establish an "Algerian Algeria." The "ultras" in both France and North Africa were infuriated by this suggestion, largely because it completely torpedoed the "gradual assimilation" approach, and anti-government riots broke out once more among the *colons* in Algiers. However, de Gaulle stood firm and surprisingly enough, the Army backed him in his determination, even to the point of firing upon European dissidents in the Algerian capital. On January 8, 1961 a great referendum took place in which voters throughout France were asked to express their wishes on the Algerian problem. More than 20,000,000 continental Frenchmen voted in this referendum and another 2,600,000 million registered their opinions in Algeria. The result was overwhelming in favor of self determination; even in Algeria fewer than half the voters (760,000) voted against de Gaulle's policy. Somehow or other, the resourceful French leader had managed to turn a colonial retreat into a victory for human freedom.

But there was to be one more act of shocking violence before the matter was settled. In April, 1961, four irreconcilable French generals, led by the onetime de Gaullist champion Pierre Salan, attempted a *coup d'état* in Algiers and even threatened to send parachutists to attack Paris itself. Again de Gaulle stood his ground, and the revolt was quickly extinguished. But the shock remained. Only at this point did the average Frenchman truly understand how much his nation owed to General de Gaulle, perhaps the only leader powerful and resourceful enough to transcend the crisis without entering into open civil war. On July 3, 1962, France formally proclaimed the complete independence of Algeria, whose newly elected native government lost no time in enrolling the infant nation as a member of the Arab League. In an incredibly short time, some 800,000 *colons,* generally referred to in France as *pieds noirs,* left Algiers and settled in the slums of the larger French cities. However, such was the health of the French economy at the moment that what could have been a severe unemployment crisis was resolved with relatively little suffering by the absorption of most of the newcomers into the lower ranks of the occupational scale.

The Algerian crisis, seen together with that of the Berlin Wall, effectively symbolized the passing of the old prewar Europe, with its highly nationalistic consciousness, its militaristic orientation, and its still largely imperialistic economy. The loss of colonies, the radical alterations in military potential brought about by nuclear weapons, and the necessity for Western cooperation in the face of the communist threat made the marching and countermarching of the previous centuries look like a checkers tournament at the firehouse, and the Congress of Vienna like a country auction. Even Versailles, with its stubborn perpetuation of ancient national hatreds, seemed to retreat into the dim past. True, the two most important men in Europe, Winston Churchill and Charles de Gaulle, still bore a nineteenth-century image in the popular mind; nevertheless, it was these very leaders who in their realistic approach to twentieth-century problems effectively dramatized the need for overcoming the pull of tradition and for accepting a new game played under new rules. But in this new game Europe was no longer the quarterback; rather, it was the football. And whatever masochistic satisfaction that it could derive from the consideration that without a football there would be no game, there was also the deflating realization that in the type of political-ideological struggle going on in the postwar years there were several footballs and several playing fields in a complicated and bewildering contest in which the new rules had not even begun to be written.

IV. THE NEW EUROPE

The decline of colonial empires and the menace of the cold war left open only one course to the politically fading nations of Europe: cooperate or die. Accustomed for centuries to pursuing a largely neo-mercantilist economy, with dependent colonies and satellites, the larger European nations were now faced with the necessity of trading more or less amicably with one another under a variety of agreements designed to render such commerce as efficient and economical as possible. Long belligerently nationalistic and thoroughly traditional in their trading activities, these countries, aided by the providential unction of Marshall Plan funds, learned that they could effectively restore their war-ravaged economies by cheerfully taking in one another's washing in a spirit of mutual defense against the threat of communist expansion.

The result was a growing material prosperity which utterly changed the appearance and habits of the major European countries. M. François Nourissier, in his incisively written study *The French,* draws this picture of his native land in the years following World War II:

A traveler . . . who had first come to France in 1945, then again in 1955, and who is now putting together impressions received in the course of a third visit would certainly be struck by the semblances of wealth today. He would notice squalid old houses still, but now crowned by TV antennas and adorned with fairly shiny cars parked in front. He would notice many new buildings also, since today we are putting up almost 400,000 housing units annually, as compared with a total of 500,000 units from 1944 to 1954. He would note that one out of every two families owns a refrigerator; that eight million cars crowd our small roads; that on the farms, tractors have increased from 56,500 in 1946 to almost a million today. He would observe that people are less poorly dressed and notice how many young people there are and how readily money circulates.[3]

The same surface indications of prosperity M. Nourissier notes in France were also observable in other countries—to a slightly lesser degree, perhaps, in Italy and Great Britain, but at an even higher level in Germany and the Scandinavian countries. Furthermore, this impression would be borne out by the statistics. In the decade following the adoption of the Marshall Plan, European domestic production (at 1954 prices) rose from 75 to 122 billion dollars annually. The Gross National Product increased at 5.4 per cent per year, twice as fast as in the United States, and by the end of the period had exceeded 800 billion dol-

[3] François Nourissier, *The French* (New York, 1968), p. 76.

lars, surpassing the American figure. Through a series of agreements stemming largely from the Office of European Economic Cooperation of the Marshall Plan, trade barriers had been extensively eliminated and wasteful duplication and competition greatly reduced.[4] Furthermore, these agreements met with enthusiastic popular endorsement.[5] People began to speak of the "Americanization" of Europe, and for once this national appelation was not projected as a dirty word. And certainly the American tourist, adrift in Europe in the late 1960s, sometimes wondered, from the growing abundance of motels, supermarkets, snack bars, and family cars whether the deeply rooted myth of old world charm was not due for what John Foster Dulles used to call an "agonizing reappraisal."

However, to this impression of prosperity, American style, M. Nourissier interjects a few disclaimers. As the tourist travels about France, Nourissier states, he will note that, for all the supermarkets, the small stores are dying a dusty death; in spite of the prosperity of the larger farms, the smaller ones are run down; in spite of the higher standard of living, there are many whose earnings are inadequate to the times.

Our financial system has always been antidemocratic, and now,

[4] The most important of these agreements were those creating the Common Market, involving France, West Germany, Italy, and the Benelux countries; the Outer Seven composed of the United Kingdom, Norway, Sweden, Denmark, Austria, Switzerland, and Portugal, and various specialized agencies such as ECSC (coal and steel), EURATOM (atomic energy for peaceful purposes), the European Investment Bank (for capital investments), the European Social Fund (for the retraining of workers), and the Overseas Development Fund (for the modernization of former colonial territories).

[5] A poll taken in 1963 showed that 71 per cent of West Germans, 75 per cent of the Dutch, 60 per cent of the French and Belgians, and 45 per cent of the Italians favored the Common Market, with only a microscopic percentage opposed in each country. The remaining percentages indicated those who registered no opinion on the matter.

instead of establishing a better balance between extremes, it is accentuating the imbalances. It is pitiless toward wages and salaries—i.e., earnings of workers, white-collar employees, civil servants, and the military—but actually tolerates tax evasion on industrial and commercial profits and on the earnings of the liberal professions. As a result, a class of people has come to exist which is not rich but at least earns a comfortable living that is not too seriously diminished by the income tax. This class is fairly large, perhaps one tenth of the population. These people are not the timid *petits bourgeoises* of once upon a time, but neither are they the holders of real wealth and its attendant power. They are simply those French people who, in a restaurant or on the road, in stores or on vacations, spend a lot of money. . . . This advantaged group is large enough . . . to make one forget that it is only a minority; its members 'serve as a screen rather than a target'; they spread 'the myth of general prosperity because one sees them often and everywhere.'[6]

And yet, with all this seeming affluence, M. Nourissier asks, is France spending its money for the right things? As he puts it, "Selling records and T-shirts to teen-agers is not building them schools; selling sunshine and bathing and vacations is not building houses. . . . A society that produces, buys, and sells luxuries is not necessarily an economically sound society. Is there not a bit of fraud here?"[7]
To readers in the United States, this reserved endorsement of the new European prosperity will sound very familiar indeed; and the more thoughtful might wonder whether the Americanization of that continent did not proceed further than the good George C. Marshall would ever have foreseen.

Still, mixed blessing though such prosperity may be, the material well-being of modern Europe did much to realize the long-held dream of a united continent. Drawn together by the fear of a possible Communist engulfment, the nations of Europe, somewhat to their own surprise, learned

[6] Nourissier, op. cit., pp. 77-78.
[7] Ibid., p. 78.

to live together without rancor and even to enjoy the economic advantages of the new order. To be sure, there was as yet no United States of Europe as a political fact, but economic rivalries were greatly reduced. And having tasted the fruits of economic cooperation and having tempered the sweetness of the ensuing higher standard of living with the saline realization that no single European nation was any longer individually defensible, it seemed unlikely that this great continuent would ever again lapse into the balkanization which had complicated its history and plagued and destroyed its inhabitants since the fall of the Roman Empire.

V. TENSIONS AND REVOLT

The "Americanization" of Europe, though limited almost entirely to material development, proved to be a powerful force in effecting profound changes in European patterns of existence and, ultimately, in European thought. Improved standards of living, increased opportunities for employment, better working conditions, and a shorter work week gave many Europeans a degree of physical comfort they had never previously known, and most of them thoroughly enjoyed the experience. Responding to the increase in general purchasing power, European merchants and manufacturers were finally overcoming the inertia of past marketing practices and were learning to cater to and develop a mass market. With tax loopholes gradually being closed and the general electorate becoming more demanding, governments were turning more budgetary attention to the convenience and welfare of the average citizen. This concern for Hans and Jacques was not a new-found altruism on the part of government; it was finally understood that a relatively satisfied middle class was the keystone of a social stability which, in former days, had been considered to be the function of the upper classes, with the persuasive backing of the army.

As a result, Europe rapidly became a continent of super-highways which supplemented its traditionally superior railway network, of excellent telephone service to supplement its overworked and less efficient post offices, and of vastly expanded housing, educational, and welfare programs. Even its creaking tradition-bound financial practices were rapidly being modernized. Payment by check was no longer considered a black art. Installment buying, virtually unknown or at least forbiddingly expensive before 1939, had become standard practice, and labels signifying membership in the popular credit-card organizations appeared in the entrances of most first-class European hotels, restaurants, department stores, airline agencies, gift shops, and florists. In short, words such as *efficiency, production, market turnover,* and *public relations* came to occupy a prominent position of respect in the European business vocabulary, and their principles began to be understood and accepted by the public. To George F. Babbitt the European business world of the 1960s would have brought back moist-eyed memories of the halcyon days of 1921 in Zenith, U.S.A. Except for pardonable difficulties with French irregular verbs or Italian rapidity of speech, George F. might even have felt relatively comfortable wandering through the streets of Paris or Milan. And at the meetings of the local Rotary Clubs, he certainly would have met many a man who talked his language in more ways than one.

This profound change in the economic complexion of European society was not accomplished without its agonies of readjustment. Old heads were bewildered—even lost —in the conflict between the middle twentieth century and traditional business methods and ideas dating back to the days of Adam Smith. Employees had to learn new skills; some even had to reform their attitudes toward the customers they served. And the heads of the family business organizations—by far the most prevailing form of European commercial establishment—had to direct considerable thought to the sensitive areas of business organization and employee relationships. No longer could the head of the family content himself with shaking the hand of every employee as he entered the shop or office in the morning, or with the inclusion of a small gratuity in the pay envelope at the holiday season. Just as in America, the workers, often backed by their unions, now expected all sorts of fringe benefits to accompany their periodically negotiated wage contracts and were audacious enough to walk out if their demands were not met.

Such changes in the economic patterns—and these are but a few of those which could be mentioned—naturally had their direct effect upon the social structure. As Ralf Dahrendorf pointed out, tensions between the old power class and the "lower orders"—of capital vs. labor, of landlord vs. tenant, and even of government vs. citizen—created a new balance wheel in what he termed the "service class," i.e., the professional managers, whose job it was to preserve order and to make the economic world function profitably for its no longer directly active owners.[8] In short order, Mr. Dahrendorf saw this class as securely stationed in the European driver's seat as its counterpart had become in the United States. Just as the French Revolution destroyed the aristocracy and World War I destroyed the nineteenth-century industrial cartel, 1945 may be remembered as the year of the beginning decline of the family business, with its paternalistic employee relationships, its fiscal policy of low capital investment and high percentage of profits, its limited market, its unadventurous development policies, and its financial system of cash on the barrelhead or, at best, of small short-term credits at high interest. It is too

[8] Ralf Dahrendorf, "Recent Changes in Class Structures," *Daedalus,* Winter, 1964, pp. 225-270.

much to expect that so revolutionary a change in the economic structure could have been accomplished without severe personal and class tensions and even open violence. The newspapers of the European mid-century gave ample evidence of these tensions, and the literary productions of the age employed the resultant social turbulence as a principal theme. But nobody expected the new system to revert to former patterns: the mass market had come to Europe, and the inevitable corollary of mass culture—however painful to traditionalists—seemed to be as permanently installed as it had become in the United States of America. Speaking of the France of 1968, M. Nourissier says (and his remarks could as well be applied to most of Europe):

. . . in less than twenty years this doddering old nation, for all that it dodders still, has become young. . . . This nation with its Marxist itch has plunged, workers included, into a vast middle-class daydream. This spent nation is experiencing a relative affluence. People of my age have witnessed this metamorphosis, have lived it—have undergone it rather than produced it—and when they look at their own country today it is with genuine curiosity. The Frenchman. today is frankly dumbfounded by his country's rapid and at times unforeseeable evolution; he finds himself confronted by a rhythm and demands from which his old European's nostalgia and indolence would, he thought, protect him.[9]

In bewildering contrast to this rising spirit of youthfulness which M. Nourissier captures so well in the above paragraph is the fact that during most of the period since 1945 the political destinies of the continent were being directed by old men whose popular image hardly coincided with the developments over which they presided—and even had initiated. There were Churchill and Atlee and Macmillan in Great Britain, Adenauer in Germany,

[9] Nourissier, *op. cit.*, p. 5.

and of course Le Grand Charles in France. True, Iberia had its antediluvian-minded dictators in Franco and Salazar, holdovers from the 1930s, and Scandinavia and the Netherlands had their aging royal families—although in all fairness one cannot charge these last nations with political arteriosclerosis. Paradoxically, the population was growing markedly younger. In the France of 1938, for example, 15 per cent of the citizen body was over sixty; by 1968 one quarter were under fifteen, one third were under twenty, and two fifths were under twenty-five with the possibility of an absolute majority under that age developing by 1979.[10] Similar trends toward youthfulness can be found in all other European countries, although the statistics are probably not quite so dramatic as those cited above.

And, as might also be expected, these young people were becoming increasingly conscious of their power. They were equally impatient with traditional methods and traditional solutions which solve nothing. Their political idol was John F. Kennedy, and they wondered why such spokesmen for youth could not be developed in their own continent. In the meantime they put increasing pressure upon their elders to develop programs commensurate with the needs and aspirations of an ever more youthful Europe. It must be acknowledged that their elders, being experienced politicians, often saw the practical expediency of heeding their demands; but it was also clear that the continuance of the older generation in power through these adaptations was regarded by most young people as being at best a stopgap operation.[11]

[10] Ibid., p. 11.

[11] Perhaps the greatest pressures for a change of traditional policies were felt in the field of education. The time-honored practice of regarding a university education as the prerogative of a small elite was to some extent modified by the more American concept of higher education as training for meeting the needs of a technological society

To many persons, especially in the United States, this "Americanization" of Europe seemed to be a laudable sign of progress. But for all the satisfaction derived from witnessing the development of a generally higher standard of living, or a more youthful political frame of mind, or a broadened and more liberalized system of education, there were other considerations (quite apart from the obvious sentimental nostalgia of the traditionalists) which caused the greatest concern to some thoughtful persons, many of them members of the same middle-income group who stood to profit most by the existing developments in European society.

One of these disquieting forces was the rise of a new institution—an efficient managerial bureaucracy. Long accustomed to the incredibly complicated and notoriously inefficient bureaucracy of government, the European was baffled and somewhat frightened by the new cult of efficiency that was rapidly developing in commerce and industry. Long accustomed also to the accepted practices of evading the law whenever possible, of ignoring the official pronouncements of the church, and of relegating the one-time "leading families" to the dustbin of history, the average family-oriented, independent-minded, stubbornly individualistic middle- or working-class European began to see his life being enveloped in a computerized, impersonal, economically determined system which, since it involved

---

calling for a high degree of skill on the part of the working citizenry as a whole. The old curricula, with their medieval rigidity and emphasis on theory and rote memorization, were often drastically revised to meet the more practical needs of the mid-twentieth century. Parenthetically, it is interesting to note that as European university programs began to take on a more American coloration, American universities were moving in the direction of demanding a more European standard of excellence in their undergraduate studies. In both Europe and the United States, of course, there has been a tremendous expansion of the college population since 1945.

his livelihood and that of his family, he could no longer evade, ignore, or effectively combat. In short, the European, like his American counterpart, began to feel the first shock of identity loss that comes with being a part of a cybernetic society, of leading a programmed existence which some nameless force, also a prisoner of the "system," has worked out for him on a mammoth and utterly impersonal electronic monster capable of performing every act of human reason without the inconvenient presence of human emotion to inhibit the process.

A second factor in the post postwar disorientation of the European was the arrival of the mass society so ominously predicted in 1929 by Ortega y Gasset.[12] This was no nineteenth-century Marxist paradise, with the proletariat taking over and eventually bringing about the withering away of the State. Rather it was the destruction of that proletariat—as in the United States—by elevating it to the status of middle-class consumer, whose incredibly vast buying power and faceless, impersonal blandness formed at once the source of energy and the visible characteristics of modern materialistic society. From a culture whose standards of value had formerly been determined by an educated and cultivated elite, European society—again like that of the United States—was becoming a desert of massminded innocuousness, where the tastes and desires of the average prevailed over those qualities of civilized and sophisticated excellence which, though practiced by no more than a very small minority, nevertheless placed their hallmark on both the surface manifestation and the inner convictions of European life.

With the rise of this pervasive collective mediocrity to the status of supreme determining force, the average citizen—himself a colorless and mediocre person—sensed the loss of those institutions which had once restrained and

12 José Ortega y Gasset, *The Revolt of the Masses,* English ed., 1932.

governed his world, and at the same time began to sense his own impotence as a unit in the ranks of mass leadership. Americans, whose ancestors' flight from Europe was in a sense an escape from these traditional restraining institutions, never experienced this bewilderment on the scale which began to prevail in Europe. The American era of mass affluence, which emerged in the 1920s and came on in a rush after World War II, was simply a material enrichment of an already largely leveled society. Europeans, despite their numerous democratic revolutions of the nineteenth century, never really began to feel the heady combination of general affluence and consumer power until the 1960s. It is only natural that the new experience should have been a source of mixed feelings, not all unpleasant, but somehow profoundly disturbing.

A third factor contributing to the general uneasiness was the effect of the increasing political vacuum. Time was when politics to the European had been as enlivening a topic as sports and sex. But those times seemed to have altered. The tone of political life, like that of the market place, became bland and mediocre. Party labels no longer meant anything; even national entities lost their color in the new trend toward collective security made necessary by the cold war and the pervading fear of the bomb. Politics is sublimated war and derives most of its thrill from the art of "brinkmanship," from the game of pushing one's opponents to the wall without having too often to crush them literally. But this game between nations, had become far too dangerous in a situation where everyone believed that the next general war could well be the last. And, in order to keep nations living in some sort of relative peace, it had become imperative to preserve a semblance of a united front on the local scene. In the ensuing semi-politeness of the political world, one derived, perhaps inaccurately, the feeling of purposeless stalemate, of a society without basic issues, of paper debates fought with little wit and less conviction. Is there any wonder that the young were turning their backs on politics or, at best, were regarding the field as one where tired old men played out the charade of their ineffectual, bumbling lives?

In Germany this turning away from politics was particularly marked. The elder generation, haunted by a pervading sense of guilt for the Hitler atrocities, sought political shelter under the obvious respectable wing of the Adenauer government. With "Der Alte" serving as a stern but benevolent father image, the war generation was content by and large to leave politics to the professionals and to make amends for the Nazi regime (in which, they would assert vehemently, they had played no part and toward which they had held no sympathies) by making expiatory pilgrimages to former concentration camps to view the gas chambers in quiet horror or by assembling old film clips of Nazi atrocities to show to school children in an effort to guarantee that "this thing shall not happen again." Although well-intentioned and undoubtedly socially useful, this constant atmosphere of *mea culpa* ultimately caused the young, who had never known the Nazis, to tire of their elders' obsession with past guilt and to wish to forget it—and the whole field of politics along with it—in an effort to get on with the business of living in the affluent, materially comfortable, and middle-class respectable Federal Republic of the 1960s.

In Scandinavia, on the other hand, the prevailing feeling among the younger generation was not disgust with their elders for having botched the job of running their society, but rather boredom with the near-perfection of the society their forbears had so resourcefully brought about. Under a highly organized system of state socialism which took care of virtually every human contingency, the young Scandinavian went through his permissive, protected, carefully organized education and subsequent working career materially content and outwardly untroubled and yet often tormented by that feeling of spiritual emptiness so well delineated in much of the provocative fiction and the superior motion pictures which emanated from this twentieth-century utopia.

With neither excessive security nor feelings of guilt to disturb their lives, French youth of this period had other reasons to reject the past: their country's humiliating and early defeat in the war, the economic disruption, housing shortages, and revolving-door governments of the postwar period, the obvious decline of former national glory in the disintegration of the French empire, and, finally, the impressive but largely backward-looking attitudes of the de Gaulle government. Politically apathetic during the 1950s, the young people of France became much more activist in the following decade and played a considerable part in the demonstration of dissatisfaction which eventually brought about the resignation of the octogenarian general as president of the Republic.

VI. THE INTELLECTUAL RESPONSE

To most continental intellectuals, the growing affluence of middle-class postwar Europe presented little attraction. Never quite recovered from the shock and destruction of World War I, which severely damaged their faith in their traditional institutions, European creative minds emerged from the second global nightmare with the feeling that their continent was culturally dead and that the long era of significant European history was finally over.[13] It must be remembered that of the continental nations which took part in World War II, *all* were defeated in the military sense, some of them at a humiliatingly early date in the

13 cf. Alfred Weber, *Farewell to European History (Abschied von der Bisherigen Zeit)*, 1946.

hostilities. Poland, Belgium, Denmark, the Netherlands, Norway, and France surrendered in 1940, although certain forces of the last-named continued to fight in defiance of the Petain government; Finland, Yugoslavia, and Greece went down in 1941, Italy in 1943, and, finally, Hitler's Germany in 1945. Other nations were occupied or absorbed, so that except for Sweden, Switzerland, and the Iberian countries, there was no continental nation that escaped either humiliation or outright military defeat in the period between 1939 and 1945. This fact, plus the horrifying spectacle of wholesale Nazi massacres of Jews; of sellouts by General Petain, King Leopold of Belgium, and other supposedly responsible political leaders to the Hitler regime; or of revolting exploitation of native populations by occupation forces on both sides did little to increase respect for governments or, for that matter, for humanity at large. There is no wonder that intellectuals, many of whom played an active part in underground resistance movements in occupied countries, should sense the eclipse of European civilization. And the aforementioned postwar reduction of that continent to the status of a pawn in the cold war between the East and West contributed even more acutely to the feelings of defeat and despair, even in those nations which were technically "liberated" by the destruction of Hitler and Mussolini.

This feeling of defeatism acted directly to bring about what one writer calls the "demythization" of European thought,[14] the decline of the "big" theories (Naturalism, Marxism, Catholicism), the authoritarian beliefs which, rightly or wrongly, gave their adherents a framework and a discipline with which to combat the ambiguities of modern existence. In their places came the philosophies of institutional non-commitment, the *depolitisation* as the

[14] Eric Weil, "Thought in Europe Today," *Daedalus*, Winter, 1964.

French call their retreat from political ideologies; the widely proclaimed, though perhaps temporary, death of God; and even the defiance of the sacred European ideal of the family in the various hirsute and sartorially extravagant youth rebellions of all complexions and degrees of calculated absurdity.

Even those less openly desirous of stopping the world in order to get off often drew lugubrious conclusions from what was occurring. Romano Guardini[15] in 1956 developed the thesis that man no longer had a place in the modern universe. Relative physics had reduced him to a mere existence, a lost cipher in a universe once fondly believed to have been expressly created for his greater glory. Mass man had destroyed all the old humanistic values, the individual human personality was an anomaly in a technological world. Man's world had once been built on concepts of self, nature, and cultural development; all of these had now been swept into the discard in the technological revolt. Man no longer was seeking experience; rather, he was seeking power, and in so doing he was creating a battery of impersonal devices which ultimately would make victims of their creators. In 1959 C. P. Snow, in a famous essay,[16] postulated the complete divorce of the sciences and humanities, and five years later Pierre Teilhard de Chardin in *The Future of Man*,[17] applying the Darwinian concept, reached the same conclusion as Guardini: Man would continue to live on as an organism, but his true existence was over; a species without a soul is dead, and science has destroyed that soul finally and irrevocably.

[15] Romano Guardini, *The End of the Modern World*, New York, 1956.

[16] C. P. Snow, *The Two Cultures* (Cambridge University Press, N.Y., 1959).

[17] Pierre Teilhard de Chardin, *The Future of Man* (New York, 1964).

Despite these gloomy pronouncements, which found a host of receptive followers, there were other writers who, similarly depressed but not yet defeated, found some hope in religion, generally of a non-institutional variety. Arnold Toynbee's monumental *A Study of History,* for example, posited an almost masochistic virtue in adversity and showed that the greatest civilizations had been those which faced some sort of powerful challenge to their very existence. Others, particularly among the older writers, found solace in a sort of non-denominational Christianity, and still others, finding little to choose between the two cultures opposing one another in the cold war, retreated still farther to the east and espoused the principles, if not the long and painful disciplines, of Zen Buddhism. Meanwhile, formal religion itself attempted with some success to find new followers by adopting an ecumenical approach to current moral and social problems, the high point of this endeavor being the surprisingly liberal *Pacem in Terris* proclaimed in 1963 by Pope John XXIII. The same ecumenical spirit, without the religious overtones, inspired the various Peace Corps activities, a program of service to needy populations started by the Kennedy administration in the United States and later adopted in one form or other by several European nations.

All of these semi-religious approaches, with the possible exception of amateur Buddhism, operated in a societal context, indicating that their practitioners had not yet come to the point of accepting the end of man as a social animal. Even the Angry Young Men of the 1950s, though often crude and violent in their reactions, were still operating within very definite concepts of social morality and directing their purgative pronouncements against what they considered to be the gross hypocrisies of the older generation, as well as against the technological monster. All were searching for values in a world which seemed to be marching rapidly toward a calculated self-destruction, all were seeking assurance that man had not yet become obsolete. And all, despite their frequent appearance of cynicism and violence, were trying to find that assurance within the confines of an organized, morally oriented social and cultural pattern.

Other groups, while no less moral in their ultimate aims, were far less social in their approach. These rebels, equally dedicated to establishing the integrity of the individual and equally revolted ("nauseated" was the term popularized by one of these groups, the existentialists) by technology on the one hand and the overwhelming vulgarity of popular culture on the other, adopted a phenomenological attitude in which all actions were judged by the conditions of the moment rather than according to any preconceived societal standards. The most discussed of these groups, and certainly the most important from the literary standpoint, was that of the existentialists, a loosely defined body whose principles could be said to have influenced at least half the leading writers of the postwar period on both sides of the Atlantic.

So much has been written on the subject of existentialism and so familiar have its vocabulary and many of its concepts become that only the briefest and most simplified summary need be given in this volume.[18] Neo-romantic in its principles, it rebels against organized society by rejecting preconceived absolutes and treating every individual action in its own context. Highly moral in its objectives, it

[18] Excellent treatments of the subject may be found in Davis Dunbar McElroy, *Existentialism in Modern Literature* (New York, 1963); Hazel E. Barnes, *The Literature of Possibility* (Lincoln, 1959); Ernst Breisach, *Introduction to Modern Existentialism* (New York, 1962); Marjorie Grene, *Dreadful Freedom: A Critique of Existentialism* (Chicago, 1948); James Collins, *The Existentialists: A Critical Study* (Chicago, 1952); Walter Kaufman, *Existentialism from Dostoevsky to Sartre* (New York, 1956).

nevertheless holds that morality is something which arises from the circumstances of the moment and that any formalized standard of moral values will inevitably fail to meet the needs of specific cases. Thus the individual must find his own morality, must make his own choices, and—most important—must accept responsibility for the consequences. If, as Emerson observed in another context, there are those who foolishly think this to be an easy, permissive philosophy, let him follow its implications for one day.

Existentialism as a term is relatively new but its ideas can be found to some degree in the earliest recorded literature, and many of the greatest masterpieces of the Western world are based upon what has come to be designated popularly as "an existential situation." (The concepts of *aidos* and *nemesis,* on which so much of the Greek drama is built, is vaguely existential; so is Hamlet's dilemma, to cite only two examples.) Philosophically, however, its roots are generally regarded as being discernible in the work of the Danish theologian and philosopher Søren Kirkegaard (1813-1855), who attempted to lead men to an inner faith in spite of the apparent meaninglessness and discontinuity of everyday human existence. Acknowledging the impossibility of finding significance or significant values in the world around us, Kirkegaard urged the individual to lead his own life, accept the responsibility of making his own free choice of actions, and find a divine faith and a proof of God's existence in the integrity of his own behavior and ideals. Truth comes from believing; each individual has his own truth, which he must accept on faith, since no tangible proofs will ever appear in this discontinuous world.

Kirkegaard was a clergyman and believed in God. His ideas were a clergyman's attempt to help man rediscover a divine spirit by a responsible and positive belief in himself. Friedrich Nietzsche, another philosopher whose

thought profoundly influenced existentialism, was an atheist. Stating in his famous *Thus Spake Zarathustra* that God
is dead, Nietzsche went on to propound a philosophy predi-
cated upon man's necessity to make his own choices and
chart his own course in a hostile universe where only the
strong can prevail. In preaching his doctrine of the Superman, Nietzsche fell into the evolutionary thesis that species
evolve upward through their ability to adapt to their environment, the weak and compassionate are crushed; only
the strong with the will to power can go onward to surpass
Man and reach the next higher stage in the evolutionary
process.

The implications of Nietzschean philosophy go far beyond the mere satisfaction of a lust for raw power over
others. They presume the following of a personal discipline and a creative resourcefulness uncommon among
ordinary human beings, a power of will and mind which
enables the individual to rise above both the hostilities of
nature and the prevailing Judeo-Christian ethic which
preaches humility toward the self and compassion and
charity toward others. The Superman finds all of these
humanitarian qualities regressive and self-defeating; he al-
lows himself no feelings of sympathy for the weak; he permits no hypocritical regard for others to obstruct his
course of Becoming, of striving toward the next higher
step in the evolutionary progress. Only by accepting the
meaninglessness of the universe in general and of human
society in particular can one divorce such a philosophy as
Nietzsche's from the reputation of predatory self-indul-
gence it has acquired in the popular mind (which sees
Hitler as a perfect embodiment of the would-be Superman)
and discern the call for exercise of character, fortitude, discipline, and creativity that Nietzsche intended.

Together, Kirkegaard and Nietzsche determine the limits of modern existentialist thought. Both assume the "ab-

surdity" of man's everyday world (though Kirkegaard postulated an inscrutable divine organization), both stress the
need for the individual to rise above this absurdity by
trusting in himself and living by his own free decisions.
They differ in their attitude toward God, one arguing that
in developing his own inner strength man can develop his
faith in a supreme being; the other postulating that, because there is indeed no such thing as a supreme being,
man must learn to be his own God and to live by his own
theology.

A further step toward the development of existentialist
thinking is to be found in the phenomenology of the German philosopher Edmund Husserl (1859-1938). Rejecting
the procedure of attempting to understand the human
mind as a phenomenon of physiological cause and effect,
Husserl accepts the world of appearances as the true reality. Preconceptions, logical deductions, even previous experience, are less important than the fact-in-itself as it
stands at any given moment. If man can learn to react to
things in themselves, he will find some sort of meaning in
his life; it is only when he tries to fit things into some
previously established format or some received standard of
moral or philosophical assumption that he becomes lost.
Each experience must be seen as an isolated phenomenon;
each problem must have its own solution, each pleasure its
own reward.

Husserl's pronouncements are followed by the widely
studied ideas of Martin Heidegger (1889-   ), who stresses
man's need to depart from the banality of his everyday life
and to live a full physical, intellectual, and social existence, accepting the total pleasures, cares, anxieties, feelings of guilt, and, above all, the certainty of death, which
are the inevitable result of following such a course. It is
only by so doing that he can achieve a sense of Being, and
it is only through this sense of Being that he can combat

the illusion of emptiness and absurdity of human existence.

Modern existentialism, as an attitude or a philosophy, adds little or nothing to the ideas already sketched in the previous paragraphs. It accepts the concept of an absurd universe and leaves it to the individual to choose the Kirkegaardian or the Nietzschean attitude toward the existence of God. It discards preconceptions, as in Husserl, and assumes with Heidegger the need for man to live a full existence.

To bring these pre-existentialist precepts into focus, let us attempt a highly simplified synthesis of the ideas of the leading exponent of atheist existentialist thought, Jean-Paul Sartre (1905-). A trenchant writer and fertile creative mind, Sartre stands at the head of the existentialist movement, not so much for the invention of new ideas as for his ability to capture and project philosophical attitudes both in expository tracts and in imaginative works of drama and fiction. In all of these works, his basic thesis is the same: the world is an outside force and not a projection of the inner self. In fact, it is more often than not inimical to the self, to the degree that its very complexity, multiplicity, and utter irrelevance result in a spiritual disgust which Sartre terms "nausea." Sufferers from this unpleasant reaction feel alienated from life, trapped in a situation from which there is "no exit" save death itself. And yet in this suicide-provoking condition, there is one loophole of escape: that of individual freedom of choice. Every man is seen by Sartre as being completely free to find his own solution to the problem of life. He may accommodate, accept the meaninglessness of his own life, and become a mere vegetable. He may, of course, take the easy way out and commit suicide. But both of these negative choices are self-defeating, as absurd and pointless as life itself. Sartre, a moralist and guarded optimist despite his depressing hypotheses, rejects both of these alternatives and suggests a much more difficult but infinitely more positive course. Man must commit himself to the task of Being-in-itself (*L'Être en soi*), of designing for himself a creative, morally responsible existence that in some measure satisfies his inner needs, whether it receives the approval of society or not. He must, of course, learn to put up with the anxiety contingent upon the necessity for his making unaided moral choices, he must accept the guilt or shame which results from his inevitable mistakes, and he must be conscious of the fact that he is living among others and will be judged, rightly or wrongly, from as many possible points of view as there are persons with whom his life comes into contact. Throughout this complex and agonizing welter of conflicting forces, he must refrain from blaming his mistakes on others (a process Sartre refers to as *mauvaise foi*—bad faith). If he can do this, he will attain a sort of qualified justification of his own existence, perhaps the nearest thing to happiness he may expect to find in this contingency-ridden world. His reward is that he truly exists, that he is spiritually alive, that he has achieved authenticity, that in a cluttered and absurd world he has somehow reached the Zarathustrian ideal of surpassing the ordinary man. And he has done it on his own, has made his own mold, has followed his own anguished choices, has received no help from a God whom Sartre, in any case, believes to be non-existent.

Such a philosophy is something far different from the hedonistic egotism associated with existentialism in the popular mind. To carry out the full implications of the Sartrean authenticity, the individual would have to attain a self-discipline which would tax even the moral seriousness of a Sophocles, the sensitivity of a St. Augustine, the creative imagination of a Dante, and the zeal of the most fanatic Calvinist. At the entrance to the dead-end existen-

tialist hell which, like Marlowe's in *Dr. Faustus,* is life itself, the new warning legend could well be inscribed:
"Abandon all Assumptions, Ye who Enter," followed by
the subscript: "No Half-Man Need Apply."

By the end of the 1960s, the events and developments
following World War II, complex and confusing as they
were, nevertheless appeared to fall into the pattern of a
worldwide moral and humanitarian revolt. Intellectuals
and young people, drawn together by the need to restore
some sense of decency after the horrors of Marxism and of
the atomic bomb, seemed to have formed a rather tentative
and uneasy alliance against the vulgarity of the burgeon-
ing middle class, the detached and possibly sinister world
of advanced technology, the apparently limitless power of
the military bureaucracy, and above all, against the nebu-
lous managerial elite whose attitudes—and human satellites—made up the vast amorphous force known throughout most of Europe as the "Situation" and in the United
States as the "Establishment." The weapons employed
against this many-headed "enemy" had been various, contradictory, and often self-defeating, ranging from violent
street demonstrations and equally violent literary denunciations (often employing a gamey admixture of obscenity
and pornography) to defiance and escape through the free-
wheeling abuse of drugs and sex. Somewhere between these
dubious—and usually exhibitionistic—extremes, however,
there had emerged a large and respectable body of valid
thought and equally worthwhile creative writing which
attempted somehow to inculcate a renewed sense of individual self-respect, which sought to develop a society
capable of a more rational and justifiable order of priorities. Above all, there was a desperate—though often floun-
dering—effort on the part of some of these dissenters to
bring the human mind to bear in a positive sense upon the
most urgent of these priorities: the need for more and bet-

ter schools, hospitals, medical care, job and housing opportunities for persons of all races and classes; the apportioning of affluence to support the world of the arts as well as that of material goods; the elimination of the deep pockets of poverty in all parts of the world; the removal, once and for all, of the spectre of the final world war. In the decades of the 1950s and 1960s, intellectuals, young people, and men of good will of all ages in both Europe and America generally found themselves relegated to the negative role of being the more or less articulate critics of the "system." It was their hope, however, that the decade of the 1970s would see a more positive application of this force of mind and humanitarian conscience to the clearly demonstrated needs of our far from equitably affluent, and still spiritually poor, society. One of their number had in the late 1940s already set the deadline; by the beginning of the 1970s all had become uneasily conscious that 1984 was now less than a generation away.

SUGGESTED READINGS

(Place of publication, when not mentioned, is New York.)

R. Albrecht-Carrié, *One Europe* (1965); L. Barzini, *The Italians* (1964); R. A. Butler, ed., *The New Conservatism* (1964); *Daedalus* (Winter, 1964), "A New Europe?"; M. Djilas, *The New Class* (1957); M. Duverger, *Le Cinquième République* (Paris, 1959); R. Guardini, *The End of the Modern World* (1957); J. Gunther, *Inside Europe Today* (1962); S. R. Hopper, ed., *Spiritual Problems in Contemporary Literature* (1952); J. Huxley, *The Human Crisis* (1963); H. Kohn, *The Mind of Germany* (1960); G. Lichtheim, *The New Europe* (1963); R. Macrides and B. Brown, *The de Gaulle Republic* (Homewood, Ill., 1960, 1963); G. Marcel, *Man against Mass Society* (1952); K. Minogue, *The Liberal Mind* (1963); H. Morgenthau, *Germany and the Future of Europe* (Chicago, 1951); F. Nourissier, *The French* (1968); M. Oakeshott, *Rationalism in Politics* (1962); J. Ortega y Gasset, *The Modern Theme* (1961); G. Orwell, *1984* (1949); *The Animal Farm* (1954); H. Peyre, *French Novelists of Today* (1967); D. Pickles, *The Fifth French Republic* (1960); J. J. Servan-Schreiber, *The American Challenge* (1968); C. P. Snow, *The Two Cultures and the Scientific Revolution* (Cambridge University Press, N.Y., 1959); W. Stahl, *The Politics of Postwar Germany* (1963); W. Stankiewicz, *Political Thought since World War II* (1965); P. Teilhard de Chardin, *The Future of Man* (1964); D. Thompson, *Democracy in France* (1952); R. M. Weaver, *Visions of Order: The Cultural Crisis of Our Times* (1965); A. Weber, *Farewell to European History* (1946); R. Wellek, *Confrontations* (1965); A. Werth, *France 1940-1955* (1956); P. Williams, *Politics in Post-war France* (1954).

Chronology for Part IV

THE RENAISSANCE

I. FOURTEENTH CENTURY

Pope Boniface VIII emprisoned by the Orsini family (1303); Clement V chosen Pope by King of France, papal court set up at Avignon (1305); John Wycliffe, who denounced the authority of the Pope and translated the Bible into English, born, Hundred Years' War between France and England began (1338); the "Great Plague" (Black Death) throughout Europe (1348); return to Rome from Avignon of Pope Gregory XI (1377); the Great Schism in the Church, Urban VI in Rome, Clement VII at Avignon (1378); Peasant Revolt in England (1381).

II. FIFTEENTH CENTURY

John Huss, who preached Wycliffe's doctrine, excommunicated (1412); termination of the Great Schism, Martin V Pope (1417); crusade against heretics (Wycliffites and Hussites) proclaimed by Martin V (1420); English driven out of France through inspired leadership of Joan of Arc (1430); first books printed in Haarlem by Coster (1446); Leonardo da Vinci, naturalist, anatomist, engineer, and artist, born (1452); Hundred Years' War concluded, Constantinople captured by Turks, driving Greek scholars to take refuge in Europe (1453); Copernicus, first modern astronomer, born (1473); Michelangelo born (1475); Raphael born (1483); Diaz rounded Cape of Good Hope (1486); America discovered by Columbus, Rodrigo Borgia Pope, Moslem power in Spain terminated by the conquest of Granada (1492).

III. SIXTEENTH CENTURY

Martin Luther posted his theses at Wittenberg, crystallizing the German Protestant Reformation (1517); Cortez in Mexico and beginning of Spain's hundred years of power (1519);

Jesuits founded by Ignatius of Loyola (1539); attempt to reform Church made by the Council of Trent (1545); Elizabeth became Queen of England (1558); Galileo, founder of the science of dynamics, born (1564); Spanish Armada defeated by England (1588).

THE SEVENTEENTH CENTURY

Inauguration of era of monarchical absolutism and French supremacy in Europe by King Henry IV (1589); nine-year-old Louis XIII became King (1610); last meeting of the Estates General before the Revolution (1614); Thirty Years' War (civil war) in Germany began (1618); Richelieu, as Chief Minister of the King, became actual ruler of France and further consolidated the aristocracy (1624); first *salon* instituted by Mme de Rambouillet (1628); French Academy founded by Richelieu to set standards of language and literature (1634); Civil War broke out in England, Richelieu died and was succeeded by Mazarin (1642); death of Louis XIII placed Louis XIV on throne (1643); Mazarin died after continuing the policy of Richelieu, leaving Louis XIV to reign as absolute monarch (1661); Royal Society (of science) chartered in England, discovery of law of gravity by Newton (1666); French Academy of Sciences founded (1666); solidity of France weakened by series of aggressive campaigns (1667-1713); the Glorious Revolution in England (1688); Dictionary finally completed by members of the French Academy (1694); Louis XIV died after reigning seventy-two years (1715).

THE EIGHTEENTH CENTURY

I. HISTORICAL EVENTS

A. *Pre-Revolutionary Europe (1696-1775)*

Peter the Great, who "westernized" Russia, succeeded to throne (1696); Kingdom of Prussia founded (1701); European politics temporarily stabilized by Treaty of Utrecht (1713); Louis XV began his wasteful reign in France (1715); War of the Polish Election strengthened Bourbon control in Europe (1733-1738); Prussia began her rise to power with succession of Frederick the Great (1740); Mme Pompadour in control of French politics (1745-1764); Peace of Aix-la-Chapelle ended eight-year War of Austrian Succession, with Prussia defeating Austria and assuming German leadership (1745); Seven Years' War realigned Europe, with England and Prussia victorious over France and Austria in Europe and England triumphant over France in India and the New World (1756-1763); Catherine the Great ruled in Russia (1762-1796); accession of Louis XVI to French throne (1774); Frederick the Great died (1786).

B. The Age of Revolution (1775-1795)

The American Revolution (1775-1783); French Estates General convoked for first time since 1614, Third Estate proclaimed itself a "National Assembly," thus beginning the French Revolution (1789); the Constitution of 1791 limited powers of French monarch, Jacobin revolt under Danton, France declared a Republic (1792); Reign of Terror in France (1793); formation of the Directory (1795).

C. The Age of Napoleon (1795-1815)

Napoleon became commander-in-chief of French Army (1795); Napoleonic campaigns in Italy (1797), Egypt (1798); Directory overthrown, Napoleon became First Consul (1799); second Italian Campaign (1800-1801); Treaty of Amiens ended war with England (1802) but fighting resumed the following year; Napoleon defeated in naval battle of Trafalgar, but victorious on land at Austerlitz (1805); Prussia decisively defeated (1806); French military fortunes declined in Peninsular War (1808-1813) and in disastrous Russian campaign (1812); revived Prussia, with help of Russia and Austria, forced Napoleon out of Germany (1813); Napoleon badly beaten by coalition of England, Russia, Austria, and Prussia and exiled to Elba, Congress of Vienna (1814); Napoleon returned from Elba, reorganized the Grand Army, but was finally defeated at Waterloo (1815).

II. INTELLECTUAL EVENTS

Publication of Pierre Bayle's *Critical and Historical Dictionary* which influenced French Deism (1697); John Locke died (1704); Voltaire's *Letters on the English* aroused French liberal thought (1740); work began on the French *Encyclopaedia* (1751); publication of Rousseau's *Social Contract*

(1762); Joseph Priestly discovered oxygen (1774); death of materialist philosopher David Hume, publication of Adam Smith's *Wealth of Nations* (1776); Linnaeus, whose classification of plants spurred interest in evolution, died (1778); death of Buffon, whose *Natural History of Animals* classified all animal species and pointed to a common origin of all animal life (1788); Immanuel Kant, idealist philosopher and author of *Critique of Pure Reason*, died (1804); Napoleon codified French laws (1804); Hegel became professor of philosophy at Berlin and propounded his mystical philosophy (1813).

GERMAN ECLECTICISM

I. HISTORICAL EVENTS

Frederick the Great ascended the throne of Prussia and Maria Theresa became Empress of Austria (1740); the War of the Austrian Succession (1740-48); the Seven Years' War (1756-63); Partitions of Poland (1772, 1793, 1795); Joseph II became Emperor of Austria upon death of Maria Theresa (1780); death of Frederick the Great (1786); abolition of serfdom in Prussia (1807); Prussia joined Russia in the War of Liberation against Napoleon (1813); Congress of Vienna (1814-15); Prince Metternich dominated European diplomacy (1815-48); liberal uprisings in Saxony (1831); German customs union effected (1835); liberal uprisings throughout Germany and Austria (1848); Prussia formed first German Confederation (1850); William I became king of Prussia (1861); German army developed under von Moltke (1859-66); Bismarck became Prime Minister (1862); war with Denmark (1864); Seven Weeks' War against Austria (1866); Franco-Prussian War (1870-71); German Empire proclaimed (1871).

II. INTELLECTUAL EVENTS

J. S. Bach died (1750); Lessing's *Minna von Barnhelm,* pioneer comedy of middle-class life (1767); *Sorrows of Werther* (1774); Schiller's *Die Räuber* published (1781); Mozart died (1791); Kant died (1804); Beethoven's *Eroica* Symphony (1804); Schiller died (1805); Goethe's *Faust, Part I* (1808); Goethe died (1832); Marx published the *Communist Manifesto* (1848) and *Das Kapital* (1867); Wagnerian Festival theatre opened at Bayreuth (1871).

POST-NAPOLEONIC EUROPE

I. HISTORICAL EVENTS

A. Conservatives vs. Liberals (1815-32)

Austrian Prime Minister Metternich, chief symbol of conservatism, dominated European politics (1814-30); the Bourbons restored in France (1814); nationalistic Carbonari Movement started in Italy (1820); Charles X succeeded Louis XVIII in France (1824); Greece became independent of Turkish domination (1829); liberal revolution in South America (1810-1830); Russo-Turkish War (1828); the liberal July Revolution in France, Louis-Philippe became king (1830); first Reform Bill passed in England (1832).

B. Liberalism Ascendent (1832-70)

Abolishing of slavery in England (1833); Victoria became Queen of England (1837); liberal rioting throughout continental Europe, Paris Revolution deposed Louis-Philippe and established Second French Republic with Louis-Napoleon as President (1848); Frederick William IV pressed for "German Union," German confederation restored (1850); Second French Empire proclaimed (1852); Garibaldi's major campaign for Italian nationalism fought (1854-61); Crimean War stopped Russian thrust toward Orient (1854-56); Napoleon III fought against Austria (1859) and interfered in Roumania, Poland, Italy, and Mexico (1856-67); abolition of serfdom in Russia, creation of Kingdom of Italy (1861); Bismarck became Chief Minister in Prussia (1862); Prussia defeated Austria and became leading German state (1866); Franco-Prussian War, Napoleon III deposed (1870).

II. INTELLECTUAL EVENTS

Rise of liberalism and nationalism in the arts (1815-32); first steam railway in England (1825); Faraday invents electric motor and electroplating (1830); Comte's *Positive Philosophy* published (1830-57); first telegraph invented (1837); *Communist Manifesto* of Marx and Engels (1848); Bessemer steel process patented (1856); Darwin's *Origin of Species* (1859); Spenser's *First Principles,* Mendel's Law of Heredity propounded (1865); invention of Gatling machine gun (1867);

Marx's *Das Kapital* (1867); Lister published discoveries in aseptic surgery (1867); John Stuart Mill, leading exponent of social liberalism, died (1873).

RUSSIAN HISTORY

Rurik, Viking, founded the Russian Empire (862); Mongol invasion (1224) which arrested Russian development for two hundred years; victory of Dmitri IV against the Mongols (1380); Ivan the Great completed struggle for independence (1480); Ivan the Terrible became Czar (1547); Feodor, last Viking king, died and Boris Godunov crowned (1605); Czar Michael Romanov crowned (1613); Peter transferred capital from Moscow to St. Petersburg and attempted to Europeanize Russia (1689-1725); Catharine II (1762-96) encouraged liberalism and European imitation; humanitarian reign of Alexander I (1801-25); Napoleon's disastrous invasion (1812); rebellion of the Decembrists (1825); Crimean War (1853-56); Alexander II abolished serfdom (1861) and introduced reforms but became reactionary as a result of revolutionary agitators; Alaska sold to the United States (1867); war against Turkey (1877-78); Alexander killed by bomb thrown by a revolutionary conspirator (1881), followed by autocratic rule of Alexander III; pogroms against Jews began (1881); TransSiberian Railway started (1891); period of revolutionary terrorism opened with a series of assassinations (1901); reforms promised by Imperial manifesto (1904); Russo-Japanese War (1904); Red Sunday massacre of strikers, defeat by Japan, revolts of units of armed services, forced electoral reforms, and the beginning of a constitution and bill of rights; government repudiation of its promises led to riots and disorders culminating in the Moscow insurrection and slaughter (1905); the first Duma clashed with the throne (1906); further terrorism and the imposition of martial law (1907); Second Duma dissolved and conservative Third Duma marked a suppressive and counter-revolutionary era (1907-12); death of Tolstoy occasion for waves of popular protest (1912); Fourth Duma instituted minor reforms (1913); World War 1 reunited Russia (1914); Rasputin assassinated (1916); collapse of Russian military power and successful revolution (1917); Treaty of Brest-Litovsk (1918); Lenin succeeded by Stalin (1924).

FIN DE SIÈCLE

I. Historical Events

Formation of Third French Republic (1871); democratic monarchy in Spain (1869-73); First Spanish Republic (1873-74) failed and Bourbons restored (1875); Turkish war weakened Ottoman Empire (1877-78); Russian reform movement terminated by murder of Czar Alexander II (1881); Triple Alliance formed by Italy, Austria, and Germany (1882); William II became ruler of Germany (1888); Bismarck dropped as Prime Minister (1891); Nicholas II became Czar of Russia (1894); Russo-Japanese War (1904-05) resulted in rapid growth of Japan; Entente Cordiale between France and England (1904); Turkey attacked by Serbia, Bulgaria, and Greece (1913); outbreak of World War I (1914).

II. Intellectual Events

Doctrine of papal infallibility (1870); first incandescent electric lighting (1878); Eastman Kodak began manufacture of motion picture film (1880); Nietzsche's *Thus Spake Zarathustra* (1883); Marconi devised wireless telegraphy and Röntgen discovered X-rays (1895); automobile manufacturing begun in the United States (1895); Chamberlain's *Foundations of the Nineteenth Century* proclaims theory of Teutonic superiority (1899); first airplane flight (1903); Einstein advances first theory of relativity (1905); Bergson's *Creative Evolution* (1909).

THE COLLAPSE OF EUROPE: BETWEEN WORLD WARS

I. Historical Events

Outbreak of World War I (1914); entrance of Italy into the war (1915); United States declaration of war against Germany and Austria-Hungary, outbreak of the Russian Revolution and armistice with Russia (1917); Wilson's Fourteen Points, armistice with Germany (1918); Versailles treaty, beginning of Russian "Red Terror," founding of Weimar Republic (1919); fascist revolution under Mussolini (1922); German inflation (1923); Dawes Plan for reparations (1924); Locarno Conference (1925); Germany admitted to League of Nations, Pilsudski becomes strong man of Poland (1926); Geneva Naval Disarmament Conference (1927); Kellogg-Briand Pact outlawing war (1928); exile of Trotsky, First Five-Year Plan in U.S.S.R., concordat between Italy and the Vatican, American Stock Market crash (1929); French evacuate the Rhineland (1930); Hitler chancellor of Germany (1933); Franco-Russian Treaty, Italian invasion of Ethiopia (1935); Spanish Civil War, new Soviet Constitution, Rome-Berlin Axis (1936); German occupation of Austria, Munich agreement on Czechoslovakia (1938); Franco victorious in Spanish Civil War, German invasion of Poland, outbreak of World War II (1939); German invasion of Norway, Denmark, Belgium, the Netherlands, France, fall of France (1940); German invasion of Russia, America enters the war (1941); Declaration of the United Nations (1942); downfall of Mussolini (1943); Allied invasion of Normandy (1944); Yalta and Potsdam Conferences, unconditional surrender of Germany and Japan (1945).

II. INTELLECTUAL EVENTS

Oswald Spengler's *Decline of the West* (1918); formation of the Third International, official origin of the Communist Party (1919); first commercial radio broadcasting, nitrogen atoms converted into hydrogen and oxygen atoms by Ernest Rutherford (1920); Alfred North Whitehead's *Science and the Modern World,* Volume I of *Mein Kampf* (1925); Lindbergh's solo flight from New York to Paris, first television broadcasts in England (1927); Sir Archibald Fleming's discovery of penicillin (1928); Ortega y Gasset's *The Revolt of the Masses* (1930); World Economic Conference at London (1933); effective radar constructed by Sir Robert Watson-Watt (1935).

EUROPE SINCE 1945

Nuremberg Tribunal condemns Nazi leaders, League of Nations formally disbands (1946); the "Truman Doctrine," India and Pakistan achieve independence, first supersonic flight (1947); Berlin airlift (1948); Organizataion for European Economic Cooperation (OEEC) established, Point Four Program started, North Atlantic Treaty Organization (NATO) established, German Federal Republic set up with capital in Bonn, United Nations adopts New York as permanent headquarters (1949); George Bernard Shaw dies (1950); André Gide dies (1951); Elizabeth II crowned queen of England, Josef Stalin dies, Konrad Adenauer becomes chancellor of the German Federal Republic (1953); violence erupts in Algeria (1954); Thomas Mann and Albert Einstein die (1955); Suez Canal crisis, revolution in Hungary (1956); Rome Treaty establishing Common Market, International Geophysical Year makes significant contribution to space exploration, Russia launches Sputnik I (1957); Nikita Khrushchev becomes premier of the U.S.S.R., Fifth French Republic established with Charles de Gaulle as president, election of Pope John XXIII, beatnik movement invades Europe (1958); first close-range moon photographs made by Lunik III (1959); Soviets make first manned space flight, Albert Camus dies (1960); Berlin Wall crisis (1961); Algeria becomes independent (1962); Pope John XXIII delivers encyclical *Pacem in Terris,* Ludwig Erhard becomes chancellor of German Federal Republic, Pope John XXIII dies (1963); Khrushchev falls from power in the U.S.S.R. (1964); Winston Churchill dies (1965); France withdraws from NATO, Kiesinger becomes chancellor of the German Federal Republic (1966); Britain devalues the pound, Konrad Adenauer dies (1967); civil rebellion in Czechoslovakia (1968); de Gaulle resigns as president of France, France devaluates the franc, men first walk on moon (1969).

INDEX